NEITHER SLAVE NOR FREE

THE JOHNS HOPKINS SYMPOSIA IN
COMPARATIVE HISTORY

The Johns Hopkins Symposia in Comparative History are occasional volumes sponsored by the Department of History at The Johns Hopkins University and The Johns Hopkins University Press. Each considers, from a comparative perspective, an important topic of current historical interest and comprises original essays by leading scholars in the United States and other countries. The present volume is the third. Its preparation has been assisted by funds from the Institute of Southern History at The Johns Hopkins University.

NEITHER
SLAVE
NOR FREE

*The Freedman of African Descent in
the Slave Societies of
the New World*

Edited with an Introduction by
David W. Cohen
and
Jack P. Greene

THE JOHNS HOPKINS UNIVERSITY PRESS
Baltimore and London

The Johns Hopkins University Press, Baltimore, Maryland 21218
The Johns Hopkins University Press Ltd., London

Library of Congress Catalog Number 79-184238
ISBN 0-8018-1374-3
Manufactured in the United States of America

Library of Congress Cataloging in Publication Data will be
found on the last printed page of this book.

Contents

Preface   vii

Notes on Contributors   ix

Introduction   1
DAVID W. COHEN AND JACK P. GREENE

1 Colonial Spanish America   19
FREDERICK P. BOWSER

2 Surinam and Curaçao   59
H. HOETINK

3 Colonial Brazil   84
A. J. R. RUSSELL-WOOD

4 The French Antilles   134
LÉO ELISABETH

5 Saint Domingue   172
GWENDOLYN MIDLO HALL

6 Jamaica   193
DOUGLAS HALL

7 Barbados   214
JEROME S. HANDLER AND ARNOLD A. SIO

8 The Slave States of North America   258
EUGENE D. GENOVESE

9 Cuba   278
FRANKLIN W. KNIGHT

10 ⌐ Nineteenth-Century Brazil   309
      HERBERT S. KLEIN

      Appendix: Population Tables   335

      Index   341

Preface

This volume grew out of a symposium on "The Role of the Free Black and Free Mulatto in Slave Societies of the New World" held at The Johns Hopkins University on April 8 and 9, 1970. Sponsored by the Department of History and the Institute of Southern History, the symposium considered earlier drafts of the chapters by H. Hoetink, A. J. R. Russell-Wood, Léo Elisabeth, Douglas Hall, Eugene D. Genovese, and Franklin W. Knight. The chapters by Frederick P. Bowser, Gwendolyn Midlo Hall, and Jerome S. Handler and Arnold A. Sio were written especially for the volume to fill important gaps noted during the symposium discussions. For the same purpose, the chapter by Herbert S. Klein, an earlier version of which appeared in the *Journal of Social History*, has also been included in a revised and expanded form.

In addition to the authors of the six initial papers, Manoel Cardozo of the Catholic University of America, Roy Glasgow of Bowie State College, Richard Graham, then of the University of Utah and now of the University of Texas, Jerome S. Handler of Southern Illinois University, Herbert S. Klein of Columbia University, Magnus Mörner of the Ibero-Amerikanska Institutet I Stockholm, Vera Rubin of the Research Institute for the Study of Man, Arnold A. Sio of Colgate University, Stanley J. Stein of Princeton University, and Barbara Stein of Princeton, New Jersey, attended the symposium and participated in the discussions.

Notes on Contributors

FREDERICK P. BOWSER has been a member of the Department of History at Stanford University since 1967. He received his university education at the University of New Mexico and the University of California at Berkeley and taught at the University of California at Los Angeles. His research interests include the role of the African and those of African descent in Latin America, with emphasis upon the colonial period. He has written *Peru and the African, 1529–1650*, and has co-edited with Robert Brent Toplin *The Afro-Latin American: Burdens of the Past*, both of which are scheduled for publication in 1972.

DAVID W. COHEN has been a member of the Department of History at The Johns Hopkins University since 1968. Educated at the University of Wisconsin and the School of Oriental and African Studies of the University of London, he is primarily interested in pre-colonial African history, with special attention being given to East Africa. He is the author of *Mukama and Kintu: The Historical Tradition of Busoga, Uganda* (1972).

LÉO ELISABETH, a native of Martinique, presently teaches history at the Lycée Schoelcher, Fort-de-France, Martinique. An *agrégé d'historie*, he attended the University of Bordeaux, where in 1954 he received the *diplôme d'études supérieures* and where he completed a study of "The Colored in Bordeaux in the Eighteenth Century." Subsequently, he has been engaged in a major study of "The Population and Economy of Martinique from 1700 to 1848" under the supervision of Professor Pierre Goubert of the Sorbonne. This study is now nearing completion.

EUGENE D. GENOVESE has been professor of history at the University of Rochester since 1969. After studying at Brooklyn College and Columbia University, he taught at the Polytechnic Institute of Brooklyn, Rutgers University, and Sir George Williams University. A specialist in the history of the American South, he has published *The Political Economy of Slavery: Studies in the Economy of the Slave South* (1965); *The World the Slaveholders Made: Two Essays in Interpretation* (1969); and *In Red and Black: Marxian Explorations in Southern and Afro-American History* (1971).

JACK P. GREENE has been professor of history at The Johns Hopkins University since 1966. He received his university education at the University of North Carolina at Chapel Hill, Indiana University, the University of Nebraska, Bristol University, and Duke University, and has taught at Michigan State University, Western Reserve University, the College of William and Mary, and the University of Michigan. A specialist in seventeenth- and eighteenth-century Anglo-American history, he has published a number of articles and books, among them *The Quest for Power: The Lower Houses of Assembly in the Southern Royal Colonies, 1689–1776* (1963).

DOUGLAS HALL, a native of Jamaica, is professor of history at the University of the West Indies, Mona, Jamaica. He studied at the University of Toronto and the London School of Economics and Political Science. A specialist in British Caribbean history, he has published many articles, as well as *Free Jamaica, 1834–1865: An Economic History* (1959); *Ideas and Illustrations in Economic History* (1964); and *Five of the Leewards, 1834–1870* (1971).

GWENDOLYN MIDLO HALL is a member of the Department of History at Livingston College, Rutgers University. She was educated at the University of the Americas and the University of Michigan, has been active in the civil rights movement, and has worked on theoretical problems of revolutionary black nationalism in the United States. A specialist in Latin American history, with particular emphasis upon comparative slave systems, she has published a number of articles in *Freedomways* and *Black World* and a book, *Social Control in Slave Plantation Societies: A Comparison of St. Domingue and Cuba* (1971).

JEROME S. HANDLER is a member of the Department of Anthropology at Southern Illinois University. Educated at the University of California at Los Angeles and at Brandeis University, he has held research positions at University College, London, and at the University of the West Indies, Mona, Jamaica, and served as O'Connor Professor of American Institutions at Colgate University in 1971–72. A student of the social and cultural life of the Barbadian slave and of the processes by which African immigrants and their descendants created cultural systems in New World environments, he has for several years been engaged in a major study of slave society in Barbados and is the author of *A Guide to Source Materials for the Study of Barbados History, 1627–1834* (1971) and a forthcoming book, *The Unappropriated People: Freedmen in Barbados Slave Society*.

H. HOETINK is director of the Institute of Caribbean Studies and professor of sociology at the University of Puerto Rico, posts he has held since 1968. Born in Holland, he was educated at the Universities of Amsterdam and Leiden and has lived in the Caribbean (Curaçao, Dominican Republic, and Puerto Rico) since the mid-1950s, except for the period 1964–68, when he served as the first director of the Center for Latin American Research and Documentation at the University of Amsterdam and professor of sociology at the University of Rotterdam. His interests range widely over the fields of slavery, race relations, and recent social history, and his principal published works are *Het Patroon van de oude Curaçaose Samenleving* (1958); *The Two Variants in Caribbean Race Relations* (1967); and *El pueblo Dominicano, 1850–1900: Apuntes para su sociología historica* (1971).

HERBERT S. KLEIN has been professor of history at Columbia University since 1969. He was educated at the University of Chicago, where he taught prior to moving to Columbia. A wide-ranging student of Latin American history, he has published many articles and two books: *Slavery in the Americas: A Comparative Study of Cuba and Virginia* (1967) and *Parties and Political Change in Bolivia, 1880–1952* (1969). He is now engaged in a study of the South Atlantic Slave trade and the settlement of Africans in Brazil in the eighteenth and nineteenth centuries.

FRANKLIN W. KNIGHT is a member of the Department of History at the State University of New York at Stony Brook. Born in Jamaica, he was educated at the University of the West Indies, Mona, Jamaica, and the University of Wisconsin. His major field of interest is colonial Latin America, and he is the author of *Slave Society in Cuba during the Nineteenth Century* (1970).

A. J. R. RUSSELL-WOOD is an associate professor of history at The Johns Hopkins University. Educated at Oxford University, he was previously a research fellow at St. Antony's College, Oxford. A student of Portuguese expansion and of colonial Brazilian social history, his principal published work is the prize-winning *Fidalgos and Philanthropists: The Santa Casa da Misericordia of Bahia, 1550–1755* (1968), and he is now at work on a study of gold and society in colonial Brazil.

ARNOLD A. SIO is professor of anthropology and sociology at Colgate University. Educated at Beloit College, the University of Chicago, and the University of Illinois, he has taught at the University of the West Indies, Mona, Jamaica. He has done extensive research on comparative slavery and the organizations of slave societies and has published several articles on those subjects.

NEITHER SLAVE NOR FREE

DAVID W. COHEN AND JACK P. GREENE

Introduction

The past twenty-five years have witnessed a growing interest on
the part of historians and non-historians alike in the structure and
functioning of the slave societies of the New World. The widespread
appearance of slavery throughout the Americas, beginning in the sixteenth century, the apparently diverse character of slavery from one
part of the hemisphere to another, and the persistence of coercive
racial and economic structures in American societies long after
emancipation are outward features which have stimulated a generation of comparative analysis and comment. A premier concern of this
recent interest has been the attempt to assess the relative repressive-
ness of particular slave systems and the relative openness of particular
slave societies. The late Frank Tannenbaum[1] was certainly not the first
writer to attempt an assessment of the relative levels of racial brutality in the slave systems of the Americas; such a comparative interest was quite evident in the pro- and anti-slavery literature that
appeared on both sides of the Atlantic during the eighteenth and nineteenth centuries. To a very important extent, however, Tannenbaum's
thin volume, together with the renewed urgency of racial issues in
the Americas, did provide most of the initial stimulus for the rapid
growth of interest in the comparative study of the origins and character of New World slavery as represented most prominently by the
work of Stanley M. Elkins, Herbert S. Klein, David Brion Davis,
Eugene D. Genovese, Winthrop D. Jordan, and Carl N. Degler.[2] The

[1] *Slave and Citizen: The Negro in the Americas* (New York, 1947).

[2] Stanley M. Elkins, *Slavery: A Problem in American Institutional and
Intellectual Life* (Chicago, 1959); Herbert S. Klein, *Slavery in the Americas: A
Comparative Study of Virginia and Cuba* (Chicago, 1967); David Brion Davis,
The Problem of Slavery in Western Culture (Ithaca, N.Y., 1966); Eugene D.
Genovese, *The World the Slaveholders Made* (New York, 1969); Winthrop D.
Jordan, *White over Black: American Attitudes toward the Negro, 1550–1812*
(Chapel Hill, N.C., 1968); and Carl N. Degler, *Neither Black Nor White: Slavery
and Race Relations in Brazil and the United States* (New York, 1971). The fact
that these writers all are white and all are North American suggests a locus of
preoccupation within the historical community of the United States with large
comparative frameworks and with certain questions within the general race
issue. This is not to say that scholars from the rest of the hemisphere have

recent work has offered not so much a new focus (attempts to comprehend the character of slavery and to measure the relative brutality of slave regimes have certainly persisted) as new tools, borrowed from sociology, anthropology, psychology, and economics, with which to dissect the institutions, attitudes, and character of the slave societies.

In *Slave and Citizen*, Tannenbaum attempted to develop two points: first, that the conditions of slavery and the brutality of race relations in the New World were not uniform, and that variations could be found in the character of slavery and race relations from one society to another; and, second, that the laws, institutions, and national traditions that European colonizers brought with them to the Americas also were not uniform, and that, in particular, variations in the conceptions of the moral nature of the slave among individual European national traditions were the basic source of the striking variations in race relations noted in the New World. In putting forward the first point, Tannenbaum took as a principal index of variation the relative status of free people of color within the slave societies. In attempting to show a direct connection between different national traditions and varying patterns of race relations, Tannenbaum gave particular attention to legislation and practices relating to manumission, here again building his argument heavily upon the legal status of the free colored.

While post-Tannenbaum scholarship has certainly carried forward a concern for the basic comparative question of relative brutality and has maintained an interest in the importance of "national traditions" in New World race relations, the most recent work is marked by a shift of concern from European ideals and colonial legislation to slavery itself, from the letter of law and tradition to the reconstructable conditions of slavery. Even so, the special importance of the free people of color[3] which Tannenbaum found so impressive has not been neglected in the rush to write the history of these societies from "below." The free colored people found within every New World society have offered to the historian what the slave has not —groups with a discernible identity, individual members of which

ignored slavery and the various historiographical and moral issues surrounding it: much of the basic groundwork has been laid, and much of the present research is being done, by scholars born and trained in Latin America, Europe, and Africa. It is to suggest only that the comparative orientation has perhaps been strongest in the United States.

[3] Throughout this volume, several somatic referent terms are used (as well as a number of non-somatic ones) to distinguish elements within the free non-white group. The editors have seen no value in pressing the contributors into some uniform usage, although *free colored* has been accepted as a general referent inclusive of all non-white freedmen with some degree of African descent. Secondarily, *black* and *mulatto* are frequently used as exclusive somatic referents, and the use of either one as a synonym for *colored* has been avoided.

were often very active and, perhaps even more important, occasionally extremely articulate.

The present volume reflects this continuing interest. Intended both to pull together what is now known and to pinpoint areas in which additional work is needed, it has two related points of focus: first, the degree to which the experience of the free colored can serve as a measure of the character of slavery and race relations in each of the slave societies here discussed; and, second, the special—and sometimes effectively pivotal—roles of this group in the evolving societies in which they lived. The first point of focus obviously shares much with Tannenbaum, while the second is the product of an emerging appreciation of the importance of the free colored in their own right.

In assessing the role of the free colored in the slave societies of the New World, an examination of rates of growth of free colored populations, manner of accretion and growth, and relative size becomes a concern of the first order. While free men of color were clearly present in the New World from the first years of the Atlantic slave trade, and there were significant numbers of free colored in every slave society, the patterns of emergence of these "communities" of free men varied considerably, as did the rates of growth and the relative sizes at particular times. At the two extremes were Curaçao, Brazil, and Martinique, on the one hand, and the British islands of Jamaica and Barbados, on the other. In several provinces of Brazil, the numbers of free colored rose above 50 percent of the total population a decade before general emancipation. Even in the late eighteenth century, the percentage of free colored in Minas Gerais surpassed 30. In the Dutch colony of Curaçao, the free colored made up more than 43 percent of the population in 1833. In Martinique, the percentage of free colored in the total population grew from 2.5 in 1696 to 32 in 1848, although the increase was not steady, dipping markedly in the 1730s and 1740s during the height of the sugar boom. At the other end of the spectrum, the percentage of free colored in the total population of Jamaica did not rise above one-tenth, even on the eve of emancipation, while in Barbados the comparable figure was less than 7 percent.

While a simple comparison of the proportions of the free colored population in several of the slave societies of the New World suggests outstanding divergences,[4] a consideration of the internal rates of growth of the free colored indicates considerably less variation. Several of the contributors have noted that, among the discernible groups in the slave society, the free colored seem to have been the only group capable of increasing through natural means. By contrast, slave and white groups tended to be incapable of maintaining their numbers, much less of sustaining a normal rate of growth. Consequently, these

[4] See Table 1. This, Tables 2 and 3, and Figure 1 are based on the population tables in the Appendix.

TABLE 1. Freedmen as Percentage of Total Population in Selected Societies

Society	1764–1768	1773–1776	1784–1790	1800–1808	1812–1821	1827–1840
Puerto Rico	—	48.4 (1775)	—	43.8 (1802)	43.6 (1812)	—
Curaçao	—	—	—	—	32.0 (1817)	43.4 (1833)
Brazil						
Minas Gerais	—	—	35.0 (1786)	41.0 (1808)	40.3 (1821)	—
São Paulo	—	—	—	18.8 (1800)	22.7 (1815)	23.2 (1836)
Martinique	2.3 (1764)	3.3 (1776)	3.7 (1784)	7.1 (1802)	9.4 (1816)	24.9 (1835)
Saint Domingue	—	—	4.0 (1784)	—	—	—
Jamaica	1.7 (1768)	2.1 (1775)	—	2.9 (1800)	—	—
Barbados	0.5 (1768)	0.6 (1773)	1.0 (1786)	2.6 (1801)	3.3 (1815)	6.5 (1833)
United States						
Upper South	—	—	1.8 (1790)	2.7 (1800)	3.4 (1820)	3.7 (1840)
Lower South	—	—	0.6 (1790)	0.8 (1800)	1.7 (1820)	1.6 (1840)
Cuba	—	20.3 (1774)	—	—	—	15.1 (1827)

Sources: The data for the United States were taken from U.S. Census Office, *Population of the United States in 1860* (Washington, D. C., 1864), pp. 600–603. Those for the other societies were derived from the essays in this volume.

4

two groups depended to a considerable degree on continual immigration and replacement. This contrast between the patterns of growth
of the free colored and the white and slave groups is, of course, much
less notable in the more temperate areas, and especially in North
America, where white settlement was much more extensive and rates
of growth were much more vigorous.

But this is not to say that the patterns of growth of the free
colored populations were similar throughout the New World—only
that they everywhere shared the common achievement of apparent
self-sustenance of population growth; moreover, with the notable exception of British North America, this achievement occurred well in
advance of both the white and slave strata.[5] Of course, the continuing
accretion of new members to the free colored group through the self-
purchase of freedom and the emancipation of children born of mixed
white and non-white unions remained a factor of importance in the
growth of the free colored population. But in each of the societies under study there was a period when the pressures created by increased
restrictions on manumissions slowed the rate of accretions to the
group and made natural replacement and reproduction the primary
generator of population growth.

The emergence and early growth of the free colored population
in New World societies were developments of enormous complexity,
and evaluating the many contributory elements is enormously difficult. What the following chapters do suggest by way of a general
pattern is that in the earlier phases of the development of the slave
society, the manumission of black and mulatto females attached to
whites in formal or informal unions and the inclusion of their offspring in the free group were the principal forms of accretion. Several
of the contributors suggest that these unions were far less transitory
than has generally been thought and that, in fact, the customs defining the responsibilities of the partners in such unions were formalized
and operated even if the white had a marriage arrangement in Europe. The fact that these unions assumed such regularity during the
early period may have ensured their survival in later years, even in
the face of strong governmental pressure such as that which Martinique experienced following the Seven Year's War.

Almost certainly, such stable unions were exceptional, and it is
highly probable that the character of interracial unions altered over
time. At first they were, for the whites, presumably unions of sexual
convenience. But later, with the emergence of a free non-white group
with some wealth and a considerable degree of assimilation to the
European society, or at least to its colonial model, the interracial
union in some societies also involved substantive economic, perhaps
even social, considerations. Discussing Martinique, Léo Elisabeth
notes instances in which such unions brought substantial financial

5 For a comparison of the growth of the free colored in several societies,
see Figure 1.

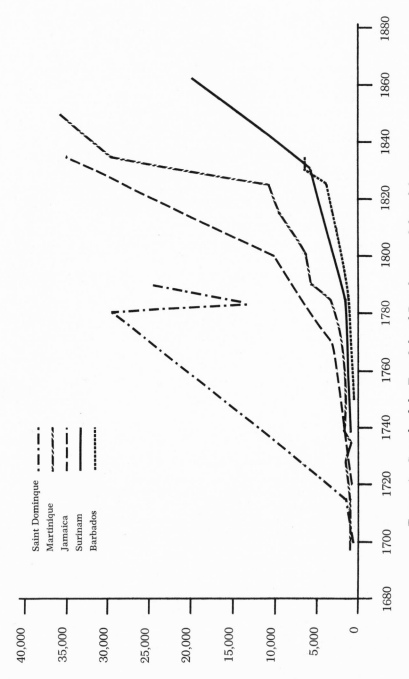

FIGURE 1. Growth of the Free Colored Population in Selected Societies

Saint Dominque
Martinique
Jamaica
Surinam
Barbados

benefits to the whites, though clearly there were exceptions even in the French Antilles. It is likely that, in later generations, unions (both marriages and less legally binding relationships) between whites and free colored must have largely supplanted the earlier white-slave unions, at least in areas where free colored were fairly numerous.

One may even suspect that, in the early phase of the emergence of the free colored (the first several generations), the complex, multi-tiered color coding system (for example, Negro, sambo, mulatto, quadroon, mustee, mustifino, quintroon, octoroon) may have been operative in terms of marriage preference and social status. A. J. R. Russell-Wood notes that an intricate but less arithmetic system survived in Brazil right through the colonial period. But elsewhere these categories became increasingly vague and confused within a century of the beginnings of the slave societies. The persistence of marriages between free colored and slave—and the increasingly restrictive legis-lation limiting subsequent manumission—made the terms *free* and *mulatto* or *slave* and *Negro* less synonymous. Equally, the differential statuses achieved by free colored of various shadings obscured the fine correlations between shade and status which white observers and administrators had readily made at an early date. Lastly, new pat-terns of manumission—through self-purchase and heroic service to state or master—made white shade preference a much less operative factor and introduced numbers of "Negroes" into the free group. One can observe, however, a tendency for the shade preference or "somatic norm image" to refocus on the more general somatic referents of mulatto and black.

The importance of the interracial union and of the associated manumissions in the early phase of the growth of the free colored population initially created age and sex anomalies. In terms of sex, the free colored groups throughout the hemisphere included dispro-portionately large numbers of females, not only as a result of the manumission of female partners in mixed marriages or sexual unions, but also as a result of the general tendency to manumit fe-male infants in greater numbers than males. This is shown quite clearly in the nineteenth-century figures for Cuba and Brazil. The sexual composition of the free colored group is all the more striking when seen against the white and slave groups, both of which were marked by a preponderance of males.

Two "selective" factors affected the sex ratio within the free colored group. The first was the increasing appearance of self-purchase as a means to freedom. Self-purchase appears to have be-come comparatively common during periods of rapid economic growth, which opened up considerable opportunities for free labor, though the practice later came under sharp fire from unpropertied white immi-grants and other anti-manumission groups in virtually every society. Where self-purchase of freedom was possible, however, males were likely to join the free colored group in greater numbers than females.

Certainly, the evidence suggests that, where the "pulling up" of wives and relatives by newly freed men was a relatively common practice, it was a reflection of the opening of the economy to colored traders and artisans. The second "selective" factor, which also moderated the tendency toward female predominance among the free colored, was the readiness of colonial authorities—notably, the French, British, and Dutch in the Caribbean, the Portuguese in Brazil, and both sides in the War of American Independence—to offer non-white combatants freedom in return for heroic service in the internecine and civil struggles of the seventeenth and eighteenth centuries.

The disproportionately young age ratio was also moderated by several factors. The first was the custom of delayed manumission, which prevailed nearly everywhere throughout the slavery era. This custom required a "manumitted" infant or child to perform involuntary service, usually to an age beyond twenty, before the manumission became effective. Similarly, testamentary bequests of freedom delayed the manumission of slaves, including that of legitimate and illegitimate offspring. A third practice which moderated the tendency toward a very young free colored population was the not altogether humanitarian practice of manumitting aged and incapacitated slaves. Such manumissions seem to have been related to declines in planting productivity and were associated with the practice of selling slaves to escape financial ruin. This practice has been well noted for the tidewater area of the United States during the nineteenth century, when slaveholders were selling their chattel to the more dynamic producing areas of the Southwest. It was at this time that state legislatures hurried to enact regulations requiring slaveholders who intended to manumit slaves to put up a bond or guarantee which would protect state and locality from having to provide for sustenance and burial of pennyless and infirm freedmen.

While the campaign to limit manumission of the helpless may be considered morally ambivalent, if not relatively humanitarian, the general trend against manumission was unequivocally strident. Waves of such legislation overtook every slave society during the late eighteenth and early nineteenth centuries, though perhaps to a lesser extent in nineteenth-century Brazil. The legislation had a number of proponents—the plantocracy, artisan and poor whites, and colonial and metropolitan administrators—and took a variety of forms, from taxes and notarial restrictions to general prohibitions. What is revealing is the timing of these waves of restrictions. In every one of the societies under consideration, the anti-manumission legislation was unassailing, if present at all, through at least the first half of the eighteenth century. In the American South and in Cuba, the hardening of manumission restrictions occurred during the sugar and cotton "revolutions" of the early nineteenth century. But such a direct relationship between agricultural transformations and the openness of manumission laws would appear to have been exceptional as well as

closely associated with the fear that the slave trade would be restricted as a result of the increasing number of attacks mounted
against it during the third and fourth decades of the nineteenth century. In this situation, even the free colored people found themselves
in a precarious position, and many fell, or were dragged back into
slavery.

Elsewhere, the relationship of periods of attack to periods of
intensification of agricultural production or the potential drying up
of sources of slaves tended to be limited. There are indications, in
fact, that the agricultural revolutions actually opened up opportunities for free colored persons—in management, in the factories, and in
all the peripheral trades that grew up around the centers of production. More important in stimulating the movement against manumission were the whites' increasing fears of economic competition
from freedmen and revolt among the slaves. The importance of these
fears is especially clear in the cases of Martinique, Curaçao, Barbados, and Jamaica, and would seem to have been operative elsewhere
as well. The revolution in Saint Domingue was only the grandest of
events that produced intense fears throughout the New World of revolts ignited by free colored and carried to the greatest possible excess
by slaves. Administrators who heard the pleadings and warnings of
white colonists were curiously and revealingly ambivalent; they noted
the increasingly important economic and military role of the free
colored but were uncertain whether this development reinforced or
threatened their authority. In almost every case, however, they tended
ultimately to heed the advice of the worried and angry whites.[6]

What is at least as significant is the fact that the statutory restrictions on manumission were often ignored, bypassed, unenforced,
or at most received only delayed attention. As a consequence, the decrease in economic opportunities permitting self-purchase, and the
increase in acceptance of "semi-freedom" without official papers, also
must be seen to have played a role in slowing down the rates of formal manumission.

Tannenbaum and others have used the relative openness of
manumission codes as an index of the coerciveness or openness of
the broader slave system and, still more generally, of colonial race
relations. Several recent studies have attacked this notion directly,
and the evidence or inferences presented here would seem to support
them. In a recent essay,[7] Eugene D. Genovese has suggested that a
relatively open system of manumissions may well have necessitated
a rigorous and brutal slave regime. Conversely, one could argue that
a relatively closed system of manumission might have appeared in

[6] Table 2 notes the changes in the percentage of free colored among the
total free in several societies.
[7] "The Treatment of Slaves in Different Countries: Problems in the Ap-
plications of the Comparative Method," *Slavery in the Americas: A Comparative
Reader*, ed. Eugene D. Genovese and Laura Foner (Englewood Cliffs, N.J., 1969).

TABLE 2. Freedmen as Percentage of Total Free Population in Selected Societies

Society	1764–1768	1773–1776	1784–1790	1800–1808	1812–1821	1827–1840
Puerto Rico	—	54.1 (1775)	—	47.7 (1802)	50.9 (1812)	—
Curaçao	—	—	—	—	62.1 (1817)	71.5 (1833)
Brazil						
Minas Gerais	—	—	65.0 (1786)	62.5 (1808)	60.2 (1821)	—
São Paulo	—	—	—	25.0 (1800)	30.0 (1815)	27.7 (1836)
Martinique	13.6 (1764)	19.3 (1776)	25.4 (1784)	40.0 (1802)	50.1 (1816)	76.2 (1835)
Saint Domingue	—	—	39.6 (1784)	—	—	—
Jamaica	16.4 (1768)	19.4 (1775)	—	25.0 (1800)	—	—
Barbados	2.7 (1768)	2.8 (1773)	4.9 (1786)	12.2 (1801)	15.7 (1815)	25.5 (1829)
United States						
Upper South	—	—	2.7 (1790)	3.9 (1800)	4.9 (1820)	5.1 (1840)
Lower South	—	—	1.1 (1790)	1.4 (1800)	3.0 (1820)	2.9 (1840)
Cuba	—	27.3 (1774)	—	—	—	25.4 (1827)

Sources: Same as those for Table 1.

the wake of a rather open system of slavery in which slaveowners were too ready to permit self-purchase or were quite accustomed to manumitting their slaves in testaments. If such models were evidenced in fact, one might view the positions of slaves and free colored, vis-à-vis authority, as inversely related. Several of the papers in this collection take up the point, though somewhat differently, suggesting that a relatively rigorous slave regime, such as that observed in Surinam and the French islands, may have resulted in a relative amelioration of conditions for the free colored as a direct result of the whites' need for allies within the slave society.

While these arguments suggest that the fear-alliance factor was a primary element in the anti- and pro-manumission surges, it is all the more notable that the anti-manumission campaigns seem to have been aimed much more at the slaves than at the "communities" of free colored. The already fully free lost little beyond an increase in their numbers as a direct result of the legislation. Though in retrospect this loss might appear to have been crucial, little free colored anxiety over their relative numbers is evidenced in the contemporary sources. The anti-manumission laws did, however, attack and affect the quasi-free—for example, the *emancipados* in Cuba and the *soi-disant libres* in the French Antilles. This rough category of quasi-free included those whose papers or backgrounds were questionable, as well as those who were bound through marriage to the slave stratum and for whom the restrictive legislation made the manumission of wives, husbands, children, parents, and siblings much more difficult and costly.

To the extent that they were enforced, the anti-manumission laws, like much of the racial legislation and many of the administrative practices in the colonies, drove a considerable wedge between the free colored and slave populations. In certain circumstances, whites conceived of the free colored and slaves as belonging to one inferior category,[8] but, in cases in which it served their interests, the dominant whites were prepared to define much more rigorously not only the interstice distinguishing white from colored but also that distinguishing free colored from slave.

As the legal and terminological distinctions made between free colored and slave became functional, the slave society assumed the character of a three-tiered structure, which prevailed throughout the New World except in much of the American South. Although the dominant group did generally perceive and define the free colored as an intermediate group between white and slave, the question of whether this stratum might be defined as a "class" or "caste" seems to be a terminological cul-de-sac. Class or caste consciousness appears to have been a relatively late-blooming phenomenon, and was first

[8] In Chapter 3, A. J. R. Russell-Wood notes the frequent use of the term *escraves fôrros* (free slaves) in Brazil and the custom of lumping free colored together with slaves.

notable in the petitioning campaigns of the eighteenth century, which were generally directed against the class legislation aimed at the free colored as a group. Its appearance is more striking still in the reactions of the free colored to the stirrings of the slave population at the end of the eighteenth century and in the first decades of the nineteenth.

A variety of explanations may be offered for the apparently slow development of such a group consciousness among the free colored. First, most of the contributors note that the free colored tended to aspire to white plantocratic or managerial status, and that such a general tendency could hardly be seen as promoting a separate group identity or reinforcing a consciousness of class.[9] Second, deep cultural divisions between assimilated and unassimilated free colored were not unusual. In Brazil, to cite a profound and perhaps exceptional instance, many free colored were first- or second-generation Africans, and many more preserved much of the tradition of their ancestors. Russell-Wood notes, as well, that a number of free colored made visits to Africa, some to the homes of their ancestors. A third explanation involves the persistence of racial distinctions within the free colored group. Although the very complex racial hierarchy was apparently short-lived, as noted above, the tendency to differentiate between free mulatto and free black survived and persisted among whites and nonwhites in every slave society (except much of the American South) right up to general emancipation. The division of free non-white militiamen into mulatto and black companies has been noted in Martinique, Saint Domingue, Curaçao, and some Brazilian towns,[10] as well as in prevailing marriage preferences and employment policies, and there are additional indications of distinctions in residence patterns. Still another explanation of the late and incomplete rise of class consciousness revolves around the fact that upward mobility was primarily effected through individual initiative or good fortune. For an individual free colored person to rise in status or wealth, therefore, he had to transcend the downward mobility or stasis that everywhere characterized the vast majority of the free colored group.

Another pattern of cleavage distinguished the established free colored, particularly of the second, third, and later generations, from the quasi-free and newly manumitted of the first generation. In some societies this pattern evidently reinforced—in fact replicated—the differentiation of mulattoes and blacks within the free group. The newly "freed" persons were typically enveloped in conditions of linger-

[9] Douglas Hall has noted another non-congealing aspect of free colored aspirations in Jamaica: because many free colored persons were in the "family" of white plantocrats and managers, their aspirations might best be described as father oriented.

[10] On the other hand, as Russell-Wood points out, whites carefully inculcated mixed companies (including whites) in rural areas with conscious concern for, and reasoned fear of, unmixed companies.

ing servitude resulting from provisos in their manumission papers or from debts incurred in self-puchase. Many of them bound themselves or "free" members of their families into states of debt peonage in order to gain the funds to free a wife, a husband, children, parents, or other relatives. In many cases the consequent creditor-debtor relationship took on the same character as the former master-slave relationship.

It is in this marginal zone between slave status and the position of free people of color that one squarely confronts the problems of defining the free colored as a "community" or as a "class" or "caste." Until the anti-manumission restrictions (together with other factors) began to limit severely the access of slaves to a free status, numbers of slaves moved each year into the borderland of freedom. When set against the total population, their numbers were of course small, but, seen in relation to the total free colored population, their numbers were considerable.[11] Several of the contributors note that the first-generation free colored constituted a substantial part of the total free colored population, at least during the early phases of the emergence of a free non-white group.

As the material presented by the contributors clearly suggests, the newly freed constituted but one band in a series of closely associated statuses which included hired-out slaves, slaves attempting to purchase their own freedom, slaves nearly free, those just declared free, those "free" but in lingering debt to their masters, those free with families still in bondage, and those longer-term free whose downward mobility or status left them in a dependent condition. The common ingredient in this cluster of free colored statuses was their persistent dependency, and their desperate position contrasts sharply with that of the free colored smallholding farmers, tavernkeepers, artisans, transporters, traders, and slaveowners, who had achieved a measure of success and had established a semblance of economic independence.

The fact that there were slaves who could be considered in the same category as nominally free men makes the problem of comprehending the role of the free colored no simpler. What the chapters here suggest is that the detectable linkages between free colored and slave (or, put another way, the very slender gap between the two) made political alliance no more likely or feasible. All were in desperate circumstances, so desperate that many freedmen sought the protection of renewed servile relationships with former masters. A more detailed study of Caribbean slave revolts, as well as of nonviolent political and social clubs and movements, may well disclose tentative, even concrete, alliances between parties from both statuses. The dis-

[11] We have too little specific data of a quantitative nature on the "newly freed," particularly for the eighteenth century. Table 3 lists the proportions of free colored among the total colored population for several societies at various dates, suggesting in every case that the annual number of slaves who became free must have been quite small in proportion to the total slave population.

TABLE 3. Freedmen as Percentage of Total Colored Population in Selected Societies

Society	1764–1768	1773–1776	1784–1790	1800–1808	1812–1821	1827–1840
Puerto Rico	—	82.2 (1775)	—	84.2 (1802)	81.9 (1810)	—
Curaçao	—	—	—	—	40.2 (1817)	52.6 (1833)
Brazil						
Minas Gerais	—	—	41.4 (1786)	54.4 (1808)	54.7 (1821)	—
São Paulo	—	—	—	43.0 (1800)	49.0 (1815)	43.5 (1836)
Martinique	2.6 (1764)	3.9 (1776)	4.2 (1784)	8.0 (1802)	10.4 (1816)	12.0 (1826)
Saint Domingue	—	—	4.3 (1784)	—	—	—
Jamaica	1.9 (1768)	2.3 (1775)	—	3.2 (1800)	—	10.1 (1834)
Barbados	0.6 (1768)	0.7 (1773)	1.3 (1786)	3.3 (1801)	4.0 (1815)	7.5 (1833)
United States						
Upper South	—	—	5.5 (1790)	8.1 (1800)	10.6 (1820)	12.3 (1840)
Lower South	—	—	1.6 (1790)	2.1 (1800)	3.5 (1820)	3.5 (1840)
Cuba	—	41.0 (1774)	—	—	—	27.1 (1827)

Sources: Same as those for Table 1.

tinction to be made here is between closeness in status, which is observable, and the self-conscious realization of closeness, which is not detectable. What we have at present, however, is the impression that the free colored almost everywhere avoided alliances, and even the appearance of alliances, with slaves until the eve of emancipation. Then, in certain cases, working alliances evolved and functioned effectively throughout much of the post-emancipation age. In other cases—and here the United States is a striking example—colored who were free before emancipation maintained a leading and privileged role over emancipated freedmen for several decades. An interesting contrast is Martinique, where, as Elisabeth notes, the free colored were so slow in anticipating and adjusting to the general emancipation of slaves that they became lost in the backwash and took their social and political lead from the dominant group of newly freed while attempting at the same time to preserve their cultural, and to some extent somatic, distinctiveness.

Where it is possible to detect exceptions to the view that the free colored eschewed all forms of alliance with slaves, these turn out to be progressive, usually anti-colonialist, movements or actions, which included not only slaves and freedmen but abolitionist whites as well. The point here is that the free colored resisted opportunities to form a common *racial* front with the slaves, typically the majority group in a slave society. It is an observation that present and future work must challenge. Certainly, our full understanding of the free colored is constrained by a tendency to see the established free colored, if not the elite, as typical of the whole group. Because the elite have been just that much more articulate, they take a prominent place in this volume. They played a key role at the upper interstice of the three-tiered structure discussed above. The line between white and colored free was, of course, much more clearly defined than was that between free colored and slave. The fact that some free colored did pass into the white group did not create links between the two tiers. In this case, passing merely reinforced the fact of social separation based on race.[12]

While in every society a considerable body of colonial legislation defined the gap between white and free colored very clearly, there were links between the two groups which tended to strengthen the colonial hand of the whites and at the same time to limit the coalition of non-white groups. Foremost was the development and use of free

[12] We might note here that passing from slavery to freedom was also likely to reinforce whatever distinctions marked the boundary between the two. The psychological dimension of passing is here underscored in Russell-Wood's study of the dependent free colored of eighteenth-century Brazil. For them, freedom was first a release from manual labor and second a search for new forms of sustenance and employment. The fact that freedmen correlated slavery with manual labor made the distinction between the two statuses all the sharper.

colored militia as the police arm of the slave society. Similarly, interracial marriage, miscegenation, the plantocratic aspirations of the
free colored, and prevalent fears of slave revolts all cemented the
tenuous but working relationship between the two minorities. More
subtle and less measurable were the opportunities created for the free
colored by the dependence of the plantocracies on them for skilled
labor and for the provisioning of the plantations.

Of course, as several chapters make clear, this service role was
not the preserve of the free colored alone. Crucial was the cheap com-
petiton offered in these fields by hired-out slaves, slaves purchasing
their own freedom, and unpropertied white immigrants. Genovese
notes the effect of such competition on the position of the free colored
in the American South. The important immigration of white workers
and craftsmen into southern cities in the antebellum period may be
seen as one of the principal factors effecting the reduction of the
small middle tier that had been present in all of the southern states in
1810, but that by 1860 was largely absent outside the Upper South
and Louisiana.

Although we have no more than a sense of the problems that
arose out of economic competition between the free colored and mobile slaves, we do see sharp conflicts between unpropertied whites and
free colored, not only in American cities, but also in Saint Domingue
and the French Antilles on the eve of the French Revolution, in Brazil
throughout the eighteenth century, and, perhaps most clearly, in
Cuba during the nineteenth century. The earliest indications of such
conflict are found within the legislation drafted to limit the range of
occupations open to free colored people—whether trading in Saint
Domingue, shipping in the French Antilles, or diamond mining in
Minas Gerais.

To say that free persons of color generally acquiesced in the
slave system, identified with the whites, and gave aid and comfort to
the plantocratic regimes is not to say that their role in the political
stirrings taking place in these societies in the late eighteenth century
was inert. Consciously and unconsciously, free blacks and free mulattoes offered the seeds of revolt or threatened revolt to the unfree
blacks. The free colored were usually among the first to raise the
issues of personal liberty and class discrimination in the societies.
Though a variety of conditions made direct alliance with slaves unlikely, the unfree blacks became conscious of world issues of which
their status and condition were a part. Elisabeth points out the way in
which the free colored took the initiative in Martinique and Guadeloupe in the midst of the French Revolution, and the way in which
protest by the free colored, even at the elite level, ignited revolt among
the unfree in Saint Domingue has been widely remarked. The fact
that the free colored were ready to act, and that their petitions and
appeals could very quickly inspire slaves to rebel, was not lost on the
white population. Even where revolt did not occur, new conditions

emerged in the vortex of widespread white fear of slave insurrections, a fear enlarged by the articulated grievances and appeals of the free colored. Apart from the strident measures adopted to preserve and enhance distinctions between slave and free colored, considerations and exceptions were given by state and plantocracy to limited numbers of free colored in an attempt to quiet free colored resentment over exclusionist policies based on race. The fact that free people of color accepted privilege when it was offered says less about commitment and corruptibility than it does about the precarious circumstances in which most free colored people lived.

Together, the ten papers in this volume provide a picture of a group whose place in the larger society was everywhere ambiguous, if not desperate, a group which came under increasing attack from the eighteenth century onward in all the societies, with the possible exception of Brazil, where the nineteenth century appears to have been a far more open period than the eighteenth. The apparently unique position of Brazil—or, as Herbert S. Klein has carefully noted, parts of Brazil—has brought considerable comparativist attention to the slave societies of the New World. Each of the papers in this collection offers comparative insight, and several, including those by Russell-Wood, H. Hoetink, and Frederick P. Bowser, are revealing comparative studies in their own right. Russell-Wood and Hoetink are not alone in using the comparative argument to demonstrate the secondary role of Iberian and northen European ethos and law in shaping the role of the free colored within Brazil, Surinam, and Curaçao. Diversity is shown to be much more closely related to specific economic conditions—at times and in particular places opening up extensive opportunities for a free, non-white, middle group, while at other times effecting the closure of opportunities for non-whites and the displacement of the free colored.

Several of the contributors suggest that the comparison of societies as whole units tends to obscure the rich variety of life among the several slave societies. The limitations of comparing large-scale units have been noted elsewhere, and the retarding effects of such a general approach are becoming increasingly appreciated by students of slave societies. Contrasts between urban and rural free colored, or between those operating at particular economic nodes—such as Minas Gerais —and those attempting to squeeze a living out of marginal soil, are suggested throughout the papers and would appear to be far more significant and revealing than those generally noted between one society and another. Interestingly, such contrasts were commonplace in contemporary observations. As Elisabeth has observed for Martinique, whites expressed an outstanding preference for militiamen drawn from the countryside and were very reluctant to induct a free colored townsman. In Brazil, the American South, Barbados, Cuba, Saint Domingue, and the Spanish mainland colonies, contrasts between town and countryside, between centers of intensive economic activity

—sugar "towns" and mining camps—and backwaters, between older settled areas and frontiers, and between areas where the free colored were under close supervision by whites and those marginal areas where they were not are sharp. As the play of national tradition is seen to be far less pronounced, the discernible variables at play in the New World must become many. A number of recent monographs, and, it is hoped, these papers as well, point the way to a new wave of more intensive local studies of parishes and towns throughout the hemisphere, studies which are likely to detail the precarious human existence of slave and freedman, as well as the varying degrees and meaning of freedom in an age of economic exploitation and aggrandizement.

FREDERICK P. BOWSER

1 | Colonial Spanish America

INTRODUCTION

Free persons of color outnumbered their slave counterparts in
Spanish America well before the struggles for political independence,
but we know surprisingly little about this important group of people.
To be sure, nearly every historian who has studied the black man and
his descendants in colonial Spanish America makes mention, and
often an extended one, of the free as well as the slave. Nevertheless,
the African in bondage is both more dramatic and easier to study
than the sometimes tortuous socioeconomic ascent of his free and
often racially mixed brother. The status of the slave, both legal and
actual, can be determined more readily than that of the free person of
color because documentation concerning the former is usually more
abundant and more precise. In the mass, if not individually, the
existence of the slave was recorded many times: in importation records, in bills of sale, in wills of masters, in letters of manumission.
The free colored is a more elusive subject for study. At the bottom of the
social and economic scale, such an individual aroused only intermit-
tent government concern, was often mentioned only in the most
general terms in the accounts of travelers, and all too rarely participated in the types of activities which generated records to document
his existence. For example, a poor mulatto in an urban area was no
more than one of the potentially unruly masses to government officials and observers, and may never have had occasion to enter into a
legal agreement which would have been preserved in notarial records.
His very existence, not to mention individuality, is difficult for the historian to uncover. By the same token, an ambitious person of African
descent seems to have made every effort to hide his racial origins,
and, unless archival research of the most painstaking sort is employed, his saga is likewise lost to us.

Despite these difficulties, continuing research will reveal much
not now known about the free colored population of colonial Spanish
America, and historians who attempt the task will significantly increase our knowledge of that area's development and civilization. We
need to understand in greater detail how thousands of slaves not only
secured their freedom but also, despite many legal restrictions and

19

much opposition from the dominant white society, achieved a better life for themselves and for their descendants. The essay which follows is an attempt to summarize our present knowledge of this complex problem in the context of the wide range of economic, social, and demographic conditions which prevailed in the Spanish American empire during its long history. More specifically, the origins, size, and legal status of the free colored population, together with its actual status, access to opportunities, and degree of assimilation during the colonial period, will be examined in relation to what we know about conditions, both local and empire-wide, which influenced relations among blacks, whites, and browns.

ORIGINS

The presence of free blacks and mulattoes in Spanish America dates from the earliest days of the conquest. Some came from Spain as part of the entourage which surrounded all prominent conquistadors and high government officials.[1] Still other blacks, who had come to the New World as slaves, distinguished themselves through military prowess and profited by the free-and-easy atmosphere of the conquest period to gain their freedom. A case in point is Juan Valiente, a slave in New Spain who fled his master's service after a disagreement, passed easily to Peru, and in 1535 joined the ill-fated expedition of Diego de Almagro to Chile. Valiente survived the rigors experienced by that party and later attached himself to the expedition of Pedro de Valdivia, who was more fortunate in his attempt at colonization. Valiente went to Chile with Valdivia as a free soldier with his own arms and horse, and the distinction of his services in the new colony earned him both a land grant and the tribute and services of a group of natives.[2] In addition, more than one conquistador freed his slaves for faithful service during the exertions of the conquest. Perhaps the

[1] For example, during the civil wars which plagued Peru in the 1530s and 1540s, the forces of Gonzalo Pizarro apprehended and hanged on Rafael Vela, described by one prominent chronicler as a mulatto relative of the luckless Viceroy Blasco Núñez Vela. See Pedro Gutiérrez de Santa Clara, *Historia de las guerras civiles del Perú (1544–1588) y de otros sucesos de las Indias*, ed. Manuel Serrano y Sanz, 6 vols. (Madrid, 1904–29), 2: 177–78. Concerning free persons of color in Spain during this period, see Ruth Pike, "Sevillian Society in the Sixteenth Century: Slaves and Freedmen," *Hispanic American Historical Review*, 47 (1967): 344–59.

[2] Rolando Mellafe, *La introducción de la esclavitud negra en Chile: Tráfico y rutas* (Santiago de Chile, 1959), pp. 49–50. Valiente later tried legally to purchase freedom from his owner, but the emissary entrusted with the task appears to have absconded with the money. His master, in turn, initiated legal proceedings to reclaim Valiente and his property, a process cut short by the death of the latter in battle. For details, see William F. Sater, "The Forgotten Race: The Black in Chile," to be published in 1972 in a collection of essays concerning Latin America and the African edited by Frederick P. Bowser and Robert Brent Toplin. According to Sater, four other blacks, presumably all free, likewise won grants of Indian tribute and labor as a reward for their services in the conquest.

most famous example concerns the black woman Margarita, slave of Diego de Almagro. Margarita waited upon Almagro faithfully while in Panama, accompanied him during the conquest of Peru, and remained with the Adelantado during the imprisonment which led to his execution. In gratitude, Almagro freed her upon his death.[3]

By all these means, free blacks and mulattoes quickly became an important group in most of the Spanish colonies. In Lima, for example, they were considered a serious problem as early as 1538.[4] However, as the exuberance and liberality of the conquest period waned, as the Spanish crown addressed itself to the hard task of building a society in America, traditional attitudes and principles came to the fore, and the processes of manumission were affected as a matter of course. As Magnus Mörner has reminded us, Spain, like most nations during this period, desired to "regulate every part of society by means of legislation," and in the Spanish case such legislation was both casuistic and particularistic, "a series of administrative decisions arrived at in certain cases and with regard to local jurisdictions."[5] Generalizations concerning the crown's intentions for the whole of America are therefore difficult to formulate, but by and large the crown did make an effort to take legislation framed for the peninsula and modify it in accordance with New World realities. Because this effort concerned the black population, both free and slave, the model was the famous thirteenth-century legal codification known as Las Siete Partidas, drawn up by the order of Alfonso the Wise.[6]

It should be stressed that the Siete Partidas was more a statement of legal and moral principles than a compilation of specific legislation.[7] That is, a body of pre-existing Spanish slave laws was not snipped out of the Partidas and applied to America; rather, the principles embodied in this compilation, although sometimes honored more in the breach than in the observance, guided Spanish lawmakers in their task. The Partidas viewed slavery as a necessary evil, as a transitory condition which did not alter or diminish the nature of the

[3] The deed of emancipation, given by Almagro's executor, is dated Lima, May 8, 1539, and is summarized in Stella R. Clemence, ed., The Harkness Collection in the Library of Congress: Calendar of Spanish Manuscripts Concerning Peru, 1531–1651 (Washington, D.C., 1932), p. 97. Margarita subsequently took her former master's name and later founded a chaplaincy in the Mercedarian convent at Cuzco to perpetuate Almagro's memory and that of his followers on the Chilean expedition. See Víctor M. Barriga, ed., Los Mercedarios en el Perú en el siglo XVI: Documentos inéditos del Archivo General de Indias, 5 vols. (Rome and Arequipa, 1933–54), 2: 184–88.

[4] James Lockhart, Spanish Peru, 1532–1560: A Colonial Society (Madison, Wis., 1968), p. 191.

[5] Race Mixture in the History of Latin America (Boston, 1967), p. 35.

[6] Las Siete Partidas del Rey Don Alfonso el Sabio cotejadas con varios códices antiguos por la Real Academia de la Historia, 3 vols. (Madrid, 1807).

[7] In the words of David Brion Davis: "It is important to note . . . that as a body of ideal law, las Siete Partidas had little relation to the living law of Castille." The Problem of Slavery in Western Culture (Ithaca, N.Y., 1966), p. 103.

slave, while liberty was proclaimed as one of the greatest of human possessions.[8] The compilation could therefore not fail to declare that freedom remained a legitimate goal for the slave, which intention society should facilitate by sanctioning such means as manumission by the master, liberation by a third person, and self-purchase with gift money.[9] By virtue of this precept, claims to freedom became privileged cases in royal courts of law.[10] As the Spanish crown and various agencies of local government slowly defined the status of the black man in America in a body of legislation noted for its repressive features, the strictures of the *Partidas* were not only adhered to but even expanded to favor the achievement of free status. As the institution of slavery evolved in Spanish America, the paths to freedom became three: manumission by the master, various forms of purchase, and (indirectly) the continuing process of racial mixture.[11] We will examine each of these paths in turn.

Voluntary manumission by the master was a fixture of slavery until its abolition. In its simplest form, freedom was granted to the slave in the master's last will and testament, or perhaps in a letter of manumission while the latter was still living, for long and faithful service. For example, Juan del Corral, a prominent builder in early seventeenth-century Lima, freed his slave Luisa Berbesi by testament in gratitude for the "fidelity and love" with which she had nursed him through various severe illnesses.[12] In another instance, Dominga Conga, aged forty-five, was freed by her mistress "for the service of God," for her faithful service to her mistress, and for the fact that

---

[8] *Siete Partidas, partida* III, *título* v, *ley* 4: "porque todos los derechos del mundo siempre ayudaron a la libertad"; *título* xiv, *ley* 5; *título* xxxiii, *regla* 1; *partida* IV, *título* v, *prólogo; título* xxi, *ley* 1; *título* xxii, *ley* 1 y 13.

[9] *Ibid., partida* III, *título* ii, *ley* 8.

[10] In a 1540 decree addressed to the *audiencias* of Spanish America, the crown commanded that if black slaves "should publicly demand their liberty, they should be heard, and justice done to them, and care be taken that they should not on that account . . . be maltreated by their Masters." I use the translation of Sir Arthur Helps, *The Spanish Conquest in America and Its Relation to the History of Slavery and to the Government of Colonies,* 2nd ed., 4 vols. (London and New York, 1900), 4: 250. The principle was obliquely reconfirmed by a decree of 1681 printed in Richard Konetzke, ed., *Colección de documentos para la historia de la formación social de Hispanoamérica, 1493–1810,* 3 vols. in 5 (Madrid, 1953–62), 2, pt. 2: 722–23.

[11] Neither in Spanish America nor in Spain was marriage considered sufficient grounds for freedom, although philosophically it was difficult to reconcile the slave's marital obligations with the master's absolute authority. *Las Siete Partidas,* which proclaimed the slave's right to marry, even against his owner's will, did not go so far as to recommend that he be given free status. The same principle was restated for Spanish America by decrees of 1525, 1538, and 1541, printed in Konetzke, ed., *Colección,* 1: 81–82, 185, 210. For an interesting discussion of the philosophical conflict between slave marriages and the master's authority, see Davis, *Problem of Slavery,* pp. 102–6.

[12] The will, dated in 1611, is printed in Emilio Harth-terré and Alberto Márquez Abanto, "El puente de piedra de Lima," *Revista del Archivo Nacional del Perú,* 24 (1960): 55–74.

she had successfully reared five children.[13] Another variation was to
free the slave children of parents who remained in bondage.[14] In still
other instances, generous masters freed their slaves out of simple
love and charity.[15] Obviously, however, manumission was not an act
of generosity to blacks who were either aged or infirm and had no one
to fall back on for support. To avoid the cost of supporting such
blacks, selfish masters occasionally freed them. The frequency of such
cases is unknown, but the Spanish slave code of 1789 saw fit to prohibit the practice.[16] On the other hand, the selectivity with which
masters freed slaves in their wills may indicate that many knew that
liberty was a cruel illusion for aged and helpless blacks.

In addition, voluntary manumission might be hedged about with
conditions prompted by a wide variety of motives. Many such cases
involved masters near death who tried to provide for the welfare of
infant and dependent slaves who would have found a simple declaration of freedom a hardship. In 1640, Martín de Ribadeneira, a free
black citizen of Lima, provided that his slave Miguel (aged ten) serve
his wife for an additional ten years, after which he was to be freed.[17]
In 1610, Juana Bañol (aged eight) was freed by her mistress on condition that she serve the convent of Nuestra Señora de la Limpia Concepción in Lima until attaining the age to become a lay sister. On the
latter date, Juana was either to pledge herself to a religious life or to
serve another four years.[18] In other instances, masters tried to balance the interests of the slave against those of dependent relatives
and friends. An Indian woman, for example, freed two female slaves
(both aged twenty-five) on condition that one serve an aged friend
of hers for six years while the other was to serve yet another friend
for a decade.[19] Often, of course, the economic interests of the masters
were quite clear. Slaves were freed, for example, on condition that
they continue to work for their former masters for a certain period of
time each day; or a black owned by a partnership might become, say,

---

[13] Archivo Nacional del Perú, Sección Notarial (hereafter cited as ANP,
SN), register of Cristóbal de Pineda (1620), August 1, fols. 245r–246v.

[14] See, for example, the following will: Horacio H. Urteaga, ed., "Cristóbal
de Burgos, Conquistador del Perú y Regidor del Cabildo de Lima," Revista del
Archivo Nacional del Perú, II (1938): 105. The document was dated Lima,
August 11, 1550.

[15] See, for example, the case of Luis de Lagama, a mulatto artisan, in
Emilio Harth-terré and Alberto Márquez Abanto, "El artesano negro en la
arquitectura virreinal limeña," Revista del Archivo Nacional del Perú, 25
(1961): 51–52.

[16] Konetzke, ed., Colección, 3: 647.

[17] ANP, SN, register of Antonio de Tamayo (1640), will of November 10,
fols. 915v–917v.

[18] Ibid., register of Francisco González Balcázar (1610), will of María de
Cabrera, December 8, fols. 837v–840r.

[19] Ibid., register of Juan Gutiérrez (1573), will of Juana de Espinosa,
September 12, fols. 972r–974r. One of the females had two small children who
were obligated for the same period of service.

one-third free upon manumission by one of the partners, in which case he would divide his time between his own occupations and continuing service to the partnership.[20] In rural areas, some masters freed large numbers of blacks but made sure that they became tenants. The former were thereby freed of the costs of slavery, assured of a fixed annual rent from the lands involved, and at the same time kept a pool of labor to draw upon at harvest time.[21]

Furthermore, intelligent and restless slaves might be placated by the promise of freedom made contingent upon a continued period of service. In 1605, for example, María de Cevallos, a slave born in Lima, was freed by her master on condition that she serve him for an additional four years.[22] In other instances, letters of manumission were granted to take effect upon the master's death.[23] Finally, some acts of manumission are difficult to evaluate. Upon his death in 1598, Juan López, a carpenter married to a slave, freed their mulatto daughter and two blacks whom he had taught the skill of carpentry. His wife, however, for reasons which escape the historian, appears to have remained in bondage.[24]

With regard to the various forms by which freedom might be purchased, Spanish American practice was actually more liberal than that envisioned by the *Partidas*. The latter compilation sanctioned the purchase of freedom by gift money, but, unlike the Roman tradition, forbade slaves to own property (*peculium*).[25] In Spanish America, however, the slave's right to *peculium* was unobtrusively, and perhaps unconsciously, restored. As early as 1526, royal officials were ordered to study the feasibility of establishing prices, depending on the slave's age and condition, which, if raised and paid by the black to his master, would entitle him to freedom.[26] It may well be that the crown had nothing more than gift money in mind, and certainly such price scales were never established for the empire as a whole, but it was not long before the custom of self-purchase took hold. In the beginning, such arrangements were entirely ad hoc and informal. Master and slave agreed on the latter's worth, perhaps with the aid of an appraisal by a disinterested third party, and the former then swore not only to free the black if this sum were paid but also that the slave could never be sold for more than this amount. All subsequent buyers of the black

[20] See Harth-terré and Márquez Abanto, "El artesano negro," pp. 27–31, for the details of these examples.

[21] See the example for eighteenth-century Venezuela in Federico Brito Figueroa, *Ensayos de historia social venezolana* (Caracas, 1960), pp. 112–13.

[22] ANP, SN, register of Juan de Altamirano (1605), July 15, fols. 561v–563v.

[23] *Ibid.*, June 1, fols. 413v–415v.

[24] Harth-terré and Márquez Abanto, "El artesano negro," p. 8, from a will dated June 3.

[25] *Siete Partidas, partida* III, *título* ii, *ley* 8; *título* xxix, *ley* 3; *partida* IV, *título* xxi, *ley* 7; *partida* V, *título* v, *ley* 45.

[26] Konetzke, ed., *Colección*, 1: 88.

were then likewise obliged to agree to these conditions. This agreement might be reached while the master was still alive,[27] or it might be embodied as an act of generosity in the latter's will.[28] Moreover, the terms might be made more generous still. In 1619, for example, a *mulata* named Ursula de Vergara, whose age is not recorded, was sold in Lima for 270 pesos on the conditions that she would be freed as soon as this sum had been raised and that the amount would be reduced by 25 pesos for each year of service. A year later, her free mulatto mother persuaded a Spaniard to loan her the requisite amount.[29]

By the seventeenth century, at least in some areas of Spanish America, these informal arrangements had become institutionalized. The famous *coartación* system of Cuba provides the most spectacular example. Under this system, eventually accepted and codified by the Spanish crown in the eighteenth century, a slave had the right to demand that his value be publicly declared by a court of law, an appraisal which he was then permitted to pay off in several installments: Once a slave became *coartado*, he also acquired the right to change masters at will, provided that he could secure a purchaser who was willing to accept his status. Indeed, in Cuba the crown eventually supported the right of a slave to assume *coartado* status against the will of his master.[30] There is some evidence that, by the beginning of the nineteenth century in Venezuela, any slave between the ages of fifteen and forty might purchase his freedom upon presentation of three hundred pesos.[31] Elsewhere in Spanish America, the self-pur-

[27] ANP, SN, register of Cristóbal Rodríguez (1640), letter of manumission of May 5, fols. 342v.–344r. In this letter, Bartolomé de Toro agreed to free Isabel Criolla, aged thirty-four and pregnant, on condition that she pay 500 pesos. The document went on to acknowledge the receipt of 300 pesos toward that end on the above date. See also *Libros de cabildos de Lima* (hereafter cited as *LCL*), ed. Bertram T. Lee and Juan Bromley (Lima, 1935–), 4: 548–51, which contains a bill of sale dated April 7, 1552, by which the city sold Antón Negro, a butcher, to one García Pérez for four hundred pesos; the bill of sale also stipulated that Negro should have the right of self-purchase.

[28] As one example among hundreds, in 1577, in a codicil to his will, Juan de Orozco, provided that Francisco Biafara, Baltasar Biafara, and Margarita Berbesi might all be free if the males paid 100 pesos each and the female paid 50 pesos, and that they were not to be sold for larger amounts. ANP, SN, register of Juan Gutiérrez (1577), codicil to will of Juan de Orozco, March 7, fols. 311r–312r.

[29] *Ibid.*, register of Francisco González Balcázar (1620), letter of manumission dated January 21, fols. 88v–90v. The mother had approved and signed the sale contract of 1619.

[30] Herbert S. Klein, *Slavery in the Americas: A Comparative Study of Virginia and Cuba* (Chicago, 1966), pp. 78 (esp. n. 62), 196–97. See also Hubert H. S. Aimes, "Coartación: A Spanish Institution for the Advancement of Slaves into Freedmen," *The Yale Review*, 17 (1908–9): 412–31.

[31] Aimes, "Coartación," p. 417; Miguel Acosta Saignes, *Vida de los esclavos negros en Venezuela* (Caracas, n.d.), pp. 305–6. As Aimes observes, such a low self-purchase price would have been bitterly opposed in areas where many slaves were expensive artisans of high earning power, but the system may have worked in Venezuela, where the emphasis was upon plantation labor.

chase system seemingly did not become so formalized, but, as Norman Meiklejohn makes clear for eighteenth-century New Granada, a slave's right to purchase his freedom for a fair price was more often than not upheld by the courts, frequently in the face of bitter opposition from slaveholders.[32]

Obviously, the right to purchase one's fredom, except in the case of gift money, would have been meaningless unless the master allowed the slave a certain amount of free time to accumulate the sum.[33] Fortunately, many masters were quite charitable in this respect. To take an example or two from seventeenth-century Peru, Gaspar Mandinga, by the terms of his master's will, was required to work three days a week on the estate of the heirs, but the rest of his time was his own, and he eventually accumulated the 200 pesos with which to purchase his freedom.[34] In the case of Polonia Negra, whose two free mulatto sons had already paid 330 pesos of the 630 required to liberate her, the master agreed that the mother was to continue to serve his household until noon each day and to sleep there at night. The rest of the day was her own, to find gainful employment with which to pay the balance of her value. Black artisans, a group discussed in more detail below, were sometimes allowed to apply a certain portion of their daily wage toward their liberation, and the same practice no doubt prevailed in other occupations.[35]

Racial mixture played a very important role in the creation of Spanish America's free black and mulatto population.[36] If the Spanish crown had had its way, the American colonies would have been populated by three distinct racial estates: the European, the Indian, and the African. The government could tolerate, and even heartily approve, the occasional marriage of a conquistador with an Aztec or Inca princess, but, beyond that, crown and church were not prepared to go. In the eyes of society, racial mixture produced types who

[32] "The Implementation of Slave Legislation in Eighteenth-Century New Granada," to be published in the collection of essays edited by Bowser and Toplin mentioned in note 2. See also Jaime Jaramillo Uribe, "Esclavos y señores en la sociedad colombiana del siglo XVIII," *Anuario Colombiano de Historia Social y de la Cultura,* 1 (1963); 53–55.

[33] There is some evidence that unscrupulous third parties advanced so-called gift money only after the slave involved promised to enter his service upon manumission, but the frequency of such occurrences is impossible to determine. See José Luis Masini, *La esclavitud negra en Mendoza: Época independiente* (Mendoza, Argentina, 1962), pp. 55–59.

[34] ANP, SN, register of Cristóbal de Arauz (1635), letter of manumission signed on November 28 by Don José de Godoy Delgadillo (executor of the estate, who had cleared the question with the other heirs), fols. 929r–933v.

[35] For examples of this practice, see Harth-terré and Márques Abanto, "El artesano negro," pp. 7–8, 10–11, 27–31. These authors also discuss the case of Polonia mentioned above. My research in Peruvian notarial records indicates that colored families were very active in accumulating money with which to free their members. Polonia is one example among many.

[36] Except where noted, I rely here on Mörner, *Race Mixture,* which is the best survey of this phenomenon.

combined the worst defects and vices of both parents, and, indeed, prejudice tended to make this view a self-fulfilling prophecy. Afro-Indian sexual unions were opposed with particular ferocity. The church feared that the African would reinforce the Indian's attachment to paganism, perhaps even infect him with the infidelity of Islam.[37] Furthermore, the products of such unions, which usually involved African men and Indian women, would be free, since in law the child acquired the mother's status.

All the efforts of crown and church to prevent racial mixture were to no avail. Spaniard, Indian, and African interacted sexually over the years to produce a bewildering variety of racial mixtures (castas),[38] and this development inevitably strengthened the formation of a large class of free "colored." Afro-Indian mixtures, of which the zambo was the purest type, were caught in a rather curious position. Usually free at birth, there was some temptation for the Afro-Indian to identify with his mother, to attempt to be accepted in her village, to work part of the lands which belonged to her family— in short, to gain acceptance as an Indian. On the other hand, the real social standing of an Indian, as distinguished from his legal condition, was generally inferior even to that of the slave.[39] If the Afro-Indian attempted to pass himself off as an Indian, he was inevitably

[37] The African became vaguely identified with Islam in the Iberian mind because the first black slaves were captured from the Moors during the reconquest or were obtained from Moorish traders who plied the Sahara route between the Mediterranean and West Africa. In the fifteenth century, as the Iberians pushed exploration and trade along the West African coast, they learned that the Arabs not only had dealt in Africans, but had also proselytized among them. Largely for this reason, in the beginning, only blacks born in the power of Christians were allowed in Spanish America. (Instructions to Nicolás de Ovando, governor of the Indies, Granada, September 16, 1501, in *Colección de documentos inéditos . . . Indias*, 42 vols. [Madrid, 1864–84], 31: 23.) Indeed, in 1503, concern over the influence of African idolatry among the Indians became so great that the introduction of blacks was briefly prohibited, but the need for labor caused the decision to be reversed the following year. (Antonio de Herrera y Tordesillas, *Historia general de los hechos de los castellanos en las islas y tierra firme del mar océano*, 17 vols. [Madrid, 1934–57], 1: 142; Ursula Lamb, *Frey Nicolas de Ovando, gobernador de las Indias, 1501–1509* [Madrid, 1956], p. 178.) Thereafter, the crown contented itself with an attempt to exclude slaves suspected of Islamic leanings. Berber and Moorish slaves were excluded as early as 1506, and the prohibition against the former was reinstated in 1531. The Wolofs, from the Guinea area, were excluded in 1532. (Herrera, *Historia general*, 1: 175; *Colección de documentos inéditos . . . Ultramar*, 25 vols. [Madrid, 1885–1932], 10: 103–4, 141–42.) Even these measures proved difficult to enforce. In 1543, for example, the government felt compelled to order the expulsion of all Berbers and Moors from Spanish America. (Fernando Ortíz Fernández, *Hampa afro-cubana: Los negros esclavos* [Havana, 1916], p. 343, n. 1.)

[38] See, for example, the lists of racial terminology in Mörner, *Race Mixture*, pp. 58–59, and the minute racial and physical discriminations recorded in Gonzalo Aguirre Beltrán, "Races in 17th Century Mexico," *Phylon*, 6 (1945): 212–18.

[39] Mörner, *Race Mixture*, p. 60.

subjected to the various tribute and labor demands of the Spanish. As a *zambo*, he might avoid such obligations,[40] but the price was the loss of whatever security and acceptance was offered by village life. The *zambo* was then forced to make his way in the larger Spanish world as a member of a despised racial group. Of course, he might have been born in one of the Spanish cities or towns, since many Indians for various reasons abandoned village life during the colonial period, and in this case his alternatives were reduced. Present knowledge does not permit further generalization, but it is clear that the lot of the Afro-Indian, product as he was of the two most despised racial groups in Spanish America, was frequently unenviable.

The fate of the mulatto, and of the still lighter products of Afro-Spanish sexual unions, was in many instances somewhat more pleasant. Sexual contact between Spanish men and African women was widespread and persistent throughout the colonial period.[41] One observer in early seventeenth-century Peru noted maliciously that the Spanish males of the colony seemed to prefer black women over their own, and ascribed the tendency to the fact that most of them had been suckled by African wet nurses.[42] Whatever the reason, black women seem to have held an overpowering attraction for the Spanish, and the inevitable result was the creation of a large mulatto group.

Because they assumed their mother's status, such offspring were, more often than not, slaves. By 1563, even the crown was forced to capitulate to social reality. In that year, it was provided that Spanish fathers were to be given preference in the sale of any children they had had by slaves who belonged to another master if the purchase was made for the purpose of liberating these offspring.[43] This decree, of course, did nothing more than sanction societal practice. From the earliest days of the conquest, compassionate Spanish fathers frequently freed their slave children and provided for them. The Peruvian conquistador Domingo de Destre, for example, had a son named Miguel by Ana Negra, slave of one Don Diego de Agüero. Destre purchased the child's freedom, and upon his death bequeathed to Miguel a farm on the outskirts of Lima.[44] Most Spanish fathers

[40] The exemption of *zambos* from the obligations imposed on the Indians was reinstated by the crown in 1659 (Konetzke, ed., *Colección*, 2, pt. 1: 480).

[41] Very rarely did affairs between Spanish women and African men come to light. For one example, see Juan Antonio Suardo, *Diario de Lima*, ed. Rubén Vargas Ugarte, 2 vols. (Lima, 1936), 2: 35–36.

[42] Boleslao Lewin, ed., *Descripción del virreinato del Perú: Crónica inédita de comienzos del siglo XVII*, Universidad Nacional del Litoral (Rosario), Instituto de Investigaciones Históricas, Colección de textos y documentos, ser. B, no. 1 (Rosario, Argentina, 1958), p. 39.

[43] *Recopilación de leyes de los reynos de las Indias: Edición facsimilar de la cuarta impresión hecha en Madrid el año 1791* (Madrid, 1943), *libro* VII, *título* v, *ley* 6.

[44] See Horacio H. Urteaga, ed., "El conquistador y poblador del Perú Diego [sic] de Destre," *Revista del Archivo Nacional del Perú*, 8 (1930): 29–39, where Destre's will of July 24, 1542, is printed.

were not so lavish, but many freed their mulatto offspring without acknowledging parenthood. In 1600, for example, Melchior de Sintra, a resident of Lima, manumitted María Mulata (aged five) "for reasons which move me." The child, along with her mother, was conveniently out of sight in Ica.[45] Others, similarly embarrassed but with even less nerve, preferred to postpone emancipation for their wills.[46] Still others, who did not wish to wait until their deathbeds, nevertheless preferred to remain anonymous.[47] There were still other variations in the manumission process. Occasionally a slave mother, if she could not prevail upon the Spanish father to liberate the child, nevertheless found another, more charitable patron, perhaps the godfather.[48] Kind masters frequently freed the children of their female slaves as a reward for faithful service or out of compassion, even though they had not sired the children. In an unusual case of 1635, for example, Don Pedro Ramírez de Valdés and his wife freed Gabriel (aged eighteen months), son of their slave María Mulata, because he was "white and blonde with a Roman nose."[49]

Very rarely, the Spanish father might free the slave mother along with the child,[50] and more rarely still one reads of marriages between Spanish men and African women.[51] In general, however, such relationships were marked by no more than concubinage, although they might be relatively long-lasting, and the products continued to be illegitimate. The example which follows may be typical of many such relationships. This case concerns one Juan Antonio, who described himself as a simple farmer when he left the duchy of Savoy in 1602, first for Mexico and then for Peru via Spain. Juan Antonio left a wife and child behind in Savoy, but this did not prevent him from having a son in Peru by María Angola, slave of Doña María de Solís, in 1607. By this time Antonio was making some money by leasing farms belonging to various religious orders, and he was able to buy the freedom of the child, named Andrés, almost immediately after birth for ninety pesos, plus eight pesos a month for room and board, with clothing to be considered a separate expense. In return, the mother was to be permitted to raise Andrés and, tacitly, to spend

[45] ANP, SN, register of Rodrigo Gómez de Baeza (1600), December 15, fol. 991.

[46] Jaramillo Uribe, "Esclavos y señores," p. 37.

[47] ANP, SN, register of Bartolomé de Toro (1630), August 8, fols. 653r–654v.

[48] Ibid., register of Cristóbal de Aguilar Mendieta (1593), letter of manumission of February 7, fols. 182v–183r; Miguel Negro (aged eight months) was freed by Manuel Correia, the padrino de bautismo, who paid 50 pesos.

[49] Ibid., register of Cristóbal de Aldaña (1635), July 17, fol. 390. Translations of quoted matter throughout this essay are the author's.

[50] See the case cited in n. 47.

[51] See the examples cited by Mörner, Race Mixture, p. 38, for seventeenth-century Santo Domingo, and Gonzalo Aguirre Beltrán, La población negra de México, 1519–1810 (Mexico, 1946), pp. 252–53, for Mexico during the same century.

considerable time at the residence which Juan Antonio maintained. Antonio, who had added the more aristocratic "de los Reyes" to his name at this juncture, managed to evade deportation as a foreigner in 1612, and at approximately the same time by word and deed he recognized Andrés as his son. Andrés came to live with his father, while his slave mother receded into the background; presumably, Juan Antonio's growing respectability in the community precluded such a liaison.

Nevertheless, relations between father and son were harmonious until 1621, by which time Andrés was fourteen years of age. At this juncture, Juan Antonio, who had accumulated a modest fortune, saw a chance to marry once again (his Italian wife had died) and thus to secure the modest dowry brought to him by one Ana Sánchez de Vergara. Ana resented the presence of the mulatto Andrés, which led to such bitter quarrels that Andrés, to his father's sorrow, left for Panama to become a carpenter's apprentice. For the next eighteen years, there was no contact between father and son, and during this interval Andrés fell in the social scale. He could make no money at carpentry and had married a *mulata,* thereby compounding his troubles. In sharp contrast, his father left an estate valued at 70,000 pesos upon his death, including a large farm, a ship, and twenty black slaves. All this property went to Doña Ana, who promptly remarried, but Andrés caught wind of his father's death and hurried to Lima to claim his inheritance. Doña Ana evidently felt that she had no choice but to receive him in her household, but by 1643 his presence had grown irksome. His "stepmother" then played her trump card. Andrés did not know that he was free, and Doña Ana, who had the letter of manumission in her possession, threatened to enslave him unless he waived all rights to his father's estate in return for 400 pesos. Andrés yielded, but later brought suit for 10,000 pesos as his rightful share of his father's estate. In 1644, he was awarded one thousand pesos; dissatisfied with this verdict, he appealed to the Council of the Indies, which refused to consider the case.[52]

The fate of Andrés is unknown, but we may observe that 1,000 pesos was hardly a munificent sum. Family histories of this sort no doubt abounded in Spanish America as the process of racial mixture continued, and, no matter how tarnished, such sagas were important, not merely in creating a *class* of free blacks and mulattoes, but also, as we shall see, in furthering the socioeconomic ascent of this class. One must also mention that racial mixture in relation to the free colored population was an increasingly complex affair as the numbers of the latter mounted. Spaniards and free black and mulatto women produced offspring who were automatically free, and these in turn

[52] Archivo General de Indias (hereafter cited as AGI), Escribanía de Cámara 510c, "Andrés de los Reyes, hijo natural que dice ser de Juan Antonio de los Reyes, sobre que se declare por hijo natural," *passim.* Compare this case with the equally melancholy one in Mörner, *Race Mixture,* p. 67.

mingled with the European and Indian elements, and with the other castes, to produce an ever-larger and more bewildering variety of free "colored." That is, the reproduction and growth of the free African element of the population, while never divorced from slavery, came generation after generation to depend less upon that institution.

Before leaving the subject of manumission, however, there are several important points to be considered. The first of these concerns the frequency of the various types of manumission and the sex and age of the slaves involved. Table 1–1 was compiled from a Peruvian sample of 320 cases of liberation for the period 1560–1650.[53]

TABLE 1–1. Types of Manumission in Peru by Age and Sex, 1560–1650

Age of Slave	Sex		Terms of Liberation				
	Males	Females	Unconditional	Future Service	Other Obligations	By Payment	For Future Payment
Over 45	8	21	15	2	1	10	2
36–45	6	22	9	1	—	16	1
26–35	9	24	7	6	—	19	1
16–25	2	19	5	4	—	10	3
8–15	9	27	16	13	—	5	3
Under 8	54	30	37	8	1	37	2
Unknown	18	71	19	21	3	32	16
Totals	106	214	108	55	5	129	28

These figures suggest that manumission operated primarily for the benefit of women and small children, who composed 82 percent of the sample, while adult males in the prime of life (aged 16–35) were rarely so favored (3 percent). This means that in the early decades of colonization, the adult free colored population of Spanish America was heavily female and that a balance between the sexes must have been achieved only slowly, as generation after generation of free male infants attained manhood. These figures also reveal that various forms of purchase constituted the most important path to liberty, followed rather closely by unconditional manumission by the slave-

[53] The sample was taken on a random basis from more than 260 notarial registers in ANP, SN. To avoid a footnote of inordinate length, I will not cite the various notaries involved. For further detail, the reader is referred to my forthcoming book cited in n. 2.

holder. This trend no doubt continued for the rest of the colonial period, and may have become even more pronounced as self-purchase became increasingly institutionalized. For example, of 954 cases of manumission discovered for Havana during 1810 and 1811, 755 involved self-purchase.[54] If this example is at all typical for the rest of Spanish America, one would expect to find more adult males entering the ranks of the free colored population, since purchase should have operated as much to the advantage of the male as to that of the female.

Other questions which await additional detailed investigation concern the attitude toward manumission held by the masters and whether or not this attitude fluctuated through time in response to economic and social forces. There is considerable evidence that when labor was scarce, particularly during periods of economic prosperity, masters became disposed to frown upon all forms of manumission, even self-purchase. Perhaps the conditions which prevailed in Cuba during the sugar boom (discussed by Franklin Knight in this volume) provide the most spectacular example of this attitude. Faced with a labor shortage in the late colonial period, the masters of New Granada likewise seem to have opposed manumission with increasing bitterness.[55] As an observer who passed through Córdoba (Argentina) late in the colonial period noted:

> There is a very large number of slaves, most of them Creoles of all conceivable classes, because in this city and in all of Tucumán there is no leniency about granting freedom to any of them. They are easily supported, since the principal aliment, meat, is of such moderate price, and there is a custom of dressing them only in ordinary cloth, which is made at home by the slaves themselves, shoes being very rare. They aid their masters in many profitable ways and under this system do not think of freedom, thus exposing themselves to a sorrowful end, as is happening in Lima.

And this attitude existed at a time when, as the same observer noted, large numbers of slaves from the confiscated Jesuit holdings were being dumped on the market.[56] On the other hand, as Mörner has observed, during an economic depression a master might encourage self-purchase, even at a low price, "since the slave could neither be advantageously sold to others nor earn his keep."[57] Clearly, more research is needed to determine the extent to which the growth of the free colored population was impeded or encouraged by developments in the larger society.

[54] José L. Franco, *Afroamérica* (Havana, 1961), p. 129.

[55] Jaramillo Uribe, "Esclavos y señores," pp. 53–54.

[56] Concolorcorvo [Alonso Carrió de la Bandera], *El Lazarillo: A Guide for Inexperienced Travelers between Buenos Aires and Lima, 1773*, trans. Walter D. Kline (Bloomington, Ill., 1965), p. 79. For many years it was mistakenly assumed that Calixto Bustamante Carlos Inca was the author of this work. See the introduction by Richard A. Mazzara concerning this problem.

[57] *Race Mixture*, p. 117.

In any event, all legal forms of manumission seem to have been more beneficent for the urban slave than for the rural counterpart. This assertion is somewhat difficult to document, but seems justified once the realities of Spanish American slavery are considered. In the first place, it is a notorious fact, almost a cliché, that the Spaniards were great town dwellers, and agriculturalists were not exceptions to this rule. Those planters who could afford to do so lived in the nearest important town, or perhaps in the colony's capital city. They visited their estates with some frequency, but day-to-day administration was usually left in the hands of a foreman. For the slave, the foreman was to the master what Saint Anthony was to God, an intermediary to a source of awesome but abstract power which seemingly rarely concerned itself with the pitiful problems of servile existence.[58] Planters did not know the slaves on their estates well, and they seem to have freed them rarely.[59] To be sure, agriculturalists of modest means who were forced to live on their estates had much more frequent contact with their blacks, a pattern which may have been widespread in the poorer colonies (for example, Cuba before the late eighteenth-century sugar boom), and a higher rate of voluntary manumission may have resulted. In the more affluent colonies, however, semi-absenteeism appears to have been the rule.

It was also difficult for the rural slave to profit from the self-purchase system. Spare time was not the problem. In theory, slaves were to attend mass on Sundays and religious holidays, but the rest of the time was to be their own, and such occasions were numerous.[60] Unfortunately, it was difficult for the rural slave to accumulate cash. Most were granted garden plots, which they worked in their spare time, but surplus produce was difficult to sell in an area where every slave had a similar plot.[61] Even skilled rural slaves (for example,

[58] See the devastating satire of plantation foremen and their excesses, written in 1791 and reprinted in Ortíz Fernández, *Hampa afro-cubana*, pp. 221–26, which confirms the thesis of planter absenteeism.

[59] I base this assertion on a mass of pinpoint data in Peruvian archival materials and upon a general survey of the printed literature concerning Spanish American slavery. If one may generalize from the evidence presented by Ward Barrett (*The Sugar Hacienda of the Marqueses del Valle* [Minneapolis, Minn., 1970], pp. 85–86), major-domos rarely praised the work of their slave underlings, and this fact may go far in explaining the infrequency of manumissions of rural slaves.

[60] In the seventeenth century, the crown calculated that there was an average of five holidays in any thirty-day period (including Sundays), but local custom operated to make for a still higher figure. According to Klein (*Slavery in the Americas*, p. 197), there were only some 290 work days per year in late eighteenth-century Cuba, although during the harvest season rural slaves no doubt worked every day of the week.

[61] Klein (*ibid.*, pp. 197–99) takes a more optimistic view, but admits that self-purchase was "principally for the skilled and urban slaves." The cacao plantations of Venezuela may constitute an important exception. Slaves there were allowed by their masters to cultivate small plots (*haciendillas*) of cacao in their spare time, perhaps largely so that their masters could secure legal

sugar technicians and carpenters) found their earning power cut by the drive for plantation self-sufficiency and by the very rhythm of agricultural labor. Most planters preferred to buy or train their own skilled slaves. Furthermore, during the harvest season, when other masters might have needed additional hands, the skilled slave was necessarily employed at home. Gonzalo Aguirre Beltrán summarizes the situation for Mexico, and his words undoubtedly apply elsewhere: "By the end of the colonial era manumission [by self-purchase] was not infrequent among urban slaves. Such was not the case in the mines, *ingenios*, and certain plantations, where the inventories of slaves frequently listed runaways but not manumissions."[62]

Even racial mixture does not seem to have favored the rural slave. It seems unnecessary to belabor the fact that planters and foremen indulged themselves sexually among their black female charges, and that many of the offspring may have been freed. However, the number of mulattoes recorded in inventories of plantation slaves indicates that many more remained in bondage.[63] On the other hand, in rural areas where both Africans and Indians were to be found, it was sometimes possible for black male slaves to marry native women (despite royal prohibitions), and presumably the *zambo* offspring were free.[64]

Finally, even if a rural slave were to gain freedom, his prospects for a substantially better life were dim. Most adults knew nothing but agricultural work, and to acquire a skill late in life was difficult. The

---

title to their holdings by demonstrating cultivation. Seemingly, the slaves were allowed to apply the resultant profits toward the purchase of their freedom and were promised possession of the *haciendillas* upon liberation. Attempts to renege the latter promise brought about bitter legal disputes in the eighteenth century. At least one estate, however, claimed that the slaves used the practice to steal the best of the crop from bushes which did not belong to them. An attempt to annex the *haciendillas* involved produced such a storm of protest that the estate finally consented to purchase the plots. Recalcitrant slaves were sold, and a stubborn free black and his wife were reduced to slavery once again and sold out of the country after their possessions were confiscated. See the essay by Federico Brito Figueroa, "La investigación sobre historia de la formación de la propiedad territorial agraria en Venezuela," and supporting documents in Eduardo Arcila Farías *et al.*, eds., *La obra pía de Chuao, 1568–1825* (Caracas, 1968), pp. 125, 152–53, 259–61, 342–43, 369–401.

[62] "The Integration of the Negro into the National Society of Mexico," in *Race and Class in Latin America*, ed. Magnus Mörner (New York and London, 1970), p. 15.

[63] In addition to a mass of pinpoint data from Peruvian archival materials, this assertion is based on Barrett, *Sugar Hacienda*, p. 79, and the remarks of Magnus Mörner in "El mestizaje en la historia de Ibero-América," *Revista de Historia de América*, nos. 53–54 (1962), p. 149.

[64] ANP, Real Audiencia: Procedimientos Civiles, 25 (1585–86), "Causa civil original seguida en el año de 1585 . . . por el Licenciado Álvaro de Torres contra Juan Gil de Montenegro y el Licenciado Sánchez de Paredes." This suit contains an inventory of 1576 which lists four plantation slaves married to *indias* (fol. 5v).

majority no doubt continued in the same capacity as free laborers or perhaps squatted on a small parcel of unclaimed land to lead a marginal existence.[65] Obviously, an emancipated rural slave who possessed some skill had a better time of it, and freed infants might be sent at the appropriate time to the nearest town for apprenticeship in some craft if anyone around them was aware that this possibility existed.

For the urban slave, the possibilities and conditions of manumission were far better. Urban slavery above all else meant household service, and this in turn meant the opportunity to be close to the master on a daily basis and to win his favor over the years. Household service was largely woman's work, and this fact may account for the high percentage of females in the sample of Peruvian manumissions. Urban slavery also required a much larger number of skilled blacks, and, as we have seen, such slaves might persuade their masters to apply a portion of their earnings toward the purchase of their freedom. Even unskilled slaves found that their earning power was greater in the towns; for example, a laundress who was permitted to work part time on her own account no doubt did not lack customers. Finally, slaves in the cities were in a much better position than their isolated rural counterparts to learn of the Spanish world and its ways. For example, a slave mother who lived in a Spanish town often knew of the demand for artisans and made an attempt to apprentice her free infant son, thereby assuring him of a better future than her own (see below). In similar circumstances, her rural sister might, through simple ignorance of the alternatives, condemn her offspring to the rewarding life of an agricultural laborer.

Important exceptions to this gloomy comparison of the lot of urban and rural slaves were those blacks who worked in the placer mines of Colombia. There, the ranks of the free were swelled not merely by compassion and racial mixture but also by the fact that mining slaves were permitted to work the streams for their own profit on Sundays and religious holidays. In this fashion, they accumulated the cash necessary to purchase their freedom, a development which their masters apparently did not object to, because most freedmen continued to labor in the mines thereafter. By the end of the colonial period it seems likely that the mining areas of Colombia contained more free colored than slaves.[66]

It should also be mentioned that manumisson, by its very nature and with the exception of small children, was restricted to slaves who had been born in Spanish America (Creoles) and to the so-called *ladinos*, Africans who had spent sufficient time in the area to acquire at least a veneer of Spanish ways. *Bozales*, slaves fresh off the boat

[65] Barrett (*Sugar Hacienda*, p. 77) cites the example of a free mulatto sugar master. More research is needed concerning the fate of the rural ex-slave.

[66] Robert C. West, *Colonial Placer Mining in Colombia* (Baton Rouge, La., 1952), pp. 88–89.

from Africa, had no chance of emancipation. In the first place, not even the most humane master was willing to manumit a slave before he had rendered a considerable stretch of service.[67] Furthermore, the bozal obviously needed a period of seasoning before he became aware that the possibility of manumission existed, and still more time had to pass before the goal could be attained. By that date, the individual had become a *ladino*. With respect to a knowledge of the legal possibilities for freedom, the urban-based creole, born a member of the society around him, was clearly in the best position.

Finally, although our discussion thus far has centered on the legal methods of manumission, many desperate slaves did not hesitate to resort to flight. This is not the place to discuss the problem of runaway slaves in Spanish America. Suffice it to say that Spanish methods of apprehension seem to have been fairly efficient. Runaways stood the best chance of success in colonies where they could flee to rugged and remote areas and there organize settlements with their fellows, or perhaps join an existing Indian community. The Spanish government, customarily short of funds, was reluctant to expend its resources in the destruction of these settlements. If local efforts to eradicate these *palenques* or *cumbes* failed, the crown was usually content to recognize the existence of the community and the liberty of its inhabitants in return for a pledge of allegiance and a promise to live peacefully.[68] Still other slaves, with some skill or craft, attempted with some success to flee from their masters for a life of freedom in another area.[69]

SIZE

By all the above means, but chiefly through the legal channels of manumission and by reproduction of their own kind, the number of free blacks and mulattoes grew steadily during the colonial period. At some point during the eighteenth century, or perhaps earlier, the size of the free colored population of Spanish America first equaled and then exceeded that of the slave population. Bearing in mind that census data for the colonial period can be considered no more than approximations, and that it was in the interest of light-hued persons partially of African descent to "pass" as Spaniards, we may selec-

---

[67] In Cuba, for example, a *bozal* could not become eligible for self-purchase until he had spent seven years on the island (Klein, *Slavery in the Americas*, p. 199).

[68] See the examples of such successful settlements cited by Jaramillo Uribe, "Esclavos y señores," pp. 42–50; Konetzke, ed., *Colección*, 2, pt. 2: 782–83; Acosta Saignes, *Vida*, pp. 264–65; D. M. Davidson, "Negro Slave Control and Resistance in Colonial Mexico, 1519–1650," *Hispanic American Historical Review*, 46 (1966): 235–53.

[69] Acosta Saignes, *Vida*, pp. 182–83.

tively survey the proportion of free colored to slave colored in Spanish America during the late colonial period.

Mexico provides the most spectacular example of the preponderance of the free colored, in part because the exuberant economy of that colony in the eighteenth century was able to tap internal sources of labor supply. According to one calculation, by 1810 there were some 624,000 *afromestizos* in Mexico, or a little more than one-tenth of the population, but only about 10,000 slaves.[70] In Uruguay, where slavery was never particularly important, a census of the Montevideo area in 1781 revealed 1,186 free blacks (of whom 603 were mulattoes) and 1,467 slaves.[71] In Argentina, a 1778 count of the bishopric of Tucumán, an important agricultural area, turned up 44,301 *"mulatos, zambos, y negros libres,"* and only 11,410 slaves from the same racial groups.[72] A 1781 census of the provinces of Quito and Guayaquil in Ecuador provided a total of 27,528 free colored with 4,684 slaves.[73] In Bolivia, where slaves were always numerically insignificant, the city of Potosí in 1758 contained 1,706 free colored and 1,300 slaves.[74]

Even in areas where the institution of slavery was strongly entrenched, the free colored were a very important element of the population. In Peru, where colored labor was extremely important along the coast, a 1792 census counted 41,404 *"gente de color libre"* and 40,337 slaves.[75] For the viceroyalty of New Granada as a whole (Ecuador, Venezuela, Colombia, and Panama), a bureaucrat in 1789 estimated a total black and mulatto population of about 500,000, of which 420,000 were free.[76] For Venezuela in particular, a partial census in 1787 counted 147,564 *"libres de color"* and 53,055 slaves.[77] For Puerto Rico, the following data are available:[78]

[70] See Ángel Rosenblat, *La población indígena y el mestizaje en América,* 2 vols. (Buenos Aires, 1954), 1: 183, 185, who relies primarily on the calculations of Aguirre Beltrán, *La población negra de México.*

[71] Rosenblat, *La población indígena,* 1: 203.

[72] *Ibid.,* p. 234. The number of free persons of African descent exceeded that of Spaniards (34,516) and Indians (35,254)

[73] *Ibid.,* p. 198.

[74] Bartolomé Arzáns de Orsúa y Vela, *Historia de la Villa Imperial de Potosí,* ed. Lewis Hanke and Gunnar Mendoza, 3 vols. (Providence, R.I., 1965), 3: 156, n. 1. I am indebted to Professor Hanke for this reference.

[75] I rely upon a copy from AGI, Estado 75, provided me by Professor James F. King. The census has been summarized in *Mercurio Peruano,* facsimile edition (Lima, 1964), vol. 1, no. 10, February 3, 1791 (preliminary figures for Lima only), and more extensively in José Antonio Saco, *Historia de la esclavitud de la raza africana en el Nuevo Mundo y en especial en los paises américo-hispanos* (Barcelona, 1879), p. 414, who was unable to date the document precisely.

[76] West, *Colonial Placer Mining,* pp. 100–101.

[77] Rosenblat, *La población indígena,* 1: 193.

[78] These figures come from Luis M. Díaz Soler, *Historia de la esclavitud negra en Puerto Rico,* 2nd ed. rev. (Río Piedras, Puerto Rico, 1965), pp. 94, 117.

Year	Whites	Free Mulattoes	Free Blacks	Slaves
1775	29,236	31,687	2,823	7,487
1802	78,281	55,164	16,414	13,333
1812	85,662	63,983	15,833	17,536
1820	102,432	86,268	20,191	21,730

Even in Cuba, soon to become the bastion of slavocracy, in 1792 the free colored population made up more than 45 percent of those of African descent (54,151 free blacks and 64,590 slaves).[79]

LEGAL STATUS

In law, the condition of free persons of color was significantly better than that of slaves, but inferior to the status of Spaniards, Indians, and mestizos. In common with Indians, free blacks, mulattoes, and *zambos* were expected to pay tribute. In the crown's view, these *castas*, who had profited by the richness of Spanish America sufficiently to free themselves and to accumulate modest fortunes, could in all justice be obligated to pay a reasonable amount of tribute annually for the peace, justice, and freedom which they enjoyed.[80] In addition, since they were obligated to pay tribute, freedom did not mean that the free colored had the right to be idle. Rather, they were hired out to Spanish masters so that their whereabouts might be known and the taxs easily collected.[81] The obligation to pay tribute was bitterly resented by the free colored as a sign of inferior status. As the liberal bishop Manuel Abad y Queipo remarked near the end of the colonial period: "The Castas are infamous by law, being descended from Negro slaves. They are liable to tribute . . . and tribute is for them an indelible mark of slavery which they are unable to erase with the passing of time or by mixing with other races in successive generations. There are many of them who by their color, features, and behavior would rise to the class of 'Spaniards' but for this impediment that leaves them depressed in the same class."[82]

Visible African pigmentation or features saddled the free person of color with the presumption of illegitimacy and inferiority. The

[79] Ortíz Fernández, *Hampa afro-cubana: Los negros esclavos*, p. 321. For Panama, see the discussion in Alfredo Castillero C., *La sociedad panameña: Historia de su formación e integración* (Panama, 1970), pp. 91–106. For Santo Domingo, see Carlos Larrazábal Blanco, *Los negros y la esclavitud en Santo Domingo* (Santo Domingo, 1967), pp. 183–84.

[80] Konetzke, ed., *Colección*, 1: 482–83, decree of April 27, 1574. The wording of this decree implies that self-purchase was considered a more important avenue to freedom than voluntary manumission.

[81] *Ibid.*, 502–3, decree of April 29, 1577.

[82] These remarks are in José Luis María Mora, *Obras sueltas*, 2nd ed. (Mexico, 1963), p. 205.

former charge was frequently true, and, along with the shadow of slave origin, led colonial authorities and the public to brand the free colored as vile, treacherous, lazy, prone to drunkenness, and, in general, infamous and immoral by his very nature.[83] Clearly, prejudice of this magnitude was a serious impediment to socioeconomic advancement. In 1549, mulattoes were forbidden to hold public office or grants of Indian tribute and labor,[84] and, as a matter of course, the ban extended to the priesthood and the professions. In the case of the former calling, the crown feared that the public would be scandalized to see "such unworthy people so highly placed," and as late as 1739 Pope Clement XII held that mulattoes were "individuals generally despised by society, unworthy of holding public office and of directing the spiritual life of others."[85] The guilds were very nearly as discriminatory. Wishing to monopolize the profits to be made from colonial demand, Spanish artisans made strenuous efforts to exclude persons of color from the rank of master, although, as we shall see, they did not hesitate to use those of African blood as journeymen.[86]

The Spanish government, whose attitude toward the mass of the free colored alternated between contempt and fear, was at pains to restrict their movements and to prohibit them from owning firearms.[87] At the same time, as foreign intrusion increased in Spanish America in the late sixteenth century and thereafter, the crown relied more and more upon colored militia units to supplement similar white contingents in warding off these attacks. In Cuba at least, the free colored who served in the militia in the late sixteenth century were armed,[88] but elsewhere, perhaps because the white population was larger, the authorities were more cautious, and these units were ini-

[83] Aguirre Beltrán, La población negra de México, pp. 187–90, 248–54; Mörner, Race Mixture, pp. 40, 68. In 1778, when the Bourbons applied to Spanish America a characteristically meticulous set of regulations concerning marriage regulations designed to prevent unions between social unequals, it was stipulated that persons under the age of twenty-five must secure the approval of their parents. Free persons of African descent, however, were exempted from this requirement, no doubt because it was assumed that most of them were illegitimate and could not locate their fathers. (Ibid., pp. 38–39.) Only colored officers in the militia came under the requirement.

[84] Konetzke, ed., Colección, 1: 256, decree of Febraury 27. It was probably assumed that a free person of color would never dare request such privileges.

[85] Ibid., 1: 607–8; 2, pt. 1: 65–67; and 2, pt. 2: 691–93. See also Aguirre Beltrán, "Integration of the Negro," p. 19.

[86] See Konetzke, ed., Colección, passim, for numerous examples; see also Manuel Carrera Stampa, Los gremios mexicanos (Mexico, 1954), pp. 223–43.

[87] Slaves, of course, even during the liberal days of the conquest period, were rarely permitted to carry weapons. Free persons of color seem to have come under the same prohibition in 1551 (Recopilación, libro VII, título v, ley 15), although local ordinances against the practice may have been framed still earlier.

[88] In Cuba, a 100-man militia company of mulattoes had been organized by 1600 (Klein, Slavery in the Americas, p. 214).

tially used in auxiliary roles where weapons were not required. In 1624, for example, when a Dutch fleet seriously threatened the Lima area, mulatto militia units were first sent to the nearby port of Surco to erect fortifications and were then ordered to return to Callao, where they were held in readiness for an assault that never came. It seems likely that they were not armed during this emergency.[89] By the eighteenth century, however, colored militia units seem to have carried weapons as a matter of routine, at least while on duty. Originally, it had been contemplated that the colored militia would be commanded by white officers, but by the middle of the seventeenth century colored men had attained this rank, and by the eighteenth century colored officers "through the rank of captain were common."[90]

The government exhibited proper concern for the manners and morals of the free African population, which was subjected, along with the slaves, to the tender mercies of the Holy Office.[91] Decrees came periodically from Spain commanding that free blacks and mulattoes be properly indoctrinated in the principles of Christianity in order that they might lead orderly and upright lives, and occasionally the crown also concerned itself with the medical care of this segment of society.[92] Various government agencies, however, went beyond these perhaps defensible concerns to regulate the lives of the free colored in various petty and galling ways. Free colored women in particular were the objects of numerous attempts at sumptuary legislation, perhaps because of the lure they held for Spanish men. As early as 1574, the crown itself confirmed ordinances for the city of Panama which commanded that colored women, whether free or slave, not use silk, pearls, gold, or mantillas in any form as wearing apparel.[93] Such regulations were promulgated with monotonous regularity throughout the colonial period, which strongly hints at their ineffectiveness, and at times included such items as slippers ornamented with silver bells, canopied beds, and rugs or cushions to

[89] Petition to the crown by the free mulattoes involved, Lima, March 18, 1627, in AGI, Lima 158.

[90] James F. King, "The Case of José Ponciano de Ayarza: A Document on *Gracias al Sacar*," *Hispanic American Historical Review*, 31 (1951): 640, n. 2.

[91] Most scholars concede that the records of the Holy Office are invaluable as documentation for social history during the colonial period, but very little has been done to tap this resource. For a hint of the possibilities as they involve the colored population, see Gonzalo Aguirre Beltrán, *Medicina y magia: El proceso de aculturación en la estructura colonial* (Mexico, 1963), and Miguel Tejado Fernández, *Aspectos de la vida social en Cartagena de Indias durante el seiscientos* (Seville, 1954).

[92] Konetzke, ed., *Colección*, 1: 435–36, 444–45, 449; 2, pt. 1: 135, 365. An interesting decree of July 21, 1623, provided that free married women of color could not be forced to attend the public dances held on the various religious holidays (*ibid.*, 2, pt. 1: 278).

[93] Diego de Encinas, *Cedulario indiano: Reproducción facsimil de la edición única de 1596*, 4 vols. (Madrid, 1945–46), 4: 387, decree of August 4.

sit on at church.[94] Even *mulatas* married to Spaniards on occasion were permitted to wear nothing more ostentatious than woolen garments, but black women, who no doubt felt their inferior status acutely in such a stratified society, could not resist aping their so-called superiors. Of eighteenth-century Lima, for example, where the Spanish women prided themselves upon the elegance of their dress and the smallness of their feet, we read that:

> The lower classes of women, even to the very Negroes, affect, according to their abilities, to imitate their betters, not only in the fashion of their dress, but also in the richness of it. None here are seen without shoes, as in Quito; and even in this particular with a precision which must be attended with infinite uneasiness by pinching up their feet in little shoes, in order to diminish their natural bigness.[95]

White women, understandably jealous of their black rivals so much favored by Spanish Lotharios, occasionally took matters into their own hands. We read, for example, of eighteenth-century Argentina:

> They [the Spanish women] do not permit slaves, or even freedmen who have a mixture of Negro blood, to wear any cloth other than that made in this country, which is quite coarse. I was told recently that a certain bedecked mulatto who appeared in Córdoba was sent word by the ladies of the city that she should dress according to her station, but since she paid no attention to this reproach, they endured her negligence until one of the ladies, summoning her to her home under some pretext, had the servants undress her, whip her, burn her finery before her eyes, and dress her in the clothes befitting her class; despite the fact that the *mulata* was not lacking in persons to defend her, she disappeared lest the tragedy be repeated.[96]

Even within the church, the free person of African descent suffered from a mild but galling discrimination. In 1614, for example, the Lima City Council prohibited the use of coffins among the African population as a serious affront to the superior status of the Spanish.[97] In the same year, a synod convoked by the archbishop of Lima ruled that no blacks, mulattoes, or Indians were to be buried in the cathedral. The crown's attorney before the *audiencia* deplored the possible effects of the harsh measure on the religious sentiments of the groups

[94] See, for example, *LCL*, 19: 401, session of September 26, 1622; Suardo, *Diario de Lima*, 1: 155, entry of April 14, 1631; Konetzke, ed., *Colección*, 2, pt. 1: 182–83; Josephe de Mugaburu and Francisco de Mugaburu (hijo), *Diario de Lima, 1640–1694: Crónica de la época colonial*, ed. Horacio H. Urteaga and Carlos A. Romero. (Lima, 1917–18), 1: 109, 171, 194, 152–53.

[95] Jorge Juan and Antonio de Ulloa, *A Voyage to South America*, 2nd ed., 2 vols. (Dublin, 1765), vol. 2, bk. 1, chap. 5. I have made slight alterations in the punctuation of this passage.

[96] Concolorcorvo, *El Lazarillo*, p. 80; see also Franco, *Afroamérica*, p. 166.

[97] *LCL*, 17: 506–7, 526.

involved, arguing that some of them "merit this and other honors," but there is no evidence that the ruling was reversed.[98] In 1669, the viceroy of Peru ruled that each colored religious confraternity could carry no more than fifty candleholders (*alumbrantes*) during the processions marking Holy Week, and that the members of such brotherhoods might not meet for mass suppers after the procession, under penalty of a month in prison.[99] In Caracas, as late as 1800, whites went to mass in the cathedral while free colored persons and slaves worshipped the Savior in two separate churches.[100] In eighteenth-century Buenos Aires, segregated seating arrangements prevailed at the theater, and free persons of African descent were excluded from the "Patriotic Society" founded in that city in 1801.[101]

ACTUAL STATUS AND OPPORTUNITIES

In practice, however, at least a portion of the free colored population of Spanish America was able to circumvent or ignore the legal disabilities directed against them and to improve their lot, despite societal prejudice.[102] The crown discovered, for example, that it was one thing to command that free persons of African descent pay tribute, but collection was another matter. In Mexico, the viceroy reported that the free colored were fleeing fixed residences and wandering from place to place rather than pay tribute, and the same thing occurred in Peru.[103] Quadroons in particular resented the obligation as a slur upon their status. In seventeenth-century Peru, they managed to secure exemption, and similar status may have been achieved elsewhere.[104] Others objected that a uniform rate was applied to all free colored persons, regardless of their ability to pay, but this aspect of the system was not changed.[105] In many instances, blacks and mu-

[98] Letter to the crown from Cristóbal Cacho de Santillán, Lima, April 16, 1617, in AGI, Lima 96.

[99] Mugaburu, *Diario de Lima*, I, 172.

[100] Mörner, *Race Mixture*, p. 62.

[101] Rosenblat, *La población indígena*, 2: 158.

[102] Mörner (*Race Mixture*, p. 57) asserts that socioracial prejudice in Spanish America increased in the eighteenth century, but my own study of the preceding two centuries convinces me that prejudice remained fairly constant during the colonial period. There is more documentation to demonstrate its existence in the eighteenth century, but this state of affairs is true for colonial-period research generally, and even Mörner concedes that continuing racial mixture served to blunt the more refined forms of prejudice (*ibid.*, pp. 68–70).

[103] Konetzke, ed., *Colección*, 2, pt. 1: 18, royal letter to Don Luis de Velasco, May 29, 1594; AGI, Contaduría 1820, treasury accounts for Trujillo (1608–11), *pliegos* 39–40.

[104] See my forthcoming book concerning the African in Peru (n. 2 above) during this period, and also Konetzke, ed., *Colección*, 2, pt. 1: 364–65, decree of 1637 to the *audiencia* of New Granada.

[105] Encinas, *Cedulario*, 4: 391, decree of August 5, 1577, to the *audiencia* of Panama.

lattoes who served in militia companies petitioned for exemption, but
the crown's policy here was contradictory, perhaps being dictated in
part by momentary financial considerations. In 1631, for example,
all free female persons of color in Peru and all free males who had
served, or were currently serving, in the militia were declared exempt.
The latter enjoyed similar privileges in Santo Domingo, Havana, and
Campeche, but the crown balked at the same request for Veracruz.[106]
The government also never hit upon an efficient method of collection.
The treasury officials were already overburdened with duties; attempts
to farm out the revenue were disappointing; special agents consumed
more in salaries than the revenue was worth; free mulattoes were
often appointed to collect the revenue, a thankless task, and many
abused their authority.[107] In general, tribute collection was spotty. In
Panama, nothing had been done as late as 1627, and for the *audiencia* of Guadalajara (Mexico) the crown was still prodding for collection as late as 1674.[108] The corollary requirement that free colored
persons hire themselves out to Spanish employers was likewise haphazardly enforced or not at all. In Lima, for example, the authorities
periodically rounded up the free colored and hired them out to Spaniards, no doubt causing a great deal of inconvenience in the process,
but in Uruguay the regulation seems to have remained a dead letter.
In Paraguay, by contrast, the manumitted colored were placed in the
charge of Spaniards who were responsible for payment of their tribute
and who were therefore given very nearly absolute authority over
these unfortunates.[109] In most areas, however, the operation of racial
mixture, by creating an increasingly mixed population, served to de-
feat the imposition of tribute and to undermine many other officially
sanctioned forms of prejudice. As an official in Mexico lamented to
the viceroy in 1770:

> The liberty with which the plebs have been allowed to choose the
> class they prefer, insofar as their color permits, has stained the class
> of natives as well as that of Spaniards. They very often join the one
> or the other as it suits them or as they need to.... A Mulatto, for
> instance, whose color helps him somewhat to hide in another
> "casta," says, according to his whims, that he is Indian to enjoy the
> privileges as such and pay less tribute, though this seldom occurs,

[106] Konetzke, ed., *Colección*, 2, pt. 1: 333–35 and pt. 2: 562–63, 586–87.
See also the individual exemption granted to a free colored person of Yucatán
in 1578 (*ibid.*, 1: 511–12).

[107] For a sample of the difficulties encountered in this connection, see
ibid., 1: 584–85, 2, pt. 2: 745–47, and my forthcoming book (n. 2 above).

[108] Konetzke, ed., *Colección*, 2, pt. 1: 306 and pt. 2: 613–14.

[109] See my forthcoming book (n. 2 above); Eugenio Petit Muñoz, Ed-
mundo M. Narancio, and José M. Traibel Nelcis, *La condición jurídica, social,
económica y política de los negros durante el coloniaje en la Banda Oriental*
(Montevideo, 1947–), 1: 339–40; and Paulo de Carvalho Neto, "Antología del
negro paraguayo," *Anales de la Universidad Central* (Quinto), 91 (1962): 44,
49.

or, more frequently, that he is Spaniard, Castizo or Mestizo, and then he does not pay any [tribute] at all.[110]

The frequency with which free persons of color were forbidden to carry arms belies the effectiveness of the above decrees,[111] yet, through their loyal service in the militia, the free colored no doubt inspired the increasing confidence of the authorities.[112] By the eighteenth century, such militia companies existed in nearly every Spanish American colony and were ordinarily divided into mulatto (*pardo*) and free black (*moreno*) units. Colored militia companies ranged in size from the very small forces organized in Chile and Uruguay to the 3,400 colored militiamen recorded in the Cuban military census of 1770.[113] These units fought against hostile Indians in Panama, were sent from Lima to the former colony in 1671 to ward off the assault of Henry Morgan, and were dispatched from Cuba to Florida, Louisiana, Mexico, and Yucatan.[114] Service was not mere parade-ground strutting; it sometimes involved considerable personal sacrifice,[115] but it also brought respect to all those who served, and, at least partly, the right to be tried in military rather than civilian courts. For the officers, in addition to modest salaries and impressive decorations, there were even more important social advantages.[116] Chiefly, these involved educational opportunities for their children.

[110] Juan Antonio de Areche as quoted and translated by Mörner, *Race Mixture*, p. 69.

[111] Konetzke, *Colección*, 2, pt. 1: 182–83, 427–28, and 2, pt. 2: 513–14, 543, 707–8.

[112] Complaints concerning the effectiveness of free colored militia units were very rare, although in 1662 the crown did instruct the viceroy of Peru to send no more such mulatto and mestizo troops to Chile, where they were considered more of a nuisance than an advantage in the struggle against the Araucanians, (*ibid.*, 2, pt. 2: 491). In Havana, the free colored militia companies complained in 1662 that they were held in such little esteem as to be forced to clean the streets at considerable economic scarifice (*ibid.*, pp. 499–500). Occasionally, no doubt in the interests of economy, the number of such units was reduced, and officers were brusquely deprived of their salaries. See the incident related in Mugaburu, *Diario de Lima*, 1: 70.

[113] Guillermo Feliú Cruz, *La abolición de la esclavitud en Chile* (Santiago de Chile, 1942), p. 42; Ildefonso Pereda Valdés, *El negro en el Uruguay pasado y presente* (Montevideo, 1965), pp. 50–53; Klein, *Slavery in the Americas*, p. 217. See also Larrazábal Blanco, *Los negros y la esclavitud en Santo Domingo*, pp. 176–77.

[114] Castillero, *La sociedad panameña*, p. 103; Mugaburu, *Diario de Lima*, 2: 4; Klein, *Slavery in the Americas*, pp. 215–16.

[115] See, for example, the complaints of the free colored of Havana and the crown's reply in "Papers Bearing on the Negroes of Cuba in the Seventeenth Century," *Journal of Negro History*, 12 (1927): 55–56, 66–67.

[116] The right to be tried in military rather than civilian courts was known as the *fuero militar*, and was valued on the presumption that the former would be more lenient. See Lyle N. McAlister, *The Fuero Militar in New Spain, 1764–1800* (Gainesville, Fla., 1957), chap. 4; Rosenblat, *La población indígena*, 2: 157–58; and Konetzke, ed., *Colección*, 3: 325. For examples of salaries and decorations, see Pereda Valdés, *El negro en el Uruguay*, p. 51, and Díaz Soler, *Historia*, p. 246.

Educational facilities in Spanish America were limited in any event, and persons of known African descent were barred from most of them. Typical was the charter of the Colegio Real de San Felipe y San Marcos in Lima, issued in 1592. Founded to educate the sons of the principal conquistadors, the school excluded all who possessed African blood, as well as the descendants of other "unworthy people and infamous men punished by the Holy Office.[117] Occasionally, the crown made a half-hearted proposal to institute some form of vocational training among the caste population. In addition, the government took some responsibility for the education of orphans. In early seventeenth-century Lima, for example, orphaned boys of all racial mixtures were assigned by parish to teachers who instructed them in reading, writing, and elementary arithmetic.[118] In general, however, the authorities in Madrid left it to the African population to provide whatever private schooling they could afford for their children, and municipal authorities were even more unsympathetic. For example, in eighteenth-century Buenos Aires, in accordance with a decision of the city council, the elementary school did not exclude children of African blood, but segregated them with the mestizos and taught them only Christian dogma. They were to mingle with the white and Indian children only at public functions, and then only under the eye of their teacher.[119] Given these attitudes, it is not surprising that the crown ignored the very rare suggestions that talented free persons of color be permitted university training.[120]

Nevertheless, many free persons of color managed in one way or another to receive at least a rudimentary education. Considerate Spanish fathers of illegitimate mulatto children no doubt often made some provisions for schooling. In the 1660s, for example, Agustín Rascón, a free mulatto resident in Cholula, was literate enough to make representations before the Mexican viceroy which argued that, as the "son of a noble father," he should be allowed to bear arms.[121] Others found white godparents or patrons who secured educational priviliges for

[117] I take my information from a 1608 copy of the charter in AGI, Lima 323. Most orphanages, however, which taught their charges to read and write, could not turn away infants, of whatever color, left at their portals, although many did not voluntarily accept those of African descent. See, for example, the charter of the orphanage of Our Lady of Atocha, founded in Lima in 1603, which is partially printed in Rubén Vargas Ugarte, comp., *Biblioteca Peruana*, 12 vols. (Lima and Buenos Aires, 1935–57), 3: 143–52.

[118] Viceroy Marqués de Montesclaros (Callao) to the crown, March 25, 1609, in AGI, Lima 35, outlines this program in reply to a royal decree of 1607 with regard to vocational instruction for the castes. The decree is printed in Konetzke, ed., *Colección*, 2, pt. 1: 134–35. Teachers' salaries were paid from unassigned Indian tributes.

[119] Rosenblat, *La población indígena*, 2: 136–37, 162.

[120] For example, the bishop of Cuzco made a proposal of this sort to the crown in a letter of February 11, 1577; see AGI, Lima 305.

[121] Konetzke, ed., *Colección*, 2, pt. 2: 543, records a decree of 1668 denying the claim.

them. The great Peruvian physician and poet, José Manuel Valdés, son of an Indian musician and a black washerwoman, received his secondary education at the Augustinian *colegio* of San Ildefonso through the intercession of his white godparents.[122] Colored militia officers relied upon their prestige and distinguished service to press for similar educational opportunities for their offspring as a matter of course, and some requested that the color bar not prevent their sons from entering the universities and the professions. Since many colored officers seem to have been artisans by profession, they undoubtedly had the economic resources with which to finance these ambitions.[123]

During the eighteenth century, ambitious free persons of color were aided in their ascent by the crown's willingness to sell certifica-tions of legal whiteness. These documents were called *cédulas de gracias al sacar*, and their sale seems to have been prompted both by financial considerations and by the government's desire to allay dis-content among prominent persons of color while at the same time supposedly leavening the ranks of the white creole elite with grateful mulattoes.[124] Perhaps because of stiff colonial opposition, this new policy was implemented cautiously, even haphazardly. For example, a tariff was not issued until 1795, and in the eighteenth century some distinguished applicants for such *cédulas* were rejected while others of seemingly identical merit had no difficulty obtaining the dispensa-tion.[125] It is also difficult to determine whether these *cédulas* were very effective in overcoming socioracial prejudice in Spanish America. In the late colonial period, a French observer in Venezuela acidly observed that the only difference such a document had made in the lives of one mulatto family was that the ladies now dared to wear a mantilla in church, a privilege which the sumptuary laws reserved for whites.[126] On the other hand, at roughly the same time in the same colony, a mulatto who held this *cédula* secured the backing of the crown in his efforts to force admittance of his son to the univer-sity in Caracas over the vehement protests of that institution.[127]

[122] Fernando Romero, "José Manuel Valdés, Great Peruvian Mulatto," *Phylon*, 3 (1942): 299. See Rosenblat, *La población indígena*, 2: 163–64, for additional examples of educated and distinguished free persons of color.

[123] See the case cited by Klein, *Slavery in the Americas*, p. 224.

[124] King ("The Case of José Ponciano de Ayarza," pp. 641–44) makes it clear that these *cédulas* were "concessions of exemptions" from existing laws whose range was wider than merely the issuance of patents of whiteness. In 1795, there were seventy-one categories of *gracias al sacar*, including the privi-lege of founding an entail.

[125] See the examples in Konetzke, ed., *Colección*, 3: 530–35, 754. In 1801, a new tariff with higher rates was issued; see King, "The Case of José Ponciano de Ayarza," p. 643.

[126] François Depons, *Viaje a la parte oriental de Tierra Firme en la América Meridional*, 2 vols. (Caracas, 1960), 1: 120–21.

[127] Ildefonso Leal, *Historia de la Universidad de Caracas, 1721–1827* (Caracas, 1963), pp. 326–32. Other free persons of color, with perhaps neither the time, money, nor inclination to secure a *cédula de gracias al sacar* from

In light of the available evidence, it seems reasonable to conclude that free persons of color found their ascent to be easiest in those occupations which held little interest for whites. The professions, of course, represented the pinnacle of ambition in the Spanish American world, and for these some university training was required. American universities were officially closed to all persons of African descent, but, prior to the eighteenth century, such exclusions were worded in such a "casual, mechanical way, as if the problem might not arise," that some mulattoes and those of lighter hue quietly enrolled and received their degrees. In the late seventeenth century, officials were scandalized to learn of the infiltration which had taken place at San Marcos in Lima, and in the eighteenth century sporadic, but determined and partially successful, efforts were made to tighten university standards in many parts of Spanish America.[128] Spanish American whites relied upon appeals to long-standing racial prejudice, particularly as these concerned the professions, while free persons of color relied upon wealth, influence, distinguished service, relatively light skin, and *gracias al sacar* to negate the arguments of their opponents. The struggle, which increased in bitterness after 1750, had produced no conclusive results by the end of the colonial period. In general, however, the whites retained crushing pre-eminence in those fields which held genuine interest for them.

It is possible to cite rare examples, such as a black lawyer,[129] but the legal profession and university faculties remained bastions of white domination. In 1737, a free colored person, who seems earlier to have obtained a decree from San Marcos, entered the competition for the Chair of Method in that institution, but his participation was quickly barred by the Peruvian viceroy.[130] In 1768, to make its own position clear, the crown barred those of African descent from receiving doctorates, a measure which was justified by reference to the "great many lawyers of obscure birth and bad ways."[131] The whites also controlled the holding of public office, an occupation legally

---

Spain, appealed to the colonial high courts (*audiencias*) for similar dispensations. Even poorer colored men preferred to claim swarthy Andalusian ancestry, or simply moved to an area where they were unknown and whose inhabitants would hopefully be more tolerant (King, "The Case of José Ponciano de Ayarza," p. 644).

[128] John Tate Lanning, "Legitimacy and *Limpieza de Sangre* in the Practice of Medicine in the Spanish Empire," *Jahrbuch für Geschichte von Staat: Wirtschaft und Gesellschaft Lateinamerikas*, 4 (1967): 37–60 *passim*.

[129] Klein, *Slavery in the Americas*, pp. 206–7, discusses the case of Don Julian Francisco Campo, a mulatto graduate of the University of Havana in civil law. Campo's white father was a high royal official on the island and no doubt used his influence to see that his son was licensed as a lawyer by the *audiencia*. Campo became so emboldened as to apply for a patent of nobility on the strength of his own and his father's services, and it was at this point that his African ancestry was discovered. Presumably, his request was denied.

[130] Lanning. "Legitimacy," p. 48.

[131] Konetzke, ed., *Colección*, 3: 340.

barred to those of African descent. With regard to minor offices such as that of notary public, however, free colored persons were able to circumvent this prohibition, in large part because such offices became saleable, and money, combined with skill and connections, was sufficient to overcome skin color.

Let us take two examples for the seventeenth century. The first concerns one Alonso Sánchez de Figueroa, a mulatto born in Badajoz and the son of a Spanish *bachiller*. Sánchez served as a scribe in a notary's office in Seville before coming to Peru, where his former Badajoz connections soon stood him in good stead. Among these connections was Pedro Pérez Landero, who was the head notary of the general visitation of the colony undertaken in the 1630s. Pérez made Sánchez his chief clerk, and the latter was soon emboldened to purchase the title of notary through agents in Spain for about one hundred ducats of his savings. Called upon to make a statement of Sánchez' competence, Pérez testified that the mulatto's script was legible and finely formed and that he was entirely trustworthy and completely in command of the various legal formulas employed in the documents of the time. Pérez also testified that Sánchez had accumulated capital amounting to some six hundred *pesos*. Another old friend from Badajoz who testified on Sánchez' behalf was Antonio Fernández de la Cruz, chief clerk of the Lima City Council. Nevertheless, the *audiencia* refused to confirm the appointment, on the grounds of race, and appealed to Spain for confirmation in accordance with its general instructions.[132] There is evidence that the appointment was eventually confirmed (see below).

A strikingly similar case came up scarcely two years later. In 1639, one Alonso de Castro renounced his office of solicitor (*procurador*) to the *audiencia* and sold the post to one José Núñez de Prado, a notary. Castro's colleagues immediately protested on the grounds that Núñez was a mulatto. Viceroy Conde de Chinchón was appealed to, and he turned for legal advice to a professor of law at San Marcos. The latter advised the viceroy to confirm the sale, pointing out that Núñez was not really a mulatto, but a quadroon, that he was a person of unquestioned ability, and that he had paid twice as much for the office (6,000 pesos) as any previous holder. The professor also pointed out that a similar case involving a notaryship—presumably that of Sánchez mentioned above—had recently been appealed to Spain, where the mulatto candidate had won a favorable decision. The viceroy accepted this recommendation and advised the crown to confirm the appointment.[133]

A few mulattoes even secured appointment through ability alone. We read of the case of Vicente Méndez in seventeenth-century

    [132] The *audiencia* of Lima to the crown, May 28, 1637, with accompanying documents from which the above information was drawn; AGI, Lima 100.
    [133] Letter of May 29, 1639, with supporting documentation; *ibid.*, Lima 49.

Panama. Méndez was a tireless and feared opponent of foreign corsairs in the area who had climbed to the rank of captain in the militia and who was much respected and loved among the unpacified Indians of the isthmus. He had managed to form a town composed of eighty Indians, and the *audiencia* of Panama had appointed him governor of the settlement. In 1686, the crown was urged by the president of that tribunal to confirm this appointment at a suitable salary, and this appeal was seconded by the bishop of Panama and by the admiral of the galleons which plied between Tierra Firme and Spain. In the face of such support, the crown could but agree to the proposal.[134]

For the late colonial period, the picture is less clear. There is evidence that free persons of color were permitted to buy certain offices in accordance with a tariff (perhaps a variation of the *gracias al sacar* principle), and for a price mulattoes were occupying ever more important posts in the colonial bureaucracy.[135] In Panama, for example, free persons of color were filling such offices as that of notary almost by default.[136] However, in the most prosperous colonies of Spanish America, competition between peninsular Spaniards and American-born creoles for a limited number of offices increased during this period, perhaps to the detriment of even the well-qualified mulattoes who could afford to pay for posts.[137]

The clergy was even more jealously guarded against penetration by the free colored. One reads, to be sure, of occasional cries of alarm on the part of the crown concerning the ordination of mulattoes, but these instances seem to have been rare indeed.[138] Colonial Spanish America produced a colored saint in the person of San Martín de Porres, but during his lifetime he was no more than a mulatto lay brother who "acquired his saintly prestige with a broom in his hand," and his beatification was delayed a hundred years.[139] The great *zambo* physician of Peru, José Manuel Valdés, professor at San Marcos, a published author in France, member of the Royal Medical Academy of Madrid, and a man armed with a papal dispensation of color, was nevertheless denied admission to the priesthood by the ecclesiastical *cabildo* of Lima.[140] In short, Spanish American whites firmly intended to preserve the income and perquisites of the church for themselves.

The medical profession was another matter. If certain stiff-

[134] Konetzke, ed., *Colección*, 2, pt. 2: 799–801.
[135] Klein, *Slavery in the Americas*, pp. 208–9.
[136] Castillero, *La sociedad panameña*, p. 102.
[137] For a general view of the creole-peninsular rivalry for office, see J. H. Parry, *The Spanish Seaborne Empire* (New York, 1966), pp. 335–37. For instances of frustrated mulatto ambition, see Klein, *Slavery in the Americas*, p. 209, and John Lynch, *Spanish Colonial Administration, 1782–1810: The Intendant System in the Viceroyalty of the Río de la Plata* (London, 1958), pp. 77–78.
[138] Konetzke, ed., *Colección*, 2, pt. 2: 551, and 3: 185–86; Romero, "José Manuel Valdés," p. 301.
[139] Romero, "José Manuel Valdés," p. 301.
[140] *Ibid.*, pp. 304–5.

necked authorities had had their way, free persons of color would have been as rigidly excluded from the practice of medicine as they were from the priesthood. The problem was that the Spaniards demonstrated no inclination to fill the corresponding vacuum. Mulattoes and other castes inevitably moved in to take their place. Some were content to operate on the margin of the law as quacks (*romancistas*), treating external ailments only by "prescribing chicken water, bread and milk, or mallows plaster." Others, however, of genuine ability and considerable training, were not content with this humble role. Valdés was one of these, and early in the nineteenth century he finally received the degrees and honors to which his talents so richly entitled him. Nor was Valdés alone. The mulatto José Francisco Báez y Llerena, who had studied under two leading surgeons, practiced surgery in Cuba for thirteen years before his credentials were challenged on the grounds that his father was a *pardo*. Arguing the case on his professional merits, Báez appealed to the crown and won. Indeed, his brother also secured from the government a ruling that the racial status of his family should not bar them from holding public office or from registering in universities for the purpose of scientific studies.[141]

In general, free persons of color made no more than modest inroads upon the whites' dominance of the professions during the colonial period, and even this progress was in many instances purchased at great psychic cost.[142] On the other hand, in many Spanish American colonies the free colored came to hold a prominent place in the arts and crafts, in some instances even a dominant position. These occupations were less lucrative and less prestigious than the professions, but they offered modest fortune and status, and were particularly vulnerable to penetration by the free person of color. Two observers of eighteenth-century Cartagena tell us why in a passage which affirms that the free colored "are the mechanics of the city; the whites, whether Creoles or Chapetones [peninsular Spaniards], disdaining such mean occupation, follow nothing below trade."[143] That is, Spanish contempt for manual labor, which was pronounced on the peninsula, assumed an even more extreme form in America, where the Spaniard found himself surrounded by a much larger service (or semiservile) population of darker hue. Under these circumstances, the ownership of land and mines, the possession of office, or, at worst, the mercantile life was the only occupation suitable for gentlemen outside the professions and the army.

This is not to say that there were no white artisans in Spanish

---

[141] *Ibid.*, pp. 302–4; Lanning, "Legitimacy," *passim*; Klein, *Slavery in the Americas*, p. 207; and Castillero, *La sociedad panameña*, p. 104.

[142] See, for example, the biography of Francisco Javier Eugenio de Espejo, a *zambo* intellectual of Quito, in Mariano Picón-Salas, *A Cultural History of Spanish America from the Conquest to Independence* (Berkeley, 1963), p. 153.

[143] Juan and Ulloa, *Voyage*, vol. 1, bk. 1, chap. 4. As before, I have made minor changes in punctuation, orthography, and translation.

America. It seems probable that many migrated there in search of economic betterment, and, as we have seen, some so fiercely resented colored competition that the latter were at least nominally excluded from the status of master in most guilds. However, powerful socio-economic trends prompted many Spanish artisans to preach one thing and practice another. Spanish master craftsmen who saw the opportunity for profit purchased slaves, trained them in their craft, and sold them to others for a handsome profit, often even as teams which could function without further expert supervision. Eventually, these white artisans took their gains and withdrew from their craft altogether.[144]

In itself, this development had no bearing on the creation of a class of free colored artisans. Theoretically, the colored could have been trained and held in servitude in an endless cycle, and many no doubt were. However, as we have seen, more and more colored artisans were allowed to purchase their freedom. In other instances, slaves were apprenticed to artisans who endowed them with a means of livelihood before liberation or with a skill whereby they could purchase their freedom. In 1557, for example, Domingo Negro (along with his seventy-year-old mother) was sold to the carpenter Baltasar Guillén on condition that the latter teach the slave his trade in order that Domingo might purchase his liberty. A year earlier, Cristóbal Negro, slave of Don Juan Sánchez, was apprenticed to the carpenter Hernando Moreno with the same objective in mind.[145] Spaniards who fathered children by slave mothers frequently adopted the same procedure. In 1587, the Dutch carpenter Miguel de Briarte apprenticed his son born of a slave mother to one Andrés de Vergara of the same craft. A similar example is that of Cristóbal Martínez, pilot major of the South Sea, who contracted with the carpenter Melchior Martínez to instruct his twenty-year-old free mulatto son for a period of three years.[146]

It was not long before free blacks and mulattoes became aware of these opportunities and apprenticed themselves in substantial numbers, first to Spanish masters, then, increasingly, to craftsmen of their own kind. One of the earliest contracts for Peru dates from 1556, when Andrés Negro apprenticed himself to the builder Francisco de Morales for four years in return for board, room, and clothing. Late in the sixteenth century the free mulatto Gregorio López and the Indian Juan Pumilla apprenticed themselves to the Spanish master Diego Felipe. In 1588, Ana de Santiago's contract with the master Pedro Falcón to instruct her *negrito criollo* son Domingo called for the latter to be provided with the usual room and board and all the necessary tools.[147]

[144] Klein, *Slavery in the Americas*, p. 144; Lockhart, *Spanish Peru*, p. 183.
[145] Harth-terré and Márquez Abanto, "El artesano negro," pp. 7–8.
[146] *Ibid.*, pp. 14–15.
[147] *Ibid.*, pp. 12, 14–15.

By the eighteenth century, and perhaps before, veritable dynasties of free colored artisans had developed in Spanish America, and with every generation their members grew lighter and married more successfully. Many joined militia units, and, as we have seen, the resulting prestige enabled them to press for still further privileges for their descendants. Not coincidentally, the activities of these men tended to force out all competition, whether it came from slaves or from white immigrants from Spain.[148]

It must be stressed that only a minority of the free colored people of Spanish America became artisans and thereby improved their prospects. The majority, while free, remained as cooks, laundresses, peddlers, musicians, and the like.[149] Occasionally, there was substantial money to be made even in these occupations. For example, Catalina de Zorita, a free colored woman, owned a bakery and confectionary in Lima in the 1540s and 1550s which was staffed by ten slaves and probably was worth several thousand pesos. Catalina, perhaps married to a Spaniard herself, arranged for the marriage of her daughter to a white; the marriage agreement included a handsome dowry, and Catalina was rarely reminded of her race to her face.[150] Other free persons of color were drawn to the land, perhaps in part to escape the vigilance of Spanish authorities, and their properties, in defiance of royal authority, were sometimes worked by Indian laborers.[151]

Manumission, however, was largely an urban phenomenon, and most free persons of color appear to have remained in the cities and towns, the world they knew best. For example, in the 1790s, nearly one-fourth of Peru's free colored population lived in Lima (10,231 of 41,404 people), and the bulk of the remainder also appear to have been urban based.[152] Undoubtedly, there were exceptions to this pattern. One may have been Colombia, where many persons of color who

[148] *Ibid.*, pp. 32–37, 59–72 *passim*; Klein, *Slavery in the Americas*, p. 144. In my forthcoming book (n. 2 above), I try to trace the origins of the free colored artisan class in greater detail. Much more research needs to be done in this connection for the other Spanish American colonies.

[149] Díaz Soler, *Historia*, p. 251, and Castillero, *La sociedad panameña*, pp. 103–4, provide examples of the concentration of free persons of color in these occupations.

[150] Lockhart, *Spanish Peru*, p. 193.

[151] *Ibid.*, p. 192; Klein, *Slavery in the Americas*, p. 145; Acosta Saignes, *Vida*, pp. 319, 321; "Papers Bearing on the Negroes of Cuba," pp. 57, 62–63; Inge Wolff, "Negersklaverei und Negerhandle in Hochperu, 1545–1640," *Jahrbuch für Geschichte von Staat: Wirtschaft und Gesselschaft Lateinamerikas*, 1 (1964): 185; Francisco Pérez de la Riva, "El negro y la tierra: El conuco y el palenque," *Revista Bimestre Cubana*, 58 (1946): 98–103. In 1745, for example, free persons of color cultivated some 2 percent of Venezuela's cacao bushes; see Brito Figueroa, "Formación de la propiedad," p. 126.

[152] With the exception of Lima, an exact determination is impossible because the 1792 census was taken by intendancy districts, which were further subdivided into *partidos*; neither division corresponds exactly to the boundaries of the colony's towns. See also Klein, *Slavery in the Americas*, p. 158.

worked in the gold placers and obtained their freedom stayed on as mine laborers. Panama seems to have been still another exception; the bulk of that colony's colored freedmen seem to have turned away from the cities to subsistence agriculture, perhaps in part because the economic decline of the eighteenth century deprived most of them of any opportunity in the urban areas.[153] Panama is also interesting because the free colored majority came to dominate the ruined town of Portobelo on the eve of independence, while the relatively more prosperous Panama City remained under white minority control.[154] Clearly, much more detailed research is needed to determine the approximate proportion of urban to rural free colored and to formulate some generalizations concerning the relative status and prosperity of each group.

ASSIMILATION

In the beginning, free persons of color exhibited a high degree of solidarity. James Lockhart states the matter well: "Free Negroes formed a coherent group or community, much like the Basques or foreigners, but even more tightly knit. Negroes married within the community, had their closest friends and worst enemies within it, loaned each other money, and preferred to do all kinds of business with each other."[155] To an extent, this cohesiveness was never lost throughout the colonial period. In every Spanish colony, there was, no doubt, a group which identified itself as free colored and derived a sense of community from that fact. But, also from the beginning, splintering was inevitable, in large part as a result of pressures from the larger Spanish society.

In this connection, Spanish racial ambivalence operated to curious effect. The authorities undoubtedly would have been pleased had all blacks remained slaves, but once the free colored community came into existence, its recognition, and even its organization, was deemed desirable. In common with many mayors in the United States today, when the governmental agencies of colonial Spanish America desired something from the free colored population, they approached those presumed to be influential within its ranks. In 1555, for example, the city fathers of Lima pondered the fact that the municipality's streets were extraordinarily filthy, and that the treasury was without funds with which to remedy the situation. Then, however, someone thought to utilize the "idle" and "prejudicial" population of free colored persons for the task. One of their number, Francisco Hernández, a "well-known family man and property owner," was appointed to supervise the task on a permanent basis. For this purpose, he was

---

[153] See the chart in Castillero, *La sociedad panameña*, p. 99.

[154] *Ibid.*, pp. 104–5.

[155] *Spanish Peru*, p. 192. My own research in Peruvian archives confirms that as late as 1650 this pattern was still very much in existence.

given a staff of office and the necessary authority to compel his fellow free persons of color to serve as the city's street sweepers.[156]

As the government expected more and more from the free colored population, it was more and more tempted formally to recognize and organize that community's existence. In the late 1620s, for example, the free mulattoes of Lima were organized into a guild, which organization and its officers were made responsible for the collection of tribute, the recruitment of the mulatto militia companies, and the collection of special contributions for various religious and civic festivities.[157] In 1631, the mulatto guild participated on a lavish scale in the festivities which honored the birth of Baltasar Carlos, heir to the Spanish throne.[158] A similar arrangement appears to have prevailed in Potosí, where an *alcalde de los negros*—in this instance a free person of color and a slaveowner—was given the power to settle minor disputes among his peers.[159] The church also institutionalized the differentiation, first by creating separate confraternities for free persons of color, and then by distinguishing between blacks and mulattoes in the organization of these groups.[160] The crown, as we have seen, made a similar distinction in the organization of militia companies.

It is likely the authorities would have been content to let the matter of racial differentiation rest at this point, but the process of racial mixture continued and, with it, the society's almost morbid fascination with racial classification. It should come as no surprise that the free colored population came to share this fascination, and to see in it the advancement or frustration of their own ambitions

[156] *LCL*, 5: 356–57, session of December 2. In seventeenth-century Cuba, the authorities pressed free persons of color into service as mail carriers, thus causing them to lose time from tending their crops ("Papers Bearing on the Negroes of Cuba," pp. 58, 64–65).

[157] It is unclear whether free blacks were also included in this guild. My information comes from a lawsuit in AGI, Escribanía de Cámara 1023b, "Pedro Martín Leguisamo, oficial de platero y vecino de la ciudad de Lima, con el Gremio de Mulatos de ella, sobre que se declarase no ser de este gremio, y sí de los españoles [1632]," *passim.* Leguisamo's mother was a *mulata*, but his father was a Basque and a *hidalgo*, and Leguisamo successfully avoided payment of tribute and service in the mulatto militia on the strength of his father's noble status. He appealed to the Council of the Indies for certification of his status as a Spaniard and as a member of the silversmiths' guild, but the council directed him to petition the viceroy instead. It might also be mentioned that the guild of mulattoes flatly refused to collect tribute from its members.

[158] Suardo (*Diario de Lima*, 1: 133–35, 137–42) describes the festivities, which included floats, theatricals, and bullfights.

[159] Wolff, "Negersklaverei," p. 185. As early as the 1560s, a similar office appears to have been created to supervise the free colored of Havana; see Pérez de la Riva, "El negro y la tierra." p. 98.

[160] AGI, Lima 301, "Relación de las ciudades, villas y lugares, parrochias y doctrinas que hay en este Arzobispado de Lima, de españolas, y de indios, y de las personas que las sirven, así clerigos como religiosos, del número de feligreses que contiene y de las confradías y hospitales que hay en los dichos lugares, sus rentas y advocaciones [1619]."

and those of their children. Intelligent free persons of color who had accumulated modest fortunes[161] were quick to observe that racial solidarity was all very well, but that whitening was the key to socioeconomic advancement.

"Eager for honor,"[162] free persons of color became extremely sensitive to racial classification and were offended when referred to by a term for darkness greater than that which they claimed. In eighteenth-century Cartagena, for example, it was noted that "every person is so jealous of the order of their tribe or caste, that if through inadvertence, without the least intention to affront, you call them by a degree lower than what they actually are, they are highly offended, never suffering themselves to be deprived of so valuable a gift of fortune."[163] Except in the most isolated and backward regions of the empire, marriages between persons of color and whites were subject to severe societal censure,[164] but, at least in Cartagena, free black and mulatto women befriended luckless, indigent Spanish immigrants, and seemingly did so out of more than simple charity. Two eighteenth-century observers describe the situation as follows:

> The Negro and Mulatto free women, moved at their [the Spanish immigrants'] deplorable condition, carry them to their houses, and nurse them with the greatest care and affection. If any one die, they bury him by the charity they procure, and even cause masses to be said for him. The general issue of this endearing benevolence is that the Chapeton, on his recovery, during the fervour of his gratitude, marries either his Negro or his Mulatto benefactress, or one of her daughters; and thus he is settled, but much more wretchedly than he could have been in his own country, though he had only his own labor to subsist on.[165]

We may therefore agree with the conclusions of Miguel Acosta Saignes that free blacks and mulattoes, although very numerous in many Spanish American colonies, basically had little sense of "class" consciousness.[166] Few outstanding cultural differences separated them from the Spanish. As slaves, they had been forced to learn Spanish,

---

[161] For examples of the economic advancement of free persons of color, see Lockhart, *Spanish Peru*, pp. 193 ff.; Wolff, "Negersklaverei," pp. 185–86; Díaz Soler, *Historia*, p. 251; Harth-terré and Márquez Abanto, "Ei artesano negro," *passim*.

[162] The phrase, that of Father Iñigo Abbad y Lasierra, refers to the free colored population of eighteenth-century Puerto Rico, and is quoted in Díaz Soler, *Historia*, p. 248.

[163] Juan and Ulloa, *Voyage*, vol. 1, bk. 1, chap. 4. For Spanish satire concerning the preoccupation of colored persons with the "whitening" process, see Ildefonso Pereda Valdés, *El negro rioplatense y otros ensayos* (Montevideo, 1937), pp. 8–11.

[164] Saco (*Historia de la esclavitud*, pp. 216–17) records a few examples of such unions.

[165] Juan and Ulloa, *Voyage*, vol. 1, bk. 1, chap. 4.

[166] *Vida*, pp. 336–37.

and the mutual unintelligibility of the various African tongues and dialects made their disappearance inevitable. No outstanding differences in dress, housing, or diet separated black from white, although living conditions enjoyed by the former were usually meaner. As Aguirre Beltrán puts it: "The view of the world held by the Negro and the mulatto at the close of the colonial period was not very different from the [white] criollo's."[167] Rent by values and ambitions imposed upon them by the larger society, free blacks and mulattoes were anxious most of all to forget their racial origins or at least to whiten themselves as much as possible. For this reason, although mulattoes made their way into the elite on rare occasions, African blood did not course through the veins of the upper class by common consent. Insinuation of African descent was one of the gravest insults that could be visited upon a respectable "white" family.[168] Father Beye de Cisneros, who addressed the Spanish Cortes in 1811 in an attempt to prevent the disfranchisement of the racially mixed in America, summarized the fragmentation of the free colored population when he said:

> I have known mulattoes who have become counts, marquises, *oidores*, canons, colonels, and knights of the military orders through intrigue, bribery, perjury, and falsification of public books and registers; and I have observed that those who have reached these positions and distinctions by reprehensible means, have been granted the corresponding honors without repugnance despite their mixed blood.[169]

That is, as early as the sixteenth century in the Hispanic world, "those who could rise," in the words of Stuart Schwartz, "did so without a backward glance."[170] The unique jumble of Spanish racial atti-

[167] "Integration of the Negro," pp. 23–26. See also the present writer's essay entitled "The Assimilation of the African: The Peruvian Experience, 1529–1650," to be published in the collection of essays edited by Bowser and Toplin (n. 2 above).

[168] Concerning this point, see the very perceptive essay by Jaime Jaramillo Uribe, "Mestizaje y diferenciación social en el Nuevo Reino de Granada en la segunda mitad del siglo XVIII," *Anuario Colombiano de Historia Social y de la Cultura*, 3 (1965): 21–48.

[169] Quoted in James F. King, "The Colored Castes and American Representation in the Cortes of Cádiz," *Hispanic American Historical Review*, 33 (1953): 56–57. The outcome of these emotional and tangled debates of the Cortes falls outside the scope of this paper, but one may note that ultimately the Spanish majority classified the colored castes as Spaniards. In the interest of maintaining peninsular dominance in all future representative bodies, however, persons of African descent were not given enfranchisement as full citizens, although a provision was made that deserving colored citizens might be so honored. In addition, the Cortes abolished the tribute requirement and provided that those of African descent might attend Spanish American institutions of higher learning and pursue ecclesiastical careers. In the end, of course, this attempted placation of the colored man was frustrated by the success of the movement for Latin American independence.

[170] "Cities of Empire: Mexico and Bahia in the 16th Century," *Journal of Inter-American Studies*, II (1969): 628.

tudes and practices assured free persons of color of just enough mobility to pervent any attempt at racial solidarity. In the late colonial period, there were explosive tensions in Spanish America, but the "Revolt of the Man with Dark Skin" was overshadowed by the successful attempt of the white creole aristocracy to wrest control of their destiny from Spain.[171] Spanish authorities were traditionally suspicious of any ties between the free colored and slave populations,[172] but conspiracies between the two groups resulting in insurrection, while greatly feared, rarely materialized.[173] Persons of mixed blood and slaves each had their grievances, but white creoles, in the best position to challenge Spanish authority, managed to carry that challenge to success and at the same time to preserve their own superiority.

In most areas, the ill-digested philosophical justifications for the struggle for independence prepared the way for an end to official racial discrimination and hastened the abolition of slavery, but social justice for the colored man was all too often lost sight of amid schemes to promote white immigration from Europe. In the meantime, the free colored person of some standing was much too busy advancing his own cause to worry about the slave population, and even those who were concerned could do little about the situation. The socioeconomic system of Spanish America, so admirably suited to absorb a limited number of free colored during the days of colonialism and slavery, faltered under the stresses of nationhood and abolition. The slaves, freed en masse after prolonged debate but with little preparation, stayed at the bottom of society, and their marginal existence provided a powerful argument for those who, often simultaneously, wished to promote white immigration and, while agreeing with currently fashionable theories of colored inferiority, to throttle forever public discussion of racial prejudice.[174]

CONCLUSIONS

Given the knowledge we have, the conclusions to be drawn from this survey must necessarily be tentative. Clearly, however, many forms of manumission were instrumental in the creation of the free

[171] The phrase is Mörner's, and *Race Mixture*, pp. 75–90, is the best account of this struggle.

[172] The government was particularly sensitive to the fact that free persons of color might be tempted to encourage slaves to run away and to aid them in their efforts (*Recopilación, libro* VII, *título* v, *ley* 22). Free colored persons sometimes complained of harassment, and worse, at the hands of would-be slave catchers ("Papers Bearing on the Negroes of Cuba," pp. 60–61, 65–66).

[173] For an exception, see Pedro M. Arcaya, *Insurrección de los negroes de la serranía de Coro* (Caracas, 1949).

[174] This issue is explored in greater detail in Mörner, *Race Mixture*, pp. 129 ff., and in various essays in the forthcoming collection edited by Bowser and Toplin (n. 2 above).

colored population—conditional and unconditional donations of liberty by the master, various forms of purchase—and in all of them
racial mixture played a subtle but influential role. Additional evidence
indicates that the manumission process may have operated to the
advantage of colored women and children, perhaps particularly in
periods of economic boom, and that urban slaves were favored over
their rural counterparts, both in the opportunity to secure freedom
and in the chance to live more than a marginal life of liberation.

At any rate, manumission and natural reproduction made for a
free colored population which increased in size and importance during the colonial period. The legal status of this group was inferior to
that of the Spaniard, but in practice conditions were considerably
better. It is true that prejudice sharply limited the access of the free
person of color to educational opportunities and therefore to membership in the bureaucracy and the professions. However, the circumstances which favored strong colored representation in the arts and
crafts also brought a measure of financial security and status, advantages which could be increased by militia service and advantageous
marriage. To "whiten" in this way was a slow and uncertain process,
but fragmentary evidence, particularly for the late colonial period,
indicates that it was a path followed with success by more and more
free colored families.

It may well be that this process, delicate and limited in a society
not noted for socioeconomic mobility, was set back by the circumstances surrounding abolition. What is more certain is that the upward ascent of the free person of color was not conducive to racial
solidarity among those of African descent. Far from it. The paradoxi-
cal nature of Spanish attitudes toward the subject of race assured that
the free person of color, despised for the very mixture of bloods which
coursed through his veins, was nevertheless rewarded for every step
taken, both cultural and biological, which approximated the white
ideal. Thus, for better or for worse, only under the most extreme circumstances did the advantaged person of color identify with those
beneath him.

H. HOETINK

2 | Surinam and Curaçao

With the exception of the years 1828–45, the Dutch possessions in the Caribbean and South America never formed a single political unit. They were, rather, separate colonies, each very different in character and situation from the other: Surinam, on the South American mainland, between French and British Guiana; and the Netherlands Antilles, formerly called the Colony of Curaçao, consisting of that island, Aruba, and Bonaire, all three of which are situated near the coast of Venezuela, and Saint Eustatius, Saba, and half of Saint Martin, in the northeastern corner of the Caribbean archipelago. Surinam was ceded to the Netherlands by the British in 1667 in exchange for New Amsterdam (later called New York); the Antillian islands were conquered from the Spaniards in the 1630s and 1640s.

As far as the Netherlands Antilles are concerned, this paper will focus on Curaçao. Aruba and Bonaire were plantations of the Dutch West Indian Company for so long that local communities of any appreciable size developed only very late in the colonial period. As for Saint Eustatius, Saint Martin, and Saba, the first two did become plantation societies (and the first of these tiny islands also achieved great commercial fame in the second half of the eighteenth century, when it was often referred to as The Golden Rock), but, compared to Curaçao, the general historical significance of all three is slight.

By limiting ourselves to a comparative description of Surinam and Curaçao, we shall be able to illustrate better how different the conditions of the free Negroes and mulattoes could become in two colonial societies subjected to Dutch authority and to similar metropolitan cultural influences.

SURINAM

Already during its English period, Surinam had become a sugar colony. By the time the Dutch took over the colony in 1667, and partly because of a recent immigration of Sephardim, the colony had some fifty sugar plantations. In the eighteenth century, coffee, cacao, and cotton plantations were added to its economic spectrum, but sugar continued to be the most important product. Nearly all these planta-

tions were located downstream on the larger rivers; only the wood
"plantations" could be found in the so called *Bovenland* (Upper
Country).

During the eighteenth century, the number of plantations rose
steadily and reached a total of 591 in 1788; the number of slaves in
that year was approximately 50,000 out of a total population of
55,000. From then on, the colony suffered a continuous economic decline: in the year of abolition, 1863, there were only 210 plantations
left; the slaves then numbered 31,380 out of a total population of
49,132 inhabitants. Of the latter number, 37 percent lived in the
colony's capital and only town, Paramaribo. The increasing numerical
significance of the urban population was a clear indication of the
decreasing economic importance of plantation agriculture. Neither
the massive immigration of contract labor from British India, which
started during the mid-nineteenth century, nor the later similar immigration from the Dutch East Indies could prevent the decline of the
plantation system; in its place came a type of agriculture predominantly based on small landholdings. In the twentieth century, bauxite
became Surinam's main product.

The turning point in the history of plantation agriculture in
Surinam came during the last quarter of the eighteenth century. In
the middle of that century considerable Dutch capital still flowed to
the colony, and speculation in tropical products, especially coffee,
created an artificial boom. In 1773, however, the Amsterdam Exchange suffered a serious reverse, which ended its easy credit and
marked the beginning of the end of Surinam prosperity. Many planters
in the colony were forced to sell their properties to metropolitan creditors, and the period of absenteeism began. Dutch-based companies
had their plantations run by administrators, some of whom were
burdened with the improbable task of supervising operations on as
many as 50 plantations. Of the 369 plantations in Surinam in 1813,
297 were the property of absentee owners.

In the period before 1773, and despite what the colony's director,
Jan Jacob Mauricius, called the *animus revertendi* (the inclination of
many colonists to make their fortunes rapidly and then leave the
country), a slow trend had been developing toward the formation of a
more stable white population group, composed not only of Dutchmen,
but also (and even more importantly) of French (mostly Huguenots),
Germans, English, and Jews, who, Sephardim and Ashkenazim taken
together, constituted more than one-third of the white population. In
1787, Jews numbered 1,311 in a population of 3,360 whites. After the
economic crisis of 1773, when many other whites left Surinam, the
proportion of the Jews increased accordingly. In 1811 they amounted
to two-thirds, and in 1830 still a little more than one-half, of the white
population. Several of them were prosperous planters, but a much
larger number earned their living as clerks or in retail businesses.
While the Jews thus formed the only group of "old" white settlers

which kept its numerical strength throughout the economic depression of the 1770s, a new category of white immigrants entered the country: the new administrators of plantations, most of whom were unmarried. As a consequence, the always unfavorable numerical balance between the sexes within the white group became still greater. Bachelor administrators and their white managing personnel often engaged in regular sexual relations with Surinamese free colored or Negro women. These relationships were called "Surinamese marriages." A simple ceremony[1] marked their beginning; normally, they ended when the male partner left for Europe. Besides these "marriages," there had always been, of course, less permanent and less regulated liaisons between white males and free colored or Negro females. It was especially the children born of the latter relations who swelled the number of impoverished colored in the colony. Others, however, mostly from the "Surinamese marriages," were well taken care of by their fathers and were even sent to Holland for further education. Because of the increase in this type of relationship in the last part of the eighteenth and the beginning of the nineteenth century, a group of "respectable" and well-educated colored people was thus being formed. We will deal with the social significance of this group later in this chapter.

First, let us look at some aspects of Surinamese slavery. The number of whites in the colony was never more than 7 percent of the total number of slaves, and most of the time it was only about 5 percent. In 1787 there were in Paramaribo two whites for every seven slaves, but in the rural rest of the country there was one white for every sixty-five slaves. Frequently, ordinances were published which demanded that there be one white overseer for every ten or twenty slaves, but these governmental stipulations do not seem to have been taken seriously.

Many documents expressed or echoed fear of the overwhelming numerical superiority of the slaves. Yet, Surinam did not have a single general slave rebellion. When revolt broke out on a plantation, the slaves sought not to broaden the revolt but, typically, to flee to the tropical jungle. By 1770, these maroons, who had succeeded in establishing their own villages, already numbered between five and six thousand persons. Some twenty years earlier, the colonial government had negotiated peace treaties with several of the groups, but fear of their increasing numbers later led to new military expeditions against them. In 1770, a military corps of Negro soldiers, freedmen and slaves (the latter being manumitted the moment they entered the ranks), was established for the explicit purpose of fighting the maroons, a task they performed loyally.

The numerical superiority of the slaves, which provoked fear,

---

[1] The mother of the girl, accompanied by a female neighbor, brought her into the bedroom of the groom. The next morning, after man and wife left, the room was visited again by her mother and the neighbor, who then proceeded to announce to the neighborhood that the marriage had become a fact.

and the isolated location of the majority of the plantations, which
made such social and judicial controls as might emanate from the
capital hardly effective, were the main causes of the generally severe
and often very cruel treatment of the slaves, especially on the sugar
plantations, and more so among field slaves than among artisan or
house slaves. After the crucial year 1773, the lot of the slaves
worsened, not only because the administrators of the plantations
probably felt even less affection for the slaves than at least some of
the former owners might have shown, but also because they had to
comply with often extreme production demands set by their metropolitan superiors. At least until the beginning of the nineteenth century, the number of deaths among Surinamese slaves was always
larger than the number of births. Not until after the end of the slave
trade in 1808 did medical care for slaves improve. Even the planters'
interest in the religious education of their slaves was slight prior to
1828, when a number of planters and high officials founded a society
for that purpose. For Van Lier, the causal link between these improved conditions for the slaves and the end of the slave trade is
obvious, and he interprets the link as proof of the "rational character"
of the slave system.[2]

During the greater part of the eighteenth century, the number of
"free people"[3] was small: between 1738 and 1787 it increased from
598 to only 650, which actually meant that it decreased vis-à-vis the
white population, from one-fourth to one-fifth of the latter group. This
small numerical increase can be explained partly by the absence of
natural increase among the free people and partly by the very small
number of manumissions made during this period. The latter, however, increased drastically during the last quarter of the century. In
1791 the number of free people was three times what it had been in
1787, in 1812 they numbered 3,075, and in 1830, 5,041. By 1830
their number was already nearly twice as large as that of the total
white population.

Of the 5,041 free people in 1830, 3,947 were colored and 1,094
were Negro, as compared to 3,033 colored and 45,751 Negroes among
the slave population of that year. Only one-twelfth of the free people
lived outside Paramaribo. The numerical superiority of colored over
Negro free people, and the fact that there were nearly twice as many
women as men in this group, clearly indicates that the composition
of the category "free people" was predominantly determined by the
masters' preference for manumitting their colored mistresses and
their offspring. The colored men among the manumitted had mostly

<hr>

[2] R. A. J. van Lier, *Samenleving in een grensgebied: Een sociaal-historische studie van de maatschappij in Suriname* (The Hague, 1949), p. 71.

[3] I use this term as direct translation of *vrije lieden*, which includes
both the colored and Negroes, and which formally has to be distinguished from
vrijgemaakten (freedmen), those who were manumitted during their lifetime,
although in many of the following data this distinction has been obscured.

been house or artisan slaves, and the latter had had some opportunity to earn income of their own with which to try to buy their freedom.

Colonial authorities in Surinam began to limit the number of manumissions during the first half of the eighteenth century. In 1733 they ordered that the approval of the Policy Council was necessary for every manumission, and one of the conditions they set was that the manumitted slave had to be able to take care of himself materially. In 1788 the authorities stipulated that every male slave manumitted had to pay one hundred guilders to the government and that every female and child had to pay fifty. In 1804 these sums were increased respectively to five hundred and two hundred fifty. In 1825 the slaves were forbidden to buy their own freedom. In 1832 an additional condition for manumission was effected whereby a slave had to be a member of an officially recognized religious organization before manumission would be extended to him. However, in 1850—some thirteen years before abolition—all restrictions on manumission were abolished. The result was a dramatic increase in the number of manumissions: between 1852 and 1856 1,492 persons were manumitted. Because the total number of slaves at that time was some 40,000, however, this frequency of manumission was hardly extensive.

Surinamese authorities always maintained a strict distinction between free Negroes and the free colored, organizing both categories into separate military companies. Similarly, they distinguished legally between those free people who were *born* free and those who were *set* free. The latter had certain obligations vis-à-vis their former masters: they were expected to treat them with respect and to aliment them if they became poverty stricken. When a childless manumitted person died, one-fourth of his inheritance went to his former master or his children.

While the largest number of free Negroes and free colored lived in poor circumstances in the capital, where they tried to sustain themselves, mostly as small shopkeepers and artisans (and in the latter case suffered from competition with artisan slaves), a certain number of the free colored came to possess greater prosperity and a better education than the rest of the free population. We observed earlier how this group consisted largely of descendants of the so-called Surinamese marriages, whose European fathers were not soldiers and sailors but belonged to the higher strata of society and bothered to take care of their Creole offspring. Some of them were educated in Europe; others received their education in Surinam, where in 1760 a governmental school for mulatto children was established.

Partly because of his preoccupation with the social impact of the exodus of whites after the economic crisis of 1773, Governor Wichers (1784–90) tried to implement a deliberate policy whereby the colored population would come to occupy the middle levels of the social structure. The sociologist and historian Rudolf van Lier, on whose valuable work *Samenleving in een grensgebied* much of this outline is based, ascribes the increasing number of manumissions in this period to the personal influence of Wichers. The number of colored in lower- and middle-level administrative positions in commerce increased at this time, as did their number in similar governmental positions. In 1809 the first colored elementary school teacher returned from the Netherlands, where he had studied, and founded his own private school. Soon more colored people came to occupy even more prestigious positions, and several decades before abolition in 1863 there were a considerable number of university-trained individuals among the "respectable" colored, some of whom were members of the judiciary branch of government; during the same period, others were appointed directors and administrators of plantations. Several of these families became members of the prestigious Dutch Reformed and Lutheran churches, whereas the poorer free people and slaves were apt to be converted by the Hernhutters (Moravian Brothers), who had established themselves in Paramaribo in 1754 or by the Catholic church. Some of the "respectable" colored families in this period came to have intimate social contacts with white families from the same socioeconomic background.

During the second half of the nineteenth century, the penetration of the colored group into the higher echelons of society temporarily stagnated, and the Jewish group (still the only permanently settled white inhabitants) again gained power and prestige. Jews succeeded in occupying many of the high governmental positions and to the extent that such posts were not reserved for the metropolitan Dutch. At least a partial explanation of this phenomenon can be found in the fact that a number of Surinamese colored who had been educated in Europe decided to leave their country and to settle in the Netherlands or the Netherlands East Indies, where the social disadvantages of their physical appearance, the existence of which still could not be denied in Surinam, were less obvious.

The rising number of colored engaged in lower and middle administrative positions was regarded as a threat by the Jews, many of whom had traditionally occupied these positions, and a mutual feeling of competition between the two groups became manifest in the course of the nineteenth century. During the first half of the century, it was mostly colored who were appointed to high governmental posts; in the second half it was mostly Jews. In passing, it may be noted that already in the second half of the eighteenth century a buffer group between the two competing categories had come into being, that of the Jewish colored, who numbered about one hundred persons. These descendants of Jewish fathers had their own congregation, or Siva, and their own temple, built with monies from white Jews and Christians.

The feelings of competition between the "respectable colored" and the Jews did not, however, prevent them from closing their ranks ever so often in common antipathy against the European Dutch public employees, who in colonial times continued to be appointed to several of the highest administrative and governing positions in Surinam. Emergent anti-colonial and national sentiments were for the most part directed against them as the chief representatives of the colonial power. Only in the second half of the twentieth century did this emergent nationalism lead to adoption, and even then somewhat reluctantly, of *Sranang tongo*, the Creole Surinam language (which had long been used by the lower strata), by the higher social classes. In other words, for a very long period the Surinam upper classes continued to reveal their Dutch cultural orientation through their language patterns.

CURAÇAO

The Dutch West Indian Company viewed the importance of Curaçao, conquered in 1634, mostly in the light of its function as a *sedem belli* in the war of independence against the Spaniards and as a strategic foothold for the salt trade and officially approved privateering activities. The company did make some efforts to cultivate plantation products (cotton, sugar, tobacco), but the arid climate of the island soon convinced the directors of the futility of such efforts. During the eighteenth century, most of the company's lands were sold to, or usurped by, European settlers, who used them to establish their "plantations." According to the Curaçao meaning of the word, a plantation included a colonial style mansion, a small irrigated area for the cultivation of vegetables and fruits, and a rather ample domain devoted to extensive goat and cattle ranching. At the end of the eighteenth century, some seventy of these plantations covered most of the island's 210 square miles. Modern capitalistic production of tropical products for the world market never became a dominant feature of the Curaçao economy.

Already in the first decades after the Dutch conquest the island began to develop into an important commercial colony. Produce from the nearby Spanish colonies was smuggled into the island and traded for merchandise from Europe and Africa. An active commercial exchange also began to take place with the French and British possessions, with Curaçao serving as a depot for European food products, arms, and slaves. As a slave depot for the surrounding region, Curaçao reached its greatest importance roughly between 1660 and 1713. Until the latter year, the Dutch participated in the sale of slaves to the so-called *asientistas*, who held monopolistic contracts with the Spanish authorities for the delivery of Negro slaves to Spanish America. In the first years of the eighteenth century an average of 8,000 slaves were imported annually from Africa on Dutch ships, most of them headed for Curaçao; between 1743 and 1753, however, the total number of imported slaves did not exceed 600. The last slave ship supposedly called at Curaçao in 1778.

Curaçao was, then, a commercial colony, and, like other imported merchandise, slaves were for the most part sold and exported again. Around the year 1700 the West Indian Company had only some 2,400 slaves in its service on the island. The virtual discontinuation of the company's agricultural activities in subsequent decades led to a drastic decrease in the number of its slaves. But the number of those owned by private masters increased, so that at the end of the eighteenth century there were approximately 4,000 slaves on the island, and in 1863, the year of abolition, a little less than 7,000. At both times slaves formed about one third of the total population.

The commercial character of the colony makes it easy to understand that a relatively large part of the slaves belonged to the categories of domestic and artisan slaves. Sizable gangs of agricultural slaves were scarce and could be found only on the large plantations in the western part of the island. In 1735, 376 slaveowners had a total of 1,391 slaves; 227 of them had no more than 1 or 2 slaves; only 38 masters had more than 10 slaves, and only 8 masters had more than 50. The largest slave gang in that year consisted of 120. This pattern of distribution of slave property maintained itself virtually unchanged until the end: in 1863 the overwhelming majority of slaveholders possessed fewer than 5 slaves.

This type of ratio between slaves and masters operated to make master-slave relationships in Curaçao relatively mild. The master's relations with his slaves were normally based on personal and face-to-face contact. Most slaveowners did not live in fear of a menacing number of slaves and were therefore probably less inclined toward acts of sadism such as could be observed in colonies where there was a higher proportion of slaves. A second factor which contributed to the relatively benign character of master-slave relations was the fact that a considerable number of white families remained on the island for many generations. This increased their emotional attachment to land and people and, incidentally, made it easier for the authorities to maintain social control over them. Such was the case with the Protestant settlers of Dutch, Westphalian, and French (Huguenot) origins and—even more so—with the Sephardim, who had established themselves on the island soon after the Dutch conquest and formed approximately one-third of the white population until the beginning of the nineteenth century. Originally dedicated to agriculture, the Jews soon transformed themselves into an economically powerful commercial elite. Third, the small size of Curaçao tended to bring the conduct of individual slaveowners under closer government scrutiny. Finally, many of the owners of plantations were hardly well-to-do (often they were—or were descendants of—civil or military officers of the company, or merchants—*rentiers*—who had great trouble in making their socially prestigious property economically viable), and this relatively low level of prosperity *may* have kept them from mistreating their slaves too frequently or too severely. Certain instruments of torture used in Surinam were unknown in Curaçao, and Curaçaoan slaves, because of their frank and undisciplined behavior, had a bad reputation on the Caribbean slave markets. The relatively benevolent treatment of the Curaçaoan slaves is reflected in their uninterrupted natural increase, a phenomenon which again stands out as an exception among slave colonies of the Caribbean region.

The mercantile character of the Curaçaoan economy had important consequences for the frequency of slave manumission. Many of the slaves were in fact "luxury servants," acting as gardeners, house servants, or coachmen; often, their manumission was less an act of charity on the part of their masters than a convenient way for the latter to free themselves of the legal responsibility for feeding and caring for their slaves in a period of economic depression. Plantation owners also manumitted old, unproductive slaves in times of prolonged drought and general poverty.

Largely as a result of the earliest of the periodic economic recessions that plagued the economy of the island, by the 1740s there were so many "free people" that a large volume of complaints began to appear about their behavior. Many of them had organized into two gangs, with the unexplainable names *Borosi* and *Japans*, and had started fighting on every conceivable occasion. It is tempting to suppose that this division correlated with that between free mulattoes and free Negroes, but, though a clear social distinction did exist between these two groups (a distinction which the government emphasized by dealing separately with them in administrative and military matters), there is no proof for the supposition. The conflicts between the *Borosi* and *Japans* resulted in a 1741 ordinance which was directed exclusively against the free people; it prohibited them from participating in any meeting of more than six persons, including weddings and burials. A 1745 decree prohibited both slaves and freedmen from walking on the streets after 9:00 P.M. without a lantern, and slaves also needed night permits from their masters. Slaves and freedmen were not allowed to carry sticks or other weapons, nor could they make music or buy liquor after that hour.

While slaves could feel they were a part of the paternalistic complex of the *Cas Grandi* (Big House) community, many free people were uprooted and lacked affective ties with any other segment of Curaçaoan society. Economically, the greatest number of free people were paupers, and in bad times their living conditions were worse than those of the slaves; socially, many of them were feared and shunned by the whites more than were the slaves. Their membership in ganglike groups must have been the response to a strongly felt psychological need.

The colonial government of Curaçao further responded to the growing number of free people by trying to limit manumissions. In the 1750s, Director Jacob Van Bosveld complained about "the too great facility of the inhabitants and owners of slaves to put these [slaves] in liberty" because he was afraid that this practice might, "at a certain moment, have unfavorable consequences." He therefore stipulated that 100 pesos had to be paid to the Dutch West Indian Company for the manumission of each male slave under sixty years of age and each female slave under fifty. It is not clear what "unfavorable consequences" Van Bosveld had in mind, but one can easily think of two: fear that a shortage of slaves would occur as soon as the then stagnating economy accelerated again; or fear of the increasing number of freedmen, which was coming to be looked upon with mounting distrust by the white population.

After this first governmental intervention in the area of slave manumission, further regulation took place in the following decades. Similar to Surinam, freed slaves and their offspring were obliged to show "all honor, respect, and reverence" to their former master, his wife, children, and their descendants. Offenses against his former master could result in the freedman's reversion to slavery. In 1813 it was decided that freed slaves would not receive their civil rights (which virtually amounted to equal status before the courts) until two years after the receipt of their letters of manumission, and in 1837 manumitted slaves were prohibited from leaving the colony. In this same period it was decreed that he who requested manumission for a slave had both to pay between three and five hundred guilders to the Treasury and to prove that the manumitted person had been accepted as a member by an officially recognized religious organization.

Of course, there were other kinds of manumission. Some resulted from genuine affection for loyal house servants or for children resulting from the sexual union of a master and a slave, while artisan slaves were allowed to buy their own freedom for a predetermined sum of money, which they could accumulate by their own labor. These slaves were called "money seekers" and had complete freedom of movement, their only obligation being to hand their master a weekly sum earned in their trade. We may note in passing that, in this way, not only did artisan slaves participate directly in the money economy but also—at least during the nineteenth century—many house slaves received an annual wage. However, if manumissions in Curaçao had taken place predominantly among house and artisan slaves, the number of colored in the category of free people would have been greater than was actually the case. It is well known that slaves of lighter color were generally selected for these privileged slave categories, especially for the group of house slaves. Yet the colored formed a minority among the free people in the early nineteenth century, a phenomenon which underlines the importance of the economic factor in the selection of slaves for manumission.

I mentioned earlier the official policy of dealing separately with free mulattoes and free Negroes. This division was, indeed, adhered to in all official documents and was institutionalized in the creation of separate military organizations for both groups. In 1789 the "corps of the free Negroes" consisted of 6 officers, 26 noncommissioned officers, and 748 soldiers. The mulatto corps in that year counted 395 soldiers. Both organizations formally fell under the supervision of the captain of the white civil guard, but both had their own commanding officers. Their specific task was to maintain peace and order among the non-white population; they were not allowed to deal with white people. Both organizations thus always became involved in whatever slave riots occurred, even when these, as was the case in 1750 and 1795, assumed the character of real rebellions. White authorities were generally fully satisfied about the way such police tasks were performed. One lieutenant of the free Negroes behaved so valiantly in 1795 that, by way of special distinction, he was allowed to fight from then on at the side of the regular white troops.

The assignment of military functions to these free people did not, however, mean that a complete social separation existed between all free Negroes and colored, on the one hand, and the slaves, on the other, during riots and rebellions. The official reports about the 1795 rebellion gave considerable attention to the numerous free Negroes and mulattoes who, continuously rambling over the island and without any means of subsistence, maintained close contacts with the rebels and kept them informed of the moves and plans of their adversaries. The reports also emphasized that free people from the French islands had taught revolutionary ideas to the slaves and had made them aware of the dramatic events in Saint Domingue.

Although the majority of the free people formed part of the lowest economic strata of Curaçao, a small number of them achieved a certain prosperity during the early years of the eighteenth century. Agriculture, as we saw, did not offer many chances for such mobility, though a few colored people owned small "plantations" and some slaves, often derived from a white planter's gift to a concubine or illegitimate son. Rather, the formation of a group of "respectable" colored took place in Curaçao's only town, Willemstad. Here, commerce in prosperous times offered a good opportunity for rapid economic advancement, provided the individual enjoyed a patron-client relationship with one of the powerful merchants. Because it was the Sephardim who, certainly from the beginning of the eighteenth century, dominated commerce and contraband trade, it was mostly colored of Jewish descent who rose to "respectability" and in time began to live together by themselves in a special town quarter. Only in the second half of the nineteenth century did other colored groups achieve a certain level of prosperity, as a result of the increased economic significance of local shipping and the support of the Catholic church[4] and its organizations, which became quite powerful during that period.

[4] Because neither Jews nor Protestants showed interest in converting the slaves, it was Catholic missionaries who, especially after the 1830s, christianized slaves and free people.

Generally speaking, prosperity and somatic traits tended to correlate: as a result of the process of social selection, the criteria for which were, in the final analysis, established by the white group, those who achieved a certain economic well-being tended to be less Negroid. Thus, it was mulattoes rather than Negroes who profited from economic protection. Within the colored group, a social differentiation based on prosperity, education, and physical traits came into being. With regard to the latter criterion, in Curaçao, as elsewhere in the Caribbean, a pre-Mendelian classification system included such terms as *sambo, grief, mestiche, castiche,* and *poestiche.* This genealogical differentiation was not of great consequence in every-day social intercourse, however, for one's biological antecedents were not always known, and one's somatic traits did not automatically inform the observer of one's genealogy and subsequent place in this classification system. Hence, a simpler division of the colored group was actually made, based, as far as racial considerations were concerned, on the observable physical characteristics of the individual.

Those colored who possessed a considerable degree of "whiteness" and a certain prosperity and minimum education were, at least by the end of the eighteenth century, no longer strictly considered colored, but were called *mesties.* They enjoyed certain privileges over the other free colored. Thus, they were officially considered "burghers," though they were still carefully distinguished from the whites. In 1789 the Dutch commissioners W. A. Grovestins, W. C. Boey, and R. Van Suchtelen noted that "in the [military] corps of the burghers all whites, both Christian and Jewish, are accepted, as are *mestiezen.*"[5]

That category "free colored," which combined light color with at least some prosperity, was equal or even superior to the group "lower white Protestants" in the economic (though not in the social) hierarchy of the insular society. The latter group consisted of small merchants and retailers, descendants of soldiers and noncommissioned officers who, because of their lower economic and educational level, were not fully acceptable to other whites—not to Jewish merchants or to Protestant plantation owners and high-ranking civil servants. Although, for reasons of social prestige, these "lower Protestants" would have preferred to keep their Dutch and religious heritage intact, many of them were forced, for lack of local partners, to contract marriages with Spanish American Catholics from the nearby continent. Among the "respectable" colored of predominantly Jewish descent, an increasing number of South American marriage partners were selected for the same reason. Both groups, the "higher colored" and the "lower white Protestants," thus became culturally Latinized. This was a painful process for the latter group, because it removed them even

[5] W. Ch. de la Try Ellis, "De Commissarissen van Zÿne Doorluchtigste Hoogheid te Curaçao in 1789," *Lux,* July, 1946, p. 6. Translations of quoted matter throughout this essay are the author's.

further from their prestigious Dutch roots, but it was a welcome development for the colored. By assimilating the Spanish American culture through their mates, the colored became more "foreign," to the extent that they became psychologically less dependent upon the Dutch colonial social system and therefore probably suffered somewhat less from the stigma of their physical appearance. Parenthetically, it may be noted that, except among a small number of "higher Protestants" and recently arrived metropolitans, Dutch had not been used as a vernacular since, probably, early in the nineteenth century; rather, *Papiamentu*, the local creole language, had become the common language, having previously served as a *lingua franca*, not only between masters and slaves, but also between Jews and Protestants.

The total number of free people, both colored and black, increased rapidly during the late eighteenth and early nineteenth centuries until, as the following figures demonstrate, they came to be twice as numerous as whites; and, at some point between 1817 and 1833, they even surpassed the total number of slaves.

	Whites	Free Colored	Blacks	Total Free People	Slaves
1817	2,780	2,240	2,309	4,549	6,765
1833	2,602	2,701	3,830	6,531	5,894

Small wonder, then, that whites were, and would continue to be, more fearful of the free people than they were of the slaves.

This fear of the free people manifested itself in repeated complaints about their undisciplined behavior and social intractability. In 1789 a report written by Dutch commissioners W. A. Grovestins, W. C. Boey, and R. van Suchtelen observed that "a mass of *mestiezen, castiezen*, and *mulatten* can be found, as well as many free Negroes and free maids, all of whom have lost completely the highly necessary ties of discipline; also, the undersigned can testify that they have never visited any colony where the Negroes are as impertinent as in Curaçao."[6] The agronomer M. D. Teenstra wrote in 1830 that "the colored men mostly are lazy and dirty drunkards, and exceptionally bold, so that the sensible thing to do is to avoid them. . . . The colored are treated with much greater contempt in Curaçao than in Surinam; with regard to the Negroes, however, the situation is the reverse."[7] The abolition of slavery in 1863 did nothing to change these

[6] C. Ch. Goslinga, *Emancipatie en emancipator: De geschiedenis van de slavernij op de Benedenwindse Eilanden en van het werk der Bevrijding* (Assen, 1956), p. 37.
[7] *De Nederlandsche West-Indische Eilanden* (Amsterdam, 1836), pp. 165–66.

attitudes. In 1898 the North American journalist W. B. Reilly remarked that "the mixed race is tabooed absolutely in Curaçao society."[8] In 1907 R. H. Rijkens wrote:

> Imitating their superiors, quite a group of young men are walking around idly and without a goal, their physical appearance showing that they belong neither to the white nor to the black race. They do not know [any trade], and refuse to perform anything by which they might elevate themselves above the common man. Their only "goal" is to dress as nicely as possible and to impersonate the gentleman, not at their own expense, of course, for they do not earn anything, but at that of their parents or other relatives, or of a silly girl, who must earn her money for them as a housemaid, or maybe by having others pay for the same favors, which she especially bestows upon him.[9]

These quotations suggest that, of the free people, it was specifically the colored who were especially despised by the white group. This disdain was directed both against the pauperized colored, who tried to hide their insecurity about their social role behind crude and coarse behavior, and against the better-educated and economically better-off colored, who were treated, especially by the "lower Protestants," with a mixture of jealousy and contempt. The more prosperous colored were, as a matter of course, socially ostracized by Protestants and Jews alike, at least as far as the more intimate social affairs were concerned, even if they belonged to the group of *mestiezen* and burghers.

With regard to the phenomenon observed by Rijkens, that of the idle group of colored youngsters who wanted to imitate the gentleman's life at someone else's expense, we may observe that, in a society where the simple forms of manual labor were immediately associated with dark skin color, the lighter colored had of necessity to develop an abhorrence for this type of work. In their poverty they wanted nevertheless to emulate the white *shon* (master). Their behavior was not just an imitation of a socially admired group, however; many of these young men were illegitimate children of white men and knew their fathers personally.

The white man maintained sexual relations, both before and during his marriage, with women from the lower Negroid strata. The owner of a plantation might have such relations with attractive female slaves from his own property; we have already noted that the light-colored offspring of these liaisons were often used as house servants and thus profited from a paternal preference which may have been partly based on the greater reliability of the bastard child. Occasionally, such an illegitimate slave was given his freedom later

8 "Curaçao, Dutch West Indies," *The Monthly Illustrator*, June, 1898, p. 9.
9 *Curaçao* (Tiel, 1907), p. 61.

in life. The white man in the city, who owned only a few slaves, often entered into erotic relations with a free colored woman.

Such sexual contracts were only partly of an incidental character; often they were institutionalized and became permanent. In the *cunucu* (countryside) or in the urban periphery, the "outside woman" lived with her children, and they were regularly visited by the white father. The frequency of this type of permanent relationship probably should be linked to the limited choice of legitimate marriage partners for white men. Both Jews and "higher Protestants" often married relatives. These *mariages de raison* were the result either of a desire to avoid splitting up the family capital or of a sheer lack of other socially acceptable candidates. The extramarital liaison may thus have assumed the functions of a complementary marriage, and an attractive "outside woman" may have provoked genuine affection from her partner, an affection which could manifest itself materially in financial care for the household and in the economic protection of the grown children.

It would seem that the Sephardim showed a somewhat greater affection and care for their "outside households" than did the Protestants. Thus, the Jewish father frequently allowed their illegitimate children to adopt their last names, or at least did not prevent them from doing so. The illegitimate offspring of the Protestant group were allowed only to suggest the blood relationship with their fathers, by corrupting his name, omitting letters from it, or changing the order of its syllables.

This greater care on the part of the Sephardim may be explained by their inbreeding, which was even more intense than that among the Protestants; thus, the institution of the "outside woman" probably became for them both more indispensable and more frequent than for the latter group. Furthermore, the Jewish father could derive greater economic benefits from the best of his illegitimate sons than could the Protestant father. The latter might give his bastard sons privileged positions on his plantation, donate pieces of arid land to them, or try to secure them small positions with the government, while the Jewish merchant and banker could employ his bastard sons as cheap and reliable personnel in his business or perhaps even give them (though admittedly seldom) a leading position in his establishment. Finally, it is possible that a somewhat greater family awareness and pride had certain favorable effects on the care of the outside offspring of the Jews. It would be altogether erroneous, however, to exaggerate the indicated differences between Protestants and Jews. Nor is there room to uncritically idealize or romanticize the relations between white men and colored or Negro mistresses. Yet it seems fair to assume that, however often they were characterized by fear and mistrust, the general relations between whites and free people, especially the colored among them, were somewhat tempered by the paternalistic relations between the *shons* and their outside households.

We have observed that in the eighteenth and nineteenth centuries several colored people owned a few slaves. As was generally the case with the "respectable colored," their behavior vis-à-vis the slaves and Negroes differed little from that of the whites. Possibly the unstable social position of the colored even caused them to show a greater aggressiveness, but we have no data at hand to confirm this suggestion. On the other hand, the Catholic religion was shared by the prosperous colored and the other Negroid groups. This fact may have had a mitigating effect on their relationship, if only because the *madrina* and *padrino*—the godparents at baptism, first communion, and marriage—were often selected from the group of more "respectable" colored. The godmother and godfather (normally not related) kept in contact with their godchild at least until his adulthood. In addition, they often served as counselors and protectors and thereby strengthened the bonds between the economically weak group and the more prosperous of the colored.

By way of summary, it may be stated that the free Negroes and the free colored in Curaçao were treated as separate social, administrative, and military categories; the colored group itself was divided into a number of "color classes" on the basis of economic, educational, and somatic criteria, which tended to correlate. Comparatively speaking, the relations of the whites with free people and slaves may be labeled as mild. Yet, because of their number and behavior, the free people, rather than the slaves, often inspired fear in the white population and thereby provoked a number of ordinances directed against them. Among the free people it was the colored, and among them the small number with a certain prosperity, who were perceived as a particular social menace by the "lower white Protestants." This small group of "respectable" colored was originally engaged mostly in commerce and later also in institutions sponsored by the Catholic church. Until well into the second quarter of the twentieth century, the governmental bureaucracy, especially its higher positions, was reserved for white Protestants. Even in the 1930s the appointment of a light-colored judge provoked some social comment.

A COMPARISON

Until 1795, Surinam and Curaçao were administered by semi-private trading companies,[10] whose authority was based upon charters issued by the Netherlands' States-General, which retained ultimate sovereignty over both areas. Within both colonies, the highest official was the director, who was a representative of his company and had, therefore, to assign priority to its economic interests. The director was

---

[10] For Curaçao this was the West Indian Company; for Surinam it was the Society of Surinam, in which, for the greatest part of the period until 1795, the West Indian Company, the city of Amsterdam, and the Van Aerssens van Sommelsdijck family each held one-third of the shares.

assisted by a *raad van politie* (policy council) in both areas, but there was an interesting difference in the way members of this council were selected.

The Dutch West Indian Company Board of Directors in Holland appointed the Curaçaoan council members, four of whom (later six) were company officials and three of whom (sometimes four) were Curaçaoan civilians. The burghers of the island had hardly any influence on these appointments. Only the fact that the captain of the (white) civil guard was an *ex officio* member of the council gave them a minimal and indirect say in governmental matters, and then solely because the officers of the guard were generally selected by the guard itself. Because the Curaçaoan population had no voting rights whatsoever until long after abolition, the free people were no worse off in this respect than were the whites.

The situation in Surinam was vastly different. The Charter of 1682—which was in effect until 1795—stipulated not only that the director had to carry out the decisions of the Court of Policy (in Curaçao the court had only advisory powers) but also that the court's members had to be selected by the director from pairs of candidates which had been constituted through the direct voting of "all the colonists." However, only the "prestigious and intelligent" members of the community were eligible for nomination. In the course of time, the right to participate in these elections was tied to some material conditions: only those who owned some real estate (house or land) were qualified to vote. This meant that not only the whites but also the freeborn and some of those set free had the right to vote (once they fulfilled these material prerequisites). We say *some* of those set free because "full blooded Negroes" were allowed to vote only if they were *born* free, a discrimination which underlined both the official distinction between those born free and those set free and that between Negroes and colored—a distinction which, as we noted earlier, was found in both colonies. There are no clear indications that formal discrimination against the free colored or Negroes existed insofar as their rights and duties vis-à-vis the judicial branch of government were concerned in either colony.

Under the jurisdiction of the companies, a number of parallels appeared in administrative directives toward the free people in the two colonies. Regulations concerning manumissions are a case in point. Such measures as had been taken to limit the number of manumissions during the course of the eighteenth century were not, it is true, taken at precisely the same date in each colony, but they were remarkably similar in content. The same can be said about the establishment of separate military corps for colored and Negroes, though it must be observed here that this separation did little more than confirm and add emphasis to a social distinction between the two racial groups which had existed since the early period of colonization. There are no indications that this particular social distinction was forced upon the non-white groups by the metropolitan or colonial authorities.

After the abolition of the companies in 1795 and the assumption of colonial authority by the executive branch of government in the Netherlands,[11] there were even closer parallels in the regulations of the two colonies. This was especially true between 1828 and 1845, when Surinam and the Dutch Antillean islands were governed as one colony by a governor general in Surinam and a governor in Curaçao. Thus, authorities in the Netherlands declared in the *Regulations with Regard to the Government Policy in the Netherlands West Indian Possessions* (1828), which applied to both Surinam and Curaçao, that "the slave is a person and not a chattel, his relation to his master is that of a pupil to his tutor or curator," and that all free citizens were to have the same rights, regardless of color or religion. Similarly, the stipulation of 1832, which forbade the manumission of slaves who were not members of a recognized religious organization, was applicable in both areas.

On the other hand, certain measures were devised to meet the particular needs of one of the regions. In 1825, for example, because of an acute lack of laborers, the authorities issued a temporary prohibition on Surinamese slaves purchasing their freedom, but they did not apply it to slaves in Curaçao. The clearest example of divergent legislation is that which dealt with abolition (1863). For economic reasons, abolition in Surinam was followed by a ten-year period during which the freed slaves, though formally free citizens, were controlled by the government and had to perform contract wage labor on the plantations. In Curaçao, such a transitional period was not required.[12]

The movement for abolition of slavery in the Netherlands began around 1840 under the direct influence of the *British and Foreign Anti-Slavery Society*, but it soon split into a Christian and a non-denominational faction and did not arouse much government response. More impressive to the Dutch government was the French slave abolition of 1848, for it led to the immediate *de facto* abolition of slavery in the Dutch part of Saint Martin, without which the slaves would have fled to the French part of that tiny island. Such a local emergency abolition accelerated at least somewhat the legislative preparations for the formal abolition of slavery in the Dutch colonies.

Generally speaking, however, the effects of metropolitan instructions or pressures, especially those intended to better the situation of

[11] In 1814 the colonies came under the supreme authority of the king, and administrative policies were determined in The Hague by the minister of colonial affairs, who until 1848 was responsible only to the king and not to Parliament.

[12] We may note in passing that in Curaçao in 1862, when the date of abolition had already been set, several slaves were still being manumitted, apparently to please them; a manumitted slave enjoyed higher social prestige than one who had received his freedom through abolition.

the non-white colonial populations, must not be overestimated. Several times during the seventeenth and eighteenth centuries, the authorities of the West Indian Company in Holland instructed their directors to have the Protestant religion taught to the (company) slaves, but such instructions brought no practical results. Similarly, the government regulations of 1828, which had been based on the recommendation of a personal emissary of the king and which formally recognized the slave as a person, produced no concrete consequences.

Because communications with the mother country were difficult, colonial officials were able to take great liberties vis-à-vis their highest superiors. The special character of the slave society in which they worked soon made them adhere to a different set of norms than that which prevailed in the metropolitan country. So long as they were not clearly in conflict with the welfare of the colony as the local directors perceived it, the interests of the planters in Surinam and of the merchants in Curaçao, generally speaking, carried more weight than did the wishes of the directors' faraway superiors.

The unwillingness to convert the slaves into members of the prestigious metropolitan churches produced a religious cleavage in the population which coincided with the social one. The whites and (especially in Surinam) some of the socially important colored families were Dutch Reformed or Lutheran, while the rest of the population became Catholic in Curaçao and Catholic or members of the Moravian Brothers' congregation in Surinam.

White population groups in both colonies were not exclusively of Dutch origin; each included not only Huguenots but also a considerable group of Sephardim. These parallels in composition led to similarities in the processes and contents of cultural contacts, both within the white group and among whites, the colored, and Negroes. The more prosperous and educated of the last two groups generally oriented themselves, as far as family organization and cultural aspirations were concerned, toward the upper white strata. Consequently, among the males of these two groups, the keeping of extra-marital sexual partners was a rather common phenomenon.

The Creole variant[13] of Dutch culture, as it manifested itself in the course of time, thus became for a considerable number of free non-whites their frame of reference *par excellence*. Only the lowest strata of colored and Negroes were forced to associate with the culture of the slaves and their immediate descendants, whose ways of life and religion were determined to a much greater extent by the vicissitudes of slavery and by African cultural retentions. The sociologically understandable inclination on the part of the middle and higher colored classes to emulate the prestigious seigneurial patterns of behavior and the cultural preferences of the white upper class, plus

---

[13] "African" and "Latin American" elements also were absorbed into this variant.

the great distance which separated them—partly because of this inclination—from the mass of slaves, helps to explain why they generally did not protest against the slave system, much less instigate the slaves to revolt.

The high positions in government which several members of the Surinamese colored group came to occupy—by filling the vacancies left by whites—influenced the social aspirations of the lower and middle urban Negroid groups after abolition. For these, education and diplomas became coveted symbols of social mobility into the governmental hierarchy, the feasibility of which had been proven by the colored elite. In Curaçao, where whites continued to dominate the governmental structure, such aspirations were to stay dormant for a long time after abolition.

Official attempts to prohibit sexual contact between blacks and whites in Surinam during the seventeenth and eighteenth centuries[14] had no practical effects on sexual relations outside of marriage, which, as we have seen, were frequent, but an unwritten social code was obviously an important deterrent to interracial marriage. The first known request in Surinam to permit a marriage between a Negress and a white man was made in 1781. As Van Lier relates this cause célèbre,[15] local officials did not immediately deny the request but referred it to the Board of the Society of Surinam in Holland. In an accompanying letter, they explained that an advantage of this marriage would be that the great wealth of the woman would ultimately be absorbed by the white group; they also pointed out that from a moral point of view marriage would be preferable to some kind of illegal relationship and that the latter would be hard to avoid if the former were prohibited. On the other hand, they dealt elaborately with the shame that would befall any white who would consent to such a union, and expressed fear that the proposed marriage would set a precedent leading to marriages between white women and Negroes. In Holland the Society of Surinam decided that there were no legal grounds to forbid the marriage but left the executive implementation of this verdict to the local authorities in Surinam. When her fiancé died, Elisabeth Samson presented herself with another white candidate. This time the local authorities did not object, and the marriage took place without unnecessary delay. A few years later Miss Samson's niece also married a white.

Although there seem to have been no enforced legal impediments against racial intermarriage either in Surinam or—as far as we can determine—in Curaçao (certainly not from the last quarter of the eighteenth century on), the frequency of such marriages was probably exceedingly low. The social value attributed to white physical characteristics was simply inculcated too deeply and spread too extensively in both areas.

[14] We lack data on similar decrees in Curaçao.
[15] Van Lier, Samenleving, pp. 66, 67.

From the above it may be concluded that, despite some important differences, a great many similar influences operated on the
political and social structure and on the cultural formation of the two
colonies: there were parallels in legislation and in executive government, as well as common administrative and social distinctions between free Negroes and free colored and between the freeborn and
the manumitted. Both colonies also manifested several of the more
general traits that were common to all slave colonies, such as the
difference in treatment of field, artisan, and house slaves and the in-
stitutionalization of sexual relations between men of the dominant
group and women of the subordinate group. Finally, the Dutch West
Indian multi-racial colonies shared a number of more specific traits
with the British, French, and Danish possessions in the Caribbean
(as opposed to the Spanish and Portuguese colonies)—namely, the
nearly total absence of absorption of the colored as marriage partners
into the white population groups;[16] and religious divisions (in all
except the French) which tended to correlate closely with the social
distinction made between whites and the most "respectable" colored,
on the one hand, and the lower social strata, on the other. Despite
their basically similar socioracial *structure*, however, the commercial
character of Curaçao and the plantation economy of Surinam resulted
in different sets of secondary economic, demographic, and social conditions, and these gave the master-slave relationship and race *relations* generally a distinct form and content in each colony. The
master-slave relationship in Curaçao could be termed mild, because
the commercial character and arid climate of the colony made large
slave gangs economically unfeasible; both the distribution of the
number of slaves per master and the numerical proportion between
masters and slaves was much less dramatic on this island than in
the slave colony of Surinam.

The small size of Curaçao and the extension and isolation of the
plantations of Surinam had opposite effects on the degree of social
control exerted by the urban and governmental milieu in the treatment of slaves. A geographical factor also explains the apparent para-
dox that a general slave rebellion took place in Curaçao but not in
Surinam; the impenetrable jungle in the latter country made the
establishment of semi-autonomous maroon communities feasible, and
these communities siphoned off many of the discontented. Similar,
and sometimes identical, legislation enacted to reduce the number of
manumissions apparently had little effect in either colony. By the
middle of the eighteenth century, recurrent periods of commercial
depression had caused a relatively large number of manumissions in

---

[16] Because the "somatic distances" between whites, colored, and blacks
may be assumed to have been the same in both Dutch colonies, the influence
of the "somatic norm image" cannot have been different, and has therefore
been left out of this comparison. For these concepts, see H. Hoetink, *The Two
Variants in Caribbean Race Relations* (London, 1967).

Curaçao; in Surinam, on the other hand, manumissions were few until the last quarter of the eighteenth century, when they increased, partly because of the favorable attitudes of one governor, but also as a result of the economic crisis which began in the 1770s. The numerical relationship between black and colored free people tended to favor the former in Curaçao, while in Surinam the latter formed a strong majority as late as 1830. This difference suggests a greater impact of economic factors on manumission in Curaçao, with its capricious economy, and consequently a greater proportion of "affective" manumissions in Surinam.

As for the numerical proportions between whites and free people, the latter were already more numerous than the former in Curaçao at the end of the eighteenth century and became so in Surinam at the beginning of the nineteenth century. The numerical proportion between free people and slaves contrasted sharply in the two areas; by the first quarter of the nineteenth century, the free people of Curaçao outnumbered the slaves, while, in 1830, there were only 5,041 free people, compared to 48,784 slaves, in Surinam. Thereafter, the rate of manumissions in Surinam accelerated; yet in the year of abolition former masters received indemnities for a total of some 32,000 slaves, while the free people in that year numbered only about 20,000. These different numerical proportions among whites, free people, and slaves go far to explain the different attitudes of whites in the two colonies vis-à-vis the other two categories: generally speaking, whites in Curaçao were more fearful of the free people; in Surinam they were more afraid of the slaves. Especially in the eighteenth century, when the number of colored was small, white opinion regarding the somewhat educated colored in Surinam was favorable. Only when increased manumissions swelled the number of free urban poor during the last years of that century and in the following decades did the image of the "the" colored become less positive; in Curaçao, on the other hand, such an unfavorable stereotype had been formed rather early in the eighteenth century.

External economic factors, especially the crisis at the Amsterdam Exchange in 1773, caused the emigration of many whites from Surinam. Only the Jewish group stayed. This white exodus had two, interrelated consequences: first, the so-called Surinamese marriages of European bachelor plantation administrators to free colored or Negro women occurred more frequently and acquired an even greater relative respectability than before, several fathers taking care of their Surinamese children with a dedication which would have been almost unthinkable if the number of European women had been sufficiently great to exert "normal" social control; second, white emigration created vacancies in government and business for which the educated colored began to apply in competition with the Jews. In logical sequence, in the first half of the nineteenth century, academically trained fathers and sons from a number of "respectable" colored families began to penetrate the highest governmental positions open to Surinamese and thus to participate in the formation of a bureaucratic colored elite, which until very recently barely had its equivalent in Curaçao.

In the latter island no exodus of whites took place. The Jewish group maintained its control over wholesale commerce, and Protestant whites maintained their claim to higher governmental positions until the middle of the twentieth century. The small number of "respectable colored" were originally mostly protégés of the Jewish group and made their living in small and middle-level commerce. At the end of the nineteenth century, their number was increased by protégés of the Catholic mission, who found employment in catholic schools, the catholic press, and similarly sponsored institutions. In the social system, however, the colored still occupied a lower rank than the traditional white elites.

Thus, developments in the two colonies lead us to conclusions which seem completely to contradict the opinion of those who attach the greatest importance to the conditions of *slavery* as an explanation for the characteristics of *race* relations. Obviously, race relations are also shaped by some factors originating outside the juridico-economic system of slavery and by others arising *after* that system had been abolished.

In Curaçao we observed a mild, paternalistic type of slavery and an early and frequent use of manumission, so that abolition was not a traumatic experience for which all mental and social preparation had been lacking; in Surinam we observed a severe, even cruel, system of slavery and a much reduced rate of manumission, except in the decades immediately preceding abolition. Yet, it was in Surinam that a colored social elite early came into being, while such a development did not occur in Curaçao.

Instead of postulating a causal relationship between paternalistic master-slave relations, on the one hand, and a benevolent attitude of whites toward free people, on the other, we might, with the situation in Curaçao in mind, advocate a completely reverse thesis: a paternalistic slave system which through frequent manumissions produces a relatively large number of free people for whom there is hardly any place in the economic structure may tend to intensify unfavorable attitudes toward them among whites. The situation in Surinam would then suggest that a cruel slave system tends to interest the whites in the creation of alliances with the free people, which may lead to the improvement of the latter's social and economic position. We certainly do not want to claim any general validity for these counterpostulates, however. The relationship between the character of master-slave relations and the status of, and attitudes toward, free people is far too complicated to allow such easy generalizations. Suffice it to say that theories which purport to base the explanation of actual group positions and social attitudes in multi-racial societies on specific conditions within the institution of slavery easily tend to fall prey to a somewhat naïve historicism, and that it seems recommendable to consider in any such analysis *all* factors related to the historical development of the *total* socioracial structure.

NOTES ON FURTHER READING

Surinam

LIER, R. A. J. VAN, *Samenleving in een grensgebied: een sociaal-historische studie van de maatschappij in Suriname.* The Hague, 1949. Unsurpassed sociohistorical analysis of Surinamese society; indispensable to anyone interested in the development of Surinamese social structure and race relations.

LINDE, J. M. VAN DER. *Heren-slaven-broeders.* Nijkerk, 1962. A valuable book on master-slave relations, especially in terms of the attitudes of Protestant denominations; partly based on research in Dutch church archives.

————. *Surinaamse suikerheren en hun kerk.* Wageningen, 1966. Deals with relations between the sugar planters in Surinam and the Protestant churches and their representatives; partly based on original research in Dutch church archives.

STEDMAN, J. G. *A Narrative of a Five Years' Expedition against the Revolted Negroes of Surinam.* 2 vols. London, 1813. An English officer's famous description of his participation in Dutch expeditions against the maroons in the last quarter of the eighteenth century and of his experiences in Surinamese slave society, including the story of his romance with a mulatto girl.

TEENSTRA, M. D. *De negerslaven in de kolonie Suriname.* Dordrecht, 1842. A pro-abolitionist's keen description of slave conditions in Surinam; especially valuable in connection with the same author's work on the Netherlands Antilles (see below).

WOLBERS, J. *Geschiedenis van Suriname.* Amsterdam, 1861. One of the best early histories of the country.

Curaçao

GOSLINGA, C. CH. *Emancipatie en emancipator: De geschiedenis van de slavernij op de Benedenwindse Eilanden en van het werk der Bevrijding.* Assen, 1956. Focuses on the role of the Catholic mission, and especially on the work of Mgr. Martinus Joannes Niewindt in the second quarter of the nineteenth century for the improvement of slave conditions.

HARTOG, J. *Curaçao: From Colonial Dependence to Autonomy.* Aruba, 1968. This is the abridged English version of the two-volume *Curaçao: Van kolonie tot autonomie,* which in turn is Part III of Hartog's *Geschiedenis van de Nederlandse Antillen;* it contains much information, part of which is based on the author's own research in Dutch and Spanish archives; though the work is rather anecdotal and does not always show narrative coherence, it is still the best historical work on Curaçao available in English.

HAMELBERG, J. H. J. *De Nederlanders op de West-Indische Eilanden.* Amsterdam, 1901. A classic work of history, based on intensive research in the State Archives of the Netherlands; contains many printed sources.

HOETINK, H. *Het patrọon van de oude Curacaose samenleving: Een sociologische studie.* 3rd ed. Aruba, 1971. Tries to analyze the development of social structure and the process of acculturation in Curaçaoan society prior to 1918.

REILLY, W. B. "Curaçao, Dutch West Indies." *The Monthly Illustrator,* June, 1898. An American newspaperman's impressions of *fin-de-siècle* Curaçao.

ROESSINGH, M. P. H., " 'Emancipatie,' 'Slavenhandel' and 'Slavernij.' " In *Encyclopedie van de Nederlandse Antillen,* edited by H. Hoetink. Amsterdam, 1969. Roessingh's articles in the recently published encyclopedia succinctly summarize our present knowledge with regard to the slave trade, slavery, and emancipation in the Netherlands Antilles.

RIJKENS, R. H. *Curaçao.* Tiel, 1907. A Dutch agronomist's view of Curaçaoan society in the post-abolition period.

TEENSTRA, M. D. *De Nederlandsche West-Indische Eilanden.* Amsterdam, 1836. Especially useful in comparison with Teenstra's work listed under *Surinam.*

Dutch Slave Trade

GOSLINGA, C. CH. *The Dutch in the Caribbean and on the Wild Coast, 1580–1680.* Gainsville, Fla., 1971. Though it deals mainly with maritime history, this important work contains valuable information on the Dutch slave trade.

UNGER, W. S. "Bijdragen tot de geschiedenis van de Nederlandse slavenhandel." *Economisch-Historisch Jaarboek* 26 (1956): 133–74. Mostly based on archival material of the Zeeland Chamber of the West India Company, this excellent article gives often surprising information on the economics of the Dutch slave trade and on the mortality of slaves and crews during their voyages.

VRIJMAN, L. C. *Slavenhalers en slavenhandel.* Amsterdam, 1943. A general and informative book on the Dutch slave trade which lacks adequate documentation.

Comparative Social Structures and Race Relations in the Caribbean, including the Dutch West Indies

HOETINK, H. *The Two Variants in Caribbean Race Relations: A Contribution to the Sociology of Segmented Societies.* London, 1967. 2nd ed. New York, 1971. A comparison between socioracial structure and race relations in the "Iberian" and "North West European" variants in the Caribbean area.

LIER, R. A. J. VAN. *Development and Nature of Society in the West Indies.* Amsterdam, 1950. A pioneering essay on the applicability of the concept of "plural" or "segmentary" societies to the Caribbean area.

A. J. R. RUSSELL-WOOD

3 | Colonial Brazil

In their chronicles, European visitors to Brazil described at
length two contrasting aspects of the society of Portugal's richest
colony. The first was the hardship of Negro slavery. The second was
the extravagant luxury of the white aristocracy. These travelers'
narratives, the political fireball of abolitionism, and recent comparative studies of slavery have tended to reduce the social structure of
colonial Brazil to a slave-master dichotomy. Other important, but
less prominent sectors of the society, such as the bourgeoisie, have
been ignored. This has been the case of the free black and the free
mulatto, whose position throughout the colonial period was ill-defined,
ambiguous, and insecure. A study of the role of the free colored con-
tributes to our knowledge not only of Negro slavery and the white
ruling classes but also of the continually effervescent and evolving
infrastructure of the society of colonial Brazil.

The demographic density of the colored population of colonial
Brazil and the conditions of life and status of the slave and freedman
varied regionally, depending on the predominant type of economy,
and at different periods. For the purpose of the following study, I
have chosen to describe in detail three major nuclei of the colored
population during the colonial era. The first was on the sugar plantations, exemplified by the Recôncavo of Bahia. The second was in the
mines, of which those of Minas Gerais were the most prosperous. As
a counterpart to these essentially rural economies, the city of Salvador (capital of Brazil, 1549–1763) provides us with examples of the
living conditions of the colored population, slave and free, within an
urban area.

This paper will treat both those free people of pure African
ancestry and those who were the offspring of black and white parentage. In colonial Brazil, as today, an infinite variety of terms and
phrases was used to describe the half-caste. In addition to describing
the color of the person, the choice of term often carried moral and
social overtones. The term *mulato* generally possessed a pejorative
connotation and was replaced in contemporary documents by the
more common *pardo*. Also used were *mestiço*, *cabra*, and *crioulo*.
Sometimes even the Portuguese felt the inadequacy of a single word

84

to describe the degree of whiteness or blackness of an individual and resorted to ill-defined phrases such as *trigueiro, corado bastantemente* (lit.: "brown, fairly colored"), *de côr fechada* (lit.: "of a closed color"), *de uma côr equívoca* (lit.: "of a dubious color"), *ao parecer branco* (lit.: "white to all appearances"), or even *de côr fula* (lit.: "of the color of the Fulah").

NUMBERS AND ORIGINS

The density of the slave population and the numerical proportion of free colored within the over-all population varied greatly from region to region and at different periods. The black slave, brought originally from Africa to work on the sugar cane plantations of the Northeast, became the cornerstone of the Brazilian economy. As such, he was inevitably subject to changing economic circumstances. During the sixteenth and seventeenth centuries the major slave nuclei were in Bahia, Pernambuco, and, to a lesser degree, Rio de Janeiro. The discovery of gold in Minas Gerais in the 1690s radically transformed the conservative, patriarchal, and stable agricultural basis of the Brazilian economy. Whites, blacks, and mulattoes deserted the coastal areas for the central plateau. Recent estimates place the entry of slaves into Minas Gerais during the years 1698–1717 at between 2,500 and 2,700 annually. The slave population of Minas Gerais was 33,000 in 1717 and increased to 50,000 in 1723 and 96,000 in 1735. Subsequent mineral strikes in Bahia, Mato Grosso (1718), and Goiás (1725) resulted in further demographic moves to those areas. In the third quarter of the eighteenth century, the general decline of the mineral deposits, already apparent in some parts of Minas Gerais in the early 1730s, led either to owners employing their slaves in agriculture or to a reverse migration to the coastal areas. A by-product of the comparatively short life span of the deposits in Goiás and Mato Grosso was the rapid fall-off in white colonization after the initial boom, which left a predominantly colored population. This was also the case in Minas Gerais, albeit to a lesser degree. In areas of lesser economic importance, the black slave was less essential for working the crops. In Pará, Amazonas, southern Bahia, Ceará, and Rio Grande do Norte, Indian labor was used extensively and black labor more rarely. In Maranhão, whose prosperity dates from the second half of the eighteenth century and where the black was a more recent element in the population, there was less miscegenation than in the plantation or mining areas of colonial Brazil. Only in the nineteenth century did the booming prosperity of São Paulo demand black labor. In the southern captaincy of Rio Grande and on the island of Santa Catarina the population was largely from the Azores and Madeira, and Indians or blacks were less frequent.[1]

[1] For general surveys of population distribution at the end of the colonial period, see Caio Prado Júnior, *The Colonial Background of Modern Brazil*

The essentially dynamic and mobile nature of the population of colonial Brazil reached its apogee in the eighteenth century. The blacks and mulattoes, slaves or freedmen, constituted the numerical majority of such population shifts. The demographic density of the slave population and the extent of miscegenation faithfully reflected those areas of highest economic intensity and productivity at different periods. The position of the free black and the free mulatto within the over-all colored population will be discussed in detail later. Suffice it to say here that the numerical increase in the free colored population was a predominantly eighteenth-century social phenomenon. This increase was largely attributable to two major factors. The first was the discovery of mineral deposits and the resulting diversity of economic opportunities afforded the slave in agriculture, commerce, or mining itself to buy his freedom. The second factor was increasing urbanization and the creation of economic and social opportunities not previously present in a patriarchal and rural society.

The means by which a slave, be he black or mulatto, could obtain his freedom in colonial Brazil were identical. The most common practice was for a slave to amass enough money to buy himself out of bondage and be granted a *carta de alforria*, or certificate of freedom, by his master. This was usually given upon payment of a sum mutually agreed to by master and slave. In those rare instances when a master refused a fair price for manumission, appeal by the slave to the governor, viceroy, or even the king generally resulted in the master's refusal being overruled.[2] It was more frequent for a slave in the cities or mining districts to buy his own freedom than for his counterpart on the sugar plantations or in the rural areas to do so. There were two reasons for this. First, the cities and mining districts afforded better economic opportunities for a slave to obtain the money necessary to buy his freedom. Second, the patriarchal plantation society may have offered a degree of protection and social security to the slave, thereby lessening his incentive to buy his freedom.

In the gold mining areas, the slave enjoyed a considerable degree of liberty. In 1719 Dom Pedro de Almeida, count of Assumar (governor of Minas Gerais and São Paulo, 1717–21), went so far as to write, "the manner of life of the slave today does not constitute

---

(Berkeley and Los Angeles, 1967), pp. 123–29, and Dauril Alden, "The Population of Brazil in the Late Eighteenth Century: A Preliminary Survey," *Hispanic American Historical Review*, 43 (1963): 173–205. Estimates for Minas Gerais are contained in Mauricio Goulart, *Escravidão africana no Brasil (Das origens à extinção do tráfico)* (São Paulo, 1949), pp. 164–71.

[2] APB, *Ordens Régias*, vol. 14, doc. 12; vol. 34, doc. 137; vol. 91, fols. 335r–336v; vol. 94, fols. 34r–35r; vol. 95, fols. 158r–160r; APMSG, vol. 14, fol. 13r, *inter alia*. The crown did not heed the warnings of Luís Cesar de Meneses (governor general, 1705–10) of the falsity of such petitions, APB, vol. 7, docs. 288, 289, 299, 300. For abbreviations used here and elsewhere in this chapter, see the list of abbreviations on p. 133.

true slavery and may be more appropriately termed licentious liberty."[3] The truth of this assertion is debatable as regards those slaves who worked in the trenches of the *lavras*, or placer mines, under the constant vigilance of overseers. But there can be no doubt of the freedom of action of the slave *faisqueiros*, or itinerant prospectors, whose owners could not afford the capital outlay necessary to develop a *lavra*. These *faisqueiros* roamed the countryside and townships, prospecting and washing for gold in any likely spot. Once a week they returned to their owners to hand over the gold dust of the *jornaes*, or daily takings. Despite severe penalties, annual municipal edicts failed to curtail the pernicious practice of the *faisqueiros* of digging out the gravel from between the cobblestones with pointed sticks, knives, and pickaxes, thereby endangering the life and limbs of every inhabitant who had to climb the steeply sloping streets of the mining townships.[4] From a life of such relative liberty to one of crime was for the *faisqueiros* but a short step. In the eighteenth century, there were numerous reports from Minas Gerais and Goiás of colored goldsmiths forging coins and falsely marking gold bars, and of the high degree of skill achieved by slaves in filing down pieces of tin so as to make them indistinguishable from gold dust and then mixing them with the *jornaes*.[5] At nightfall such *faisqueiros* congregated in the numerous stores and taverns which flourished in the mining areas. Whores and unscrupulous storekeepers soon induced the *faisqueiro* to part with his *jornaes*. Many a slave, rather than face the wrath of his master by returning empty-handed at the end of the week, preferred to escape to one of the many *quilombos* of fugitive slaves which existed in and around every mining township. While it is abundantly clear that much of the gold dust acquired by these slaves was spent on women and *cachaça*, the fiery sugar cane brandy, many slaves nevertheless scraped together by fair means or foul enough to buy themselves out of bondage within a comparatively short period of time.

The slave in the Diamond District was rigorously watched by an overseer while working and was subjected to probing searches at the

---

[3] "Sendo certo q' não he verdadeira escravidão a forma em q' hoje vivem quando com mais propriede selhe pode chamar liberde licencioza" (Assumar to the *Ouvidor* of the *Comarca* of Rio das Velhas, 21 November 1719, APMSG, vol. 11, fols. 170r–171r. Translations throughout this essay are the author's unless otherwise noted.

[4] Assumar suggested to the crown on 10 May 1720 that the privilege of exemption from confiscation of mining instruments or slaves in civil cases be granted to miners with *lavras* to encourage this form of mining, APMSG, vol. 4, fol. 245. Penalties for *faisqueiros* ranged up to fines of 3½ *oitavas*, 15 days in jail, and 50 lashes in the pillory. See Edict of Municipal Council of Vila Rica, 5 January 1761, APMCMOP, vol. 77, fols. 5v–6r). For other examples see APMCMOP, vol. 32, fol. 86; vol. 33, fols. 9v–10r; vol. 35; fols. 78r–79r; vol. 60, fols. 16v–17r and 130, *inter alia*.

[5] Assumar to Crown, 28 June 1721, and royal reply of 16 May 1722, APMSG, vol. 20, doc. 45. For later reports see APMSG, vol. 5, fols. 123v–124r, and APMCMOP, vol. 65, fols. 46v–52v.

end of the day's work. But this greater vigilance was offset to a high degree by the greater facility with which a skilled slave could conceal a diamond on his person and by the fact that such stones could bring a higher price than gold dust. As the miners of Serro do Frio pointed out to the town council of Vila do Príncipe in 1732, the slaves stole from under the very noses of their masters, "and, even if the latter stood over the bowls and were possessed of more eyes than Argos and sight sharper than that of the lynx, it would avail them nought."[6] Slaves developed great skill in concealing diamonds, and buyers for good stones were not difficult to find. As had been the case in the gold areas, storekeepers readily acted as "fences" for stolen contraband. Indeed, they actively encouraged slaves to take slave girls, as concubines, to use the store as a meeting place, and to buy the girls' freedom with stolen diamonds. In such cases the storekeeper took a cut on the sale of the stones and kept the proceeds for the slaves until they were enough to manumit the girls.[7] Nevertheless, as the district judge of the county of Serro do Frio informed Dom Lourenço de Almeida, when a slave managed to conceal a really big stone, he did not squander it on drink or women, but sold it to an itinerant buyer, storekeeper, or even a fellow slave who had been instructed by his master to act as an intermediary.[8]

Slaves of artisans and shopkeepers also had ample opportunity to buy their freedom. In the "mechanical trades," the master was frequently more overseer than practicing artisan, supervising the work of slaves and then adding the finishing touches himself. Writing in 1711, the Jesuit Antonil remarked that Angolan slaves who had been raised in Luanda proved the best pupils in learning a trade.[9] A slave who was skilled as a carpenter or stonemason was often permitted by his master to undertake casual labor as a *jornaleiro*, for which no municipal license was necessary. Such dayworkers were allowed to keep all or part of their earnings. Nevertheless, few slave artisans reached a high enough standard of proficiency to submit themselves for examination by the guild judges (*juízes de ofícios*) and be granted a license by the town council to practice as qualified artisans. The one outstanding exception was the art of "barber" (*barbeiro*). We shall be returning to this subject later, but I should point out here that this profession was virtually a colored monopoly and predominantly one of slaves. As in the case of the artisan slave

---

[6] "Sem q' a estes lhe baste o estarem com mais olhos q' os de Argos, e com a vista mais perpiscaz [*sic*] que a dos linces sobre as bateas" (APMSG, vol. 27, fols. 119r–123r).

[7] APMSG, vol. 27, fols. 111v–114v and 137.

[8] Letter of 30 May 1732, APMSG, vol. 27, fols. 141r–142v.

[9] André João Antonil, S.J., *Cultura e Opulencia do Brasil, por suas Drogas, e Minas, com varias noticias curiosas do modo de fazer o Assucar; plantar e beneficiar o Tabaco; tirar Ouro das Minas e descubrir as da Prata* (Lisbon, 1711), bk. 1, chap. 9.

dayworker, such slave "barbers" had unusual opportunities to make social contacts and to earn enough money to buy their freedom.

Commerce also afforded intelligent slaves a degree of liberty and opportunities to buy their freedom. The majority served behind the counter in their masters' stores or taverns, but a few achieved the responsible post of cashier in a deposit or warehouse, thereby gaining entry to the business community. A slave with initiative could not only further his master's commercial interests but undertake small dealings on a commission basis on his own account. In this the slave had to be careful not to arouse the jealousy of rivals by being over-successful, as was well illustrated by the chastening experience of Francisco da Cruz. Francisco was a mulatto slave in Salvador at the end of the eighteenth century and held the post of cashier in his master's provision warehouse. He enjoyed the complete confidence of his owner, who was well satisfied by the substantial receipts directly attributable to Francisco's diligence. Francisco's reputation for business acumen and honesty spread and he was commissioned to undertake small business deals by third parties. Rivals noted his growing prosperity and maliciously spread the rumor that this was derived from fiddling the returns of his master's business rather than from his own honest effort. Francisco was jailed and tortured before he was finally released on payment of bail.[10]

Another branch of this petty business was undertaken with the full knowledge and consent of the master. Female slaves were actively encouraged to go out on the streets with trays loaded with cooked meats and African foods and drinks for sale. In Minas Gerais the presence of large numbers of such peddlers on the gold *lavras* and along the diamond-bearing rivers severely distracted the miners from their labors. Under pressure from slaveowners, who saw a large proportion of the *jornaes* of their slaves being spent on food and drink bought from such women, town councils and governors forbade these itinerant hawkers in the mining areas on pain of severe penalties, but with little effect. In the cities this type of vending was organized by the lady of the house, to whom the slaves handed the day's takings, receiving a percentage in return. At the end of the eighteenth century, the regius professor of Greek in Salvador, Luís dos Santos Vilhena, commented on the frequent sight of slaves of the most noble families peddling their wares on the streets. Other slaves peddled boxes of cloth bought by their owners from foreign ships in return for gold coin or contraband goods from the Portuguese "factories" on the West African coast, on which no duty had been paid to the crown. The nobility and wealth of the owners of such slaves effectively protected them from prosecution by the fiscal authorities, many of whose officers were receiving kickbacks on the profits. A similar protection racket applied to the sale of fish, which was the monopoly of certain

[10] APB, *Ordens Régias*, vol. 86, fols. 276r–277r.

wealthy households. Slaves known as *ganhadeiras* bought the fish at source and resold them at a higher price.[11] It is easy to see how a slave girl working under such patronage was soon able to buy her *carta de alforria*.

An extension of this was slave prostitution. The charm and sexual attraction of the colored woman, exalted often enough in song, verse, and prose, need no further description here. In 1709 the crown, acting on the complaint of the councillors of Salvador that slave girls were inciting the male populace by their "lascivious dress," ruled that no slave girl could wear silk or adorn herself with gold jewelry.[12] For the most part these girls simply hustled on the side to earn money normally denied them by their regular domestic duties. In Minas Gerais, slave *faisqueiras* were banned from the mining areas because experience showed that their daily earnings were more frequently earned with their bodies than with their mining tools. In this they were aided and abetted by storekeepers (the whites being the worst offenders) who hired out rooms in the back of their shops, despite severe penalties for this offence. Many slaveowners turned a blind eye on this practice, while others forced their slaves into prostitution and lived off their immoral earnings.[13]

Slaves employed in rural areas had little hope of ever being able to purchase their freedom. By law, every master was required to grant his slaves one day a week (in addition to Sunday) to cultivate their own plots of land. In practice, slaves were often denied this right and were forced to chop wood, mend fishing nets, or clear scrub by masters determined to work their slaves to the limit. Those slaves who did have plots of land invariably planted manioc, which was easy to grow, even on poor land. In 1781 it was estimated that, in theory, a slave with only twenty days' labor could plant and harvest enough manioc not only to feed himself but also to have a substantial amount for sale. Unfortunately, this rosy picture of slaves buying their freedom effortlessly through the sale of manoic flour failed to take into account such everyday hazards as thieving neighbors and the destruction of crops by ants, wild boars, and stray cattle.[14]

[11] Luiz dos Santos Vilhena, *Recopilação de noticias soteropolitanas e brasilicas, contidas em XX cartas, que da cidade do Salvador, Bahia de todos os Santos, escreve hum a outro amigo em Lisboa*, 2 vols. (Bahia, 1922), 1: 127–32. Cf. similar practices in Vila Rica by the "escravas da Sociedade," APMCMOP, vol. 54, fol. 3.

[12] Crown to Luís Cesar de Meneses, 23 September 1709, APB, *Ordens Régias*, vol. 7, doc. 616, in response to the council's request of 15 December 1708. Earlier crown prohibitions were contained in a letter to the governor of Rio de Janeiro of 20 February 1696, ANRJ, *Códice 952*, vol. 8, fol. 41. See also Amédée-François Frézier, *A Voyage to the South-Sea and along the Coasts of Chili and Peru in the Years 1712, 1713, and 1714* (London, 1717), p. 304.

[13] APMSG, vol. 27, fols. 58r–59r; APMCMOP, vol. 63, fols. 172v–175r; C. R. Boxer, *The Golden Age of Brazil, 1695–1750: Growing Pains of a Colonial Society* (Berkeley and Los Angeles, 1962), p. 138.

[14] Eduardo de Castro e Almeida, *Inventario dos documentos relativos ao*

An indirect method used by slaves to purchase their freedom was the intermediation of a brotherhood. Blacks and mulattoes, slave and free, had their own brotherhoods. The statutes of such brotherhoods often carried the clause that, if the financial position of the brotherhood were sufficiently strong, a loan could be granted to any slave brother to enable him to buy his freedom. The slave was required to petition the governing body of the brotherhood, at which time he would name a guarantor for the amount of the loan and announce the consent of the viceroy or governor that the loan be made for this purpose.[15] The brotherhood of Our Lady of the Rosary and Ransom in Rio de Janeiro, which was comprised of free and captive blacks and mulattoes, had been founded for the express purpose of aiding those slaves who wanted to buy their freedom. It also presented to the crown appeals by slaves whose masters had adamantly refused all offers for manumission.[16]

A black or mulatto slave could also receive his liberty gratuitously by means of a will made by an appreciative master. The female slave was more likely to be such a beneficiary than was the male. In her case, freedom usually included any offspring she might have. One example will illustrate this process. Pedro Mendes Monteiro, a bachelor of Bahia who died in 1744, left a will granting his creole slave girl and her two-year-old daughter their freedom. The mother received outright payment of 50$000 and household linen. The daughter was provided for by a trust fund of 400$000, a handsome sum in those days. This capital was to be placed on loan, and annual interest was to be applied to the upkeep of mother and daughter until the latter married, whereupon the total sum would constitute her dowry. Legal recognition by white masters of the paternity of children born of slave girls was rare. In such cases the mother's freedom was conditional, being granted once she had fulfilled the clauses of the master's will concerning the children's upbringing. Usually a daughter of such parentage was granted a dowry, and financial provision was made for a son to be apprenticed to a trade.[17] Sometimes a philanthropist donated the sum required to buy the *carta de alforria* of the child of a slave girl.[18]

Freedom granted to a slave could be revoked at a later date if subsequent behavior showed the favor to have been undeserved. In

Brasil existentes no Archivo de Marinha e Ultramar de Lisboa, 8 vols. (Rio de Janeiro, 1913–36), 2: doc. 10907; Vilhena, *Recopilação de noticias*, 1: 188–89.

[15] *Compremissio da Virgem Sanctissima May de Deus N.S. do Rosario dos pretos da Bahia, 1686*, chap. 16. I am indebted to the Reverend Canon Manuel Barbosa for allowing me to consult these statutes.

[16] ANRJ, *Códice 952*, vol. 3, fol. 202r.

[17] ASCMB, vol. 42, fol. 204. For other examples see A. J. R. Russell-Wood, *Fidalgos and Philanthropists: The Santa Casa da Misericórdia of Bahia, 1550–1755* (London, Berkeley, and Los Angeles, 1968), pp. 182–83, to which should be added ASCMB, vol. 41, fols. 37r–38v, 70r–79r.

[18] ASCMB, vol. 15, fol. 10.

1795 the prior and friars of the Carmelite monastery of Salvador instituted legal proceedings to re-enslave a former slave to whom they had granted freedom, but who had subsequently proved disobedient and had made calumniatory remarks about his former masters. The judge upheld the friars' complaint and sentenced the culprit to servitude once again, convicting him "as the law decrees for repaying by ingratitude the favor of having been granted his freedom."[19]

The legal distinction between slave and freedman constituted a less clear-cut division that did the ethnic difference between black and white. The white population of colonial Brazil looked upon any colored person as a slave, regardless of whether or not he could produce a *carta de alforria*. One example will illustrate this fact. The dark-skinned Caetana Franca, a native of Madeira and a free woman, was brought to Brazil against her will and was then sent to Minas Gerais to be sold as a slave. In 1719 the governor, Dom Pedro de Almeida, ruled that the onus was on her to prove her status as a free person—no easy task for a single woman without financial means in the interior of Brazil who would have to contend with the chronic delays of the Portuguese colonial bureaucracy.[20] Also victims of this attitude were Amerindians and those native Goans and Chinese who had been lured onto homeward-bound Indiamen by promises of lucrative employment in Lisbon and sold in Salvador to cattle drovers who resold them in Minas Gerais.

Brief reference must be made to those slaves who gained their freedom illegally, and usually only temporarily. These were slaves who had fled from their masters and formed into small groups known as *calhambolas* or *mocambos*, who in turn joined together to form the *quilombos*. At various times more than four or more than seven fugitive slaves were legally held to constitute a *quilombo*.[21] Throughout the colonial period such bodies of armed slaves terrorized roads and even townships, raping, murdering, destroying property, stealing goods, and burning crops. The *quilombo* that survived longest and was the largest in Brazil was at Palmares in the captaincy of Pernambuco. In existence at the time of the governorship of Diogo Botelho (1602–8), it was finally subdued in 1694 after resisting seventeen expeditions (including two by the Dutch). At this date it occupied some 4,500 square leagues and was comprised of a series of heavily fortified settlements, each with permanent houses and a chapel, and each under the jurisdiction of a council of elders. One interesting fact was that, whereas any slave who fled there of his own volition was accorded the status of a freedman by the elders, a slave captured in the

[19] "Incurso na pena da Lei, como ingrato ao beneficio da Liberde" (OCB, *Livro de Memorias da Provincia Carmelitana da Bahia*, pp. 191, 310).

[20] APMSG, vol. 14, fol. 13r; A. J. R. Russell-Wood, "Class, Creed, and Colour in Colonial Bahia: A Study in Prejudice," *Race*, 9, no. 2 (1967): 151.

[21] Contracts of *capitães do mato* of 1722 and 1735, respectively, APMCMOP, vol. 6, fols. 60v–62r, and vol. 28, fols. 155r–158v.

course of an attack was treated as a slave. Such a slave could, however, achieve his freedom by inducing another slave to join the *quilombo*.[22] Smaller groups of runaway slaves continued to occupy the townships and countryside of colonial Brazil, and in the 1790s a *quilombo* in the mountains of Andrahy in the captaincy of Bahia counted 1,000 souls behind elaborate defenses with their own king and captains.[23] Local punishment of fugitive slaves tended to be arbitrary. In 1735 the town council of Vila Rica ordered that an offender's hand be severed at the wrist.[24] A royal decree of 1741 ruled that a runaway slave in a *quilombo* should be branded on the shoulder with the letter **F** when caught the first time and lose an ear the second time.[25]

Finally, reference must be made to Portuguese legislation concerning the freeing of slaves. Portuguese crown policy toward colored subjects in Asia, Africa, and Brazil was far from uniform. In Brazil, Amerindians and the offspring of white-Amerindian parentage (*mamelucos* and *caboclos*) fared far better than blacks or mulattoes, against whom there was evident discrimination. From 1755 to 1758, Pombaline measures emancipating the Amerindian were not matched by royal decrees favoring the black or mulatto slave. In fact, a 1755 law which declared the enslavement of Amerindians to be illegal specifically excluded Amerindian-Negro offspring born of black slaves. A royal *alvará* of 19 September 1761 ruled that no black slaves should be sent to Portugal six months after publication of the decree in Brazil and Africa, or a year after its publication in Asia, and that any slaves who did land after this period would automatically be granted their freedom. This law did not apply to slaves already in Portugal. Only in 1773 were they emancipated, and no corresponding law was passed for Portugal's overseas dominions.

Under extraordinary circumstances, the slave could obtain his freedom by legislation of purely local application. A slave could be

[22] Ernesto Ennes, *As Guerras nos Palmares (subsídios para a sua história)* (Rio de Janeiro, São Paulo, Recife, and Porto Alegre, 1938); Edison Carneiro, *O Quilombo dos Palmares*, 3rd ed. (Rio de Janeiro, 1966); and R. K. Kent, "Palmares: An African State in Brazil," *Journal of African History*, 6 (1965): 161–75. See also Stuart B. Schwartz, "The Mocambo: Slave Resistance in Colonial Bahia," *Journal of Social History*, 3, no. 4 (1970): 313–33.

[23] APB, *Ordens Régias*, vol. 86, fols. 242r–245r; vol. 89, fols. 42r–47r; *Memorias historicas e politicas da Provincia da Bahia do Coronel Ignacio Accioli de Cerqueira e Silva: Annotador Dr. Braz do Amaral*, 6 vols. (Bahia, 1919–40), 3: 326–31.

[24] APMCMOP, vol. 28, fols. 155r–158v. On *quilombos* in Minas Gerais, see "Cartas do Conde de Assumar ao Rei de Portugal sobre os quilombos e castigo delles," *Revista do Archivo Público Mineiro*, vol. 3, pp. 251–66, and vol. 8, pp. 619–21; Francisco António Lopes, *Os palácios de Vila Rica: Ouro Prêto no ciclo do ouro* (Belo Horizonte, 1955), pp. 125–29. See also Boxer, *The Golden Age of Brazil*, pp. 172–73.

[25] *Provisão* of 3 March 1741, ANRJ, *Códice 952*, vol. 30, fol. 264 and accompanying documents.

granted his *carta de alforria* by the viceroy or governor as a reward for denouncing infractors of the law to the authorities. For example, a wave of church robberies in Salvador led the viceroy in 1738 to promise freedom to any slave who provided information leading to the arrest of the culprits.[26] In Minas Gerais, denunciations played a prominent part in the maintenance of law and order and the enforcement of fiscal measures. Slaves received their freedom in return for denouncing the sale of firearms, shot, and powder to slaves, evasion of payment of the royal fifths (*quintos*), illegal export of gold from the mining areas, and the smuggling of diamonds. Denunciations made by slaves against their owners out of malice or as threats led to frequent abuse of this method. The royal decree of 3 December 1750, which re-established taxation by fifths, made specific reference to these disadvantages and suspended the practice of accepting denunciations as a legal expedient, although the king allowed that he would reconsider this step if the miners asked him to do so.[27]

Although sanctioned by law, the granting of *cartas de alforria* evoked considerable opposition from governors, town councils, and private citizens in colonial Brazil. The principal objections were made on economic and political grounds. The economic opposition was based on three premises. First, the slave had been brought from West Africa to work on the plantations and in the mines of Brazil. The stability of the Brazilian economy and the income of the Portuguese treasury depended on these sources of wealth. Therefore, the practice of giving slaves, who constituted the essential labor force, their freedom jeopardized the economies of both colony and mother country. Second, it was alleged that, as freedmen, former slaves contributed nothing to the economy and were of no benefit to the community. Third, as freed people, former slaves enjoyed an unusual degree of liberty, would become property owners, and would thereby threaten the commercial supremacy of whites. This last fear was particularly prevalent with regard to mulattoes, who, it was alleged, either as bastard sons or adopted children (*crias de casa*), frequently inherited possessions, businesses, houses, and plantations. The advocates of these views severely overstated their case. The practice of passing *cartas de alforria* was never so prevalent as to constitute an economic threat. Also, inheritances of rich estates by mulatto bastard sons or adopted children were the exception rather than the rule. Finally, the allegation that, as freedmen, the former black or mulatto slaves contributed nothing to the colonial or national exchequer was less than just. They were subject to the same taxes as their white counterparts

[26] APB, *Ordens Régias*, vol. 69, doc. 47. On legislative measures see C. R. Boxer, *The Portuguese Seaborne Empire, 1415–1825* (London, 1969), pp. 265–66.
[27] APMCMOP, vol. 33, fols. 26r–27v, and APMSG, vol. 11, fols. 279r–280r. In Mawe's time a slave finding a diamond weighing an *oitava* was freed; see Boxer, *The Golden Age of Brazil*, p. 218; royal *alvará* of 1750, chap. 11, APB, *Ordens Régias*, vol. 47, fols. 130r–135r.

and similarly made voluntary donations for such diverse purposes as the construction of barracks, royal marriages, or the restoration of Lisbon after the 1755 earthquake. It was the concept rather than the reality of colored economic and commercial participation which troubled the white apologists of these views.[28]

The political opposition to *cartas de alforria* may be summed up in the phrase "threat to white security." The white settlers of colonial Brazil were uncomfortably aware of their numerical inferiority as compared with the colored population. Royal decrees and local laws were specifically aimed at reducing the social, economic, and political rights of blacks and mulattoes, slave and free, and at fortifying the position of the whites as the dominant sector of the community. Nevertheless, the crown, governors, and town councillors remained on tenterhooks throughout the colonial period, fearful of a possible "black rebellion." Such fear tended to result in hasty and arbitrary legislation by governors and town councils. The count of Assumar, a talented if autocratic administrator, issued an edict in 1719 prohibiting any master in Minas Gerais from granting a *carta de alforria* to a slave unless he had first submitted a petition to the governor and received permission. Assumar imposed severe penalties for infractions, pending a royal order revoking this measure. Listing the reasons that had led him to take this step, he concluded: "But the greatest evil of all is that, otherwise, this land would be populated by free blacks, who, because of their primitive state, do not maintain the public order. Within a short time all government would be in the hands of such blacks."[29]

Moral and humanitarian objections to the manumission of slaves were also advanced. Such diverse personalities as the Jesuit Antonil, the count of Assumar, and the Greek professor Vilhena condemned slave prostitution as a means of gaining freedom.[30] There can be no doubt that the strength of the desire to "escape the yoke of servitude" led slaves of both sexes to commit not only immoral, but also criminal, acts. There was also an unsavoury and inhumane side to the granting of *cartas de alforria*. A healthy slave represented a

[28] See APMSG, vol. 18, fol. 1r, and vol. 27, fols. 130v–131r, for defense of the colored economic role. Cf. Dom Lourenço de Almeida to the Crown, 20 April 1722: "e seguro a VMag^de que sendo os mulatos de todo o Brasil m^to prejudiciaes, por serem todos inquietos, e revoltozos; estes das Minas hão de ser muito peyores, por terem circunst^as de ricos" (*ibid.*, vol. 23, fols. 110v–111r.

[29] "Mas o mayor [inconveniente] de todos q' he povoarse este pais de negros forros q' como brutos não conservão a boa orde͂ na Republica, e viria esta dentro de pouco tempo a ficar em mãos dos d^os negros" (*bando* of 21 November 1719, APMSG, vol. 11, fols. 282v–284r).

[30] Antonil, *Cultura e Opulencia do Brasil*, bk. 1, chap. 9; Assumar to Crown, 28 November 1719, APMSG, vol. 4, fols. 238r–239r; Vilhena, *Recopilação de noticias*, 1: 47–48. The Mariana City Council suggested to the king in a letter of 5 May 1755 that slaves be granted their freedom gratuitously as rewards for good service instead of being required to buy their freedom "por termos indecorozos" (APB, *Ordens Régias*, vol. 54, fol. 99).

financial investment and was a symbol of social prestige. The fact
that some masters placed sick slaves in the hospitals of the *Misericórdia* and met the cost of their treatment is well documented.[31] But this
was the exception rather than the rule. Many masters allowed their
slaves to buy their freedom because age, sickness, or injury prevented
them from working. The most cursory glance at the collections of
cartas de alforria reveals the frequency of the phrase "useless for any
form of labor."[32]

A slave who was granted freedom gratuitously by the terms of
his master's will had little cause to be overly grateful for his emancipation unless this was accompanied by a legacy. The majority of
slaves knew no trade and lacked the technical, and often physical,
capacity to benefit from their new-found freedom. Vilhena suggested
that those blacks and mulattoes who fell into this category should be
placed under the guidance of a tutor, who would advise them as
freedmen and so prevent their falling victims to their "primitive im-
pulses."[33] His comments are eloquent testimony to the fact that the
signing of the *carta de alforria* was only the initial step in the transition from slavery to freedom and was followed by the prolonged and
painful process of physical, psychological, and mental adaptation to
a new economic and social reality.

The number of blacks and mulattoes who obtained their freedom
within the slave society of colonial Brazil is the subject of controversy.
Statistical demographic analysis for the period is fraught with difficulties. The first census was not ordered by the crown until 1776.
Divided into age groups and sexes, with annual birth and mortality
rates, this census offers no information on the ethnic composition or
the civil status of the population. Previous to this date, population
polls had been taken irregularly with three specific purposes in mind.
The first had been ecclesiastical and had recorded the number of
communicants at Easter. The second had been military and had been
taken to establish the number of able-bodied men available in the
various parishes for militia service. The third had been fiscal and had
been limited to the gold mining areas, where a capitation tax on
slaves had been imposed from 1735 to 1750. The fragmentary nature
of such data is readily apparent. Easter records specifically excluded
children, Indians, and unbaptised slaves. The Portuguese in Brazil
went to considerable lengths to avoid enrollment for military service.
The capitation tax proved difficult to enforce effectively in areas
where isolation and terrain afforded secure hiding places for slaves.
In the light of these difficulties, hypotheses based on the available

[31] Russell-Wood, *Fidalgos and Philanthropists*, pp. 182, 281.

[32] These *cartas* merit detailed, statistical study. Every individual *cartório*
handled the cases of its own clients, a fact which makes over-all chronological
consultation difficult. The APB contains 1,384 volumes of such records for
Bahia for the period 1644–1915.

[33] Vilhena, *Recopilação de noticias*, 1: 134–35 and 2: 940.

figures are, at best, questionable, and the establishment of numerical relationships between different sectors of the population for every captaincy is well nigh impossible.

Once these caveats have been made, however, the information available for the major nuclei of the eighteenth-century colored population of Brazil—the northeast, Minas Gerais, and Rio de Janeiro—suggests four broad conclusions. The first is the increase in the colored population of Brazil during the second half of the eighteenth century and the first two decades of the nineteenth century. The second is the increase, within this colored sector, in the number of mulattoes. The third is the increase in the number of free colored persons, with a marked predominance of free mulattoes over free blacks. The fourth conclusion is that there was a higher degree of miscegenation in the northeast and in Minas Gerais than in any other region of Brazil.

The census taken in Salvador in 1775 revealed that the urban population of 35,253 was composed of 12,720 whites, 4,207 free mulattoes, 3,630 free blacks, and 14,696 slaves. By 1807 the total population had increased to 51,000. Similarly, the population which had been 36 percent white and 64 percent colored in 1775 had increased its colored sector to 72 percent (20 percent mulattoes, 52 percent blacks), whereas its white sector had decreased to 28 percent. For the captaincy of Minas Gerais the invaluable codex compiled by Caetano da Costa Matoso (crown judge at Vila Rica, 1749–52) indicates a decrease in the slave population between 1735 and 1749 from 96,541 to 88,286. This was matched by a decrease in the number of free colored persons from 1,420 to 961. In 1776 the total population of Minas Gerais was 319,769: 70,769 whites, 82,000 mulattoes, and 167,000 blacks. Statistics for the years 1786–1821 are best illustrated by the following table:

	1786	1805	1808	1821
Whites	65,664	78,035	106,684	136,693
Free Mulattoes	80,309	92,049	129,656	152,921
Free Blacks	42,739	48,139	47,937	53,719
Slave Mulattoes	20,376	24,997	15,737	22,788
Slave Blacks	153,759	163,784	133,035	148,416
Totals	362,847	407,004	433,049	514,537

These figures suggest an increase in the number of free colored persons in the over-all population from 35.0 percent in 1786 to 40.3 percent in 1821. Among these free colored, the mulattoes increased from 65.1 percent to 73.3 percent in the same period. Even in São

Paulo, where until the middle of the eighteenth century Tupí rather than Portuguese was the common language, the 1797 population of 158,450 was made up of 89,323 whites, 38,640 blacks, and 30,487 mulattoes. In 1800 this population had increased to 95,349 whites, 34,311 blacks, and 39,884 mulattoes. Statistics for Curitiba, Parana-guá, and Rio Grande do Sul during the late eighteenth and early nineteenth centuries reveal similar increases in the mulatto sectors of the population. The enormous influx of some 24,000 Portuguese and 4,000 foreigners into Rio de Janeiro in the period 1808–22 (total population in 1817, 110,000) led Spix and Martius to comment that European features were less rare in Rio de Janeiro than in Bahia.[34] As we shall see later, however, this demographic increase in the number of free colored persons, and especially of mulattoes, was not matched by any amelioration in the legal position, civil status, or living conditions of freedmen in colonial Brazil.

ECONOMIC ROLE

The colored person in colonial Brazil, be he slave or freedman, black or mulatto, was compelled to recognize that all norms governing commercial and social conduct had been established by a white minority. Failure to conform to these precepts was less tolerated in a colored person than in a white person and could result in the former being victimized, censured, and condemned by law without being permitted to offer any defense. The colored person faced the basic problem of how best to achieve a degree of integration in this economically and socially "white world." In this struggle for integration, two premises held true. The first was that a free-born black or mulatto had a better chance than his slave counterpart, who had been born a slave and had later been granted or bought his freedom. This was primarily psychological, although economic and social considerations were contributory factors. Slavery stifled initiative, decision-making ability, leadership, and the capacity for self-control. All that was demanded of a slave was physical exertion. It should come as no surprise, then, that the slave, having crossed the threshold into the free world clutching his freshly signed *carta de alforria*, was often totally unprepared to face the demands of a competitive society in which

[34] José Honório Rodrigues, *Brasil e África: Outro Horizonte*, 2nd ed., 2 vols. (Rio de Janeiro, 1964), 1: 53–54; Mauricio Goulart, *Escravidão africana*, pp. 139–71. Population figures for Minas Gerais for the years 1786, 1805, 1808, and 1821, published in the *Revista do Archivo Público Mineiro*, vol. 4, pp. 294–96, differ slightly from those for 1821 published by W. L. von Eschwege, *Pluto Brasiliensis* (Berlin, 1833), pp. 595–96. See also Octávio Ianni, *As metamorfoses do escravo: Apogeu e crise da escravatura no Brasil meridional* (São Paulo, 1962), pp. 45, 70, 84–95; Thales de Azevedo, *Povoamento da cidade do Salvador*, 3rd ed. (Salvador, 1969), pp. 181–200, 232; Fernando Henrique Cardoso, *Capitalismo e escravidão no Brasil meridional* (São Paulo, 1962), pp. 41–43.

those very qualities were the most highly prized. Many ex-slaves totally failed to adapt to their new condition. Moreover, with only a few exceptions, the slave of the *senzala*, or slave quarters, had no more than a domestic relationship with the white members of a household and thus had received no grounding in the social habits of a free society. One evident exception were those slaves who, either as concubines or as adopted children, were well accustomed to exposure to white society. The second premise was that, generally speaking, a mulatto or a not-too-dark Negro had a better chance than did the black of being assimilated into the "white world." This ethnic factor could be of greater importance in conditioning the degree of assimilation of a colored person than whether or not he had been born free or a slave. A light mulatto, even when born a slave and later manumitted, frequently had a better chance of acceptance in the white commercial or social community than did a black whose father and grandfather had been free men.

Faced with this situation, the free black and free mulatto could opt for one of three possibilities. The first was to take the utmost advantage of any commercial opportunities and attain financial independence within the competitive society. The second was to compromise, allowing oneself to be reabsorbed into the system of slavery as an overseer or a salaried laborer. The third was to reject the challenge as having the odds too heavily weighted against the free colored person and to drift into casual employment and vagrancy.

The role of the free black and the free mulatto in the economy and commerce of colonial Brazil was restricted to a certain degree by the antipathy of the white populace toward colored commercial participation and competition. Fiscal measures were more strictly enforced against colored shop owners and traders than against their white colleagues. Penalties were more rigorously imposed. Taverns and stores under colored ownership were the first to be searched for arms, powder, and shot. Travel by a colored trader from one township to another or to the rural areas in the necessary course of business was regarded with suspicion. More than once the suggestion was made that the free colored be required to register in their parishes of residence and take out licenses for travel.

Municipal legislation frequently referred to *escravos fôrros* (lit.: "free slaves"). Often, no distinction was made between slaves and free blacks and mulattoes in the enforcement of penalties for illegal trading. Itinerant peddlers were forbidden in the mining areas, and penalties of up to 100 lashes, loss of wares, three months in jail, and a fine of 20 *oitavas* were imposed, regardless of whether the infractor was a slave or a free colored person.[35] The possession of slaves by a free colored person was also viewed with distrust. It was feared that

[35] APMSG, vol. 27, fols. 58r–59r. Cf. *ibid.*, vol. 21, fols. 13v–14r, 21; *ibid.*, vol. 27, fols. 15, 42; APMCMOP, vol. 13, fols. 11, 36v, 42r; and *ibid.*, vol. 43, fol. 32.

the authority exercised by a colored master over his slaves could lead to the formation of colored nuclei with colored leadership within cities and towns, which, it was believed, would threaten the maintenance of law and order. In 1719 in Minas Gerais, the count of Assumar passed the draconic edict that no free colored person should possess a slave and that those who did should dispose of them within two months or have them confiscated. Moreover, no free black or mulatto would be permitted to own a food store.[36] This measure would have effectively stifled all colored commercial enterprise. Fortunately for the colored population, it was later revoked, but the attitude of distrust toward all forms of colored commercial interests persisted.

The severest clash between free colored enterprise and colonial legislators occurred in the Diamond District (Distrito Diamantino) of Minas Gerais. Regulations concerning the extraction and disposal of diamonds were intended by their severity to impress upon the inhabitants of that area that all mineral-bearing lands were crown property. Harsh decrees promulgated by the governor, Dom Lourenço de Almeida, in January, 1732, included one ordering the expulsion of all free blacks and mulattoes, not only from the diamond district, but from the county (comarca) of Serro do Frio under penalty of imprisonment, whipping, confiscation of property, and deportation to the colony of Sacramento on the River de la Plata. Pleas by the district judge of Serro do Frio for moderation were ignored. Dom Lourenço also brushed aside the representation made by the town council of Vila do Príncipe, which stressed the good conduct of the free colored inhabitants and the useful contribution they made to municipal funds by paying taxes on stores and taverns. The council also pointed out that their sudden exodus would present problems for creditors in the collection of debts. In his rejection of these appeals on behalf of the colored community, the governor's trump cards were two appeals made to him by the miners, who had asked for the expulsion of all free colored persons as a condition for the acceptance of Dom Lourenço's modified terms for mining. The town council had refused to pass these on to the governor. In his reply, Dom Lourenço severely chided the councillors for their support of such a "bad type of people" and "harmful rabble" (má casta de gente and prejudicial canalha) and openly suggested that sexual alliances with free colored women had led the worthy councillors to forget their duty to the community.[37] In September, 1732, the count of Galvêas replaced Dom Lourenço as governor, and free blacks and mulattoes were allowed to remain in Serro do Frio.

Commerce and agriculture were the two fields in which the free

[36] APMSG, vol. 11, fols. 282v–284r.

[37] The extensive correspondence is in ibid., vol. 27, fols. 89v–100v, 104r–108r, 108v–134v. See also Joaquim Felício dos Santos, Memórias do Distrito Diamantino da Comarca do Serro do Frio, 3rd ed. (Rio de Janeiro, 1956), pp. 63–66; and Boxer, The Golden Age of Brazil, pp. 207–8.

colored person had the greatest opportunity to gain a regular livelihood and even attain a certain prosperity. The first brought the free
black and the free mulatto into direct competition with the white, but
offered higher returns and greater possibilities for social integration.
Lack of capital effectively prevented a free colored person from engaging in major commercial ventures. Possession of a provision store,
which usually doubled as a tavern, offered the maximum financial
security and the highest social position to which the free colored person could aspire. Municipal registers for the colonial period record
single free colored women and free colored couples possessing not
only such stores but one or two slaves as well. They were subject to
the same municipal fiscal regulations that governed white store owners and to periodic inspections of goods and weights and measures.
Such *vendas* sold everything from food, drink, clothing, and domestic
items to firearms, knives, agricultural tools, and mining bowls
(*bateias*). Specialization in a single product was rare. One free black
who did specialize successfully was Bernardo de Almeida, who went
to Serro do Frio in 1731 to sell clothes and textiles. An inventory of
his possessions made two years later revealed considerable affluence,
for, in addition to the clothes and textiles he had for sale, he also
possessed diamonds, valued at more than 8,000 *cruzados*, and two
horses.[38]

Stores under colored ownership were objects of suspicion for the
authorities. No doubt many were entirely above board in their financial dealings, but there are good grounds for believing that in many
cases the suspicions were justified. In the mining areas, these stores
served as meeting points for slaves returning from the mines. Much
gold dust never reached the masters, but was spent on food, drink,
and women. Clandestine activities of such storekeepers included the
harboring of fugitive slaves and the supplying of food and arms to
quilombos. The imposition of curfews and regulations ordering that
the counters be in full view of the street did not end such malprac-
tices, despite heavy punishments for infractions.

For every free colored person who did achieve this financial stability and independence through small commerce, there were hundreds who eked out a living as *taboleiros* or as go-betweens for foodstuffs, occupations equally practiced by slaves. The first were colored
women who carried trays of sweetmeats and other foods for sale
through the streets. They were required to obtain a license from the
town council to ply their trade legally. More often than not, this requirement was ignored, or the vendeuse reached an arrangement with
the municipal fiscal officer, who turned a blind eye to her activities in
return for a cut of the takings. In Minas Gerais the presence of such
itinerant peddlers of both sexes was strictly forbidden in the mining

[38] APMSG, vol. 18, doc. 52. At this period the silver *cruzado* of 480rs.
was valued at between 2s. 6d. and 3s. sterling (Boxer, *The Golden Age of
Brazil*, p. 355).

areas. A more permanent variant of such activities was the selling of wares and vegetables in the marketplace under the direct surveillance of market inspectors.

The free colored were prominent as go-betweens in the black market in foodstuffs, which was a conspicuous feature of colonial Brazil. Reference has been made to slave *ganhadeiras* in this context. The free colored person lost the patronage of a wealthy family, but had the edge over the slave in extra mobility and financial independence. After buying at source, he could resell to the highest bidder or channel the produce through four or five intermediaries before the final sale was made. This wheeling and dealing process was known as *carambola*. In Salvador at the end of the eighteenth century, the sale of meat and fish was largely governed by such intermediaries. Free colored women formed liaisons with soldiers or low-ranking officers who simply commandeered a catch of fish or raided butchers' shops and gave the fish and meat to their lovers to sell. Similar practices existed for agricultural produce. Groups of free colored persons and slaves gathered outside the cities and townships to buy flour, beans, fruits, vegetables, and poultry directly from the smallholder for resale. In the interior, imported goods such as dried fish, cheese, salt, and olive oil, and luxury items such as wines, were often in short supply because racketeers hoarded commodities for sale at exorbitant prices.[39] In 1747 the attorney of the *Misericórdia* of Vila Rica complained to the town council that there were fifteen sick people in the hospital, but that he could not get a supply of chickens for their diet because none reached the town for sale on the open market.[40]

The free black or free mulatto who was an artisan had a secure, if unprofitable, livelihood. In order to open his own shop he had to obtain a license from the town council. This was granted only after examination in the theory and practice of his trade by the guild judges. All such examinations and licenses were recorded in the municipal registers. Qualified artisans were required to renew their licenses each year and to abide by the terms of employment and prices established by the guild regulation (*regimento*), which was modified annually. A study of these registers reveals the scarcity of free colored people among these qualified artisans, and no free colored person ever held the prestigious office of guild judge. The few free blacks or mulattoes who did obtain the licenses were invariably carpenters, tailors, or shoemakers. The register of payment of fifths in Vila Rica in 1715 mentions one Pedro Nunes, a free black potter who possessed not only a pottery but also a store and four slaves, but

[39] See Vilhena, *Recopilação de noticias*, 1: 127–31, for Salvador. Municipal legislation against this practice in Minas Gerais was not effective, although it was repeated annually; see, for example, APMCMOP, vol. 32, fols. 87v–88v; vol. 33, fols. 6r–7r, 61r–62r, 76v–77v, *inter alia*. See also Francisco António Lopes, *Os Palácios de Vila Rica*, pp. 183–86.

[40] APMCMOP, vol. 54, fol. 3.

this was quite unusual for an artisan.[41] There can be no doubt that throughout the colonial period in Brazil the so-called mechanical trades were dominated by white artisans and that the free colored person was not accepted as a professional equal. He remained, as did the slave, an assistant or dayworker.

The professions of "barber" and midwife provide the notable exceptions to this rule, being monopolized by the colored. In a somewhat fruitless attempt to reduce the large numbers of "quack" practitioners in colonial Brazil, the law required all "barbers" and midwives to produce a license in order to practice openly. This was issued only after application and payment of a fee to an examination panel composed of a local commissioner, nominated by the chief surgeon of Portugal (*cirurgião-mór do Reino*), and two qualified doctors. All licenses granted by this panel had to be sent to Portugal for confirmation by the chief surgeon. A sampling taken of the number of "barbers" in Salvador for the years 1741–49 and 1810–22 reveals that, of a total of 101 municipal examinations held in the first period for all artisan trades, 38 were of "barbers," and all of these were colored. Of the 38, 17 were slaves and 21 were free blacks or mulattoes. The figures for the second period were 68 licenses, 33 of which were for "barbers" (20 slaves and 13 free colored persons). Registers of other municipal archives confirm the predominance of colored "barbers" in the colonial period. Sometimes the license granted to a "barber" also permitted him to act as a "tooth-puller."[42] An idea of the salary commanded by a free colored "barber" may be gained from the fact that in 1705 the *Misericórdia* of Salvador appointed a full-time colored "barber" for work in the hospital at an annual salary of 20$000.[43]

Whereas the art of "barbering" was equally open to slaves and the free colored, that of midwifery was usually limited to free female blacks or mulattoes. A related activity, though not subject to licensing, was wet-nursing. Large numbers of foundlings—white, mulatto, and black—were a prominent aspect of Brazilian urban life. According to Portuguese law, the upkeep of foundlings constituted a municipal responsibility. Town councils hired free black or mulatto women as wet-nurses, but were frequently negligent in paying their wages.

[41] *Ibid.*, vol. 2, fol. 7r. The shortage of qualified colored artisans in São Paulo in 1767 was noted by Roger Bastide and Florestan Fernandes in *Brancos e negros em São Paulo*, 2nd ed. (São Paulo, 1959), pp. 25–27; for Salvador see AMB, vols. 189–93, and for Vila Rica see APMCMOP, vols. 17, 44, 57, 58, 74, 85, 108, 115. When Herbert S. Klein asserted that, "as freedmen, Negroes and mulattoes dominated almost all the skilled trades" ("The Colored Freedmen in Brazilian Slave Society," *Journal of Social History*, 3, no. 1 (1969): 47), he was presumably referring to a numerical domination by colored artisan apprentices; archival registers leave no doubt that the skilled, qualified, professional artisan in the colonial period was invariably white.

[42] AMB, vols. 191, 193.

[43] ASCMB, vol. 850, fol. 269v; for comparable salaries of other employees, see Russell-Wood, *Fidalgos and Philanthropists*, p. 380.

Often totally dependent on regular payments to meet day-to-day costs, these wet-nurses frequently sold, neglected, or even killed their charges. Crown pressure on councils to improve services for found-lings or to provide elementary instruction for them was ineffectual because of the perennial dearth of funds alleged by town councils throughout Brazil in the colonial period.[44]

Agriculture offered limited opportunities for the free black or the free mulatto to be his own master and achieve financial stability. The basic problem was that slave labor was essential to help clear scrub, plant, and harvest, if the owner of the property was to realize any worthwhile return. Few of the free colored could afford a slave, and cultivation depended on the efforts of the laborer's family. In the northeast it was common practice for a sugar planter to rent out part of his land to sharecroppers (lavradores de canas), who often possessed considerable wealth and social prestige. At the other end of the financial and social scale there was room for the free black or free mulatto to be the tenant of a modest area. The agreement between the tenant and the owner of the plantation could take many forms, but basically the issue was whether or not the tenant was under an obligation, as part of his contract or lease, to have his cane crushed in the plantation owner's mill.[45]

The cultivation of tobacco recommended itself to the freedman of limited means. Capital outlays were small, and an adequate finan-cial return could be obtained from a small area of land. The tobacco industry in the Bahian Recôncavo was developed in the late seven-teenth and eighteenth centuries, not on plantations, but on small-holdings, by families without slave labor. The whole family turned out to harvest and clean the leaves, but the heavy work of twisting and rolling the leaves was left to the men of the family.[46]

The cultivation of manioc was likewise a smallholder economy, but did not offer more than barely subsistence-level returns for the majority of planters. For the most part, families simply encroached as illegal squatters on the outlying areas of cane plantations. For those who did pay rent, it was purely nominal. For example, in the mid-seventeenth century, a free mulatto with a small plot of land in the Recôncavo paid an annual rent of two chickens and one cockerel on Saint John's Day.[47] At the end of the eighteenth century, Vilhena

[44] Russell-Wood, Fidalgos and Philanthropists, pp. 295–319. Despite severe legislation by the town council, foundlings remained a serious problem in Vila Rica, Francisco António Lopes, Os palácios de Vila Rica, pp. 187–90, and A. J. R. Russell-Wood, A Craftsman of the Golden Age of Brazil: Manuel Francisco Lisboa (Belo Horizonte, 1968), pp. 29–35. An attempt by the crown in 1721 to oblige councils to provide elementary education for illegitimate children failed; see APMSG, vol. 23, fols. 6, 101.
[45] Antonil, Cultura e Opulencia do Brasil, bk. 1, chaps. 2, 3, 7, 12.
[46] Ibid., pt. 2, chap. 5.
[47] ASCMB, vol. 13, fol. 88v; for illicit squatters see ibid., vol. 14, fols. 20r, 160.

described such squatters or smallholders as rural beggars who lived on corners of plantations and rented tiny plots for a pittance. The available evidence supports this grim picture of the living conditions of such families, whose plots of poor land barely provided enough flour for the family's needs.[48] Naturally, there must have been exceptions. The townships of Boipeba, Camamú, and Cairú, in the southern part of the captaincy of Bahia, were the main suppliers of manioc flour to Salvador in the seventeenth and eighteenth centuries and enjoyed modest prosperity. In the nineteenth century, it was proposed that travel by the free colored from Salvador to the Recôncavo be restricted in order to preclude the possibility of their inciting slaves to revolt. The chief of police agreed that this measure was fine in theory, but that it would be totally impracticable, resulting in the stoppage of all food supplies to the city because such trade was the virtual monopoly of free mulattoes.[49] Subsiduary occupations, such as fishing and pig and chicken raising, offered similarly precarious livelihoods.

Gold mining and diamond washing do not appear to have attracted many free blacks or mulattoes. In the early nineteenth century, the German engineer Eschwege, who spent several years in Minas Gerais, classified the free black as forming part of "the poorest class of all." Slaves were essential for mining, and few free blacks or mulattoes ever had enough capital to employ slaves. There were outstanding instances of colored owners of gold mines, such as the Encardideira mine of the semilegendary Xico Rei. Eschwege referred to the creole José Rodrigues and the black José de Silva, masters of seventy-seven and sixty slaves, respectively, as owning placer mines near São João del Rei in 1780.[50] But these were truly exceptional and merely prove the general rule. The majority of freedmen who did mine joined the crowds of slave faisqueiros, panning a few grains of gold on the outskirts of townships. Perhaps a few used their freedom of action to venture into the rough hills of Minas Gerais, driven on by the hope of making a "strike" which would bring wealth, crown privileges, hereditary concessions, and even social acceptance.

The free black or free mulatto willing to renounce part of his independence could find employment as an overseer in agriculture, cattle raising, or mining. In fact, this was a possible first step toward social integration in the free world. The freedman who was intelligent enough to gain an understanding of the mechanical processes of crushing and preparing the raw sugar cane, or mining techniques,

---

[48] Vilhena, Recopilação de noticias, 2: 941.

[49] I am indebted to Arnold Kessler for this information.

[50] Von Eschwege, Pluto Brasiliensis, p. 596. General surveys of the colored person in Minas Gerais are Aires de Mata Machado Filho, O negro e o garimpo em Minas Gerais, 2nd ed. (Rio de Janeiro, 1964); Edison Carneiro, Ladinos e crioulos: Estudos sôbre o negro no Brasil (Rio de Janeiro, 1964), pp. 11–25.

was well on the way to leaving behind the "black world" of the *senzala* and was poised on the threshhold of the "white world" of the "big house." To a great extent, the degree of acceptance within the white community depended on his professional skills, which in some fields spelled profit or loss for the plantation owner on a crop.

There was a place, albeit small, for free colored labor on the sugar plantation. Whereas the slave produced the raw material—that is, the cane—the free black or mulatto was often responsible for the various technical processes that yielded the finished product. The most important post held by the free colored was that of "master of the sugar" (*mestre de açúcar*), who was contracted for the entire crop or was paid according to the amount of sugar produced. In 1711 his salary could have been 120$000 for a crop. He presided over the *casa da caldeira*, where the cane juice underwent repeated boilings until it reached the consistency of a syrup. The skill of the "master" in this important process consisted in maintaining the boiling juice at the right temperature. The "master" was assisted in this hot and heavy work by a free colored person known as the *banqueiro*, who received a wage, and the *soto-banqueiro*, usually a mulatto or creole slave, who merely received some reward for his services. Other posts held by free colored people were those of chief overseer (*feitor-mór*) and the lesser overseers in charge of personnel (*feitor dos partidos*) or the crushing house (*feitor de moenda*). It is not clear whether other posts, such as that of overseer for the distribution of sugar or overseer in charge of the cleaning of the juice, were held by free colored persons or slaves. In addition to employment in the actual sugar process, a cane plantation offered free blacks and mulattoes employment in subsidiary occupations such as looking after cattle, fishing, or supplying wood, or in skilled jobs such as stonemasonry, tile making, or carpentry.[51]

Cattle ranchers also employed the free colored as overseers of an outlying ranch or as drovers. One example from the end of the seventeenth century will illustrate this. Manuel Álvares Pereira was bound to Salvador by his post as treasurer in the mint and as a member of the council on tobacco. These responsibilities prevented him from visiting regularly his extensive cattle ranches on the São Francisco River and in the hinterland of the captaincy of Piauí. He employed as the overseer of one of these ranches a free creole who had his own team of cowboys, horses, and even slaves.[52] Free blacks, mulattoes, and Amerindians were also contracted to drive the herds of cattle from the interior of the captaincies of Pernambuco, Ceará, Bahia, and Piauí to the cattle mart at Capoâme, some eight leagues from Salva-

[51] Antonil, *Cultura e Opulencia do Brasil,* bk. 1, chaps. 5–9, and bk. 2, chaps. 9, 11; Vilhena, *Recopilação do noticias,* 1: 173–201.

[52] ACDB, *caixa* 3, *pasta* L: Miguel de Abreu e Sepúlveda to Manuel Álvares Pereira, 5 May 1695.

dor, or over the rough trails following the São Francisco River for sale in Minas Gerais at higher prices.[53]

Free blacks and free mulattoes were also employed as overseers in the gold and diamond regions. The general level of technical knowledge of mining remained deplorably low throughout the colonial period. The suggestion made by the count of Assumar in 1719 that the crown should send out miners from Saxony to instruct the Portuguese of Minas Gerais does not appear to have borne fruit.[54] Slaves usually had a better basic technical knowledge than their masters. Many originated from gold-mining regions in West Africa and brought with them such techniques as the use of wooden bowls (bateias) for washing and the stretching of cattle hides over a wooden frame (canoas) to retain the gold dust.[55] Free blacks and mulattoes placed this knowledge at the disposal of white miners in the gold and diamond districts by supervising the slaves working in the troughs and trenches.

Despite the range of opportunities open to them, the challenge of a free society proved too great for many colored people. They drifted from employment to casual labor, and from casual labor to the large numbers of beggars and prostitutes who plagued every town and city in colonial Brazil. Sometimes this downward path was the result of a psychological inability to adapt to the stresses and strains of a competitive society. On other occasions it was due to economic factors such as lack of capital, destruction of a crop, or loss of the breadwinner of the family. Old age, sickness, and blindness also were insurmountable problems. But all too frequently this renunciation and physical and mental auto-destruction were entirely voluntary, motivated by the prevailing colonial ideology that manual labor was degrading and fit to be done only by slaves. Whites and free-born blacks and mulattoes, even former slaves who had bought or been granted their freedom, firmly adhered to this concept. Vilhena referred to the "poor white trash" who chose to live "acquainted with hunger" rather than accept employment. Eschwege described the newly manumitted slave as punch-drunk on his liberty, rejecting all authority, working only in order to be able to buy food and drink, and ending as a beggar or in jail. Among contemporary observers, however, there was unanimous agreement that the free mulattoes were the worst offenders in this respect. Excessively vain because of the degree of white blood in their veins, it was charged, they rejected offers of employment and preferred to live a life of moral torpor, drunkenness, and pauperdom. In 1732 the count of Galvêas, governor of Minas Gerais, wrote: "With respect to free mulattoes, these are all the more insolent because their white blood fills them with so much pride and vanity that they flee from all servile labor, and thus the

[53] Antonil, Cultura e Opulencia de Brasil, pt. 4, chap. 3.
[54] Assumar to Crown, 12 December 1717, APMSG, vol. 4, fols. 208v–209r.
[55] Von Eschwege, Pluto Brasiliensis, pp. 305–6.

majority of them live a life of idleness." For his part, Eschwege characterized the free mulatto as "living with his arms folded and considering work as something unworthy of him." This applied not only to males but to females. Vilhena regarded the large number of whores in Salvador as directly attributable to the fact that "the daughters of this country have an outlook such that the child of the poorest and most abject man, the most miserable little mulatto girl, would more easily work in a brothel than serve a duchess, if there were such in this country."[56]

The Portuguese crown and municipal authorities in colonial Brazil failed to face the social and economic causes of such poverty. There was no policy of social rehabilitation or financial assistance for indigents. The only organizations that accepted responsibility for colored people who had fallen on evil days were the lay brotherhoods. The philanthropic efforts of the colored brotherhoods, such as Our Lady of the Rosary, were limited to their own brothers, slave or free, and consisted of dowries, alms, and burials. Ironically enough, the staunchly white and "Old Christian" brotherhood of the *Misericórdia* was the only body that offered comprehensive social assistance to people of all races and denominations. The *Misericórdia* offered dowries to free colored girls of marriageable age. Colored people were accepted as patients in the brotherhood's hospital. Slaves and colored indigents were treated free of charge, but occasionally the brotherhood was the beneficiary of a will made by a free black or free mulatto in recognition of such assistance. An extension of the hospital was a service for foundlings. These children were brought up at the expense of the brotherhood, which had its own staff of paid wet-nurses. At a suitable age, foundlings were lodged with a respectable family. The boys were apprenticed to a trade and the girls were granted a dowry, which enabled them to marry. The *Misericórdia* also employed lawyers to defend without charge any colored person, slave or free, in the courts. Finally, the *Misericórdia* operated a comprehensive burial service for all sectors of the community, including charitable burials for slaves and the free colored.[57] In these philanthropic acts the brotherhoods of colonial Brazil remedied to some extent the total neglect of these problems by church and state. By offering financial assistance and social rehabilitation to the free black and the free mulatto, the brotherhoods contributed substantially to enabling the free colored to accept the economic challenge of a competitive society.

[56] "E no q' respeita aos mulatos forros, que estes são mais insolentes porq' a mistura q' tem de brancos, os enche de tanta soberba, e vaidade que fogem ao trabalho servil, cõ que poderião vivir, e assim vive a mayor parte delles como gente ociosa" (Galvêas to Crown, 7 October 1732, cited in royal reply of 17 June 1733, APMSG, vol. 18, fol. 1r. See also Vilhena, *Recopilação de noticas* 1: 134–35, 139–40, and 2: 927; Von Eschwege, *Pluto Brasiliensis*, p. 596.

[57] Russell-Wood, *Fidalgos and Philanthropists*, pp. 192–93, 227–28, 246–57, 281–82, 309–14.

SOCIAL ROLE

The social integration and progress of the free black and the free mulatto in colonial Brazil was deliberately obstructed by crown policy. Whereas Amerindians and the offspring of Amerindian-white parentage were protected by Portuguese legislation, the black and the mulatto were the objects of official and unofficial discrimination and prejudice. This severely limited their role in the society of colonial Brazil.[58]

The free black and the free mulatto were discriminated against by laws which frequently failed to distinguish between slaves and the free colored. Discriminatory legislation against free blacks and mulattoes was particularly in evidence in regulations concerning the carrying of arms and dress. One of the first measures taken by António de Albuquerque Coelho de Carvalho upon assuming office as governor of Minas Gerais and São Paulo in 1710 was to prohibit any black, mulatto, Carijó Indian or half-caste, slave or free, from carrying firearms or swords on pain of a public whipping in the pillory. The crown and later governors passed similarly worded legislation and extended the list of prohibited weapons to include daggers, knives, clubs, and pieces of wood sharpened to a point.[59] These laws did not apply to colored soldiers on duty and were subject to relaxation in special circumstances. The *capitão-mór* of the captaincy of Sergipe pointed out to the king in 1751 that one reason for the impunity enjoyed by the *quilombos* of fugitive slaves was that most of the "bushwhacking captains" (*capitães do mato*) and their bands were colored and were forbidden to carry arms by the terms of the law.[60] The better-educated mulattoes of Rio de Janeiro and Minas Gerais petitioned the crown for relaxation of the law forbidding their carrying of swords. After receiving the report of Governor Gomes Freire de Andrada, Dom José I granted this privilege in 1759.[61]

The use of certain types of dress and adornment was also legally forbidden for blacks and mulattoes. Reference has already been made to restrictions imposed on slaves in this respect. A law of 24 May 1749 aimed at reducing ostentatious extravagance in dress contained one clause specifically devoted to the dress of free blacks and free mulat-

[58] For discussion of racial prejudice and discrimination, see C. R. Boxer, *Race Relations in the Portuguese Colonial Empire, 1415–1825* (Oxford, 1963), pp. 101–21, as well as his *The Portuguese Seaborne Empire*, pp. 259–66, 280–81, 312, and "The Colour Question in the Portuguese Empire, 1415–1825," *Proceedings of the British Academy*, vol. 47 (London, 1961), esp. pp. 130–37. See also Russell-Wood, "Class, Creed, and Colour in Colonial Bahia," pp. 133–57.

[59] *Bando* of 18 July 1710, APMSG, vol. 7, fol. 8r; for other examples see, *Revista do Archivo Público Mineiro*, vol. 7, pp. 276–77, and APMSG, vol. 11, fols. 268r, 279r–80r.

[60] Letter of 16 September 1751, APB, *Ordens Régias*, vol. 76, doc. 78 and accompanying docs.

[61] ANRJ, *Códice 952*, vol. 37, fols. 129r, 131r–32r; Boxer, *Race Relations*, p. 117.

toes. The king had been informed of "the great inconvenience caused in the overseas conquests by the liberty with which blacks and mulattoes, offspring of a black or mulatto father or of a black mother, clothe themselves in the same way as white people." The king henceforth forbade any black or mulatto to wear silk or fine wool, jewels or gold or silver adornments, on pain of confiscation of the offending article and a fine estimated at its full value (or a whipping, if the culprit was penniless) upon the first offense, and life exile to the island of São Tomé upon a second offense. This clause of the law was revoked on 19 September 1749, pending further consideration.[62] I do not know whether or not it was re-enacted, but in 1781 a Bahian lawyer commented on the blacks' and mulattoes' common use of silk in their dress.[63]

At the local level, justice for the free colored was arbitrary and frequently brutal. There was one set of laws and punishments for whites and another for colored persons. An edict promulgated by the governor of São Paulo on 27 March 1732 against gold smuggling carried the penalties of banishment to Angola and a fine of 2,000 cruzados for white offenders, whereas free blacks, mulattoes, and Amerindians were also banished but in addition received 400 lashes.[64] A similar distinction was made in the acceptance and use of evidence. In Minas Gerais in 1719, in a legal case in which a white man was accused of stealing gold from a free black woman, the ruling handed down was that "it would be uncivil and undignified to defame a white person with the name of thief in any case involving a black without superabundant evidence of his guilt." It was a wonder that the litigant, having given up all hope of ever seeing her property again, limited herself to requesting that the judge "not permit that she be victimized for the mere fact of being black."[65]

All too often law enforcement officers and judges did not even look for evidence before sentencing a colored person. The case of the slave António Fernandes, who was sentenced to be tortured on an unsubstantiated murder charge simply because he was a "base person and a slave," has been described elsewhere.[66] The free colored person was no less likely to be a victim of arbitrary justice. Bernardo de Almeida, a free black, went to Vila do Príncipe in the early 1730s to sell cloth. A priest charged him with having bought a diamond from the priest's slave and having encouraged him to escape. Acting on the priest's word alone and without circumstantial evidence, the local

---

[62] "Por ser informado dos grandes inconvenientes, que resultão nas Conquistas da liberdade de trajarem os negros, e os mulattos, filhos de negro, ou mulatto, ou de mãe negra, da mesma sorte que as pessoas brancas" (law of 24 May 1749, clause 9, APB, Ordens Régias, vol. 50, fols. 28r–34v, and supplementary alvará, ibid., fol. 35).

[63] Castro e Almedia, Inventario dos documentos, vol. 2, doc. 10907.

[64] Boxer, "The Colour Question," p. 132, n. 1.

[65] APMSG, vol. 14, fols. 9r, 54v–55r.

[66] Russell-Wood, Fidalgos and Philanthropists, pp. 256–57.

magistrate arrested Almeida and confiscated his belongings. He was kept in jail for three months and was not finally released until the slave reappeared and, despite torture, testified to the innocence of Almeida. Even after releasing Almeida, the judge refused to return his confiscated property, having reached an agreement with the priest over its disposal. Only after Almeida had appealed to the crown were his belongings restored to him.[67] The privilege granted by Dom João V to the governors of Rio de Janeiro, São Paulo, and Minas Gerais to hold private courts composed of crown judges of the respective captaincies in order to pass sentence on blacks, mulattoes, Carijó Indians, and half-castes, including the death penalty, did nothing to deter authorities from imposing penalties as they willed.[68]

Public office in the service of the crown, municipality, judiciary, church, or religious orders was closed to any black or "mulatto within the four degrees to which mulattism [mulatismo] constitutes an impediment."[69] A testimonial of "purity of blood" (pureza de sangue) was required of every candidate for public office. This involved the questioning of witnesses, lenthy inquiries within Brazil, and often the sending to Portugal for testimonials taken in the candidate's birthplace confirming that he was of unquestioned white parentage and of "Old Christian" stock. In the case of a married man, this stipulation was equally applicable to his wife. Crown officials planning to marry in Brazil were first required to petition the king for permission, which was granted only after the proposed wife's antecedents had been checked and approved. Marriage without this permission resulted in dismissal for crown officials and dishonorable discharge for a soldier. There are many examples of the crown's insistence upon "purity of blood."[70]

The church and religious orders maintained a similar insistence upon "purity of blood" in their statutes, although here the degree of enforcement varied from order to order.[71] The evidence suggests that there was less discrimination against colored people by religious orders in Portugal than by those in Brazil. As late as 1754, when Salvador counted three convents, the daughters of a sergeant major of the city's garrison requested royal permission to go to Portugal to become nuns "because in the aforesaid city of Bahia the convents do not admit as novices any girl stained with Negro blood, even though the supplicants are not very dark-skinned."[72] In the 1760s, a white citizen of Salvador found it easier to send his two illegitimate daugh-

[67] APMSG, vol. 18, doc. 52 and accompanying docs.
[68] Privilege granted to Minas Gerais by an order of 23 February 1731, APMSG, vol. 27, fol. 85r. This privilege was extended to Goiás; see APB, Ordens Régias, vol. 52, doc. 49; vol. 69, doc. 56 and accompanying docs.
[69] "Mullato dentro nos quatro graos em q' o mullatismo hé impedimento," APMSG, vol. 29, doc. 17.
[70] Russell-Wood, Fidalgos and Philanthropists, pp. 140 and 246, n. 1.
[71] Boxer, Race Relations, pp. 118–19.
[72] Russell-Wood, Fidalgos and Philanthropists, p. 329.

ters by a slave girl to a convent in Portugal than to gain their admission to one in Brazil.[73]

From 1642 onward, the Overseas Council in Lisbon formulated all colonial legislation. Frequently, the councillors had no direct knowledge of local conditions, and governors had to modify and interpret the letter of the law to suit the local situation. In colonial Brazil, the perennial shortage of whites, especially away from the coastal ports, compelled the authorities to overlook Negroid characteristics in a candidate for public office, provided they were not too prominent and the skin color was not too dark. This degree of tolerance varied from region to region. In Salvador, the city council was dominated for much of the colonial period by the white landowning aristocracy. It would have been inconceivable for a colored person, no matter how light-skinned, to have even aspired to the office of city councillor.[74] But in Minas Gerais, a shortage of pure-white candidates for the councils of the mining townships led to the acceptance of mulattoes as councillors in the early eighteenth century. In 1726, however, Dom João V ordered that this tolerance should cease and that henceforth only whites—husbands or widowers of white women—should hold such posts. The king noted that, whereas previously there had been some excuse for accepting mulatto candidates, there were now sufficient families of "clean birth" to make it "unseemly that they [such posts] should be held by people with this defect." The measure was also intended to reduce concubinage, but the king advanced an administrative reason for the ruling as well. During the absence of the district judge (*ouvidor da comarca*), his duties were to be fulfilled by the senior town councillor (*juiz ordinário*). Dom João V feared "that it could happen that this post [of district judge] would be held by people notoriously defective and stained, leading inevitably to loss of respect for such posts."[75]

Despite the crown's insistence upon "purity of blood," there was

[73] APB, *Ordens Régias*, vol. 64, fols. 48r, 49r.

[74] C. R. Boxer, *Portuguese society in the tropics: The Municipal Councils of Goa, Macao, Bahia, and Luanda, 1510–1810* (Madison and Milwaukee, 1965), p. 77. Cf. Crown to Galvêas, 16 February 1739, which ordered greater scrutiny of candidates for the city council because "se vira o anno passado, sendo pessoas prohibidas pella Ley, tanto na limpeza de sangue como nas calidades por estes terem o exercicio de taverneiros com logeas abertas" (APB, *Ordens Régias*, vol. 35, doc. 42). It is not stated whether or not this censure applied to persons of colored or "New Christian" origin.

[75] "Se fas indecorozo q' elles sejão ocupados por pessoas em q' haja semelhante defeito . . . será tal vez em ocasião q' se vejão ocupar aquelles lugares por pessoas notoriamente defectuozas e maculadas, seguindose naturalmente por esta cauza menos reverencia aos mesmos lugares" (Crown to Dom Lourenço de Almeida, 27 January 1726, based on a resolution in the Overseas Council of 26 January 1726, APMSG, vol. 29, doc. 17; the original proposal by the Overseas Council to the king is cited in Augusto de Lima Júnior, *A Capitania das Minas Gerais* [*Origens e Formação*] 3rd ed. [Belo Horizonte, 1965], pp. 124–25).

a similar degree of flexibility in making other appointments. In 1736, acting on a royal order, the town council of Vila Rica appointed in each parish judges and scribes (*juízes da vintena*), whose responsibilities were the maintenance of law and order, minor judicial questions, and public works. In 1748 the attorney of the council protested that some judges were mulattoes. He demanded that these be suspended because their appointment was illegal and constituted a threat to public order. The councillors overruled this objection "because the effective enforcement of the law depends on good service and not on an accident of birth." Noting that in many parishes white men had refused to hold these posts, the council approved the election of a black as parish judge of Ouro Branco later the same year.[76]

This local tolerance extended to military appointments. As late as 1806 the count of Ponte, governor of Bahia, complained that it was impossible to maintain the infantry regiments of the troop of the line at full strength because of the shortage of white men, and that it was often necessary to enlist as soldiers "rather dark individuals."[77] The pseudomilitary post of *capitão-mór* of the captaincy of Sergipe was held in the 1720s by a mulatto woman's son who was himself married to a woman of mixed blood. The whole question of appointments of free colored persons to public posts was summed up by Gomes Freire de Andrada (governor of Rio de Janeiro, 1733–63, and of Minas Gerais, 1735–63) and Rugendas, an artist who visited Brazil in the early nineteenth century. The first noted that wealth, rather than color, was the chief criterion for municipal office. The second related the anecdote of how he asked a mulatto if the local *capitão-mór* was a mulatto and received in reply, "He was, but is not any more."[78]

To be sure, there were some rare instances of the crown overruling local discrimination against colored subjects, but in general the official policy was one of determined racial discrimination. In the face of this policy the contribution of the free black and the free mulatto to the public life of colonial Brazil was inevitably negligible. Only two persons of mixed racial parentage achieved high office in government or in one of the religious orders.

The first was the guerrilla leader João Fernandes Vieira (16?–81), born on the island of Madeira and allegedly the illegitimate offspring of a comely mulatto whore. His claim to fame is based on his leading role as a military leader in the revolt known as the "War of Divine Liberty" against the Dutch in northeastern Brazil (1644–54).

---

[76] "Porque a bondade da Ley não consiste no asidente mas sim no bom prosedimento" (APMCMOP, vol. 52, fols. 169r–171v and 177v–178r).

[77] "Individuos de qualidades escuras" (Count of Ponte to Prince Regent, 17 July 1806, APB, *Ordens Régias*, vol. 102, fol. 251.

[78] APB, *Ordens Régias*, vol. 18, doc. 59, on the *capitão-mór* of Sergipe; Boxer, *Race Relations*, p. 117; and João Maurício Rugendas, *Viagem pitoresca através do Brasil*, 5th ed. (São Paulo, 1954), p. 94.

For his services he was rewarded by two commanderies in the Order of Christ, absentee membership on the Council of War at Lisbon, and land concessions in Brazil. João Fernandes Vieira was governor of Paraíba from 1655 to 1658 and of Angola from 1658 to 1661. The second was António Vieira, S.J. (1608–97), whose paternal grandmother had been a mulatto serving woman in the household of the counts of Unhão. Born in Lisbon, António Vieira was educated in the Jesuit college in Salvador and was ordained in 1634. A brilliant scholar and preacher, Vieira championed the Portuguese in their struggle against the Dutch and was a staunch defender of the rights of the Amerindian. As a confidential adviser to Dom João IV, he traveled widely in Europe on diplomatic missions and was the prime force behind the founding of the Brazil Company in 1649. Palace politics, Messianic beliefs, and tolerance for "New Christians" led to his trial and imprisonment in 1667. Although released on the accession of Dom Pedro as prince regent, Vieira failed to regain his former prestige at court. In 1669 he went to Rome and remained there until 1675, when he returned to Portugal. Still regarded with suspicion at court, Vieira left for Salvador in 1681 and died there.[79]

Despite their different spheres of influence, the success stories of João Fernandes Vieira and António Vieira, S.J., have several points in common. Neither was born in Brazil. Neither was the offspring of a slave. Both were light mulattoes who achieved prominence at a time when Portugal was threatened politically, militarily, and economically. The very nature of their talents relegated considerations of "purity of blood" to a subordinate level. Finally, as seventeenth-century figures, they lived at a time when the free black and the free mulatto in Brazil had not yet, by increasing numbers and militancy, aroused the antipathy among the white population which was to characterize Brazilian society in the eighteenth century.

The social role and integration of the free colored in colonial Brazil depended on a series of interrelated factors. The application of the concept of a social pyramid to the slave society of colonial Brazil, one having a broad base of slaves and an apex formed by a mercantile or landowning aristocracy, is acceptable, but only with certain reservations. The first caveat is that this social pyramid was juxtaposed, interrelated, and often coincident with ethnic, religious, and economic pyramids. These ranged from the black slave, who practiced religious beliefs originating from West Africa, to the white, "Old Catholic" aristocracy of blood or wealth. Religion, financial means, and color contributed to the degree of social acceptance and

---

[79] The definitive work on João Fernandes Vieira is José António Gonsalves de Mello, *João Fernandes Vieira: Mestre de Campo do Terço de Infanteria de Pernambuco*, 2 vols. (Recife, 1956). Short biographies of both Vieiras appear in C. R. Boxer, *The Dutch in Brazil, 1624–1654* (Oxford, 1957), pp. 271–76, and, by the same author, *Salvador de Sá and the Struggle for Brazil and Angola, 1602–1686* (London, 1952), pp. 165–67.

integration of the colored person. The lighter the mulatto's skin was, the greater were his chances of social acceptance; but then, as now, wealth could buy whiteness. The second caveat is that, within this social structure, vertical and horizontal mobility was great, as were regional variations in social composition. In eighteenth-century Brazil, the traditional class structure underwent violent transformations and saw the emergence of a bourgeoisie and a "meritocracy." Privileges, formerly the exclusive prerogatives of the gentry and aristocracy, came to be enjoyed by other sectors of society. This phenomenon was accompanied by ideological change. Whereas, in the sixteenth and seventeenth centuries, business interests had been regarded as distasteful and improper for anyone of the gentry or aristocracy, the eighteenth century saw the total acceptance of such activities. A mercantile class came to play a more prominent role in Brazilian society and in many instances took over public posts formerly considered the monopoly of the landowning aristocracy. To a lesser degree the free black and the free mulatto in small trades benefited from this change of attitude and were less reluctantly accepted by society.[80]

Nevertheless, the free colored person had to fight to overcome stereotyped attitudes of discrimination and prejudice, which were deeply imbued in the private white sector of the community. These rivaled official policy in their intensity and severity. Racial inferiority, which was attributed to all blacks, mulattoes, and half-castes, was equated with social inferiority. A "person with infected blood" (*pessoa de sangue infecta*), or with a "defect of blood" (*defeito de sangue*), was automatically a "base person" (*pessoa vil*) and a "person of the lowest social standing" (*pessoa de ínfima condição*).[81]

The antipathy felt for blacks and mulattoes is well illustrated by the terminology used to describe them. The black never ceased to be a slave in the minds of whites, and was referred to frequently as "nigger" (*pretinho*) or "brutish black" (*prêto bruto*). The mulatto aroused dislike because of his seeming arrogance and pretensions. Antonil described mulattoes as "proud and corrupt people who prized themselves as bravadoes." Vilhena used similar terms when in the late eighteenth century he described mulattoes as "presumptuous . . . , haughty, and good-for-nothing." The general attitude was summed up by the interim governors of Bahia, who in 1765 described Salvador as a city "where the lowest classes are made up of insolent and arrogant mulattoes and brutish blacks."[82]

[80] A. J. R. Russell-Wood, "Mobilidade social na Bahia colonial," *Revista Brasileira de Estudos Políticos* (Belo Horizonte, 1969), pp. 175–96.

[81] Russell-Wood, "Class, Creed, and Colour in Colonial Bahia," p. 154; cf. Boxer, *Salvador de Sá*, p. 219.

[82] Antonil, *Cultura e Opulencia do Brasil*, bk. 1, chap. 9; Vilhena, *Recopilação de noticias*, 1: 46, 139; and APB, *Ordens Régias*, vol. 66, fols. 398r–400v, cited in C. Ott, *Formação e evolução étnica da cidade do Salvador*, 2 vols. (Bahia, 1955, 1957), 2: 111–14.

The degree of acceptance of colored people by the white community varied from class to class and from region to region. The staunchest defenders of white ethnic superiority were the Third Orders and the *Misericórdia*, whose statutes forbade colored membership and even insisted upon white employees. Commissions were appointed to examine each application, and a general inquiry was held by the governing body. A typical example is the Third Order of Saint Dominic, established in Salvador in 1723. Regulations for the questioning of witnesses, formulated in 1757, specified seven set questions concerning candidates for membership. One of these served to verify that the candidate, his parents, and his grandparents were "Old Christians . . . without any trace of Jewish, Moorish, or mulatto blood, or of any other nation which has been censured."[83]

The free blacks and free mulattoes who were best able to play a prominent role as individuals in the society of colonial Brazil were the *crias de casa*, illegitimate children sired by a white man, or adopted children who had been brought up as members of white families. Adoption was extremely common in colonial Brazil. Brought up within a white family and endowed with social graces and administrative authority, such children sometimes inherited cattle ranches, sugar plantations, and other property. This aroused the ire of governors, who viewed colored ownership as a threat to the national security. Vilhena harshly denounced clerical concubinage, not on moral grounds, but because of the evils of illegitimate mulatto offspring inheriting property and possessions.[84] The influence and power exercised by such mulatto landowners was considerable in the rural areas of the interior, but it is doubtful that they enjoyed the same acceptance in the urban society of Recife, Rio de Janeiro, or Salvador during the colonial period.

The free colored who seem to have been least capable of social assimilation were those slaves who had left Africa as adults and had been granted or had bought their freedom in Brazil. Whereas the creole had acquired at least a working knowledge of Portuguese, many slaves or former slaves proved incapable of learning Portuguese. In 1702 the crown had recommended to the governor general that *ladinos*, the more intelligent colored who had been in Brazil for some time, but who also spoke their native African languages, should be used as interpreters and catechists for new arrivals. This suggestion was rejected by the archbishop of Salvador and by the prelates of the religious orders, on the grounds that the missionaries themselves did not know the African languages; not only might new arrivals be badly instructed in the Catholic doctrine, but they might be

[83] "E preguntando ao quarto dise, q'os pais e avos do Pertendénte são Catholicos Romanos tidos e havidos por Christãos Velhos sem raça de Judeo, mouro, ou mulato, nem de outra infecta nação reprovada" (VOTSDB, *Livro 2 do Tombo*, fols. 208v–209v).

[84] Vilhena, *Recopilação de noticias*, 1: 138–39 and 2: 282–83.

subjected to malicious influences by unscrupulous *ladinos* who abused their position. Nevertheless, a year later, Dom Rodrigo da Costa reported to the king that Jesuit missionaries were teaching slaves in the *Recôncavo* of Bahia in the language of Angola. Evidently this was a purely local effort on the part of the Jesuit order, for in 1719 the count of Assumar complained to Dom João V about the lack of doctrinal teaching of slaves in the mining areas. One reason for this was that many slaves did not possess an adequate command of Portuguese, and the local priests did not speak the African languages. He suggested that Jesuits who had mastered the languages of Angola and the Mina Coast should instruct the clergy, and that the bishop of Rio de Janeiro should appoint to the parishes only those priests who had shown proficiency in these courses.[85]

The collective role of the free black and the free mulatto was limited by official measures, on the one hand, and by tensions and tribal distinctions within the black community, on the other. The colored community was torn by internal tensions and antagonisms, of which the following were the most apparent: antagonism between Brazilian-born free blacks and mulattoes and African-born slaves who had gained their freedom by purchase or legacy; antagonism between freemen and slaves, which was caused primarily by the former abusing and flaunting their liberty; and antagonism between the blacks (*prêtos*) and the mulattoes (*pardos*).

Three examples will illustrate the strength of these differences. In 1756 the slaves of a *quilombo* near São João del Rei, in league with groups of runaway slaves from other parts of Minas Gerais, planned to attack the town on Maundy Thursday at a time when the whites would be in church. This plan resembled a similarly abortive raid on Vila Rica in 1719, but the interesting fact about the 1756 attack was that the object was to kill not only all whites but also all mulattoes.[86] The second example concerns the brotherhood of blacks and creoles dedicated to Our Lady of the Rosary in the diamond-mining encampment of the Tijuco. In 1771, after violent disputes with the black brothers, the creoles broke away to form their own brotherhood.[87] The "Tailors' Revolution" in Salvador in 1798 furnishes a third example. The leadership of this revolt was exclusively mulatto. The only black invited to participate not only refused but betrayed the uprising.[88] There was considerable truth in Vilhena's observation that these

[85] Crown to Dom João de Lencastre, 12 April 1702, and reply, APB, *Ordens Régias*, vol. 13, docs. 72, 72a; Rodrigo da Costa to Crown, 22 October 1703, *ibid.*, doc. 82; Assumar to Crown, 4 October 1719, APMSG, vol. 4, fol. 234v.

[86] APMCMOP, vol. 65, fols. 236v–237v; see Francisco António Lopes, *Os Palácios de Vila Rica*, pp. 127–28, for the Vila Rica revolt.

[87] Aires de Matta Machado, *Arraial do Tijuco: Cidade de Diamantina* (Rio de Janeiro, 1944), pp. 162–63.

[88] In his report Dom Fernando José de Portugal referred to "por certa opposição que ha entre pardos e pretos"; see Affonso Ruy, *A primeira revolução social brasileira (1798)*, 2nd ed. (Salvador, 1951), p. 92.

antagonisms played a positive role in maintaining a balance between the numerically superior colored population and the whites.[89] The only two instances of the colored population achieving some degree of solidarity and cohesion were the militia companies and the brotherhoods.

With the exception of the troop of the line and the dragoons, the military in colonial Brazil was organized not as a standing army but as a series of local militia groups, which were convoked in times of emergency and disbanded again afterward. Such groups were formed in towns and in the rural areas. Their structure varied regionally and at different periods, but usually the various companies were loosely regimented to form a *terço*. These militia companies multiplied, especially in the eighteenth century. They were composed mainly of companies of whites, but annexed to the regiments were companies of free blacks and free mulattoes under their own commanders. For security reasons and because of the difficulty of finding enough free blacks or free mulattoes within a single area to make up a regiment, colored militia groups did not exceed company standing in the rural areas.[90]

These colored companies each counted some sixty strong and were composed of all sectors of the free colored population. Companies of free mulattoes and half-castes (*pardos e bastardos fôrros*) were the most common in eighteenth-century Minas Gerais, followed by companies of free blacks and free mulattoes (*prêtos e pardos fôrros*), free blacks and free mixed-bloods (*prêtos e mestiços fôrros*), and even of Amerindians and half-castes (*indios e bastardos*). The ethnic composition varied from region to region, *mamelucos* being more common in Minas Gerais and São Paulo than in Bahia or Pernambuco. It appears that an official effort was made to compose such colored companies of a mixture of blacks, Amerindians, and mulattoes, possibly for security reasons.

The creation of colored companies was officially justified as preparation "against any contingency." Nowhere did they multiply as rapidly as in Minas Gerais, where the population contained a high proportion of colored people, both slave and free, was extremely mobile, and was notorious for its resistance to authority. The duties of these companies were less military and more general law enforcement in nature; they included patrolling roads, escorting bullion, arresting fugitive slaves, attacking *quilombos*, and capturing smugglers of gold and diamonds. In the cities, militia regiments were formed of free blacks and free mulattoes led by officers of their own color. The regiments of the infantry militia composed of free blacks were commonly known as the Regiments of the Henriques and existed in the major cities of colonial Brazil. Urban militia regiments of mulattoes were usually formed at a much later date than their black counter-

[89] Vilhena, *Recopilação de noticias*, 1: 135–36.
[90] APB, *Ordens Régias*, vol. 7, docs. 517, 518.

parts. The fourth militia regiment in Salvador was composed of mulattoes, and was established by the count of Povolide, acting on instructions contained in a royal letter of 22 May 1766.[91]

The crown's attitude toward the multiplication of colored companies of rural militia was mixed. On the one hand, their military value could not be denied. The free creole mulattoes of Vila Rica reminded the governor in 1762 that, "with the help of God, the natives of the American continent can survive for a considerable length of time on tree roots and game, of which there is a superabundance."[92] Moreover, blacks and mulattoes proved to be experts at opening up trails through heavy forest and scrub. On the other hand, the crown feared that such companies, composed exclusively of colored men under their own commanders, might pose a threat to the white population, especially in the more isolated rural areas. A royal decree of 21 April 1739 ordered that no new companies of the free colored should be established. This order did not apply to the urban militia regiments of Henrique Dias or to the mulatto regiments, and even in the rural areas colored companies continued to be prominent until the end of the colonial period.

Dom João V made several attempts to enforce a policy of integration in the rural militia companies, so that colored and white would serve together, as was the practice in the regular troops of the garrisons. On several occasions in the 1720s, the king refused to confirm appointments made by governors of Minas Gerais of colored officers in command of exclusively colored companies. The king had ordered that ethnic segregation should cease and that militia companies should be raised from the inhabitants of a given area, regardless of color.[93] This order was ignored. In 1731 Dom João V again ordered the amalgamation of colored militia soldiers in white companies and the future formation of all companies on an integrated basis. The count of Sabugosa (viceroy, 1720–35) agreed to comply, but in 1733 the king again found it necessary to order the integration of the militia companies of free mulattoes and free blacks with the white companies. However, within three years the viceroy was obliged to revert to the former basis of color differentiation because white soldiers refused to serve alongside colored soldiers.[94] It was the same story in Minas Gerais. In 1736 the acting governor, Martinho de Mendonça de Pina e de Proença, informed the king that enforcement of a royal order for the amalgamation of companies of free blacks, mulattoes, and *mamelucos* with white companies "would horrify the

[91] *Ibid.*, vol. 95, fols. 214r–216r.
[92] APMCMOP, vol. 78, fols. 147r–148v.
[93] APMSG, vol. 29, doc. 75.
[94] *Ibid.*, vol. 17, fols. 30v–31r; Crown to Sabugosa, 13 January 1731, and reply of 10 June 1731, APB, *Ordens Régias*, vol. 27, docs. 16, 16a. See also Crown to Dom Lourenço de Almeida, 13 January 1731, APMSG, vol. 29, doc. 136.

inhabitants of this region, would impede the efficiency of the militia, and would result in no white person serving in the militia without great indignation and unless he were compelled to do so."[95] This repugnance at integration was not limited to the white militia soldiers. In the 1720s the officers of the mulatto militia companies petitioned the crown for the creation of an exclusively colored regiment with their own officers. Later in the century similar appeals were made on the grounds that white officers and soldiers refused to acknowledge colored officers and soldiers as equals and heaped insulting epithets on them.[96]

The colored infantry militia regiments and companies in the urban and rural areas never did constitute the threat to security which had been feared. But there can be no doubt that the urban militia regiments of free blacks and free mulattoes acted as a platform for colored demands, which became increasingly insistent as the eighteenth century progressed. These demands centered on three issues: pay, privileges, and the eligibility of colored militiamen for the senior posts in their regiments.

From the outset, officers of colored militia forces in both rural and urban areas, received no pay. Only when on special duty did they receive an allowance to defray costs. This situation was accepted in the rural areas, but, in the cities, colored officers pressed for regular wages. In the course of the eighteenth century the crown responded to these demands and granted the colored officers of the Henrique Dias regiments of Bahia and Pernambuco improved basic pay and uniform allowances.[97] Acting on a recommendation of the Overseas Council, Dom José I ordered that the colored officers of the militia regiments of free blacks and free mulattoes of Pernambuco should receive the same pay as the officers of the white militia regiments. Dom João (prince regent, 1792–1816; king, 1816–26) extended this concession to all free black officers in the Henrique Dias regiments throughout Brazil.[98]

Equality of privileges was also demanded by the militants of the colored regiments. White regular troops refused to salute colored officers and regularly insulted them. The law of 1773 which abolished slavery in Portugal contained the clause that colored persons freed thereby should be eligible for all posts, honors, and privileges.

[95] "As ordens de VMag^de prohibem haver companhias separadas de negros forros, mullatos, e mamelucos mandando q' servão juntamente com os brancos nas mesmas companhias, o q' neste Paiz cauzaria orror aos moradores, envelheceria [sic] o exercicio das ordenanças, e faria q' sem grande violencia, e indignação não concorressem a ellas os brancos" (letter to Crown, 18 December 1736, APMSG, vol. 44, fols. 129v–132v).

[96] APB, Ordens Régias, vol. 25, doc. 33; vol. 91, fols. 228r–235v.

[97] Ibid., vol. 8, doc. 106; vol. 42, docs. 98, 98a; José António Caldas, Notícia geral de toda esta capitania da Bahia desde o seu descobrimento até o presente ano de 1759 (Bahia, 1951), p. 342.

[98] APB, Ordens Régias, vol. 91, fols. 228r–235v.

Although applicable only within Portugal and not in the overseas empire, this clause severely rankled the free colored (especially mulattoes) in Brazil and served to make them take stock of their underprivileged position. In the 1790s the officers of the mulatto militia regiment of Salvador asked the king to clarify the intent of this clause because colored persons in Brazil were still denied access to posts in the judiciary and in the regular, paid troops. They also claimed that the privilege granted to all officers of militia regiments to wear bands on their caps had been denied by the governor general. Finally, the mulatto officers asked that the privilege be restored whereby officers and soldiers of militia companies should be tried by military tribunals (*foro militar*) in civil and criminal cases.[99]

The third issue concerned the eligibility of colored soldiers for the senior ranks of the urban militia regiments of free blacks and free mulattoes. The third regiment of the Salvador militia, the Henriques, and the fourth regiment, composed of free mulattoes, had always had officers of their own color. In 1796 the governor, Dom Fernando José de Portugal, submitted to the crown a proposal for the reform of the command structure of the regiment of free mulattoes in Salvador. This proposal advocated the abolition of the senior posts held by mulattoes—those of colonel, lieutenant colonel, and adjutants—and the replacement of these by a white sergeant major to command the regiment and two white adjutants with the rank of captain who would be transferred from the troops of the line. Evidently the governor acted without awaiting royal approval, relieving the colored officers of their posts and nominating the white sergeant major and adjutants. Royal approval was then granted on 17 August 1796. The mulatto officers immediately protested to the crown. A full inquiry was held, and on 13 January 1800 the Overseas Council submitted its report, which was in wholehearted support of the colored officers.

This report represents a landmark in the history of race relations in colonial Brazil, and it is worthwhile to summarize the major points made by the councillors. First, the abolition of posts held by mulatto officers was at variance with recent royal policy whereby the prince regent had ordered the creation of militia regiments of mulattoes elsewhere in Brazil. Second, the mulatto regiments were important in military terms, and the officers' loyalty might diminish if promotion beyond the rank of captain was closed to the colored. Third, white officers might scorn colored subordinates because, in Brazil, "to be mulatto or black is considered a personal defect and not a chance of nature." Fourth, there were mulattoes serving voluntarily in the regiments of the line who possessed the necessary military knowledge to hold senior posts in the mulatto militia regiments. This report was sent to the governor with a top-secret letter which clearly revealed the ambiguous official attitude toward colored militia forces. On the one

[99] *Ibid.*

hand, the governor was told to weigh the necessity of not discouraging mulatto officers by denying them senior posts; on the other, he was reminded of the desirability of not promoting mulattoes to such a degree that they might threaten public law and order. By a resolution of 23 July 1802 the prince regent revoked his previous approval of 17 August 1796 and ordered a return to the original command structure.[100]

The brotherhood was the only form of communal life permitted to colored people in colonial Brazil. Blacks and mulattoes, slave and free, had their own brotherhoods dedicated to Our Lady of the Rosary, Our Lady of Succor, Our Lady of Grace, Saint Benedict, Saint Ephigenia, and Saint Anthony of Catagerona. In the eighteenth century these were common to all villages and towns of colonial Brazil. In the cities the brotherhood of Our Lady of the Rosary could count branches in virtually every parish. On the sugar plantations of the northeast the slaves were permitted, even encouraged, to celebrate the festivals of Saint Benedict and of Our Lady of the Rosary in the plantation chapel.[101] The primary objects of such brotherhoods were devotional and philanthropic. The festival of the patron saint was celebrated every year. Social aid took the form of alms, medical assistance, occasional dowries, prison aid, and burials, and it was limited to brothers and their immediate dependents.

Every colored person in colonial Brazil, be he African-born or Brazilian-born, slave or free, black or mulatto, could be a member of a brotherhood, provided he was of good moral conduct and able to pay his entry fee and subscription. Generally speaking, the colored brotherhoods accepted people "of any quality and condition." In this they were far more tolerant than many white brotherhoods, which demanded proof of "purity of blood," both ethnic and religious. Legacies to colored brotherhoods came from white as well as colored members. But there were some colored brotherhoods which limited their membership to certain sectors of the community. These could be Angolan, creole, or tribal, such as the brotherhood of *Senhor Bom Jesus das Necessidades e Redempção des homens prêtos* in Salvador, which admitted only Gege, or the brotherhood of *Nossa Senhora da Boa Morte* of Nago-Yorouba of the Ketu nation.[102]

    [100] *Ibid.*, fols. 227r–235v (prince regent to governor, 20 April 1800, and the council's report); the institution of examinations is discussed in *ibid.*, vol. 100, fol. 163. The report of the commanding officer, essential reading for any student of race relations, is partially published in Castro e Almeida, *Inventario dos documentos*, 5: doc. 25053; missing is the opening part, which is to be found in APB, *Cartas do Governo a Sua Magestade*, vol. 142, fols. 386r–388r. I am indebted to Arnold Kessler for bringing this last reference to my attention.
    [101] Antonil, *Cultura e Opulencia do Brasil*, bk. 1, chap. 9.
    [102] P. Verger, *Flux et reflux de la traite des nègres entre le golfe de Bénin et Bahia de todos os Santos du dix-septième au dix-neuvième siècle* (Paris and The Hague, 1968), pp. 527–28. Ott (*Formação e evolução étnica*, 1: 65) maintains that the brotherhood of the Redenção admitted only Nagô, but he does not cite any source for this assertion.

These colored brotherhoods multiplied in the eighteenth century. In the face of considerable physical and economic difficulties, many built their own churches. In the early eighteenth century in Salvador there were six brotherhoods for blacks and five for mulattoes. By 1720 in Minas Gerais, in the mining towns of Vila Rica, São João del Rei, Sabará, and Ribeirão do Carmo, there were seven brotherhoods of blacks and one of mulattoes. In the latter part of the century there was a great increase in the number of mulatto brotherhoods in the mining areas especially, and elsewhere there was a similar increase in newly established brotherhoods or in new branches of already existing brotherhoods for the colored.[103]

All lay brotherhoods were governed by a *compromisso*, or statutes, whose terms had to be approved by the crown. The governing body was elected annually and was presided over by one or more "judges" (*juízes*). Some brotherhoods placed limitations on those who were eligible for the office of "judge." The brotherhood of Our Lady of Grace of the Tijuco, while admitting whites, blacks, and mulattoes, ruled that only creoles could be elected "judges."[104] Often, where membership of a brotherhood was mixed—for example, creoles and Angolans—each sector had equal representation in the governing body. The statutes of 1686 and 1820 of the branches of the brotherhood of Our Lady of the Rosary established in Salvador in the church of the Conceição da Praia and in the Pilourinho, respectively, ruled that Angolans and creoles should elect their own "judges," both male and female.[105]

The colored brotherhoods, no less than the militia, served as a mouthpiece for the aspirations and demands of free blacks and free mulattoes. It is interesting to note that the demands made by the colored brotherhoods coincided entirely with those already discussed in relation to the militia: equality of privileges and the right to self-government without white intervention. But, while the militia's demands had been resolved internally and through normal administrative channels, those made by the colored brotherhoods involved not only the crown and governor general or viceroy but also the arch-

---

[103] Fritz Teixeira de Salles, *Associações religiosas no ciclo do ouro* (Belo Horizonte, 1963), pp. 31–36.

[104] *Ibid.*, pp. 40–41.

[105] See *Compremissio da Virgem Sanctissima May de Deus N.S. do Rosario dos pretos da Bahia, 1686,* chap. 6, in the archives of the church of the Conceição da Praia. See also VOTRB, *Compromisso da Irmandade de Nossa Senhora do Rosario dos homens pretos* (1769, reformed in 1820), chaps. 5, 8, 12, 15. Both *Compromissos* state categorically (chaps. 4 and 3, respectively) that admittance is open to all, and not just to creoles and Angolans, as affirmed by Ott, *Formação e evolução étnica*, 1: 65. For the brotherhood of Saint Anthony of Catagerona (1699) of creoles and Angolans, see Manoel S. Cardozo, "The Lay Brotherhoods of Colonial Bahia," *Catholic Historical Review*, 33, no. 1 (1947): 12–30. See also A. J. R. Russell-Wood, "Aspectos da vida social das irmandades leigas da Bahia no século XVIII," in *O Bi-centenário de um monumento bahiano*, Coleção Conceição da Praia, vol. 2 (Salvador, 1971), pp. 143–68.

bishop, local clergy, and a large section of the white population, which felt its own interests were threatened.

The prime source of conflict of interests concerned burial privileges. Throughout colonial Brazil the *Misericórdia* held the virtually exclusive prerogative to bury people within the urban areas. In the seventeenth century in Salvador, the *Misericórdia* authorized a few colored brotherhoods to possess litters for the funerals of their own brothers. In 1685 the first branch of the brotherhood of Our Lady of the Rosary was founded in Salvador. This brotherhood grew rapidly in importance and soon became the most vocal mouthpiece for colored rights. In 1720 it petitioned the crown for concession of the privilege to possess and use a covered bier. This petition was rejected by the crown on this occasion, but, in the course of the eighteenth century, colored brotherhoods not only received royal permission to possess their own litters, but some were even allowed to own biers for the burial of members.[106]

The second issue concerned the office of treasurer and the role of the local parish priest in the administration of the colored brotherhoods. During the colonial period it was customary for black brotherhoods to have a white treasurer, whereas mulatto brotherhoods usually had one of their own color. In the late seventeenth and early eighteenth centuries it was also common practice for the scribe of black brotherhoods to be white, although no definite ruling governed this post. A regular clause of the statutes of colored brotherhoods ruled that the local parish priest should be present at all meetings of the governing body and at elections. Whereas Our Lady of the Rosary of Salvador had been the leading colored contender for equal burial privileges, the black brotherhood of Saint Benedict, composed of slaves and freedmen, took up the cause of independent colored self-government. In 1788 the "judges" and governing body of the brotherhood in Salvador directed a petition to the crown.

This petition, a reading of which is essential for an understanding of race relations at the end of the colonial period, asked that the clause of the brotherhood's statutes which stipulated that the posts of treasurer and scribe should be held by whites be revoked. The brotherhood reasoned that, whereas formerly it had been rare to find blacks who could read, write, and count, now the majority could. The governing body requested this reform with the express understanding that, in the years when a Brazilian-born black was treasurer, an African-born black should be scribe, and vice versa, in alternate years. The crown ordered a full inquiry. White opposition was voiced in the bitter report to the governor by the current scribe and treasurer of Saint Benedict, who underlined five reasons why these posts should continue to be held by whites. First, many blacks were slaves and

---

[106] This issue is fully discussed in Russell-Wood, *Fidalgos and Philanthropists*, pp. 93–94, 213–14, 216–20.

would not have the confidence of the public if elected. Second, only a minority was literate and could count, especially among the African-born brothers, and the number of eligible candidates would soon be exhausted. Third, many brothers were unemployed or were artisans and lacked the financial means to comply with the royal order that the scribe and treasurer should possess property and have financial resources. Fourth, blacks were incapable of administration and were subject to discord, especially when there was a mixture of creole and African-born members. Fifth, a white scribe, treasurer, and chaplain provided a stabilizing influence. Despite such adverse comments, the governor recommended in 1789 that the granting of this privilege would not constitute a precedent, because six black brotherhoods already had blacks as scribes and treasurers. He suggested, however, that, if this privilege were extended to the brotherhood of Saint Benedict, it be done on condition that the incumbents of these posts were freedmen with some financial resources.[107]

The colored brotherhoods played a vital role in furthering the adaptation and social integration of the free black and free mulatto in colonial Brazil. Whereas for the slave they could be instrumental in buying his freedom, for the freedman they afforded a degree of protection against exploitation by a highly competitive society. For both, the brotherhood spelt unity and the sharing of colored problems and aspirations. The common ground of religion meant that colored and white brotherhoods participated in the same funerals, processions, and civic functions, and may have contributed to the colored brotherhoods' acceptance by the white population.

The demands made by the militia regiments and brotherhoods are indication enough of growing unrest among the colored population of Brazil in the eighteenth century. The most remarkable example of this was the so-called Tailors' Revolution at Salvador in 1798. The aims of this were ill-defined but were broadly as follows: the overthrow of the regime and establishment of a republic; the opening of official posts to colored people and whites equally, ability being the sole criterion; the abolition of slavery; the opening of the ports to free trade. This revolt differed from earlier outbreaks in Bahia and Minas Gerais in having a large proportion of mulattoes among its most active leaders, although it is possible that there was a following among the white gentry, some of whom would have stepped in if the revolt had succeeded. On 12 August 1798 bulletins were posted urging the overthrow of the regime and preaching the ideals of equality, liberty, and freedom. Such notices contained a large military content, inviting all soldiers of the militia and of the troop of the line to participate,

---

[107] APB, *Ordens Régias*, vol. 78, fols. 275r–286r. In 1826, the Brotherhood of Our Lady of the Rosary of Salvador asked for the reform of their *Compromisso* on similar grounds; see ANRJ, *caixa* 288, doc. 50. The *Compromisso* (VOTRB) of 1820, chap. 16, stipulated that members of the governing body should be freedmen.

and promising better basic pay for soldiers and promotion for officers, regardless of color. The plot was betrayed and easily suppressed. A leading witness was Joaquim José de Sant'Ana, a black who had bought himself out of slavery and was then captain of a company of the Henriques. The plotters had counted on his support and that of his company, and had tried to undermine his loyalty by suggesting that a white would be appointed sergeant major of his regiment, a post coveted by Sant'Ana. The suspects who were arrested included twenty-five free mulattoes, two free creoles, eleven slaves, and eleven whites. Ten of the free mulattoes were regular or militia soldiers. The four ringleaders, all free mulattoes, were hanged, and the remaining conspirators were exiled, jailed, or lashed in the public pillory. The Tailors' Revolution was not a racial revolt; it was a warning to the authorities of the extent of discontent among the colored population of Brazil at the end of the eighteenth century.[108]

That selfsame lack of unity which characterized the social life of the colored population of colonial Brazil also extended to the cultural sphere. Slaves had been brought from a wide variety of regions at different periods of the slave trade and did not possess a common culture. The cultural traditions which did survive did so despite official repression, which was deliberately aimed at destroying colored solidarity in any form.

The authorities were afraid of any colored person exercising authority over others. Some blacks had been members of ruling dynasties in Africa before being sold into slavery by rivals or enemies. In Rio de Janeiro in 1736, the appearance of a slave claiming to be the son of the king of the Congo was immediately reported to Dom João V.[109] In Brazil, such slaves enjoyed great prestige among the colored population and usually gained their freedom rapidly. They were chosen as godfathers at the weddings and baptisms of slaves and of the free colored. This practice was forbidden in Minas Gerais in 1719. Parish priests were ordered to accept only whites as godfathers, ostensibly on the grounds that because of their "brutal nature" blacks could not instruct their charges in the Catholic doctrine as well as "whites, who have been brought up on the milk of the Church."[110] Restrictions were placed on any type of colored festivity, including

[108] The basic study of this revolt is Ruy, A primeira revolução. Ideological studies are Luís Henrique Dias Tavares, Introdução ao estudo das idéias do movimento revolucionário de 1798 (Salvador, 1959), and Katia M. de Queirós Mattoso, Presença francesa no movimento democrático baiano de 1798 (Salvador, 1969). Many commentators on this revolt have failed to take into account (1) the highly selective process of choosing witnesses, many of whom were ignorant of the events but who served to screen participation by the white gentry, and (2) the shift in objectives between inception and abortive realization.

[109] APB, Ordens Régias, vol. 32, doc. 87.

[110] APMSG, vol. 11, fols. 171v–172v, 184r, 282v–284r; vol. 4, fols. 238r–239r.

baptisms and marriages, if the accompanying party numbered more than ten people. The discharge of firearms on such occasions also was forbidden.[111] It was customary for slaves from the Congo and Angola to elect a king and queen annually. Antonil referred to this practice in Bahia, and it also occurred in Rio de Janeiro and in Minas Gerais. Although forbidden in Minas Gerais, such coronations were celebrated in the distant county of Serro do Frio until 1720, when the governor prohibited this "act and solemnity, which is so at variance with the humble position of slaves." Similar measures prohibited dances and the beating of the *atabaques*, or drums.[112]

African cultures managed to survive in Brazil for three reasons. First, there was a continual influx of slaves who spoke their native languages and practiced African customs rather than adopt those of Brazil. Second, such laws as those just cited were not enforced. Dancing in the streets by colored persons was forbidden, but it was unofficially permitted in Rio de Janeiro because the majority of the colored there were Angolans or Benguelans and were of peaceful disposition. Vilhena observed that, at the end of the century in Salvador, blacks of both sexes danced through the streets to the beat of drums and spoke African languages. In 1814 the prince regent ordered strict enforcement of the law forbidding street gatherings by colored persons, slave or free.[113] The third reason was that oral tradition, passed from father to son, played a prominent role in African cultures. Transportation to Brazil, slavery, and emancipation failed to eradicate this practice. Generations after emancipation, families continued to repeat the same traditions and stories that had been brought from Africa by their slave forefathers.

One important aspect of this cultural transmission was the bringing of African religions to the New World. The impact of these religions on Brazil varied at different times and places. In Salvador

[111] *Ibid.*, vol. 27, fols. 14v–15r, and APMCMOP, vol. 54, fols. 122v–123v; the prevention of such festivities was one of the responsibilities of the *capitães do mato* as stated in their *Regimentos* (APMCMOP, vol. 32, fols. 210r–212r).

[112] "Faltava remediar no Cerro do frio o erro q' ainda hoje selhes consente la, que nas suas festas aclamem e coroem os negros Reys e Raynhas, acto e solemnide que como tão repugnante com a condição humilde de escravos em q' se devem conservar, ha tempo selhes prohibio em todas estas outras Minas, e porq' importa mto fazellos reconhecer a sugeição sem a menor liberde e q' nem pella memoria lhes passe este estimullo e incentivo de mayoria e superioridade que elles no q' a affectão bem mostrão o mto q' a dezejão, portanto ordeno q' selhes não permita daqui em diante este genero de celebride" (*bando* of 20 May 1720, APMSG, vol. 11, fol. 288v). The election of kings and queens also occurred in brotherhoods (António Lopes, *Os palácios de Vila Rica*, pp. 194–97) and in *quilombos* (APMCMOP, vol. 54, fols. 114v–119v); see also Antonil, *Cultura e Opulencia do Brasil*, bk. 1, chap. 9.

[113] Vilhena, *Recopilação de noticias*, 1: 135; APB, *Ordens Régias*, vol. 116, fols. 128r–130r. This order was opposed by some slaveowners on humanitarian grounds, and the governor was ordered to ensure that these views received no publicity in the press (*ibid.*, fol. 228r).

the strongest cultural impression was made by the Nagô. Their religious practices and beliefs fall roughly into two interrelated groups. The first was the worship of the Oriṣa, or gods and goddesses, each being the personification of a natural phenomenon and possessing his (or her) own attributes. The second was the worship of family ancestors, rulers of African dynasties, and the founders of sects in Brazil, and the practice of elaborate funeral rites. The objects of this veneration took on bodily forms and were (and still are) called the Egun, the cult being known as the Egúngún. The origins of these cults in Brazil are shrouded in mystery. What is perhaps an early reference to the Egúngún is contained in the writings of the Jesuit Antonil in 1711.[114] The count of Povolide (governor of Pernambuco, 1768–69) was forced to take steps against friars and clerics arrested in houses where blacks from the Mina coast were celebrating African religious rites.[115] Inventories made by the police in Salvador during raids on *quilombos* in the Cabula district in the early nineteenth century list objects of ritual significance. The liturgy and ceremonies of these cults have been described elsewhere. My purpose here is merely to suggest the important role played by the free black in the preservation of these cults.[116]

These sects were persecuted during the colonial period and continued to be persecuted into the early twentieth century. The greater mobility and freedom of action of the free black enabled him not only to return to Africa to perfect his ritual knowledge but also to found *terreiros*, or cult centers, albeit clandestinely, in Brazil. One example will illustrate this. The chief of the *terreiro do Mocambo* on the island of Itaparica in the Bay of All Saints was the African-born Marcos Pimentel, otherwise known as Marcos the Old. This was an Egúngún cult house. Marcos the Old had bought his freedom and had returned

---

[114] "E se, em cima disto, o castigo fôr frequente e excessivo, ou se irão embora, fugindo para o mato, ou se matarão per si, como costumam, *tomando a respiração* ou enforcando-se, ou procurarão tirar a vida aos que lha dão tão má, recorrendo (se fôr necessario) a artes diabolicas" (Antonil, *Cultura e Opulencia do Brasil*, bk. 1, chap. 9, italics added). The inducement of death by holding one's breath is part of the tradition of the death cult.

[115] René Ribeiro, *Religião e relações raciais* (Rio de Janeiro, 1954?), p. 44. I am informed by Deoscoredes M. dos Santos that the priest of the first cult of Xango in Bahia was a slave.

[116] Much research is still to be done on the Egúngún, but an introduction to the subject is Juana Elbein dos Santos and Deoscoredes M. dos Santos, "Ancestor Worship in Bahia: The Égun-Cult," *Journal de la Société des Américanistes* (Paris), 58 (1969): 79–108. For the Oriṣa see P. Verger, *Note sur le culte des Orisha et Vodoun à Bahia, la Baie de tous les saints au Brésil et l'ancienne Côte des Esclaves en Afrique* (Dakar, 1957), a definitive work. A popular description is given by Donald Pierson in *Negroes in Brazil: A Study of Race Contact at Bahia* (Carbondale and Edwardsville, Ill., 1967), pp. 275–317; see also Roger Bastide, *O candomblé da Bahia* (São Paulo, 1961), Edison Carneiro, *Religiões negras* (Rio de Janeiro, 1936), and the numerous works of Nina Rodrigues, Artur Ramos, and Manuel Querino.

to Africa to perfect his ritual knowledge and initiate his son, known as Marcos the Young, into the secrets of the cult. After some years in Africa, both returned to Bahia. Marcos the Young became chief of the *terreiro de Tuntum*, also on Itaparica. According to tradition, Marcos the Old was sentenced to death by the elders of the cult after having caused the death of a person through the use of his ritual powers; he died seven days later on the beach. The chronology of the founding of the *terreiro do Mocambo* is uncertain, but Marcos the Young died almost a centenarian in about 1935, so it may well have been in existence in the last years of the colonial period. There is every reason to believe that those African cults present in Brazil in the early nineteenth century were born of a cultural tradition and ritual practice already present at an earlier period.[117]

The free black and the free mulatto played a significant role in the arts in colonial Brazil. The studies of Francisco Curt Lange have revealed the importance of the mulatto in eighteenth-century vocal and instrumental music, especially in Minas Gerais. A royal marriage, a governor's visit, or the arrival of a new high-court judge was celebrated by public processions, performances by the artisan guilds, theatrical pieces, and dances, in all of which the free colored were prominent.[118]

The free colored also served as artisans in the construction and decoration of churches, but comparatively few have been identified. The outstanding exception is António Francisco Lisboa, *O Aleijadinho*, born in the 1730s in Vila Rica, the bastard son of a Portuguese master carpenter and his slave. Although the victim of a disease which was probably leprosy and resulted in muscular atrophy and partial paralysis, *O Aleijadinho* dedicated himself to church art and received numerous commissions for work in wood and stone from the lay brotherhoods that flourished in the mining area. Perhaps his greatest works were the twelve prophets, sculpted in soapstone, and the starkly realistic wooden figures of the Way of the Cross at Congonhas do Campo.[119]

[117] I am deeply indebted to Deoscoredes M. dos Santos and Juana Elbein dos Santos for permission to use unpublished material based on their extensive research on the Egúngún cult. Their hospitality enabled me to accept an invitation to attend the cult ceremonies on the island of Itaparica in 1965.

[118] See Francisco Curt Lange's *Archivo de música religiosa de la "Capitania Geral das Minas Gerais" (siglo XVIII) Brasil: Hallazgo, restauración, y prólogo* (Mendoza, 1951); "La música en Villa Rica (Minas Gerais, siglo XVIII)," *Revista Musical Chilena*, nos. 102–3 (1967–68); and "As danças coletivas públicas no período colonial brasileiro e as danças das corporações de ofícios em Minas Gerais," *Barroco* (Belo Horizonte, 1969), vol. 1, pp. 15–62, as well as sources there quoted.

[119] Studies on the Aleijadinho are too numerous to enumerate, but reference should be made to Germain Bazin, *Aleijadinho et la sculpture baroque au Brésil* (Paris, 1963), and to *Antônio Francisco Lisboa, o Aleijadinho*, Publicações da Directoria do Patrimonio Histórico e Artístico Nacional, no. 15 (Rio de Janeiro, 1951), and articles in the *Revista* of the same department.

Even more spectacular, in social terms, was the achievement of Manuel da Cunha (1737–1809). A slave in Rio de Janeiro, he was encouraged by his master to study painting under João de Sousa and was sent to Lisbon for further training. Upon his return, Manuel was bought out of bondage by a local philanthropist and executed religious works for chapels in Rio de Janeiro. His main contribution to Brazilian art was that he was the first artist in Brazil to distinguish himself as a portraitist. His most famous subject was Gomes Freire de Andrada, whose government in the years 1733–63 extended over the greater part of Brazil. This portrait was later hung in the city council of Rio de Janeiro.[120]

CONCLUSION

The role exercised by the free black and the free mulatto reveals much about the conditions of life and status of the colored population as a whole in colonial Brazil. The Portuguese crown followed a discriminatory policy against all blacks and mulattoes. No separate policy was formulated specifically for the free colored. Legislation on colored issues was founded on ethnic criteria and totally failed to recognize any distinction in civil status between slave and free colored. Distrust, fears of "black rebellion," and a complete lack of understanding of the social reality of the free colored sector of the population characterized the crown's attitude. For this, the crown was not solely to blame. Governors, city councillors, and influential private citizens were haunted by fears (usually unfounded) of uprisings, economic competition, and black dominance and advised the crown accordingly. It was easier to repress than to understand or tolerate. The result of this official phobia was that it was easier for a colored person to go to Portugal and enter a convent, religious order, or university and to practice a profession than it was in Brazil.

Official discrimination and widespread social distrust did much to limit the role played by the free black and the free mulatto in colonial Brazil. Neither fish nor fowl, master nor slave, the free colored stood uneasily between the "black world" of the slaves and the "white world." In a social "no man's land," he was the butt for the antagonisms and tensions of all sectors of the community. With the exception of the militia companies and the brotherhoods, themselves not entirely free of internal racial divisions, the free colored population was characterized by its lack of over-all solidarity or cohesion. As a class, it failed to find a place in the social structure of colonial Brazil. Those few individuals who did achieve prominence or notoriety did so as individuals and in the face of convention. They did not exercise mass influence over the colored population. At no time were they epic figures, representatives of a collective social ideal.

[120] Nair Batista, "Pintores do Rio de Janeiro colonial (notas bibliográficas)," *Revista do Patrimônio histórico* (Rio de Janeiro), 3 (1939): 103–21.

Nonetheless, the free black and the free mulatto made their presence increasingly felt during the eighteenth century. A demographic increase in the over-all colored population and increasing opportunities for the free colored in the mining areas and growing urban centers contributed to this social phenomenon. The growing numbers of brotherhoods and militia regiments, both of which were encouraged by whites as stabilizing factors, were indicative of this increased prominence. It must be emphasized that such brotherhoods and regiments were regarded as individual groupings of colored persons and never as representatives of a unified social class.

This increasing prominence of the free colored sector in colonial Brazil fed the flames of two much-debated controversies. The first concerns the alleged mildness or harshness of slavery in Brazil. Advocates of the "mildness" thesis cite the presence of a large free colored sector in a slave society as evidence of the milder and more open form of slavery in Brazil. But Sir Richard Burton's comment that "nowhere, even in Oriental countries, has the 'bitter draught' so little of gall in it" severely overstated the case, even for the mid-nineteenth century. There is no qualitative evidence from the colonial period which indicates that slavery in Brazil was harsher or milder than slavery in the colonies of other European nations. For those slaves who were whipped to death, worked to exhaustion in the mines or cane fields, or thrown into pools of piranhas or between the grinders of the sugar mills, there were others who were granted dowries, received financial or medical assistance, were freely accepted as members of patriarchal families, or were given their freedom. In Brazil, as elsewhere, there were good and bad masters, just as there were good and bad slaves. The form of expressing this dominance varied. Treatment of the slave depended not only on human factors but, to an equal or greater degree, on the different working conditions that existed in gold mines and on cane plantations, tobacco holdings, or cattle ranches. General comparative studies of slavery in Brazil, the West Indies, and the United States blur the importance of the economic factor in determining slave conditions. Of greater relevance would be studies of slave conditions in specific types of economic areas—for example, in mining in the Spanish American or Portuguese American empires. In colonial Brazil there were many opportunities for slaves to become free. This suggests that colonial Brazilian slavery may have been less rigid and more open. It should not be inferred from this, however, that slavery was more mild in colonial Brazil than elsewhere.

The second controversy has been waged by academics over the alleged "social ascent" of the free colored person, especially the mulatto, during the colonial period. The very phrase "social ascent" has led to much misunderstanding by suggesting a Brazilian equivalent of "from log cabin to White House." There can be no doubt that some free blacks and even more free mulattoes did achieve financial autonomy and a degree of social acceptance in the white community. It cannot be overemphasized, however, that such autonomy and acceptance were achieved within very limited spheres. Used in reference to the free colored in the colonial period, the term "social ascent" can mean little more than the limited social acceptance of individual colored persons by whites of the lower bourgeoisie and artisan class. In financial terms, ownership of a small shop represented success for a free colored person. Colored owners of mines and plantations and owners of thirty or forty slaves were vivid exceptions to the general rule. The lifting of previously imposed restrictions forbidding the carrying of arms and the wearing of certain types of dress by free mulattoes in the mid-eighteenth century should not be regarded as evidence of social ascent, because of the limited application of such a privilege. With the exception of the demographic increase in the free colored population, especially on the part of the mulattoes, in all other respects—juridical, economic, and social—the position of the free colored person in the colonial period continued to be characterized by its static nature and the absence of general upward progress or amelioration. Whatever vertical mobility there may have been always remained within certain limits. At no time did a mulatto, no matter how light-skinned, entirely cast off his ethnic origins and gain total integration into the white ruling class. All but a very few free blacks and free mulattoes in colonial Brazil were born, lived, and died in a social, economic, and ethnic penumbra.

BIBLIOGRAPHICAL NOTE

The material available in English on colonial Brazil is limited. The best general surveys are C. R. Boxer, *The Golden Age of Brazil, 1695–1750: Growing Pains of a Colonial Society* (Berkeley and Los Angeles, 1962), and Caio Prado Junior, *The Colonial Background of Modern Brazil*, English ed. (Berkeley and Los Angeles, 1967). The only documented study of race relations is C. R. Boxer, *Race Relations in the Portuguese Colonial Empire, 1415–1825* (Oxford, 1963), pp. 101–21. This counterbalances the over-optimistic but excellent and classic studies of Gilberto Freyre, *The Masters and the Slaves: A Study in the Development of Brazilian Civilization*, English ed. (New York, 1946), and *The Mansions and the Shanties: The Making of Modern Brazil*, English ed. (New York, 1963). Chapters in Donald Pierson, *Negroes in Brazil: A Study of Race Contact at Bahia* (Carbondale and Edwardsville, Ill., 1967), and in Carl Degler, *Neither Black nor White: Slavery and Race Relations in Brazil and the United States* (New York, 1971), are of interest. The colored brotherhoods are discussed in A. J. R. Russell-Wood, *Fidalgos and Philanthropists: The Santa Casa da Misericórdia of Bahia, 1550–1755* (London, Berkeley, and Los Angeles, 1968).

Race relations are a constantly recurring theme in monographs on colonial Brazil, but there is no satisfactory study of the slave, let alone of the free colored, throughout Brazil during the colonial period. The pioneering studies, frequently re-edited, of Nina Rodrigues (*Os Africanos no Brasil* and *O animo fetichista dos negros bahianos*), Artur Ramos (*O negro no civilização brasileira*), and Manuel Querino (*A raça africana*) are introductory works but appear somewhat old-fashioned by the standards of modern sociological methodology. In the absence of detailed studies, much information on the conditions and standing of the slave, the free black, and the free mulatto in the colonial period can be gleaned from the opening chapters of socioeconomic monographs dealing primarily with race relations in different areas of nineteenth-century Brazil. These include L. A. da Costa Pinto, *O negro no Rio de Janeiro: Relacões de raça numa sociedade em mudança* (São Paulo, 1952); Roger Bastide and Florestan Fernandes, *Brancos e negros em São Paulo*, 2nd ed. (São Paulo, 1959); Florestan Fernandes, *The Negro in Brazilian Society* (New York, 1969); Fernando Henrique Cardoso and Octávio Ianni, *Côr e mobilidade social em Florianópolis: Aspectos das relações entre negros e brancos numa comunidade do Brasil meridional* (São Paulo, 1960); Octávio Ianni, *As metamorfoses do escravo: Apogeu e crise da escravatura no Brasil meridional* (São Paulo, 1962); Fernando Henrique Cardoso, *Capitalismo e escravidão no Brasil meridional* (São Paulo, 1962); and Emilio Viotti da Costa, *Da senzala à colônia* (São Paulo, 1966).

For bibliographical details on specific topics—for example, the slave trade, brotherhoods, religious cults, and artistic works—the reader is referred to the notes accompanying this chapter.

ABBREVIATIONS

ACDB	Archives of the Convent of Santa Clara do Desterro, Salvador
AMB	Municipal archives, Salvador
ANRJ	National Archives, Rio de Janeiro
APB	Public archives of the state of Bahia
APMCMOP	Public archives of the state of Minas Gerais; registers of the municipal council of Vila Rica do Ouro Prêto
APMSG	Public archives of the state of Minas Gerais; registers of the secretaria do governo
ASCMB	Archives of the Santa Casa da Misericórdia, Salvador
BNRJ	National Library, Rio de Janeiro
OCB	Archives of the Carmelite Order, Salvador
VOTCB	Archives of the Third Order of the Carmelites, Salvador
VOTRB	Archives of the Third Order of the Rosary, Salvador
VOTSDB	Archives of the Third Order of Saint Dominic, Salvador

LÉO ELISABETH

4 | The French Antilles

INTRODUCTION

Early in the seventeenth century, the French made their first Caribbean settlements in the Lesser Antilles. At first, metropolitan interest centered on the Saint Christopher holdings, but, by the 1660s, metropolitan attention had shifted to Martinique, which had first been occupied by France in 1635. The transfer of the governor general to Martinique in 1669 was an obvious mark of the move away from the earlier center; perhaps even more important was the migration of Saint Christopher settlers to Martinique, particularly after 1689, when twenty years of peace between English and French settlers on Saint Christopher came to an end.

Almost from the days of the first arrivals of Africans and the earliest appearances of slavery in the French islands, persons of color managed to obtain their freedom, and, in certain instances, free men of color owned slaves in numbers comparable to the whites. Some free persons of color were integrated into the white group, not only economically and socially, but also racially. But in the records of the early period of slavery in the French islands, it is often difficult to distinguish or to isolate emancipated slaves from other free persons of color. The French islands were a singular and lasting refuge for the Carib Indians, and the Caribs were generally considered to have been free always. While the Indians were in certain cases ascriptively and legally distinguished from the free colored of African and slave descent, they were in other instances lumped together with the emancipated people of color.

The legal framework in which the statuses of the free colored were embedded, as well as the related ascriptive terminology, was complicated by patterns of miscegenation in the societies of the French Windward Islands. Theoretically, the offspring of Indians and Europeans by mixed relations were called mestizos. From the 1730s, however, this term was applied to anyone of mixed origin whose complexion and features veered more toward white than toward black. On the other hand, the direct descendant of a European and a Negro was, in the literature, sometimes termed a mulatto. Similarly, however, the meaning of this term became increasingly vague and more

134

difficult to apply with each succeeding generation. These difficulties were revealed in 1763, when the duke of Choiseul informed the authorities of the Windward Islands that all "free Negroes" were to be denied permission to leave for France. The vagueness of the appellation required an explanation, and in a second letter the duke specified that he meant any "Negro man or woman, mulatto or mulatress," without discrimination of sex, including people from India and Indians, "who simply constitute another type of colored people." In Martinique in 1767, the general phrase "mameluke, mestizo, mulatto, or Negro, and, as a rule, any colored people" had to be used to avoid any misinterpretation of a local ordinance.[1]

It was also difficult to distinguish between the "Negro" in the "pure" sense and other non-whites of mixed origins. In the literature, the term "Negro" came to have all the ambiguity, or at least the non-specificity, of the term "colored man." Although in law and practice and in many specific instances distinctions were made between emancipated and non-emancipated free persons of color, and between free "colored" people and free "Negroes," what is significant is that whites began to perceive of these groups of varying origins as linked to one another or as one. They also saw them as a social group which was not slave, but which could never, theoretically, obtain the privileges of the upper social stratum—in short, as a group which was perceived of, and came to function, as an "intermediate class."

The attitudes of whites which underlay this conception of the free colored as an intermediate social class, reinforced to some extent by racial distinctions, were slow to develop. In the early period of the French islands, the white colonists had no singular or common attitude toward the colored subjects. The *Code Noir* of 1685, for example, called for full assimilation of the free colored. Prejudice, however, tended to sustain itself in the face of legislation.

Supported by local authorities, planters were to transform the notion that freedmen owed respect to their former masters into the insistence that colored people in general were required to show respect to whites in general. This shift was fundamental to the broad attack which the white group made upon the status of the free colored population. The system of exclusion was erected without plan; as usual, usage was there before the law.

As we follow the campaign of attack on the *Code Noir* and the growth of constraints on the position of the free colored in the societies of the French islands, it will become clear that, if any factor

---

[1] Archives Nationales des Colonies, B117, June 30, 1763, fol. 337 (hereafter cited as Colonies). The quoted examples are rather late, but some others can be traced back to the early eighteenth century. To be sure, in the early period, a certain number of those who were closer to whites in complexion and standard of living were not included among the "colored people." The second letter of Choiseul is to be found in *ibid.*, August 29, 1763. Translations of quoted matter throughout this essay are the author's.

helped to protect, even to promote, the rights of the free colored, it was the condition of war. Although the *Code Noir* was published in 1685 during a period of peace, and the peaceful reign of Louis Philippe was favorable to the colored people in the French colonies, in general, wartime offered more opportunities to the free colored population. Not only did the authorities relax their attention in wartime, but the free people of color offered a source of military support which was by no means negligible. War also increased the numbers of freedmen because, from the earliest period, the local government enlisted slaves with the promise of emancipation to those who distinguished themselves in military campaigns. In peacetime, whites saw the free colored as useful in hunts for runaway slaves. Beyond that, the local administration heard endless lamentations from eminent white persons bewailing the growing numbers, or increasing role, of the freedmen. It should be noted that the first regulation instituting strict control of freedmen dates from 1713, when the Treaty of Utrecht was bringing an end to the War of the Spanish Succession.

The growth of the planting economy in the French islands did not favor the free colored. Before the introduction of sugar, the island's economy was based on peasant proprietorship and the cultivation of smallholdings. Free colored peasant farmers had much in common with poor white farmers. Economic fluctuations affected them just as they did poor whites. After 1726, the access of free colored farmers to capital was effectively blocked, and this group felt the effects of this handicap fully.

At first, patterns of cultivation, especially of tobacco, were favorable to peasant proprietors, and direct access to capital was relatively unimportant. But, by 1680, tobacco planting had been largely replaced by sugar cane. In general, this crop demanded ever-increasing investments, both in labor and in capital goods. Proprietors who could not keep pace were pitilessly eliminated. Sugar cane cultivation wiped out the weaker—in effect, the peasant—proprietors. By 1710, the agricultural transformations brought about by the sugar revolution were practically completed on Martinique, and even the lands reserved for grazing cattle were being planted in cane.

In terms of wealth and status, the sugar planter occupied one of the top positions on the social scale. He was able to amass a fortune, something that could not be achieved in other colonial activities. With assiduous disrespect for the laws, these estates could survive for a considerable period of time. Avoiding the *coutume de Paris* and the Civil Code, these estates, unlike those of smallholders, were not thoroughly broken up after the death of the owner. In the case of bankruptcy, the large estates were held together and sold unparceled. Crises, whether they affected individuals or, in the case of massive disasters such as earthquakes and hurricanes, the whole economy, tended to accelerate the process of land concentration and the concomitant emergence and consolidation of a planter class that was increasingly hostile to any economic competition from the free colored population and intent upon preserving the slave system intact.

PATTERNS OF MANUMISSION AND GROWTH

At first, French law permitted slavery only in the islands. The ownership of slaves in metropolitan France was, in theory, impossible, and the mere contact of a slave with French soil was sufficient grounds for manumission. After 1691, however, the correspondence between the ministers of the navy and island administrators revealed a growing concern for problems arising from the application of this principle. Some ship captains signed on slaves to complete their crews, and other slaves stowed away on vessels bound for France. On their arrival in France, these slaves automatically became free. The complaints of the aggrieved slaveholders were forwarded by the local administrators to France, and the monarchy, respecting the law of property, accepted the principle of indemnities linked with fines levied against the ship captains.[2]

But these punitive measures were considered insufficient; the principle of emancipation itself was under fire, and the persistence of the white colonists can be illustrated by a number of cases. In 1696, for example, according to the intendant Robert, white residents of Martinique claimed that a royal decree allowed them to retain possession of the slaves whom they had taken to France as servants and that it was only just that the same regulation should apply to kidnapped or fugitive slaves.[3] After investigation, the minister, who could find no such decree on record, reaffirmed the principle of liberation on French soil.[4] Versailles reacted similarly in 1698 in regard to the Saint Dominguan slaves who had been taken prisoner during the expedition against Cartagena and had been returned to the island after passing through France.[5]

This decision did not, however, stop the administrators of the islands from pleading before the minister again in 1704, when Intendant Mithon argued that for thirty years, at least since the attachment of the islands to the royal domains, the law had not been applied in Martinique.[6] They argued that the liberation of childbearing families would ruin the owners of such families, and that there were already too many freedmen in the islands. In 1705, convinced that he

---

[2] Ibid., B14, October 4, 1691, fol. 104.
[3] Ibid., C8A.7, May 26, 1696.
[4] Ibid., F249, October 12, 1696, fol. 818.
[5] Ibid., February 5, 1698, fol. 926 (letter to Ducasse from the minister of the navy).
[6] Ibid., C8A.15, June 29, 1704 (letter from Machault to the minister of the navy); ibid., November 24, 1704, fol. 347.

could not oppose the interests of the colonists without at the same time harming the public order, the minister decided to approve the existing order of things: those slaves who refused to return to the islands could not be forced to do so, but those who went back of their own volition would lose their liberty.[7]

This first breach of the old principle was soon to be widened. An edict of October, 1716, legalized temporary slavery in France, ostensibly to increase the size of the labor force in metropolitan France. But, despite the formal changes in law, the application of the new edict was uneven. Colonists continued to return to France with those they wished to emancipate, the old customary law of automatic liberty continued to be applied, and the new edict was enforced. Whatever the application of the law, the number of colored persons in France increased steadily. In 1753, the minister contemplated the expulsion of slaves from France, but relented on the grounds that the experience they had gained in France would only be used against the colonies.[8]

After the Seven Years' War, the administration considered transporting this foreign population, slave and free, to the colonies, but this proved impossible because of colonial resistance.[9] Metropolitan officials made strenuous efforts to restrain the numbers of arrivals, but they had little effect; the number of free colored persons continued to increase, and legal cases concerning them multiplied before the Tribunal of the Marble Table of Paris, which systematically refused to admit that slavery or even temporary slavery existed in France.[10] Finally, in October, 1777, after long negotiations with the Parlement of Paris, a new declaration was published. In the spirit of its sponsors, the declaration banned the entry of any colored man into France. Additionally, it called for the taking of a census of those colored who already dwelt there, with a view toward expelling them in order to obviate all the problems that had arisen during their stay in France. But, here again, the administration did not get as much as it would have liked, because the new declaration applied only to those colored who were slaves. During the Revolution, all colored people who were found in France were freed and given full citizenship rights by the decree of September 28, 1791, but slavery quickly reappeared. Finally, under Louis Philippe, the statute of April 26, 1836, au-

7 *Ibid.*, F425, October 24, 1715.
8 *Ibid.*, F258, fol. 741.
9 *Ibid.*, F390, fol. 107 (letter of Fenelon, governor of Martinique). See also Emilien Petit, *Traete sur le gouvernement des esclaves*, 2 vols. (Paris, 1777), 2: 99. The latter explains that free colored acquired the spirit of equality in France. In the preamble of the declaration of 1777, it is precisely stated that the colored people who return to the colonies bring with them the spirit of independence and intractability.
10 This tribunal was reserved for foreigners, and slaves were considered as such for the purposes of the court.

thorized the liberation of all slaves in advance of their embarkation for France and the freeing of those who were already there.[11]

Up to 1685, no precise legislation concerning manumission in the islands, as opposed to metropolitan France, was applied. Each slaveowner manumitted as he saw fit. In one respect, custom seemed to acknowledge one pattern of manumission—that of social birthright. Dutertre, de Blénac, and Labat all thought that the mulattoes were more like Europeans than Africans, which seemed to assure them of having a "vocation for liberty,"[12] and Dutertre wrote in 1667 that, in the times of the noblemen-proprietors, governors declared all mulattoes free at the age of twelve "to punish the sins of their fathers."[13] In 1681, Governor General de Blénac considered that this freedom should be automatically acquired by mulattoes in Martinique. But, in order to indemnify the owners, mulattoes would not become free until the age of twenty, after they had completed eight years of work, unless their fathers had bought their freedom.[14] Father Labat noted that, before 1672, mulattoes were freed at the age of twenty-four; he believed that it was after 1674 that the old saying *"partus sequitur ventrem"* was adopted.[15] The latter date is of great importance because, after this time, the attitudes and principles that had tended to favor the mulattoes began to weaken. Also after this time, mulattoes were forced to submit to the same humiliations and penalties to which black runaway slaves were subjected.[16] The age at which mulattoes were liberated thus seems to have gradually crept upward. Furthermore, this custom does not seem to have been systematically applied. In any case, it began to come under fire in the 1670s. In 1673, M. du Ruau-Palu claimed that in 1636 the commander de

[11] On the problems of metropolitan emancipation see L. Peytraud, *L'esclavage aux Antilles Française d'après les documents inedits des Archives Coloniales* (Paris, 1891), chap. 4; and Shelby T. MacCloy, *The Negro in France* (Lexington, Ky., 1961).

[12] Y. Debbasch, *Couleur et Libertè* (Paris, 1967), 1: 23.

[13] Jean Baptiste Dutertre, *Histoire générale des Antilles,* 4 vols. (Paris, 1667–71), 2: 477 ff. We should note that twelve was, in the seventeenth century and during almost all of the eighteenth, the age at which children began to work and the master began to pay a poll tax for his young slave.

[14] Colonies, F3.248, December 3, 1681. It should be noted that at this time the repurchase of children was compulsory. This custom was attacked in Guadeloupe in 1681. We do not know the date at which it ceased to function, but not until the law of July 18, 1845, did it reappear in the form of a legal right.

[15] Martinique and Guadeloupe passed from the French West Indies Company into royal hands in 1674.

[16] Père Jean-Baptiste Labat, *Voyage aux îles de l'Amerique,* 2 vols. (Paris, 1931), 2: 219. This feeling in their favor may have lasted longer in Saint Domingue because the minister of the navy allowed the administrators to be more tolerant in conferring freedom on mulattoes, "who were enemies of the Negroes" (Colonies, B61, June 29, 1734, fol. 437).

Poincy had declared the mulattoes to be slaves.[17] In 1681, when the judges of Guadeloupe decided in a particular case that a mulatto should remain a slave, the intendant Patoulet spoke out against "these types of people who could not be kept under control once they were freed."[18] Thus, even before the publication of the edict of 1685, certain notables, backed by a part of the administration, already favored limiting the extent and character of manumissions.

After 1685, they did not relax their pressure, and, in 1704, Intendant Mithon ruled that there were too many freedmen;[19] but it was Governor General Phélippeaux, a few years later, who was mainly responsible for the first official infringement of Article 55 of the Code Noir.[20] His quick temper and his bad relations with Intendant de Vaucresson had led him to side with a certain Mme. La Palu, a widow, who claimed possession of a colored woman named Babet. We do not know all the details of this affair, which took place in Martinique, but in it we find all the classic features: personal entanglement, a claim for respect due to whites, and accusations of immorality against freedmen and freedwomen. Fortified by these pretexts, in June, 1711, Phélippeaux demanded a regulation which would put an end to the right of every inhabitant to manumit his slaves. He felt that manumission should no longer be permitted without official sanction and that all deeds of manumission should be registered with the High Council.[21] Despite the opposition of the intendant, in a decree of October, 1713, the king forbade manumission thereafter without the permission of either the governor general and the intendant or specially named governors and trustees. In cases of infraction of this rule, "Negroes" were to be declared ownerless and sold for the benefit of the king.[22] After 1713, then, initiative in these matters passed to Versailles, where the annual records from the islands were received.

But in Martinique, to take one example, this prohibition did not prevent manumission or the continued growth of the free colored group, at least not for a few years. Up to 1726, the number of free colored continued to increase dramatically.[23] The ministers in Versailles were thus forced to take new and more drastic steps to limit manumissions. In 1721, they forbade free minors to manumit their slaves.[24] In 1722, the Naval Council proposed that freedom be granted

[17] Colonies, F3.91, November 30, 1673 (memoir of Mr. du Ruau-Palu, general agent of the Compagnie des Indes, Martinique).

[18] Ibid., F3.248, December 5, 1681.

[19] Ibid., C8A.15, November 24, 1704, fol. 347.

[20] Article 55 of the edict of 1685: "Masters, from the age of twenty, may set free their slaves by all deeds between the living or because of death, without being obliged to give the reasons for the manumission, nor do they need consent, although they are still minors under the age of twenty-five."

[21] Colonies, C8A.18, June 3, 1711, fol. 118. See also the letter dated April 6, 1713, which is found in the same register.

[22] The word "Negro" is used here to mean "colored people."

[23] See pp. 147–51 below.

[24] This ordinance did not concern servants.

only to those slaves who, by acts of devotion, had saved the lives of their masters, mistresses, or the children of their owners. Writing in 1723, Intendant Blondel stated that, although there were too many "free Negroes" in the colonies, he nevertheless felt that the restrictive proposals would simply force the slaves to run away. As a compromise, he suggested a general scrutiny of deeds of manumission, which would permit an accurate evaluation of their number. This would also control conditional manumissions.[25] These suggestions do not appear to have been followed, however, because Governor General de Feuquières and Intendant Blondel later assured the minister that permission would be granted only according to the conditions stipulated in 1722.[26]

During the next half-century, other regulations made manumission still more difficult. In 1726 the government at Versailles forbade all deeds of gift between white and colored persons, including wills. This ruling was used to put an end even to guardianships, which in turn made it possible to annul the liberal provisions of Article 56 of the *Code Noir.*[27] The application of this restriction explains, in part, the decrease in the number of freedmen, which is noticeable in the 1733 census figures for Martinique. On the other hand, it was the large number of freedmen in Saint Domingue which preoccupied the authorities after 1734.[28] Consequently, the statute of 1736 seems to have corresponded essentially to the needs of the latter island. It renewed the royal decree of October 1713 and further forbade the baptism of children whose mothers had not been legally manumitted. The baptism of children of color had been one of the oldest traditions of the islands; it had definitely not been contrived as a means of circumventing the 1713 statute. An examination of the parish registers of Martinique indicates that the baptisms were not increasing at this time. This assessment is reinforced by a letter from Champigny and d'Orgeville, governor general and intendant, respectively, who informed the minister that, in the Lesser Antilles, baptismal manumission had no legal standing whatever.[29] The direct inscription of the

[25] Colonies, C8A.32, November 11, 1723, fol. 267.
[26] *Ibid.,* C8A.35, September 1, 1724. We must add here that another motive for manumission remained admissible. Liberation for services rendered for the public liberty could be granted as a reward for fighting against enemy forces in case of war or in hunting down runaway slaves. Service in the *maréchaussée* (the militia), or later in the *chasseurs de montagne*, was soon considered essential to the granting of certain liberties. During the Restoration, this was the only means by which colored persons could obtain their legal freedom. Only those liberties granted by Rochambeau during the Revolution were attacked by the administrators of Britain, the empire, and the Restoration.
[27] Article 56 of the edict of 1685 said that slaves who had been made residuary legatees by their masters, or named as executors of their masters' wills or guardians of their children, should be deemed freedmen.
[28] Colonies, B61, June 29, 1734, fol. 439.
[29] *Ibid.,* C8A.47, December 6, 1736, fol. 82.

names of freedmen in the register procured them only a de facto
liberty. This was also held to be true for freedom granted by will.
After the Seven Years' War, the local statute of 1767 even forbade
notaries to accept deeds of manumission unless they were accompanied by the permission of the authorities.[30] Going even further, the
administrators of 1789 forbade manumission by will[31]—a prohibition
that was again decreed in 1805, though it was then stated that people
of one class could not benefit from wills drawn for persons of other
classes. Only under Louis Philippe was the liberal *Code Noir* provision
of 1685 reinstated.

Another part of the liberal *Code Noir* which came under attack
concerned intermarriage and the rights of manumission through marriage. The compilers of the *Code Noir* strove to render West Indian
society more moral by favoring intermarriage between free people and
slaves, and Article 9 of the *Code* was quite explicit in creating another
legal path to manumission: "When a slave marries her master she
becomes free!" Illegitimate children were to be freed along with the
mother.[32] Article 13, which stipulated that it was not sufficient to
marry in order to be free, simply protected the master's rights.[33]
Father Labat records how these two articles were applied in Martinique between 1694 and 1695. A certain Dauphiné, having come to
Martinique five or six years before, was infatuated with a mulatto
woman who gave him "*effets.*" Unable to get her master's consent, he
abducted her and married her. The owner, supported by Father Labat,
lodged a complaint with the intendant. The marriage was declared
null and void. Dauphiné was convicted, fined, and had to pay costs.
Luckily, he found a supporter in an ecclesiastic at Fort-Royal, and
everything was settled by compromise.[34]

Later on, the procedure that came to be applied was the following: (1) purchase of the freedom of the woman and her children;
(2) manumission; (3) marriage. Thus, at this date, marriage did not
in practice directly entail freedom. In 1727, for example, the validity

[30] Statute of February 11, 1767, Martinique Code of Laws, 2: 502 ff.

[31] Departmental Archives of Martinique, Upper Council, December 23,
1789, fol. 235.

[32] Article 9 of the edict of 1685 specified that a freeman who had one
or more children from concubinage with a slave, as well as the slaveowner
who accepted it, had to pay a fine of 2,000 pounds of sugar; if the freeman
was the proprietor of the slave in question, then she and the children were
to be awarded to the hospital without ever being liberated. Article 9 notwithstanding, if the slaveowner was not married to anyone else at the time of
his concubinage, he was to marry his slave according to the rites of the church;
the aforementioned slave was there upon set free and the children were both
freed and legitimated.

[33] Article 13 provided that, in case a male slave married a freewoman,
the children, either male or female, were to be free like their mother, despite
the fact that their father was a slave. If the father was a freeman and the
mother a slave, the children were to be slaves as well.

[34] Labat, *Voyage*, vol. 1, pt. 2, pp. 212–13.

of a marriage contracted eighteen years before was contested at the time of the husband's death. In spite of the opposition of the attorney general, the Upper Council of Guadeloupe declared this marriage to be valid. The matter was then brought before Intendant Blondel in Martinique. The latter reversed the council's decision on the grounds that the Negress "was not a free woman."[35] In 1775, the administrators wanted to profit by the apparent contradiction of Articles 9 and 13 of the Code Noir by taking away the right of manumission by marriage, but the Upper Council opposed this. Actually, the administrators achieved the same end by demanding preliminary permission, which was required for all other liberties. This interpretation even permitted the prohibition of marriages between free colored people and those who were slaves or merely nominally free. In addition, in 1785, Viscount de Damas forbade marriages between free people of Martinique and slaves who had been manumitted abroad.[36] In 1789, Article 13 of a local ordinance in Martinique forbade marriages between free colored people and slaves on this island and made preliminary manumission obligatory. This law also specified that marriage did not manumit children.[37] Finally, the advocates of rigorous prohibition of mixed marriages attained their goal in 1805, when the higher authorities approved Article 3 of the decree of promulgation of the Civil Code, which forbade the intermarriage of people of different classes.[38] The authorities also applied similar decrees to Guadeloupe and French Guiana.

In the 1820s, these restrictions were eased somewhat. In 1827, the Privy Council of French Guiana finally lifted the ban on intermarriage, but, in order to limit the effects of this ruling, the administrators insisted upon the preliminary permission of the owner and stipulated that the ban would be removed only in cases in which there were already children from the relationship. When in 1828 the Privy Council of French Guiana allowed a free colored man to marry his slave after he had manumitted her and legitimized the three children she had borne him, the minister of the navy considered this decision a binding precedent and requested the governor of Martinique to look into the possibilities of a return to the provisions of the edict of 1685,

[35] Colonies, C8A.37, March 18, 1727.
[36] Departmental Archives of Martinique, Privy Council, July 13, 1829, fols. 109 ff. This interpretation of Articles 9 and 13 was adjudged abusive, but was deemed necessary in order to halt the rapid increase in the number of freedmen.
[37] Ibid., Upper Council, December 23, 1789, fols. 234–35.
[38] Article 3 of the decree of November 7, 1805, Martinique Code of Laws, 5: 78, reads: "The laws of the Civil Code relating to marriage, adoption, recognition of illegitimate children, the rights of illegitimate children to the estates of their fathers and mothers, to liberties granted by wills or gifts, to official or dative guardianship, could be valid in the colony only between whites and whites, without any of the aforesaid dispositions being effected between one class and another, by any direct or indirect means."

although the Privy Council of Martinique took a stand against this view in 1829.[39] This restrictive legislation was finally abolished in September, 1830, during the reign of Louis Philippe. A later law dealing with intermarriage, the statute of June 11, 1839, was even more liberal than the Code Noir and greatly increased the number of manumissions. From then on, a slave was manumitted not only by being married to his or her master but even if he or she married a free person with the simple consent of the master. The law was retro-active, for anyone who had married a slave could claim that his or her spouse's master had given his consent.

One of the most efficacious ways devised in the Lesser Antilles for combatting the rapid increase of freedmen was taxation. The idea originated at an early date. It certainly was present in the custom which required the fathers of illegitimate children to pay a fine for the benefit of the church. The tax in question was at first assigned to the hospital—that is to say, to the church. Later, when the adminis-tration was larger, the tax was seen to be a by no means negligible benefit. In 1723, Governor General Pas de Feuquières and Intendant Bénard informed the minister of the navy that they had agreed to ap-prove the manumission granted by will to the Negro Paul and to his wife Marguerite on the condition that the heirs should pay "of their own free will" 200 livres to the hospital. At the same time, Paul himself would pay 400 livres.[40] At first the demand for payment was refused. The heirs then made various offers, and finally the slaves were taxed according to their ability to pay.

In 1745 the minister proposed a scheme to make the taxes on all the islands uniform. He suggested a tax of 1,000 livres for a man and 600 livres for a woman, except when freedom had been legally acquired in conformity with the Code Noir.[41] The administrators of the Windward Islands replied that it was more profitable to vary the tax according to the age of the applicants and their capacity to pay. By this procedure they sometimes got as much as 1,000 crowns—three times as much as the sum proposed.[42] A royal decree abolished this tax in February, 1766. The decree may have been effective in Saint Domingue, but in Martinique the tax did not disappear until 1831, during the reign of Louis Philippe. It had been a heavy burden on the budgets of the applicants for manumission.[43]

---

[39] Departmental Archives of Martinique, Privy Council, July 13, 1829, fols. 107 ff.

[40] Colonies, C8A.31, January 18, 1723.

[41] Ibid., B81, July 8, 1745, fol. 46.

[42] Ibid., C8A.57, January 20, 1746.

[43] The highest assessments had been those made in 1789. See Depart-mental Archives of Martinique, Royal Council, December 23, 1789, fol. 235: from birth to three years, 1,000; from three to seven years, 1,650; from seven to twelve years, 2,400; from twelve to forty years, 4,000; from forty to fifty years, 2,400; from fifty to sixty years, 1,000.

So effective were the statutes of 1713 and 1736, as well as the other methods taken to limit the number of freedmen, that there developed in the islands a new intermediary class between freedmen and slaves which was composed of those people who, having been unable to obtain de jure liberty in the islands, had obtained deeds of liberty abroad. This group was referred to as the *soi-disant libres* (nominally free), a term used by the administrators of the Lesser Antilles as early as 1723 and somewhat later in the parish records.[44] Prior to the French Revolution, the local governments on the islands paid considerable respect to these *soi-disant libre* deeds of emancipation, especially when they were not contested[45] or when they were old.[46] Thus, at least occasionally, the deeds served as a springboard to a legally free status. A striking example was Magdeleine Roblet. When she baptized her son Charles on December 2, 1751, she was clearly designated a *soi-disant libre*, or nominally free, woman. By 1761, however, she was being referred to as a "free mulatto," and, by the time of her marriage to Sieur Marcher, an upper-class white, on June 28, 1768, there was no mention of either her color or her status.[47]

During the Restoration, beginning in 1824, authorities in France tried to regularize the status of these *soi-disant libre* individuals. But the upper classes and the local governments on the islands looked upon this effort as an opportunity to take a firm stand and could not be persuaded to accept the directions of the metropolis. Despite a ministerial letter of May 2, 1828, which forbade the sale of all those individuals who for a long time had enjoyed a nominal state of liberty as unclaimed property, one Marie-Anne, a nominally free woman for thirty-six years, had been sold, as had a number of her children. The fact that she had also been listed in the census as "free" and had paid the poll tax required of all "free" people, that her children had been inscribed as "free" in the records of the civil authorities, and that her sons had served as freedmen in the militia clearly shows how precarious this nominal freedom was and how weak a deed of liberty granted abroad was as a guarantee of free status.[48]

Despite the precariousness of such a status and despite the fact that the practice of sending slaves abroad to obtain their freedom was prohibited in 1764,[49] the practice seems to have been very heavily

[44] Colonies, C8A.32, November 17, 1723, fol. 266.
[45] *Ibid.*, C8A.47, December 6, 1736, fol. 82.
[46] Adrien Dessales, *Histoire générale des Antilles*, 5 vols. (Paris, 1847–48), 3: 411 ff. In 1775, the administrators of Martinique declared that anyone who could produce a baptismal record for their mother which showed that she was "free" would be considered free.
[47] Departmental Archives of Martinique, parish registers.
[48] *Ibid.*, Privy Council, 1829, fol. 113.
[49] Decree of July 12, 1764, Martinique Code of Laws, 2.

used following the Seven Years' War,[50] as masters either sent slaves they wished to manumit abroad to get a deed of manumission or simply had certificates of freedom sent from abroad to the slaves.[51] Indeed, this practice appears to have been so common that we can only begin to estimate the number of nominally free in the French islands. The following table does, however, give some idea of the size of this group at the beginning of the reign of Louis Philippe.[52]

MANUMISSIONS PROMULGATED

By virtue of the statutes
of July 12, 1832, and April 29, 1836

From the end of 1830 to the application of the statute of July 12, 1832		Soi-Disant Libre			Slaves		
		Men	Women	Chil-dren	Men	Women	Chil-dren
Martinique	5,597	2,374	3,782	3,115	2,242	3,989	3,317
Guadeloupe	1,798	928	1,691	1,738	2,127	3,720	3,460
French Guiana	371	109	138	84	337	584	625
Bourbon	230	76	85	45	972	1,877	2,043
Total	7,996	3,487	5,696	4,982	5,678	10,170	9,445
		14,165			25,293		

Because the many manumissions issued from 1830 to 1832 mostly entered the same category as those which were grouped under the heading of *soi-disant libre*, this group ballooned, particularly in Martinique, where it was, in fact, more numerous than all those who had fallen into the official free category in 1826.[53] While many of these *soi-disant libre* had bought their freedom, they did not generally pay the poll tax for freemen. Their legal status was closer to that of the slaves than to that of the free, and their de facto status was equally low.

The early census returns provide only fragmentary data on the number of free colored people in the Antilles. While "whites, mulat-

[50] Colonies, B123, 1765, fol. 283: letter of the minister of the navy.
[51] National Archives of Martinique (SOM), Miscellaneous, box 666, dossier 3, January 30, 1838 (hereafter cited as SOM).
[52] Population, Cultivation, Trade, and Shipping Tables, Paris, 1851, SOM, p. 673.
[53] See p. 151 below.

toes, and blacks" are mentioned, no distinction is made between "free" and "slave" statuses.[54]

	Whites	Mulattoes	Blacks
Martinique, 1664	2,681	16	2,704
Saint Christopher, 1671	2,810	93	4,468

Between 1687 and 1694, the Caribs were entered separately in the census returns. The following figures include all the French possessions in tropical America.[55]

	1687	1688
Negroes	10,975	10,959
Negresses	9,197	8,926
Negro boys and girls	7,086	7,110
Mulattoes	638	734
Mulatto women	339	337
Caribs		
Free	299	312
Indentured	—	164

From 1696 in Martinique, 1697 in Guadeloupe, and 1703 in Saint Domingue, it is possible to note the growth of the free colored population, for this group was thenceforth noted in a separate entry. The remaining difficulty, then, is the probable lack of precision of the figures. The figures for Martinique are clearest.[56]

[54] Colonies, G1.470 (Martinique census) and G1.417 (Saint Christopher census). The fact that mulattoes were listed separately has led certain authors (for example, T. Baude, *L'affranchissement des esclaves aux Antilles Françaises* [Fort-de-France, Martinique, 1948], and E. Hayot, "Les gens de couleur libres du Fort-Royal, 1672–1823," *Revue Française d'Histoire d'Outre-Mer*, nos. 202 and 203, 1969) to consider them not only as being free but as being the only free colored people. In order to accept this hypothesis, we must exclude the Caribs and note that at that time there was not a single black who was free.

[55] Dessales, *Histoire générale des Antilles*, 2: 453 ff. He also records that, in 1687, nine Caribs were slaves. In 1688, the term "indentured" was perhaps used to replace "slave" when referring to non-free Caribs.

[56] The figures for 1696 were taken from Colonies, G1.470. Those for 1700 were taken from Alexandre Moreau de Jonnès, *Recherches statestiques sur l'esclavage colonial et les moyens de le suppremer* (Paris, 1842), p. 17. Those for 1715 and 1726 were found in Colonies, C8A.21, January 21, 1716, fol. 250, and C8A.37, February 16, 1727, fol. 14. The others were drawn from Dessales, *Histoire générale des Antilles*, 4: 574 ff.

148   LÉO ELISABETH

	1696	1700	1715	1726
Free Colored	505	507	1,029	1,304
Whites	6,435	6,597	8,735	10,959
Total free population	6,940	7,104	9,764	12,263
Percentage of free colored in total free population	7.2	7.1	10.5	10.1
Slaves	13,126	14,225	26,865	40,403
Total population	20,066	21,329	36,629	52,666
Percentage of free colored in total population	2.5	2.3	2.8	2.4

	1731	1734	1738	1751
Free Colored	1,204	810	1,295	1,413
Whites	11,957	12,705	14,969	12,068
Total free population	13,161	13,515	16,264	13,481
Percentage of free colored in total free population	8.6	5.9	7.9	10.4
Slaves	46,062	53,080	47,778	65,905
Total population	59,233	66,595	74,042	79,386
Percentage of free colored in total population	2.0	1.2	1.7	1.7

These figures indicate that from the early eighteenth century the number of free colored people among the total free population was very small, and that among the total population it was almost insignificant. It should be noted, however, that Intendant Mithon first argued that their number was excessive in 1704.[57] In Guadeloupe, the number of free colored was even smaller, and the percentages of free colored among the total free population and the total population were hardly more significant. In 1697, the free colored numbered 275 in Guadeloupe, or 10.6 percent of the total free population; they comprised only 3.7 percent of the total population of the island.[58]

About 1726, the free colored population of Martinique reached a

[57] Colonies, C8A.15, November 24, 1704, fol. 347.
[58] These figures were taken from Dessales, *Histoire générale des Antilles.* For Guadeloupe, one of the best studies is G. Lassere's "La Guadeloupe: Étude geographique" (thesis, University at Bordeaux, 1961), 1: 301 ff.

high point, but the role of this group in the society was already diminishing as a result of the repressive legislation introduced from 1713 onwards, legislation which ultimately impeded the group's numerical growth. After 1726, a substantial drop in numbers and percentages can be detected. This decrease is also found in the rather sparse figures we have for Guadeloupe: in 1730, the free colored there numbered 1,262; in 1767, they numbered only 762, or less than 1 percent of the total population. Later there was a resurgence in numbers, and we find, 1,175 in 1775 and 1,300 in 1784. Generally, however, the situation seemed more favorable in Saint Domingue. There were 500 free colored there in 1703, 1,500 in 1715, and around 3,000 in 1755.[59] We have no other figures, but we know that in 1734 the minister of the navy was astonished to note that in the previous year there had been a sharp increase in the number of colored people in Saint Domingue at the very moment when the opposite was occurring on Martinique.[60] To account for this variation, we must remember that the economy of Saint Domingue was in full swing and that the Lesser Antilles were undergoing an economic decline which began with the destruction of the cocoa plantations in Grenada in 1724 and in Martinique in 1727. Then, a series of natural catastrophes struck the islands, especially Guadeloupe. The year 1739 was terrible, and the small planters and farmers bore the brunt of the disaster.[61] An additional factor was the decree, published in 1724 and renewed in 1730, which subjected free colored people to the poll tax.[62] One result of these pressures was that a number of colored people emigrated. The administrators insisted that the free colored émigrés should go to the neutral islands.[63] Thus, in 1735, Governor General de Champigny estimated that there were about eighty free persons of color on the island of Saint Lucia.[64]

While the 1730s were marked by a decline in both the percentage and the absolute number of free persons, by the beginning of the Seven Years' War, the free colored in Martinique were regaining the numerical position relative to whites which they had reached around 1715. Not until after this war, however, did they reach a position among the total population comparable to that which they had held at the beginning of the century.[65]

[59] M. L. E. Moreau de St.-Méry, Description de la partie Française de Saint-Domingue, ed. Maurel and Taillemite, 4 vols. (Paris, 1958), 1: 8.

[60] Colonies, B61, June 29, 1734, fol. 437.

[61] See p. 148.

[62] See pp. 153–54 below.

[63] These islands were Dominica, Saint Lucia, and Saint Vincent.

[64] Colonies, C8A.46, December, 1735. This figure appears to be relatively low. The question therefore arises whether some of the colored émigrés did not go to Saint Domingue.

[65] The figures for 1764 were taken from Dessales, Histoire générale des Antilles, 5: 610; the other figures were published in Moreau de Jonnès, Recherches statestiques, p. 17.

150   LÉO ELISABETH

	1764	1776	1784	1789
Free Colored	1,846	2,892	3,472	5,235
Whites	11,634	11,619	10,150	10,636
Total free population	13,480	14,511	13,622	15,871
Percentage of free colored in total free population	13.6	19.3	25.4	33.3
Slaves	68,395	71,268	79,198	83,414
Total population	81,875	85,779	92,220	96,158
Percentage of free colored in total population	2.3	3.3	3.7	5.4

After 1764, much enhanced by the inclusion of the nominally free of the previous generation, the growth of the free colored population continued inexorably.[66] Only in 1784, however, did the colored people in Guadeloupe reach a numerical position among the free which was comparable to that of 1730, and in 1789 they still had not regained their place in the total population. In 1784, they numbered approximately 1,300—about 10 percent of the total free population. By 1789, they numbered 3,058.[67] To summarize, then, at the beginning of the French Revolution the free colored of Saint Domingue must have accounted for about 40 percent of the total free population, those of Martinique for about 33 percent, and those of Guadeloupe for 18 percent.[68] Their position among the free people at this time was relatively strong, and they had the potential to play an important part against the whites, should the occasion present itself. In terms of the bulk of the population, however, they constituted an insignificant minority: about 5 percent in Saint Domingue and Martinique and 3 percent in Guadeloupe.

The abolition of slavery by the decree of the National Convention in February, 1794, affected only Guadeloupe because Martinique was to be occupied by the British beginning in March, 1794. In 1802, slavery was re-established in Guadeloupe, and Richepanse ordered a scrutiny of all manumission papers. The efficacy of this operation is manifested in the census figures of 1804. The free colored numbered 3,058 in 1789, 14,310 in 1802, but only 6,705 in 1804. Contrary to

[66] See pp. 145–46 above.
[67] See Lasserre, "La Guadeloupe," 1: 302–3.
[68] There were said to be 12,000 free people in Saint Domingue in 1760 and 28,000 in 1789; see Debbasch, Couleur et Liberté, 1: 80 ff. The figures given here were taken from Moreau de St.-Méry, Description, 1: 85. The percentage of free colored given in relation to the total population was calculated from the same author's figures. Compare Colonies, F134, fol. 354.

the opinion of Debbasch[69] that a stable balance between the whites
and free colored had been attained by 1821, it was not until the beginning of Louis Philippe's reign that the number of free colored suggested the numerical balance Debbasch was looking for.

In Martinique, on the other hand, the upward trend remained
steady. The number of free colored almost doubled between 1789 and
1816, and, by the latter date, it equaled the number of whites.[70]

	1789	1802	1816	1826
Free Colored	5,235	6,578	9,364	10,786
Whites	10,636	9,826	9,298	9,937
Total free population	15,871	16,404	18,662	20,723
Percentage of free colored in total free population	33.3	40.0	50.1	52.0
Slaves	83,414	75,584	80,800	81,142
Total population	96,158	91,988	99,462	101,865
Percentage of free colored in total population	5.4	7.1	9.4	10.5

From the beginning of Louis Philippe's reign, the situation
changed rapidly.[71]

	1831	1835	1848
Free Colored	14,055	29,955	36,420
Whites	9,362	9,000	9,490
Total free population	23,417	37,955	45,910
Percentage of free colored in total free population	60.0	76.2	79.7
Slaves	86,499	78,076	67,447
Total population	109,916	116,031	120,357
Percentage of free colored in total population	12.8	24.9	32.0

[69] Debbasch, *Couleur et Libertè*, p. 263.
[70] These figures were taken from Moreau de Jonnès, *Recherches statestiques*, p. 17.
[71] These figures have been published by various writers, including Baude.
A striking contrast between Martinique and Guadeloupe may be noted: in

We do not know the figures for 1830, but the jump between 1826 and 1831 was due to the issuing of regular certificates to several thousand nominally free colored people. Between 1831 and 1835, the number of free colored doubled, as did their proportion in the total population. After 1835, there was a relative slowing of growth which suggests that, while the government of Louis Philippe did succeed in legitimizing the position of the nominally free, it failed in its program of progressively liberating the true slaves.

An examination of the numerical growth of the free colored pinpoints some of the factors which seem to have played a part in restricting the role which the free colored people played in the larger colonial society prior to the Revolution.

SOCIAL POSITION

Before the advent of the *Code Noir*, the free colored, particularly if they were not of mixed blood, apparently did not encounter any formidable restrictions in the legislation of the colonies. By Articles 57 and 59 of the edict of 1685, even the newly manumitted slaves of African origin were accorded privileges not given to whites of foreign origin or French immigrants.[72] The manumitted person did not need naturalization papers. Moreover, he was considered a creole, and as such did not have to pay a poll tax. While the principles laid down in these two articles were quite clear, Articles 35, 39, and 58 provided more specific pretexts for discrimination against freedmen: theft, the sheltering of runaway slaves, and lack of respect due to former masters and their families.[73]

Guadeloupe the free colored represented only 24 percent of the total population in 1848; see Lasserre, "La Guadeloupe," 1: 232, 233.

[72] Article 57 of the edict of 1685. See, for example, Dessales, *Histoire générale des Antilles*, 2: 470: "Déclarons leur affranchissement fait dans nos îles, leur tenir lieu de naissance dans nos dites îles, et les esclaves affranchis n'avoir besoin de nos lettres de naturalité pour jouir des avantages de nos sujets naturels, dans notre royaume, terres et pays de notre obéissance, encore qu'ils soient nés dans les pays étrangers."

Article 59 granted to manumitted slaves "the same rights, privileges, and immunities as are enjoyed by free-born people."

[73] Articles 35, 39, and 58 of the edict of 1685. See, for example, *ibid.*, pp. 465, 466, and 470:

Article 35. "Les vols qualifiés, même ceux de chevaux, cavales, mulets, boeufs ou vaches qui auront été faits par les esclaves ou par les affranchis seront punis de peines afflictives, même de mort si le cas le requiert."

Article 39. "Les affranchis qui auront donné retraite dans leurs maisons aux esclaves fugitifs, seront condamnés par corps envers le maître, en l'amende de trois cents livres de sucre par chacun jour de rétraction, et les autres personnes libres qui auront donné pareille retraite, en dix livres tournois d'amende par chacun jour de rétention."

Article 58. "Commandons aux affranchis de porter un respect singulier à leurs anciens maîtres, à leurs veuves et à leurs enfants en sorte que l'injure

These were fundamental articles, and they constituted the sources of later legislation which contributed to the creation of the "intermediate class" of free people of color: freedmen precluded by law from developing institutions and behavior which might generate links or feelings of solidarity with slaves. At the same time, this legislation precluded the free colored from all posts which might obligate a white to pay respect to a free person of color.

Poll Tax

Among the legal measures which were used to effect a rather clear distinction between the white creoles and the free colored, the poll tax was of great importance, for it ultimately placed a substantial and unequal burden on the free colored community. However, it was not so much the tax itself but the authorized exemptions from the tax which reinforced the racial distinctions that were hardening amid the colonial population. Originally, du Parquet, the early proprietor of Martinique, had exempted "white children born on the island" from this universal tax.[74] But, in 1691, a bylaw of M. de Baas exempted "all women and white girls from any country whatsoever," as well as "male and female creoles."[75]

The intentions of the local administration on the islands were always quite clear, even though the specific terms were not spelled out. For that reason Intendant Begon deemed it necessary to hand down a regulation in 1684 to make colored people submit to the poll tax.[76] However, this regulation could not be enforced, partly because of opposition to it, and partly because it was contrary to Article 59 of the *Code Noir*.[77] In 1689, the idea was renewed, however, and Intendant Dumaitz decided that Begon's ruling would not be applied to free-born mulattoes whose mothers were free mulatto women, but that it would be applied to all other colored people.[78] The preserva-

---

qu'ils leur auront fait soit punie plus grièvement que si elle était faite à une autre personne. Les déclarons toutefois francs et quitte envers eux de toutes autres charges, services et droits utiles que leurs anciens maîtres voudraient prétendre, tant sur leurs personnes que sur leurs biens et successions en qualité de patrons."

[74] Dutertre, *Histoire générale des Antilles*, 3: 157. The promise of du Parquet was renewed by de Tracy's ordinance of March 17, 1665. Debbasch (*Couleur et Libertè*, p. 27) believes that the mulattoes were subject to poll taxes. I am not so sure of this, because of the ease with which they seem to have entered the white group during this period.

[75] The interpretation of the regulations cited here is made all the more difficult by the ambiguous use of the term "creole." The Larousse Dictionary today considers that the word signifies a white born in the islands, but there is no basis for accepting this narrow interpretation, particularly in reference to the early period.

[76] See, for example, Colonies, C8A.9, May 26, 1696.

[77] See note 72 above.

[78] Colonies, C8A.6, May 26, 1689, fol. 136.

tion of a limited exemption for the free colored was marginally supported by some administrators who felt that free persons of color might otherwise give up their useful employment in the Lesser Antilles and migrate elsewhere.[79] But, in 1723, this last exemption clause was removed when Governor General Pas de Feuquières and Intendant Bénard informed the minister of the navy: "The tax collector says that he is astounded that some Negroes enjoy rights which *foreign whites*—a term including both foreign- and French-born— do not enjoy, and that it would be proper to cease giving such exemption to people of slave origin."[80] They argued that giving exemptions to free colored people would only encourage them to be disrespectful to whites. The minister gave way in the face of this opposition, and a statute of July 25, 1724, subjected all colored people to the poll tax.[81]

Mixed Marriages

One of the most consequential rights, because of its social consequences, was the freedom to contract mixed marriages. Since 1669, years before the *Code Noir*, Dutertre had expressed his disapproval of marriages between white women and mulattoes.[82] And, in 1667, official attempts had been made in Guadeloupe to restrict all mixed marriages.[83] Thus, in spite of the liberal tendencies of the *Code Noir*, efforts were being made to limit, penalize, and even forbid such unions. In 1727, on the pretext of discouraging unions between whites and slaves, the intendant of the Lesser Antilles asked for a royal decree forbidding the superiors of the religious orders to dispense with the posting of bans unless the "father, mother, guardians, and nearest relatives of both parties asked for them together."[84] This requirement of broad family approval was intended to render any proposed marriage between a white man and a colored woman practically impossible. Moreover, Europeans could not marry freely if they held important posts or were soldiers.

[79] *Ibid.*, C8A.9, May 12, 1697. The administrators of the Lesser Antilles thanked the minister for maintaining the exemption, telling him "cette grâce contribuera beaucoup à retenir ces sortes de gens dans les îles françaises étant donné que la nécessité de payer des droits a ci-devant engagé plusieurs d'entre eux à se retirer parmi les Caraïbes."

[80] *Ibid.*, C8A.32, September 27, 1723.

[81] See, for example, *ibid.*, C8A.34, January 25, 1725.

[82] Dutertre, *Histoire générale des Antilles*, 2: 479.

[83] Colonies, F3.133, fol. 36. See also, for example, Debbasch, *Couleur et Libertè*, p. 49. The December, 1667, decision of the Upper Council of Guadeloupe forbade "all monks, priests, and ecclesiastics to celebrate any marriage between a white and a black without the knowledge of the governor or the commander in chief of this island, and no notary may draw up a contract for such a marriage without the written permission of the aforesaid governor or commander in chief without having the deed nullified and having to pay a fine."

[84] Colonies, C8A.37, March 18, 1727.

Soon mixed marriages were additionally restricted by the application of penalties. In 1703, the Upper Council of Martinique refused to accept the validity of the claims of nobility of two brothers because they had married mulatto women. Reporting this to the minister, Governor General Machault supported the idea that they be deprived of their rank as nobles because of their shameful alliances, which would endow Negroes with the glorious status of gentlemen.[85] On this basis, the minister then generally approved the original decision of the Upper Council. In contrast, the patterns of control of mixed marriage on Saint Domingue were much less well established. In 1731, having observed that in the quarter of Jacmel at Cayes "there were very few pure whites" because of their frequent marriages with blacks, an administrator requested and obtained the authorization of the minister to exclude all whites thus married from all government posts.[86]

All of these measures proved to be insufficient, however, and a demand for a legal ban began to develop. It seems to have been expressed for the first time in Guadeloupe in 1711,[87] and in 1724 it appeared in Article 6 of the Louisiana Code, which prohibited marriage between whites and blacks. For some years, segregationists tried unsuccessfully to enact this measure in the Antilles. Finally, in 1741, in reply to a question from one of the administrators of French Guiana, the minister of the navy agreed that the mixing of white and Negro blood should not be allowed,[88] and in 1768 this letter was utilized against all persons of mixed blood in the colonies.[89] After the Seven Years' War, the proponents of a "legal" interdict became more and more active. Around 1780, it was rumored in Saint Domingue that a law would be introduced to forbid certain kinds of marriages in the colonies. Actually, this law had been prepared, but it was never published, probably in great part because it was not really necessary.[90]

[85] Ibid., C8A.15, September 21, 1703. Note that the council's decision was made in response to a specific case. After the Seven Years' War, the principle was applied not just to the occasional case but to everyone. Marchault's use of the word "Negro" certainly referred to children of color in general. Later, more specific appellations, such as "half-breed" or "quadroon," were used.

[86] Ibid., C9A.33, letter dated July 5, 1734. For Debbasch (Couleur et Liberté, p. 58), these prohibitions did not apply to descendants of Amerindians, but he himself showed that it was necessary to institute proceedings in order to have this fact accepted.

[87] Oruro Lara, La Guadeloupe (Paris, 1929), p. 52.

[88] Colonies, C14, September 18, 1741, fols. 89–90.

[89] Ibid., F3.91, January 13, 1768, fol. 120. The content of the letter of 1741 was known in the Lesser Antilles; see M. Santineau, Histoire de la Guadeloupe sous l'Ancien Régime, 1635–1789 (Paris, 1928), p. 354.

[90] Colonies, F3.92, fol. 494. For the period 1790 and 1799, Hayot ("Les gens de couleur libres," pp. 80–81) found only one case of a mixed marriage at Fort-Royal. For the period 1799 to 1825, the closing date of his survey, he was unable to find another. This is not astonishing, for these marriages were rigorously forbidden after 1805.

Illegitimacy

Thus we see that, from the beginning of the eighteenth century, mixed marriages faced more and more insurmountable obstacles. These restrictions in turn encouraged illegitimacy. Since the seventeenth century, the authorities had struggled to curb illegitimacy, though their efforts seem to have been limited largely to those illegitimate unions established between whites and slaves.

Articles 9 and 13 of the *Code Noir* prescribed penalties for moral laxity, but at the same time they encouraged people living in concubinage to marry.[91] The conflict created by these two principles made the enforcement of the penalties difficult. Apart from a few specific cases, legal prosecutions under the *Code*'s provisions had been abandoned by the beginning of the eighteenth century. Several lawsuits produced embarrassing charges against whites. Father Labat, for example, tells how a female slave ridiculed an overzealous priest before a tribunal in Martinique by stating that the priest was the father of her child.[92]

With regard to mixed marriages, the principle that the colonists immediately accepted was that one could not take the word of a slave against that of his master. More than twelve years after the publication of the *Code Noir*, certain prominent persons decided that Article 9 ought to be applied only to suppress concubinage between whites and slaves. Thus, colonial society admitted concubinage between colored people and their slaves, as well as that between whites and colored women. These whites could even look after the up-bringing of their illegitimate children in cases of necessity, though they could not legitimize them. Shortly before the Revolution, Dessales expressed the attitude of the whites on this subject quite well. "A white who marries a colored woman legally lowers himself from the status of a white and becomes the equal of the manumitted; he deserves to be classed beneath them."[93] Marriages between colored people and slaves were fought with the same vigor so as to avoid augmenting the number of freedmen and freedwomen.[94]

One can see how ineffective—in fact, counterproductive—the restrictions on mixed unions were by examining the illegitimate birth statistics that Hayot established for Fort-Royal between 1727 and 1823. We notice that from 1727 to 1749 the number of illegitimate births was slightly less than that of legitimate ones, 166:173. Between 1749 and 1759 the figures inverted to 100:91. Then, between 1800 and 1823, the situation changed dramatically as, apparently,

---

[91] Articles 9 and 13 of the edict of 1685; see p. 142 above.

[92] Labat, *Voyage*, 1: 215 ff.

[93] Dessales, *Histoire générale des Antilles*. In his third volume, page 292, Dessales reproduces quotations from the "Annals" of his grandfather Regis Dessales, which were written in 1786.

[94] See pp. 142–43 above.

the old restrictions broke down completely. During that time there were only 425 legitimate births for every 1,000 illegitimate ones.[95]

Names

Today, many colored people in the Antilles are known by what seem to be Christian names, names which they use as surnames. This practice makes it relatively simple to distinguish persons of color from whites in older records, but the practice developed gradually, and some persons of color have the same surnames as whites. To explain this seeming anomaly, it has occasionally been argued that, in the early stages of colonization, certain manumitted persons took the names of their former masters. While this is possible, what is quite certain is that some family names were passed on to illegitimate children. This can be demonstrated by examining parish registers, for priests inscribed the names of the fathers of illegitimate children there. This curious practice was called into question in 1752 by a few prominent persons who had been annoyed by the publication of their names at the weddings of persons of color.[96]

The principle that certain names belonged solely to white families was first publicly propounded about 1752. Not until 1763, however, was the first decree forbidding colored people to adopt the names of whites promulgated in Guadeloupe.[97] The same prohibition was extended to Martinique and Saint Domingue in 1773.[98] In the decree issued in Saint Domingue, it was precisely stated that mothers must give their illegitimate offspring names drawn from African tradition, their work, or their color.[99] A decree issued in 1803 in Martinique obliged colored freedmen and freedwomen to take a surname, though not that of their masters or of any white, under pain of a fine.[100] Finally, a royal decree of 1836 made it obligatory for the newly manumitted to take a surname. This name could not be that of a family existing on the island unless consent had been granted. Some freedmen chose their own names, but the majority could not. Occasionally, those who received their certificates of manumission plumbed the depths of mythology, their trades, and nature. In other cases, anagrams of the masters' names were used. A special case was the formation of names based on maternal christian names. This practice was accepted in Martinique after the interdictions of 1773–

---

[95] Hayot, "Les gens de couleur libres," pp. 65 ff.

[96] Colonies, C8A.59, August 21, 1752 (letter from Intendant Hurson).

[97] *Ibid.*, F3.236, fol. 176.

[98] Durand-Molard, *Code de la Martinique*, 5 vols. (Saint-Pierre, 1807–14), 3: 151.

[99] Colonies, F3.269.

[100] Durand-Molard, *Code de la Martinique*, 3: 589. These distinctions were made to eliminate the possibility that a white man bearing the same name as a colored man might be suspected of being colored himself. See, for example, Satineau, p. 352.

74. For example, at Anses d'Arlets in 1787, Joseph, the free mulatto son of Rosine, a free Negress, married Rose, the free mulatto daughter of Beatrice, a free Negress, on June 26. It is quite clear that neither had inherited his or her father's name, so, in July, 1788, Joseph became Joseph Rosine.[101]

Education

Access to education is an important factor in determining the role which a group may come to play in a society. Hayot has surveyed the signatures of free colored people in the parochial registers at Fort-Royal, beginning with 1710. His figures indicate that, after 1750, only a few could not sign their names. This would be highly significant were it not possible that the same influential persons of color had been chosen as witnesses, godfathers, and godmothers. A study of the notarial registers of the French Admiralty offices presents a much less rosy picture. The registers of the Admiralty offices at Bordeaux, for example, reveal only eighty-five signatures among 3,242 slaves and 358 free colored.[102] The distribution of these signatures is as follows: fifteen between 1740 and 1767; sixty-seven between 1768 and 1787, forty-five of which were recorded between 1772 and 1778; and three (colored students) in 1777. These eighty-five persons can be classified as follows:

Men	Women	Age
4	3	Over 30
24	2	21–30
28	8	19–20
11	1	Under 16
2	2	Unknown

All were creoles except one slave from Saint Domingue. All were mulattoes except one mestizo, two Negresses, and two Negroes. Only twelve of the total were slaves. All things considered, if one looks strictly at the free colored, rather than at the entire colored popula-

[101] Departmental Archives of Martinique, parochial registers of Anses d'Arlets.
[102] Concerning the problem of the education of colored people in France, see Raimond's ideas for the pre-revolutionary period in "Observations into the Origins and the Spread of Prejudices," p. 7, cited by Debbasch in *Couleur et Liberté*, p. 89. In Raimond's opinion, it was after 1740 that colored parents began sending their children from Saint Domingue to France. On the other hand, it is interesting to note that the nuns in the Cap district of Saint Domingue had more colored girls than white in their schools.

tion, their education was considerable. From 1737 to 1787, of the 206 freemen and the 152 freewomen who registered at Bordeaux, 73—or slightly more than one-third—knew how to sign their names.[103]

After the Seven Years' War, expansion of the education of colored people in Martinique began to be regarded as a danger. On May 8, 1765, the Upper Council ruled that it was improper to employ colored people in notaries' offices and forbade them to follow this profession. In 1802, Villaret-Joyeuse tried to close the schools of the colored people of Martinique because he believed that "the abuses of enlightenment are often the base of revolution."[104]

In any case, in the West Indies, free colored people received only an elementary education until the time of the July monarchy. After 1830, they began to seek higher education in France, for this was a period when the professions began to be opened to them. The students who sought such education were chiefly the sons of artisans and merchants—that is, town citizens. Many stayed in France, thus considerably decreasing the number of colored with higher education in the islands.[105]

Economic Role

As early as the end of Louis XIV's reign, the notables of the Windward Islands and the colonial administrators demonstrated their hostility to the growth of the position of free colored in the colonial

[103] Departmental Archives of Bordeaux, Admiralty Office of Guyenne, ser. B.

[104] See, for example, Hayot, "Les gens de couleur libres," p. 95, or H. Gisler, L'esclavage aux Antilles Françaises (Fribourg, 1965), p. 89. The text is based on Colonies, C8A.105. Villa ret Joyeuse failed in his appeal. In 1805, Moreau de Jonnès noted the particular care which colored people took to educate their children, but he was surely thinking only of the colored elite when he said that almost all of them could read and write. His view is approximately the same as Hayot's.

[105] After about 1840, the elementary education of free colored children on Martinique was handled mainly by the Brothers of Christian Education of Ploërmel, to whom the minister of the navy and the colonies had given a contract on May 16, 1837. They opened nine boys' schools between 1840 and 1848, the first being opened at Fort-Royal. On April 7, 1841, this school was run by four brothers of Ploërmel and had an enrollment of 262 pupils, all colored. By 1850, the pupils numbered 438, including 15 whites. Another school was opened at Saint-Pierre, where there were four brothers and 260 colored pupils on April 17, 1841. By 1850, there were eleven brothers and 978 pupils, including 6 whites. At the same time, there were two brothers and 140 pupils, including 6 whites in Trinité; three brothers and 260 pupils at Marin; three brothers and 220 pupils at Lamentin; two brothers and 119 pupils, including 5 whites, at Saint-Esprit; six brothers and 140 pupils at Mouillage; two brothers and 168 pupils at Vauclin; and two brothers and 170 pupils, including 10 whites, at François. After 1842, girls were looked after by the nuns of Saint Joseph de Cluny, who opened seven schools between 1842 and 1848. In 1850, they had thirteen schools with 2,170 pupils. In theory, these schools had been opened for slaves, but the local authorities reserved them for free colored children. These figures were supplied by B. David by personal communication.

economy. Colored transporters were the first to arouse jealousy. As far back as 1710, de Gabaret, governor of Martinique, had informed the minister of the navy that there were a number of passenger boats on the island, most of which belonged to free Negroes. He recorded his view that the boat fares were too high and the enterprises in need of regulation. The administration then tried to finance a transportation business, but the attempt failed because of the scarcity of funds.[106]

Tavernkeepers were the second free colored group to come under attack. The reports of Intendant Mithon in 1704 and of Governor General Phélippeaux between 1711 and 1713 suggest that tavernkeeping was one of the most important occupations of the free colored people. According to Mithon, these tavernkeepers were "thieves and receivers of stolen goods." According to Phélippeaux, they also sheltered "run-away slaves, and, above all, Babet and her sisters were very insolent."[107] Clearly, the disturbances attributed to the colored innkeepers should not be exaggerated. As Phélippeaux himself hinted, the disturbances he attributed to Babet and her sisters did not amount to much, inasmuch as "all the inhabitants of Saint-Pierre shrug their shoulders when these facts are mentioned."[108]

Tavernkeeping was not the most prominent occupation of the free colored, but it was certainly one of only a few paths to financial success. One notable instance of such success was that of Marie, sis-

---

Hayot has observed that nine colored teachers and schoolmasters were listed in the parochial registers of Fort-Royal between 1788 and 1821; see his "Les gens de couleur libres," pp. 50 ff.

[106] Labat (*Voyage*, p. 195) narrates the story of Louis Galère, a free Negro who had set up a very prosperous passenger-carrying company between Saint-Pierre and Fort-Royal. In 1694, "Louis Galère had been carrying on that trade for two or three years and had been so successful, though others had imitated him, that, when I left the island, he owned more than twenty slaves, three or four passenger boats, and a fishing 'seine,' which constituted a rather large fortune." See also Colonies, C8A.19, September 10, 1713 (letter of Vaucresson); C8A.17, December 12, 1710 (letter of Gabáret); and C8A.19, October 6, 1713. In 1713, there were twenty-five passenger boats at Saint-Pierre.

[107] The Mithon statement is found in Colonies, C8A.15, November 20, 1704. For Phélippeaux's remarks, see *ibid.*, C8A.18, May 24, 1712, fol. 297. Intendant Vaucresson declared in 1713 that there were more than 200 taverns at Saint-Pierre, but he did not say that their owners were all colored people; see *ibid.*, C8A.19, June 20, 1713. Hayot ("Les gens de couleur libres," p. 36) notes that there was one at Saint-Pierre in 1768; see Colonies, F3.248. But, by 1775, there seem to have been quite a few at Saint-Pierre; see Departmental Archives of Martinique, Royal Council, 1775, fol. 126. Hayot counted twelve taverns in the parish registers of Fort-Royal between 1786 and 1823. In 1824, a ministerial dispatch recommended the exclusion by all prudent measures of all free colored people from the trades which could be carried on only under the scrutiny of the police, such as tavernkeeper, innkeeper, and so forth; see Baude, *L'affranchissement des esclaves.*

[108] Phélippeaux's letter is found in Colonies, C8A.19, April 6, 1713, fol. 75.

ter of the aforementioned Babet. A gift she was said to have made to an administrator's wife was supposed to have been worth 500 crowns, and Babet herself gave financial assistance to a widow La Palu, who claimed that Babet was her slave. Perhaps because of the financial success of these enterprising women, Governor General Phélippeaux sought a law forbidding newly freed slaves to become tavern-keepers.[109]

Such a law would necessarily have conflicted with Articles 47 and 59 of the *Code Noir*. Nevertheless, the whites of the islands were, at least from the beginning of the eighteenth century, extremely hostile to the acquisition of wealth by free persons of color. An ordinance dated February 3, 1720, forbade the participation of free colored persons in the gold and silver trades. The most important of the early ordinances restricting participation of the free colored in the colonial economy was the royal decree of February 1726, which ran directly counter to Articles 56, 57, and 59 of the *Code Noir*. The decree declared that free persons of color could not receive the bequests of white persons.[110] Significantly, the reverse was not proscribed. It is not clear who pressed for the application of the 1726 decree in the Windward Islands. Even Dessales regarded it as ridiculously unenforceable—the parties could always establish an arrangement outside of a formal will, and evasion was facilitated by the use of trusts. When local authorities found enforcement impossible, they simply held that it was the central government's responsibility to see that the decree was obeyed.[111] In the end, the decree was not promulgated at all in Saint Domingue, though the local tribunals eventually took a similarly restrictive stance on bequests.

The purpose of the 1726 royal edict seemed to be to discourage concubinage between whites and blacks by placing white and non-white children on very different legal footings; it also provided the leaders of the islands with a tool to curb guardianships. Dessales, for one, thought it a "strange sight" that, in 1727, a "rich mulatto" of "honorable birth" should be the guardian of a white girl in Saint Domingue. This guardian, Bathelemy Loppes, was closely watched by the authorities, and, once his conduct had, as one might expect, been censured by the authorities, he was arraigned and convicted of having squandered his ward's fortune. As far as Dessales was concerned, Loppes' color had nothing to do with his case.[112] Obviously,

---

[109] *Ibid.*, C8A.18, May 24, 1712, fol. 297.

[110] For the texts of Articles 56, 57, and 59, see notes 27 and 72 above.

[111] See Dessales, *Histoire générale des Antilles*, 4: 233. Dessales neglected the likelihood of converse evasion. The descendants or trustees of a benefactor more than occasionally failed to keep the word of the trusts which they were to guarantee. The heirs or trustees occasionally went so far as to attempt to sell the intended beneficiary of the trust.

[112] Dessales (*ibid.*) quotes M. L. E. Moreau de St.-Méry's *Lois et constitution des colonies françaises de l'Amérique sous le vent*, 6 vols. (Paris, 1784–89), 3: 198.

however, the full system of colonial justice was neither blind to color nor oblivious to the racial divisions and jealousies in the society. The famous Babet won a case before the judges,[113] but the governor general rejected the decision. More explicit were the complaints lodged against Governor General Ricourd and Intendant de la Varenne in 1717 by several free colored persons who had been unable to sustain proceedings against some white persons. The judges had admitted their cases before the court but the intendant had proceeded to place the colored litigants in the position of the accused and found them guilty because *"tous les nègres et négresses libre sont des scélérats pour la plupart et des recéleurs."*[114]

Notwithstanding these early efforts to restrict the economic activities of the free people of color, it was only after the Seven Years' War that attempts to destroy the free colored community became obsessive. The competition of free colored people was increasingly seen by whites to be dangerous in all fields except smallholder farming. A royal decree forbade free colored people from practicing medicine, surgery, and pharmacy in 1764, and another, in 1765, prohibited the employment of free persons of color as, or in the offices of, clerks of court, notaries, and bailiffs. At this time, whites frequently complained that there were too many colored persons in the trades. Finally, on January 3, 1788, a decree compelled free colored people to apply for permits to carry on trades other than that of farming.

To these measures were added several others which were merely vexatious. For instance, in 1765, free people of color were prohibited from assembling for feasts, and, in 1781, it was forbidden to designate free colored people as "Monsieur" or "Madame" in official deeds. In Martinique, this series of decrees was for the most part abolished in 1789, but the new codes of 1799, 1802, and 1805 generally reinstated the prohibitions of the 1760s. Only one curious modification was made. On March 12, 1806, a new decree allowed white people to receive donations from colored persons and to become the guardians of their children. These discriminatory provisions finally disappeared at the beginning of Louis Philippe's reign.

The restrictive legislation of the eighteenth century suggests that the free colored had an important place in the colonial economy and that they offered threatening competition to the resident whites. Many colored people were in the small trades and crafts. As early as the beginning of the eighteenth century, they distinguished themselves in the building trades. Father Labat notes that the colored joiners were greatly valued by the colonists and that the work of a Negro was actually preferred over that of a white.[115] According to

[113] Colonies, C8A.18, March 31, 1711, fol. 18.
[114] *Ibid.*, C8A.23, 1717, fol. 107.
[115] Labat, *Voyage* (1722 ed.), 3: 429.

Hayot, their craft at Fort-Royal was the oldest and one from which several persons of prominence emerged with considerable fortunes. For the period from 1700 to 1823, Hayot has counted 210 joiners, 36 of whom were given the title of *maître*.[116]

Beyond the small traders, craftsmen, and perhaps a larger number of smallholder farmers, the free colored "community" played a limited role in the economy of the Antilles. The free colored of Saint Domingue, however, seem to have been considerably better off than those of the Windward Islands. Yet, one must be somewhat skeptical of the claims that show great achievements on the part of free colored persons in Saint Domingue. Most of these claims—such as that made by Oge in 1789 that the free colored community owned one third of the riches of the island and could pay patriotic contributions amounting to six million francs, "which would represent but the fiftieth part of their wealth"[117]—were clearly directed toward a metropolitan public weighing the desirability of allying with an overseas colored elite. Whatever the exaggeration, free colored people were often seriously regarded by the whites as tireless workers whose enrichment was to be feared. Such was the view of M. de la Rochalar in Saint Domingue in 1731, when he pointed out that, thanks to their thrift, the blacks could purchase properties more easily than whites. Already in these years, people were noting the great enterprise of women of color and of the numerous whites who desired to benefit, and did benefit, from marriages to them.[118]

While numbers of free colored were in the trades and crafts, before the Revolution, anyway, most of the free colored were peasant farmers. In the rural areas, they often played the role of pioneers.[119] In Martinique, they got nothing but small land grants. All the same, by 1717, Louis Tiffaigne, a freedman at Anses d'Arlets, had accumulated properties worth more than 80,000 francs.[120] He was clearly an exception, however. In 1732, Governor General Champigny and Intendant d'Orgeville noted that "just about the only landowners who till the earth themselves are the free colored" and, further, that they produced little but foodstuffs.[121] In 1734, a report indicated that the part the free colored played in producing the tapioca meal needed by the large plantations was rather important. De Givry, a commissioner

[116] Hayot, "Les gens de couleur libres," pp. 20 ff. It should be noted that, at this time, few colored workers were being trained in France. European workers sometimes married colored women, and the result was often that their skills were handed down through the mulatto family.

[117] Debbasch, *Couleur et Libertè*, p. 159.

[118] Peytraud, *L'esclavage aux Antilles Française*, chap. 3.

[119] Debbasch, *Couleur et Libertè*, p. 80. In particular, Debbasch cites Moreau de St.-Méry to show the role of colored pioneers in Jeremie parish. The role of pioneer also belonged to the free colored settling on the neutral islands.

[120] Colonies, C8A.23, 1717, fol. 107.

[121] *Ibid.*, C8A.43, September 17, 1732.

from the Admiralty, informed his superiors that the price of meal was rising every day and that the trouble arose from the fact that "several small farmers and even mulattoes and free Negroes had given up the growing of the crop," replacing it with coffee.[122] He offered the opinion that free colored people should be prohibited from growing coffee.

Thus, while some of the prominent whites of Martinique thought that export crops should be reserved for whites, it was never suggested that the free colored should be excluded from farming altogether. Until 1788, they were allowed to engage in it without a license. Increasingly, whites drew distinctions between the free colored in farming and those in non-agricultural occupations. During the Restoration, in a dispatch dated February 25, 1824, one minister strongly advised militia recruiters to pick the petty officers from among the free colored people who were agriculturalists.[123]

In Saint Domingue, where much more land was available, there were, as already noted, a few large landowners of color. According to Malouet, some owned sugar refineries and two or three hundred slaves.[124] Before the Revolution, upward mobility for the free colored of Saint Domingue typically involved the movement of artisans to commerce and then to the ownership of land, but with fewer restrictions on the aggrandisement of estates than has been noted for Martinique. By contrast, for the Martiniquan free colored, the primary route to a higher economic standing was certainly through urban proprietorship. One source, Moreau de Jonnès, argued that persons of color owned considerable numbers of houses at Saint-Pierre and Fort-Royal in Martinique and at Pointe-à-Pitre in Guadeloupe.[125] It seems that towns, in particular, provided a milieu which was favorable to the upward mobility and enrichment of the free colored community. This fact may very well account for the overcrowding of the towns at the beginning of the nineteenth century and especially under Louis Philippe.[126]

[122] *Ibid.*, C8A.47, April 11, 1736.

[123] Baude, *L'affranchisement des esclaves*, p. 26.

[124] Pierre-Victor Malouet, *Collection de memoires et correspondances officielles sur l'administration des colonies*, vol. 5 (Paris, 1802), p. 127.

[125] Alexandre Moreau de Jonnès, "Recherches historiques sur les affranchis ou gens de couleur libres des îles de la Martinique et de la Guadeloupe . . ." (1816), Public Records, SOM, DFC, Martinique, no. 518.

[126] Debbasch (*Couleur et Libertè*, pp. 261 ff.) quotes the reports of Inspectors Pichon (Public Records, SOM, Guadeloupe, no. 282, p. 41) and de la Mardelle (*ibid.*, Martinique, no. 249, pp. 46 ff.). These records suggest that there were *"grands commerçants de couleur"* in the Antilles during the Restoration. We must not, however, exaggerate the number of these elite few. In 1829, the Privy Council of Martinique reported that at least half of the freed slaves were not landowners (Departmental Archives of Martinique, Privy Council, 1829, fol. 110), though this may be an underestimation of the true proportion. What seems clear is that success for the free colored was not so difficult in the towns as in the country, where they were excluded from the

Several writers in the eighteenth century compared the motivation and enterprise of white and colored citizens. In the early part of the century, observers noted the considerable economic enterprise of free women of color. Assertions of laziness on the part of freedmen did not become pronounced until after the Seven Years' War.[127] They become notably marked under Louis Philippe. The apparently gradual appearance of the white ascription of idleness and sloth to the free colored community is a problem which merits serious study. This theme of opprobrium arose in the face of the fact that the newly freed had very often used their wages to purchase their freedom. Looking beyond the tides of "thieves and concubines," it is clear that the enterprise of the free colored, while increasingly attacked by colonial legislation throughout the eighteenth century, was sustained over a very long period by a motivational base associated with the self-purchase of manumission.

THE FREEDMAN AND SLAVERY

As the free colored labored and occasionally found success in their enterprise, some became slaveowners, and this seems to have occurred throughout the history of the Antilles up to the time of abolition. It was only under Louis Philippe, however, that the numbers of slaves owned by the colored people of Martinique became apparent. In 1844, there were 76,117 slaves in Martinique, 12,348 of which belonged to persons of color. There were at this time 36,626 free persons of color, or roughly three freedmen for every slave owned by a freedman. At the same time, there were 9,139 whites and

---

best lands. Moreover, under Louis Philippe, town workers generally earned more. Concerning the size of the free colored population in the towns of Martinique, Hayot ("Les gens de couleur libres," p. 21) gives the following figures for 1822:

	Whites	Free Colored	Total Free	Slaves
Fort-Royal	1,127	1,642	2,769	6,431
Saint-Pierre	2,854	2,755	5,609	12,413

It should be noted that some of those recorded here as "slaves" were actually de facto free colored people.

[127] See, for instance, Jean-Marie Pardon, La Guadeloupe depuis sa découverte jusqu'à nos jours (Paris, 1881), p. 170: "The town worker works little, two or three days a week; his pay is enough for him for the rest of the week." A similar statement is found in the Public Records, SOM—for example, in box 156, dossier 1299, September, 1836. The problem is also raised in a report dated January 25, 1765, and preserved within the Martinique Code of Laws, 2: 309.

63,769 slaves owned by whites, or, roughly, one white for every seven slaves owned by whites on the island. So, while colored people, on the whole, possessed less human chattel, their interests in regard to slavery tended to converge with the interests of white planters. This explains, at least in part, the apparent contradiction that, while frequently charged with harboring runaway slaves, the free colored community was basically responsible for their capture.

In various ways, the white colonial community managed to hinder the growth of feelings of racial solidarity between the free and slave colored. They succeeded in doing so, for the most part, by tempering the enforcement of segregation laws and by granting exceptions and favors to a certain number of free colored people.

Outwardly, the free colored formed a racial group that some people have called the "intermediate class." The word "class" should not mislead us, however, for in this instance it encompasses various social levels or statuses. At the top were the people whose freedom had perhaps been recently secured, but who, by education and way of life, were closely connected with the white artistocracy. For instance, Alexandre Dumas, the son of General Dumas, was the grandson of the marquis de la Pailleterie. The great leaders at the beginning of the Revolution—Oge and Raimond—belonged to the group whose color was not far from that of the whites. At the foot of the ladder were people whose status was much nearer that of the slaves; some of these had been born in Africa. This stratum included some colored slaveowners, but all were small owners, and they presumably emancipated their slaves more readily. Their own emancipation and the emancipation of their relatives were often intimately bound up with their position as slaveowners, and some of their slaves were in fact close relatives. In some instances, the small slaveowners kept their relatives in the bonds of slavery until they had repaid the money paid for them. More often, until the reign of Louis Philippe, they held their fathers, mothers, concubines, children, and other relatives in an official state of slavery because they were unable to pay the emancipation tax. The slaveowner himself was often in debt to another freedman or to a white for his own manumission or for debts contracted while manumitting others. It was a complex cycle.

Notarial records and parish registers provide the details of a large number of cases of this kind. At notary Lefébure's office in Fort-Royal, a deed dated April 22, 1777, reads: "Marguerite, called Bichonne, and Judith, both free colored women at Fort-Royal, fully satisfied and pleased with the good behavior and work of their daughters Madelon, a sixteen-year-old creole Negress, and Marie-Adelaïde, an eighteen-year-old creole mulatto, their slaves," wanted to reward them by freeing them, but they could not pay the emancipation tax. Thus, they entered into an agreement with the chevalier de la Bretonnière, a major in the Martinique regiment, who would take the girls in as maidservants for two years, paying board and lodging but not wages. At the end of the period, he would emancipate them at his own expense.[128]

RESISTANCE TO OPPRESSION

The people of color in the French Antilles were not always quiet in the face of suffering and repression, but it was not until the time of the French Revolution that the first instances of violent collective resistance occurred on the islands. Before then, the emigration of trained workers to neutral islands, or the threat of such migration, and petitioning were the principal implements of resistance—the former being effective, the latter usually not.

Petitions by the free colored began to appear rather early, though, beyond an occasional reference to them in the records of those to whom they were addressed, we know little about the earliest ones. The first petitions appear to have been motivated by the inequities discerned in the application of the poll tax discussed earlier in this chapter. Thus, in 1727, a petition signed by the colored people of Martinique reached Versailles. In this case, the free colored were not at odds with all white planters, for some had joined them in petitioning against the general capitation out of fear that an inequitable poll tax would drive the "useful" free colored from the island.

Following the Seven Years' War, petitioning freedmen could usually count on the support or assistance of protectors in metropolitan France, a pattern of political alliance that continued into the revolutionary period. By the beginning of the Revolution, however, the role of the intermediaries had been considerably reduced by pressures from the white communities on the islands. Toward the end of 1789, Seneschal Ferrand des Beaudieres, a white man, was hanged for assisting with a petition presented by the colored communities of Léogane and Petit Goâve. A few months later, in June, 1790, the violent edge of revolution was sharpened when thirty-four free colored militiamen were hanged in Saint-Pierre rioting after having followed up a petition calling for permission to participate in the Corpus Christi procession with a physical demonstration. The whites who had assisted with their petition were attacked. Even when the intermediaries in the colonies and France began drifting away, petitioning went on through direct appeals to local administrators, the central power, or metropolitan public opinion, a section of which generally supported the free colored beginning in the 1770s.

In this regard, developments in Saint Domingue played a key role in linking events in metropolitan France with the issues raised by the free colored in the Antilles. By the 1780s, the free colored elite from Saint Domingue were attempting to organize the free colored community and to build support for themselves in France. Working

[128] SOM, Notary, Lefébure, 1777.

with a core of wealthy Saint Dominguan mulattoes in Paris, Raimond on the eve of the Revolution founded the Sociéte des Colons Americains, a nearly stillborn group which could not even claim the support of the colored elite in France.[129] Their position was ambiguous. They were not democrats. Because many were slaveowners, their attempts to build ties with the Club Massiac failed, and they subsequently turned for support to the Society of Friends of the Blacks.

Mainly because of their inability to break out of their own class, the elite leaders of the Saint Dominguan free colored population rapidly lost the initiative they had demonstrated earlier. On the island itself, a white proletariat had arisen in the towns, apparently from the number of poor whites who had recently landed in the West Indies. These people were indisposed to cooperate with the free colored, with whom they competed for work and power. On many issues, they were able to place themselves between metropolitan decrees and the local free colored, blocking attempts to grant civil rights to the free colored.

Even when they had the opportunity, the free colored of Saint Domingue were unwilling to form political alliances with the slaves, and, when the slaves revolted, the moment of opportunity passed. In 1796, two free mulattoes, Villate and Rigaud, gained political control of some of the countryside, but they themselves were not united, and they eventually became embroiled in conflicts with Negroes. By 1800, the old free colored community represented by Rigaud had been effectively eliminated from participation in the government of the island by Toussaint and his followers.

By contrast, on the eve of the Revolution, the free colored in Martinique were able to make more effective use of their ambiguous place in society. As in Saint Domingue, in the late 1780s the poor whites of Martinique were emerging as an important political force and were prepared to act against the free colored. Concerned about the excitement among the island's "patriots" (largely poor whites, but also including some businessmen), Governor de Viomesnil in September, 1789, began to move tentatively toward an alliance with the free colored of Fort-Royal. After the June, 1790, massacre over the Corpus Christi incident, the free colored themselves began to swing toward alliance with the "aristocrats," or supporters of the *ancien régime*. By 1791, the coalition of wealthy landowners and free colored was effectively in control of the Windward Islands.

By 1792, the free colored clearly were in an ascendant position, for, after a period of public restlessness following the news of the

[129] See Debbasch, *Couleur et Libertè*, pp. 144 ff. See also G. Debien, "Gens de couleur libres et colons de Saint-Domingue devant la Constituante," *Revue d'histoire de l'Amérique Française*, March, 1951, pt. 3, p. 15; and *idem*, "Les colons de Saint-Domingue et lax Revolution: Essai sur le Club Massiac, August, 1789–August, 1792" (Ph.D. diss., Faculty of Letters, University of Paris, 1953).

flight of the king, they took the initiative in rallying the Colonial Assembly at Fort-Royal to the side of the republic. The new alliance of free colored and republicans enabled the colored population to participate in the administration and in the officer corps of the militia on a large scale. By the end of 1793, however, a Martiniquan planter, de Percin, began to rouse his friends to revolt against the domination of the government by persons of color. The insurgent planters appealed to the British, and the emerging conflicts among race, class, and national loyalties began to cause divisions among the free colored. In the early months of 1794, the republican alliance collapsed, some free colored moved to the British side, which was considered faithful to the old regime, and eight years of British occupation began.

Under the British, the restrictive laws of the post–Seven Years' War period were reimposed. The abolition of slavery decreed by the National Convention on February 4, 1794, was not applied to Martinique, because of the occupation by Britain. By contrast, in Guadeloupe the abolition decree had been promulgated, and Britain's attempt to occupy that island was cut very short. The older free colored group played a considerable role in the government of Guadeloupe between the end of the British occupation in 1794 and the re-establishment of strong metropolitan control in 1802. It was a period of progressive liberalization for the free colored; however, with the arrival of Governor Richepanse in 1802, the old restrictions on the free colored were reintroduced and slavery was reinstated. Though the free colored followers of a Colonel Delgrès, himself a mulatto, revolted, there was little movement toward alliance with the slaves. Rather, just the reverse occurred—the free colored of Guadeloupe moved quickly to the side of the British when they saw that because of Britain's occupation the abolition decree would be set aside.[130]

During the Restoration, a violent reaction swept down upon the free colored communities of the French Antilles. It seems to have been particularly virulent in Martinique, where, at the time, the free colored were more numerous than whites. The few ministerial initiatives aimed at easing the system of oppression were resisted by the privy councils on the islands. In Martinique, the public outcry was considerable as well. Thus, in 1820, the free colored people of Fort-Royal, having ventured to hand a petition to de la Mardelle—who had arrived to preside over the reorganization of the system of justice —became the objects of violent outburst from the white *colons*. The whites were prepared to take advantage of the slightest pretext in order to crush the "plots" of the free colored.

Significantly, the free colored did play an active role amid the remonstrations and rising fears of the whites. They remained the core of the local militia and were used to repress the "plots" which the whites attributed to the very same free colored community. An exam-

[130] Lassere, "La Guadeloupe," 1: 287.

ple of the overreaction of the whites in Martinique was the response to a pamphlet printed in France by a mulatto named Bisette and a few friends in the early 1820s. An appeal for the rights of the colored,[131] the pamphlet was distributed in France and in Guadeloupe without raising particular objection. But in Martinique in 1823 it was seen as the germ of a new plot, and the violence of the repression resulted in a wave of emigration and a decrease in the free colored population of the island between 1822 and 1826. In the aftermath of the Bisette case, the white colonists were in complete control. The system of segregation was stiffened; one clear example was the separation of the registers of births, marriages, and deaths of the whites from those of the free people of color.

The revolution of July, 1830, traditionally has been regarded as the inauguration of a more liberal era. Thus, in 1831, the government permitted the organization of free colored societies on the island, albeit they had to be *"patriotique et fraternelle."* The liberal initiative did not go unchallenged, however.[132] Resistance among whites was extreme in Martinique, where it resulted in the Grand Anse riot of 1833.[133] In addition, though the political rights of the free colored were nominally enlarged, their actual rights were limited by the relatively inaccessible property qualification.

Because the possibilities for alliance with white political movements were few, movements toward alliance with the slaves were effected in the 1830s. Residing in France, Bissette actively participated in the battle for the civil rights of the colored and in 1834 founded the *Revue des Colonies.* The civil rights struggle led Bissette toward alliance with the metropolitan abolitionists, and perhaps this precluded the possibility of the free colored struggle becoming an anti-French struggle. Quite clearly, the appeals of the free colored were aimed at placing the colonies on the same footing as the mother country. The application of metropolitan laws was seen as the best means of securing that equality, which in turn would enable them to snatch local power from the hands of the ruling class.

CONCLUSION

For the free colored of the French Antilles, post-revolutionary society did not differ very much from the society they had known in the 1770s and 1780s, but the Revolution itself did have enormous

---

[131] The text of the pamphlet is recorded by Joseph-Elzéar Morenas, *Precis historique de la traite des Noirs et de l'esclavage colonial* . . . (Paris, 1828), and by Baude, "L'affranchissement des esclaves," pp. 127 ff.

[132] Baude ("L'affranchissement des esclaves," p. 9) relates that in February, 1833, M. Dupotet, the governor of Martinique, was recalled to France under the pressure of local reaction because he had declared in a speech that it was time to put an end to "that trifling classification of men because of the color of their skin."

[133] Maurice Nicolas, *L'affaire de lax Grand Anse* (Fort-de-France, 1960).

repercussions. For the first time, the free colored were inspired to take note of their position in colonial society and of their potential strength. Perhaps most important, however, was the fact that they were unable to conceive of a society different from the one they already knew. This fact was clearly most debilitating in respect to their stand toward the slavery issue. They did not seek the help of the slaves, nor did they offer much succor to them. The free colored advocated equality, but only vis-à-vis themselves and the white ruling class. They sought alliances, but primarily with the white ruling class. During the Revolution, when such an alliance seemed unlikely, they took the initiative and placed themselves at the center of power. Because they were unable to reach out beyond their group, however, their success lasted less than a year, at which time the planters sought Britain's help to restore the old regime. Even then, the unity of the free colored was tenuous, and it eventually collapsed.

After 1830, the political initiative of the free colored fell into the hands of a few mulattoes, such as Bissette, who resided in France. It was only at this late date that the free colored became absorbed in the anti-slavery struggle. It is significant that activists such as Bissette came to understand that slavery was responsible for the misfortunes of free people of color only after a long exile from the islands. The political activities of those free colored who remained on the islands are less well recorded, though evidently more moderate. Thus, when the Second Republic proclaimed the abolition of slavery, the old free colored elite—whose numbers had not dramatically increased during the liberal era of Louis Philippe—lost the initiative once again and followed the political direction of the newly emancipated slaves. They served, though, as a moderating influence, as, for instance, in the profound split which developed between Schoelcher, the Caucasian and a keen enemy of white colonial society, and Bissette, the man of color who favored reconciliation and forgetting the past.

5 | Saint Domingue

Emancipation and the status of the free population in slave systems in the Americas have been discussed by a number of contemporary historians. They have generally treated the attitudes toward racial differences held by the various colonizing powers as the crucial question in determining the ease of emancipation and the quality of life available to the free people. Neglecting the problem of social control and viewing the slave systems as static, or as developmental in the direction of growing humanitarianism with the passage of time, they have assembled fragmentary and sometimes distorted evidence to prove or disprove a preconceived theory. Saint Domingue is a particularly interesting colony in which to examine the problems of emancipation and the status of a free population in a slave society. Of great economic importance to France, it was administered by a centralized bureaucracy, and documentation is abundant.

From the evidence relating to formulation of policy, it is clear that pre-existing attitudes toward race were relatively insignificant. Pressures upon and within the society were intense, and policies stemming from attitudes toward race were luxuries the policy makers could not afford. Fundamental military, economic, social, and political concerns were crucial. These concerns were conflicting in themselves, and changes in policy toward emancipation and the status of the free reflected which concern, or concerns, was of paramount importance at any given period of time. The metropolis jealously asserted its right to determine policy in its own interests, and little sentimentality crept into policy discussions. "The property rights of the masters have never been the reason for tolerating slavery in the colonies," wrote a high colonial official. "The establishment of the lands was, and is, the sole aim, in the interest of commerce."[1] Emilien Petit maintained that the French government should encourage or restrict emancipation in the interests of the stability of the colony, regardless of the desires of the masters. His strategy was a middle

---

[1] Emilien Petit, *Traité sur le gouvernement des esclaves*, 2 vols. (Paris: Knapen, 1777), 2: 68. Translations from this and all other sources cited herein are the author's.

course: restrict emancipation to keep enough hands, but do not restrict it so much that it produces a dangerous state of despair among the slaves, because "only the hope for liberty can sustain or animate the fidelity of the slaves in a state of degradation and poverty and attach them to their masters, or to white blood, which amounts to the same thing."[2]

The Predominance of Military Considerations during the Pre-Plantation Period

During the early years of colonization of the French Caribbean, it was difficult to obtain white colonists. Before the rise of the slave plantation systems, there were few attractions for them. At the same time, rivalry over control of the islands was intense, not because of the economic value of the islands themselves, but because the British and French islands were viewed as bridgeheads to the gold- and silver-producing Spanish mainland colonies. Once the Spanish territorial monopoly of the Caribbean had been breached, the principle of effective occupation determined which power would control which islands. Emancipation was encouraged, and freedmen enjoyed a relatively high status because the colonizers needed to count as many heads as possible, and because the free colored, and at times even the slaves, were effectively used for military purposes. While the military role of the slaves and the free colored population was apparently less prominent in the British colonies, which quickly became colonies of economic exploitation and for which white settlers were easier to obtain, the free colored population was the major source of military strength in the Spanish and French Caribbean. In Saint Domingue, Africans were the principal military and police force from the earliest years of colonization, even after the rise of the slave plantation system, and this situation was an important factor in the success of the Haitian Revolution. As Jean-Baptiste Dutertre reported in the middle of the seventeenth century:

They are valiant and hardy in the face of danger, and, during all the desperate encounters which our colonists of Saint Christopher Island have had from time to time with the English, they have been no less redoubtable to this nation than their masters. M. d'Enambuc used them advantageously to repulse the British, and M. le Commandeur de Salles, seeing himself in this year 1666 with the choice between victory and death, used them to chase these irreconcilable enemies of our nation from the island. And they have so well done their duty, setting fires everywhere while our Frenchmen were in battle, that they have made no small contribution to the famous victory which France won over England.[3]

[2] *Ibid.*, p. 69.

[3] Jean-Baptiste Dutertre, *Histoire générale des Antilles habitées par les français*, 4 vols. (Paris, 1667–71), 2: 499.

Throughout the history of Saint Domingue, officials in the islands mobilized free blacks, mulattoes, and slaves, not only to participate in the frequent colonial wars of the Caribbean, but also to pursue fugitive slaves and to defend the border with Spain. In 1695, they offered slaves 10 écus for each enemy head and each deserter returned to an officer, and freedom for taking an enemy officer or flag or for saving the life of a subject of the king.[4]

Even after the rise of the slave plantation system, Africans continued to be used for military and police purposes—an important factor in the success of the Haitian Revolution. Thus, in 1709, the government routinely mobilized trusted plantation slaves, "experience having proved that one can make very good use of the *Nègres des Habitans*,"[5] and in 1721 it organized a company composed of whites and mulattoes to guard the Spanish border and provided that, in default of whites, free blacks also could be received into the company.[6] In 1724, the government conscripted free blacks into military service and organized them into the *Compagnie de Nègres-Libres*, which was divided into from three to four squadrons, each under an officer. The main duty of this company was to pursue fugitive slaves.[7] When the *Maréchausée*, a militarized police force, was reorganized in 1733, its archers were chosen from among free blacks and mulattoes.[8] In 1740, the king, complaining that the white colonists were too "soft," even in defense of "their own property," recommended an increase in emancipations to augment the military strength of the colony; the free Africans, he noted, had always been regarded as "the principal force of the colony."[9]

As the slave plantation system developed, however, internal security problems became more severe and exerted pressure against using Africans for military purposes. Following the Mackandal conspiracy, exposed in 1758, masters expressed their fear that the arming and military training of slaves would undermine discipline, and they insisted upon training and leading their own slaves. It was decided that slaves would in no case be allowed to form a separate body of troops.[10] The government continued to rely heavily upon the free colored population for defense, however, and in 1762 it organized a *Compagnie de Chasseurs de Gens de Couleur* consisting of volunteer

[4] M. L. E. Moreau de St.-Méry, *Loix et constitutions des colonies françaises de l'Amérique sous le vent*, 6 vols. (Paris, 1784–89), Arrêt du Conseil de Guerre pour la defense de la Colonie en cas d'attaque, February 17, 1695.
[5] *Ibid.*, Ordonnance des administrateurs touchant les Nègres à armer en temps de guerre, September 9, 1709.
[6] *Ibid.*, Ordonnance des administrateurs, March 27, 1721.
[7] *Ibid.*, Règlement fait par le gouverneur de Cap, pour la Compagnie des Nègres-Libres de la dépendance de la même ville, April 29, 1724.
[8] *Ibid.*, Ordonnance des administrateurs, January 20, 1733.
[9] *Ibid.*, Lettre du ministre à M. de Larnage sur les milices, June 3, 1740.
[10] *Ibid.*, Ordonnance des administrateurs, March 12, 1759.

free blacks and mulattoes.[11] Though this body of troops was supposed to be disbanded at the end of the war in 1763, it was still in existence in 1768, when the commanders were ordered to use it in the pursuit of fugitive slaves and deserters, and for policing the neighborhoods.[12]

In 1779, the king, expressing full confidence in the attachment and fidelity of his free colored subjects, formed a *Corps de Chasseurs Volontaires de Gens de Couleurs de St. Domingue* consisting of 600 volunteers,[13] and, in 1780, the commander in chief ordered a general conscription of free men of color. Thereafter, all blacks, mulattoes, and free colored men between fifteen and sixteen years of age were ordered to serve one year in the *Compagnies de Chasseurs-Royaux* of their department, and no emancipation could be ratified until the subject had served one year in the said companies.[14] Upon the departure of most of the garrison on a major expedition, the commander in chief ordered the commander of the *limonade* battalion to call up the colored militia to help garrison the island.[15] Two old captains of the *Nègres-Libres*, both aged ninety-six, were given life-time [*sic*] pensions from the government. According to the order, "The said Etienne Auba has always given to his numerous family as well as to the people of his color the best example of respect, of obedience and of submission to the government as well as to the whites."[16]

Moreau de St.-Méry boasted of the excellent soldier the French had made of the mulatto. His worth had been proven in his conscription into the *Maréchausée*, into the *Chasseurs* formed by M. de Belzince in 1762, and into the *Compagnies de Chasseurs-Royaux*, which marched on Savannah, Georgia, in 1779. It was the mulattoes, he wrote, who usually pursued fugitive slaves. He pointed out that military life had its attractions for the idle and pleasure-loving, and that the mulatto was content with little, living off roots and tropical fruits. He needed almost no clothes, could stand the sun, and could climb mountains with agility. But he should not be confined to the barracks at night, because "night belongs to pleasure."[17] It is, unfortunately, only too rarely that poetic justice is dished out as it was in Saint Domingue, where this cynical policy of degrading and exploiting a population to fulfill the military needs of the rulers backfired so thoroughly.

[11] *Ibid.*, Ordonnance du gouverneur général, March 12, 1779.
[12] *Ibid.*, Ordonnance du roi, April 1, 1768.
[13] *Ibid.*, Ordonnance du gouverneur général, March 12, 1779.
[14] *Ibid.*, Ordonnance du commandant en chef par interim, May 26, 1780.
[15] *Ibid.*, Lettre du gouverneur général au commandant du bataillon de limonade, April 15, 1782.
[16] *Ibid.*, Ordonnances des administrateurs, July 8, 1776, and August 11, 1779.
[17] M. L. E. Moreau de St.-Méry, *Description topographique, physique, civile, politique, et historique de la partie française de l'Isle Saint-Domingue,* 4 vols. (Philadelphia, 1797), 1: 103–4.

POLICY TOWARD EMANCIPATION AND THE
NEEDS OF PLANTATION AGRICULTURE

The colonizing powers initiated the slave systems with few pre-conceptions about encouraging or discourging emancipation. It eventually became evident that, if no restrictions were placed upon emancipation, the free colored population would grow rapidly. During the pre-plantation period in Saint Domingue, the existence of a large free colored population was a military advantage. The development of a plantation system, however, brought with it hostility toward the emancipation of slaves and vigorous attempts from the metropolis to limit severely the right of the master to emancipate his slave at will, the obvious reason being that a slave plantation system required large numbers of slaves to work in agriculture. Freed slaves tended overwhelmingly either to abandon agriculture and flock to the cities and towns, thus creating a serious problem of social control, or, where land was available, to engage in subsistence agriculture. In either case, they rarely offered themselves on the labor market. This tendency was a major factor leading to the decline of the sugar industry in Jamaica following the emancipation of slaves there.[18] Abolition also resulted in a labor shortage in the coffee regions of Brazil, where freedmen found that they could meet their necessities by working two or three days a week and preferred to "buy leisure" rather than earn more than enough to acquire the most rudimentary necessities.[19] In contrast, on small islands like Antigua, where neither land for subsistence agriculture nor employment in towns was available, labor costs did not increase after the abolition of slavery, and the plantation system continued to thrive.[20]

In colonies where economic alternatives to plantation labor existed, slavery or another form of forced labor, either direct or indirect, was necessary to ensure the existence of plantation agriculture.[21] Maintaining an adequate labor force on the estates was an essential concern of those policy makers who encouraged plantation agriculture, and, consequently, restrictions upon the right of masters to emancipate slaves at will were characteristic of societies evolving in this direction.

[18] Noel Deerr, *The History of Sugar*, 2 vols. (London: Chapman & Hall, 1950), 2: 362–70.

[19] Celso Furtado, *The Economic Growth of Brazil: A Survey from Colonial to Modern Times* (Berkeley and Los Angeles: University of California Press, 1965), pp. 153–54.

[20] Deerr, *History of Sugar*, 2: 368.

[21] For a discussion of forced labor among white settlers of Puerto Rico during the nineteenth century, see Sidney W. Mintz, "Labor and Sugar in Puerto Rico and Jamaica," *Comparative Studies in Society and History*, 1, no. 3 (March, 1959): 273–83.

THE EVOLUTION OF FRENCH POLICY REGARDING EMANCIPATION

French policy evolved from placing no restrictions whatsoever upon emancipation to deliberately increasing limitations that would make it very difficult indeed for the master to emancipate his slave. During the strategic period of colonization, the *Code Noir* allowed masters twenty years of age or older to emancipate their slaves without the consent of their parents. This right was revoked in 1721, for the stated reason that young masters were abusing it and thereby ruining their estates, a fact which resulted in a "considerable prejudice to our colonies, the principal utility of which depends upon the labor of the Negroes, who give value to the lands."[22] By the early eighteenth century, a government permit was required for emancipations.[23] The master had to petition for the right to emancipate his slave, stating the reasons why he wished to do so. The petition then had to be approved and ratified by a government official.[24] Hostility was expressed toward testamentary emancipations on the grounds that sick masters at the mercy of their slaves were often forced to emancipate them against their will and that the impatience of the slaves often hastened the death of the master.[25]

In 1775, a royal ordinance imposed a heavy tax upon emancipations: at least 1,000 livres for each male, and 2,000 livres for each female, under the age of forty for a permit to emancipate, unless the master could prove extraordinary service to himself or to the colony.[26] Subsequently, tax-free emancipations were allowed only for military service, such as that of a drummer in the army for eight years, chasing fugitive slaves, or performing other military duties or outstanding services.[27] This was a continuation of an earlier policy. Earlier in the eighteenth century, several slaves had been emancipated for service to the colony, usually for the denunciation or capture of fugitive slaves,[28] and some slaves had been promised freedom for outstanding acts of bravery on the battlefield.[29]

The growing hostility of the metropolis toward emancipation was also manifested during the eighteenth century in a steady under-

[22] Moreau de St.-Méry, *Loix*, Déclaration du roi, December 15, 1721.

[23] *Ibid.*, Ordonnance des administrateurs généraux des isles, August 15, 1711, and Ordonnance du roi, October 24, 1713.

[24] *Ibid.*, Ordonnance de l'intendant en fonction, portant concession de la liberté a un de ses esclaves, avec la ratification du général, October 10 and 11, 1721.

[25] Petit, *Traité sur le gouvernement*, 2: 70.

[26] Moreau de St.-Méry, *Loix*, Ordonnance du roi, May 22, 1775.

[27] *Ibid.*, Ordonnance des administrateurs, October 23, 1775.

[28] *Ibid.*, See also Arrêt du Conseil du Cap, August 6, 1708; Ordonnance des administrateurs, February 10, 1710; Ordonnances des administrateurs, June 28, 1734; and Arrêt du Conseil du Cap, July 9, 1750.

[29] See, for example, *ibid.*, Arrêt du Conseil de Guerre, February 17, 1695, and Ordonnance des administrateurs, September 9, 1709.

cutting of the principle that a slave became free upon touching the soil of France.[30] By 1762, the institution of slavery had taken firm root on French soil, and one official felt called upon to complain that "Paris has become a public market where men are sold to the highest bidder; and there is not a bourgeois or a worker who does not have his black slave."[31]

ILLEGAL FORMS OF EMANCIPATION

Flight and the establishment of colonies of *marons* was a widespread and effective means by which slaves freed themselves. These techniques dated from the earliest years of colonization in the French Caribbean. Before 1665, the Dutch brought 1,200–1,300 black slaves to Martinique and Guadeloupe and sold them cheaply and on credit.[32] M. Houel, the administrator of the colony, having more confidence in his slaves than in the French colonists, made the mistake of arming his slaves and teaching them to use firearms. The slaves outnumbered the French, and at the end of 1656 there was an uprising led by two slaves named Pedre and Jean le Blanc. Their plan was to massacre the masters, keep their wives, and set up two Angolan kingdoms on the island of Guadeloupe, one at Basse-Terre and the other at Capesterre. Intertribal rivalries carried over from Africa led to disunity, and some of the conspirators failed to show up at the appointed time and place. About forty slaves armed themselves and seized several plantations. Pursued by the militia, they headed for the woods. The militia hesitated to follow them. For ten or twelve days, they pillaged the plantations and massacred the French settlers. The French militia obtained twenty Brazilian slaves to carry food and serve as guides in pursuit of the rebels. Following the capture of the conspirators, the two Angolan kings were quartered, and several of their followers were subjected to various forms of torture.[33]

Simultaneously, mass desertions of slaves occurred in Guadeloupe. Those who left returned for relatives they had left behind and to convince others to follow them. They fled to the Indians, who received them well at first, but later discovered that the slaves could be profitably sold to the Spanish. Desertions became so massive that

[30] *Ibid.*, Extrait de la lettre du ministre à M. Ducasse, February 5, 1698; Extrait de la lettre du ministre à M. Ducasse, March 11, 1699; Lettre du Ministre sur les Nègres amenés en France, June 10, 1707; Ordonnance du roi, April 28, 1694; Déclaration du roi, October 28, 1694; Edit du roi, October, 1716; Déclaration du roi, December 15, 1738; Lettre du ministre aux administrateurs, June 30, 1763; Règlement de l'intendant, August 29, 1769; Déclaration du roi, August 9, 1777; Arrêt du Conseil d'État, September 7, 1777; and Ordonnance du roi, February 23, 1778.

[31] Paul Trayer, *Étude historique de la condition légale des esclaves dans les colonies françaises* (Paris, 1887), pp. 95–96.

[32] Dutertre, *Histoire des Antilles*, 3: 201.

[33] *Ibid.*, 1: 500–502.

every house lost some slaves. In response to a rumor that all the slaves were going to leave on a certain day, masters put their slaves in irons. But in spite of draconian measures, mass desertion spread to even the most devoted slaves. Punishments only made them leave more quickly. "One was reduced to such an extremity at Martinique," wrote Dutertre, "that one dared not say a cross word to a black, nor make the slightest correction without his fleeing to the woods. Even the *Negresses* fled, running off with little infants seven or eight days old."[34]

Search parties sent after the slaves could not locate them. The slaves led groups of Indians in raiding the plantations in broad daylight, stealing, killing, running off slaves, and burning homes. This situation lasted for two years, until the French authorities decided that the only solution was to clear out the Indians, who were giving the slaves boats in which to escape and offering them asylum. The French authorities finally reached an agreement with the Indians not to receive fugitive slaves.[35]

The fugitive slaves were called *marons*. They developed techniques of guerilla warfare which closely resemble contemporary methods. The tactics of Francisque Fabulé are a good example. A tall, powerful slave with a martial air, Fabulé declared himself the leader of 300–400 *marons*, organizing his followers into groups of 25 or 30 and dispersing them around the island. They descended on isolated estates at night and stole arms and provisions, though at first they did not kill anyone. The settlers feared the possibilities of the situation and offered Francisque his freedom if he would return and bring in some of his followers. Francisque agreed at first to these terms and then reneged. Instead, he joined the Indians and blocked the roads, burning down estates and massacring their owners. The French settlers decided to fight, but they did not get far. Thick forests, rocks, cliffs, and mountains blocked their path. After hunting the *marons* for a month, the French militia captured only five or six fugitives, who happened to have foot trouble and could not run. "The rest, not at all wishing to fight, sought their health in flight." Four or five Frenchmen died of snakebite. Because the pursuit was proving more costly to the French than to the fugitive slaves, the militia asked to be demobilized to attend to neglected crops, and the authorities adopted a new tactic: offering rewards for the return of fugitives, paying the reward, and pardoning the fugitives. These tactics made inroads upon Fabulé's followers, and within a few months he agreed to surrender in return for his freedom. A treaty was signed which stated that the island had been devastated by fugitive slaves, and, since Francisque Fabulé was the leader of a large band, he would be given his freedom and a thousand pounds of tobacco, and no punishment

34 *Ibid.*, 2: 537.
35 *Ibid.*, 1: 502–4.

would be inflicted upon the members of his band. He brought in 6 or 7 of his followers, collected a reward, and was given an official hug, his freedom, and a sword to wear. Thereafter, he brought in large numbers of fugitives in return for additional rewards.[36]

The pattern established in the lesser French islands was carried over to Saint Domingue, where maroon colonies also thrived. Escaped slaves set up communities, elected their leaders, cultivated the soil, built houses, and constructed barricades against invaders. Operating from these bases, fugitives hid in the cane fields during the day, robbed passers-by on the highways at night, and went from plantation to plantation seizing cattle. They often hid in the slave quarters, gathering information about what went on in the master's house so that they could steal without being noticed.[37] Mass desertions of slaves, especially in wartime, were common. The authorities complained that

> they leave in bands, and desert to the foreigners with whom we are at war. Several of the colonists have had the misfortune of seeing themselves deprived of the cultivation of their lands, and reduced to seeking the help of their friends to provide for their families. And it is certain that ... the enemy has not taken as many as those who have given themselves up voluntarily, and a great number who remain do so only for the return of some and the desertion of others from the island.[38]

Colonists lived in fear of being suddenly ruined by the loss of all their slaves. Planters who went to bed at night owning 100 or 200 slaves could not be sure of waking up the next morning with even one.[39]

Flight was greatly facilitated because two-thirds of the island was in Spanish hands. The Spanish part of the island was undeveloped, thinly populated, and its slave system was relatively mild. Colonial rivalries between France and Spain made the authorities of the Spanish part of the Island very uncooperative in returning fugitive slaves. Attempts to eliminate the Spanish part of the island as a refuge for fugitive slaves met with little success. In 1728, a secret treaty was signed with the Spanish to allow a French agent to go to the city of Santo Domingo to claim all the fugitive slaves there. The agent spent 23,700 livres in this undertaking, which failed because a revolt took place at Santo Domingo when he arrived. The colonists would not allow themselves to be taxed to pay his expenses, and the

---

[36] *Ibid.*, 3: 201–4. For the treaty signed with Francisque Fabulé, see Moreau de St.-Méry, *Loix*, Arrêt du Conseil de la Martinique, March 2, 1665.

[37] *Ibid.*, Arrêt du Conseil de la Martinique, October 13, 1671, and Arrêt de règlement du Conseil de Léogane, March 16, 1705.

[38] *Ibid.*, Arrêt du Conseil de Léogane, July 1, 1709.

[39] *Ibid.*, Mémoire des administrateurs au Conseil Supérieur du Cap, July 7, 1721.

cost was eventually assumed by the king of France.[40] It was not until 1776 that a treaty was negotiated between France and Spain for the purpose of mutual restoration of escaped slaves.[41]

Colonial officials were well aware of the danger implicit in the existence of permanent pockets of slave military power: "A colony which has the misfortune to have to fear establishments of slave deserters enters, from that moment, into a state of war, the danger of which can only increase with time."[42] Large maroon bands and guerilla bases were never successfully eliminated during the colonial period in Saint Domingue and were still in existence at the outbreak of the Haitian Revolution.[43]

THEFT AND THE MARKET

The market was very important to the economic, social, and religious life of West Africa, and the blacks, especially the women, were skilled in buying and selling. Within Saint Domingue, the French colonists depended upon the slave-operated markets to trade goods and especially to provide the cities and towns with food. Colonial authorities had to recognize that the colony depended upon these slave-operated markets. When the *Code Noir* of 1685 outlawed these markets, the authorities in Saint Domingue protested that they were absolutely necessary to the commerce of the colony, and the French government changed the law the next year to allow them to continue.[44]

The West African brought with him complex ideas about property. In Dahomey, which had the greatest cultural influence in Saint Domingue, everything belonged, in theory, to the king: land, horses, implements, slaves, money, even the person of the subject. But no king would dare claim his rights, because of fear of the tribal ances-

[40] *Ibid.*, Arrêt du Conseil du Petit-Goave, March 6, 1728; Arrêt du Conseil du Cap, December 6, 1728; and Extrait de la lettre du ministre à M. Duclos, January 18, 1735.

[41] *Ibid.*, Commission d'un commissaire de la nation françoise auprès du gouvernement Espagnole de Santo Domingo, January 15, 1776; Ordonnance des administrateurs concernant les Nègres Espagnoles pris en marronage, March 30, 1776; Ordonnance des administrateurs concernant les frais de restitution des esclaves fugitifs ramenés de l'Espagnole, April 16, 1776; Traité définitif de police entre les cours de France et de l'Espagne sur divers points concernant leurs sujets respectifs à St. Domingue, June 3 and December 4, 1777; and Lettre de l'intendant à l'ordonnateur du Cap touchant le prix des Nègres françois mariés dans la partie Espagnole, January 28, 1778.

[42] Petit, *Traité sur le gouvernement*, 2: 165. Petit was referring to a peace treaty signed between the Assembly of Jamaica and Cudjoe, a leader of fugitive slaves, in 1739. A French translation of the treaty was published in *ibid.*, 2: 165–77.

[43] C. L. R. James, *The Black Jacobins*, 2nd ed. rev. (New York: Random House, Vintage Books, 1963).

[44] Edit du roi, March, 1685, or *Code Noir*, art. 7. The original, complete text is published in Lucien Peytraud, *L'esclavage aux Antilles françaises avant 1789* (Paris, 1897), pp. 158–66.

tors. There were two other types of property. One was the property of the sib, or extended family. It was owned collectively and was administered by the oldest male member. The other was private property, which could be held by men or women. It included the houses a person built and the trees he planted, regardless of who owned the land. Private property was the money earned, the produce of one's labor, utensils, guns, mats, pipes, and magic charms, which often consisted of herbs and medicines discovered in the forest. The discoverer could sell the formula to others for their use. There were complex rules for the inheritance of personal property.[45]

French law denied all property rights to slaves. Anything the slave might acquire through industry, gift, or any other way belonged legally to the master. A slave could not give or will anything he possessed to members of his family or to friends. He could not make a valid contract to dispose of goods.[46] This simplistic view of property rights entirely excluded the slave, but was impossible to enforce in Saint Domingue because the slaves controlled the internal market and because, in addition to the legal market, an illegal one was created by the slaves to dispose of stolen goods. Indeed, the illegal market tended to supplant the legal one. Colonial officials complained that slaves were stealing indigo and other merchandise that was easy to carry and were selling it to black-market operators traveling from plantation to plantation; and this illegal trade was thriving to the extent that the public markets were poorly attended.[47] The *procureur du roi* described the systematic operations of the black market:

> several persons buy indifferently from slaves indigo, horses, clothing, and other merchandise without troubling to find out where the slaves could have obtained these goods. The slaves conspire with the house slaves to steal the indigo from the drying houses and the horses from the fields, break into the storehouses, and pass the stolen goods from one neighborhood to another, from hand to hand among the slaves, until it is finally sold to several bad-intentioned individuals who receive it, give some recompense to the slaves for their thefts, and then resell it to merchants or exchange it for other merchandise.[48]

Slaves used monopoly price-fixing to profiteer on food sold in the cities and towns. They waited along the highways, stopping all the supplies headed for the market, and then resold them at high prices. These practices were so effective that the Council of Cap complained that officers from the merchant fleet, the clergy, the House of Charity, and private families were suffering from lack of eggs, poul-

---

[45] Melville J. Herskovits, *Dahomey: An Ancient West African Kingdom*, 2 vols. (New York: J. J. Augustin, 1928), 1: 78–95, 51–63.

[46] *Code Noir*, art. 28.

[47] Moreau de St.-Méry, *Loix*, Arrêt du Conseil du Petit-Goave, January 8, 1697.

[48] *Ibid.*

try, and vegetables, and some people were being forced to eat meat on the days forbidden by the church, for lack of fresh foods.[49]

The slaves of Saint Domingue used their control of the internal markets, both the legal and illegal ones, to amass sums of money with which to purchase their freedom. Cabarets owned by free blacks became centers of vice, the proceeds of which went toward the purchase of freedom for more individual slaves. Colonial officials concluded that most of the disorder among slaves came from the "facility which the colonists have of giving them freedom in return for sums of money," because, once a sum was agreed upon, they

> abandon the service of their masters, engaging in private affairs under the pretext of working by the day in return for a small recompense which they promise to their said masters. Others abandon themselves to all kinds of vices to amass the sums agreed upon, getting together in the houses of those who have already been freed, most of them having cabarets, and fraternize with whites who are low enough to receive them and suffer their infamous and immodest commerce.[50]

Through control of the internal market, the blacks in Saint Domingue exercised a considerable amount of economic power, amassing wealth through legal and illegal channels, much of which went toward the increase of the free black population.

RACISM AS AN INSTRUMENT OF SOCIAL AND POLITICAL DOMINATION

As the slave population began heavily to outnumber the white population in the countryside, the obvious symbol of visible racial differences was seized upon as a means of convincing the slaves of their own innate inferiority. Overt racist policies were instituted during the last half of the eighteenth century in Saint Domingue, and perhaps because this period preceded the flowering of racist theories during the nineteenth century, as the institution of slavery itself was seriously challenged, French ideologists did not find it necessary to attempt to convince themselves of the innate inferiority of the Africans. They contented themselves with trying to convince the Africans. Containing the slaves and maintaining the social order were frankly acknowledged as the reasons for racist policies. A *memoire du roi* dating from 1777 was blunt.

> Whatever distance they may be from their origin, they always keep the stain of slavery, and are declared incapable of all public functions. Even gentlemen who descend to any degree from a woman of

[49] *Ibid.*, Arrêt du Conseil du Cap, February 7, 1707.
[50] *Ibid.*, Ordonnance des administrateurs généraux des isles, August 15, 1711.

color cannot enjoy the prerogatives of nobility. This law is harsh, but wise and necessary. In a country where there are fifteen slaves to one white, one cannot put too much distance between the two species, one cannot impress upon the blacks too much respect for those they serve. This distinction, rigorously observed even after freedom, is the principal prop of the subordination of the slave, by the opinion that results that his color is inextricably linked with servitude, and nothing can render him equal to his master.[51]

A book officially endorsed by the French government stated that "interest and security demand that we overwhelm the black race with so much disdain that whoever descends from it until the sixth generation shall be covered by an indelible stain."[52] The very spectacle of free blacks was dangerous for slaves, it declared, because color should be absolutely identified with slave status.[53]

Along with the tendency to restrict emancipation, identify blackness with slavery, and degrade the free colored population, as plantation agriculture flourished, there was also a tendency to create a caste system, which fomented mutual antagonisms among people of varying degrees of African descent by establishing distinct legal and social categories in accordance with the percentage of admixture of European blood, the number of generations of legitimate birth, and the number of generations removed from slavery.

ORIGIN OF THE COLONIAL ELITE OF SAINT DOMINGUE

Early egalitarian policies toward race contrasted sharply with discriminatory policies characteristic of the late colonial period. The *Code Noir* guaranteed in unequivocable language full citizenship rights to slaves emancipated in the French islands, considering them the same as native-born French citizens, regardless of where the slaves had been born (Articles 57, 58, and 59).[54] These measures were no doubt motivated by the desire to count as many heads as possible at a time when the principle of effective occupation determined control of the islands. The population factor, especially the shortage of white women, was certainly very important in promoting racial

---

[51] Antoine Gisler, *L'esclavage aux Antilles françaises (XVIIe–XIXe siècles): Contribution au problème de l'esclavage* (Fribourg: Editions Universitaires Fribourg Suisse, 1964), pp. 99–100.

[52] Hilliard d'Auberteuil, *Considerations sur l'état présent de la colonie française de St. Domingue*, 2 vols. (Paris: 1776–77), 2: 73.

[53] *Ibid.*, 2: 84.

[54] Article 59 reads: "We give to the freedmen the same rights, privileges, and immunities enjoyed by free-born persons; we will that the merit of an acquired liberty produce in them the same effects upon their persons as well as their property as the good fortune of natural freedom causes to our other subjects." Some later versions of the *Code Noir* read, "Voulons qu'ils méritent une liberté acquise," but this is an inaccuracy stemming from the growth of racism. The original *Code Noir* reads, "Voulons que la mérite d'une liberté acquise."

equality in early Saint Domingue.[55] As Dutertre wrote: "There are many of these mulattoes in the islands who are free and work for themselves. I have seen some fairly handsome ones who have married Frenchmen. This disorder was more common before than it is today because the number of women and girls in the Antilles prevent it; but at the beginning of colonization it was terrible and almost without remedy."[56]

Interracial unions, both informal and legalized, continued on a large scale throughout the history of the colony. The *Code Noir* exerted pressure on the master to marry his slave concubine, thereby freeing her and legitimizing their children, under penalty of fine and confiscation of the concubine family (Article 9). Before the promulgation of the *Code Noir*, it was accepted practice that the offspring of unions between white men and black women be automatically emancipated when they reached the age of twenty-one. The *Code Noir* followed the Roman principle that the status of the new-born child followed the condition of the mother, and, thereafter, formal emancipation in writing was required. French colonists in Saint Domingue expressed dissatisfaction with this provision, and an administrator in Saint Domingue proposed in 1697 that a law be passed declaring all mulattoes free as soon as they reached the age of twenty-one. The minister of the colonies agreed to propose such a change in the *Code Noir*, "which was formulated without having examined this question in depth."[57] It is evident that Article 9 was frequently violated. Many children were emancipated because they were "children of free men." This would have been legal if the father was not the master, or if the master had married his slave concubine. But most of these children were probably sired by their mother's master.[58]

There was strong sentiment in favor of emancipating the natural children of the master throughout the history of the colony, and these children were an important source of the free colored population. As late as 1735, mulattoes were specifically excluded from the policy of sharply restricting the emancipation of slaves. Instructions to the colonial authorities read: "You should not follow the same policy with the mulattoes. I know that they are the declared enemies of the blacks."[59] As late as 1777, Emilien Petit favored freeing the

[55] For some interesting concepts about the impact of population patterns on the racial attitudes and organization of colonial society, see Marvin Harris, *Patterns of Race in the Americas* (New York: Walker, 1964), and Winthrop D. Jordan, "American Chiaroscuro: The Status and Definition of Mulattoes in the British Colonies," *William and Mary Quarterly*, 19, no. 2 (April, 1962): 183–200.

[56] Dutertre, *Histoire des Antilles*, 2: 513.

[57] Moreau de St.-Méry, *Loix*, Extrait de la lettre du ministre à M. Dacasse, February 5, 1698.

[58] Peytraud, *L'esclavage aux Antilles*, p. 199.

[59] Moreau de St.-Méry, *Loix*, Extrait de la lettre à le marquis de Fayet, March 29, 1735.

mulatto children of white planters and making the fathers responsible for their care until they came of age. He explained:

> It is to the affection of their concubines that whites have owed the discovery of several conspiracies. . . . the children born of these concubinages form a class of freedmen who are always distinguished from the other classes of free colored people, with whom they have few ties, and whom they despise. The freedman who depends upon his master or patron for his subsistence will not easily risk seeing himself deprived of it. One would find fewer guilty parties among the mulattoes if they had something to lose.[60]

Racial mixture was not discouraged in pre-plantation Saint Domingue. The *Code Noir* was not concerned about preventing the fusion of the races, either physically or legally.[61] A judgment rendered by the Council of Martinique in 1698 declared that the *Code Noir* aimed only at the vice of concubinage. Far from preventing racial mixture (*le mélange des sangs*), it was concerned only with augmenting the colony, because it discharged the master who married his slave concubine from paying the fine.[62] As late as 1713, the administrators were remarkably free from preoccupation with *le mélange des sangs* typical of the late colony. Pointing to widespread concubinage of slave women, they complained that masters kept their concubines and their children openly in their homes, "exposing them to the eyes of all with as much assurance as if they had been procreated from a legitimate marriage."[63]

Throughout the history of the colony, whether by virtue of the provisions of the *Code Noir* or otherwise, legal intermarriage was far from unusual. In 1703, the king refused to receive the titles of nobility of several French noblemen because they had married *mulatresses*.[64] A report dating from 1731 indicated that intermarriage was almost universal in some parts of Saint Domingue:

> In the inspection which M. de la Roche-Allard has made in Cayes in the neighborhood of Jacumel, he reported to me that there are few whites of pure blood. . . . the whites ally themselves willingly in marriage with the blacks because the latter, through their frugality, acquire property more easily than the whites.[65]

A nephew and cousin tried unsuccessfully in 1746 to prevent their white relative's marriage to a *mulatresse*. The court ordered the publication of the bans and required the curé to proceed with the

[60] Petit, *Traité sur le gouvernement*, 2: 72–75.
[61] Peytraud, *L'esclavage aux Antilles*, p. 156.
[62] *Ibid.*, p. 202.
[63] Moreau de St.-Méry, *Loix*, Ordonnance des administrateurs, December 18, 1713.
[64] *Ibid.*, Lettre du ministre au gouverneur général des isles, May 4, 1703.
[65] Peytraud, *L'esclavage aux Antilles*, p. 207.

marriage, under penalty of seizure of his stipend.[66] Even during the last few decades of the colony, marriage between white masters and their slave concubines and between impecunious white Frenchmen and comfortably placed women of color were common enough to inspire bitter comment. Hilliard d'Auberteuil wrote that the *Code Noir* was "subject to great abuse."

> How many *Negresses* have profited from it and appropriated the entire fortune of their masters, brutalized by libertinage and incapable of resisting their power over feeble and seduced souls. . . . The wealth of families has been sacrificed to passion, has become the price of debauchery, and respectable names have fallen, along with the best lands, to legitimized mulattoes.[67]

On the other hand, white men who married *filles de couleur* were accused of doing so for money. In the 1770s, there were about 300 white men, several born gentlemen, who were married to *sang-melées*. "They make these women whom cupidity has induced them to marry miserable; [and] their children, incapable of filling any civil function, . . . [are] condemned to share the humiliation of slaves."[68] Emilien Petit favored outlawing intermarriage, under penalty of nullification, a prohibition which was "necessary to prevent unions so contrary to the growth of the white population, and to maintain the superiority of white blood, which such misalliances degrade."[69]

The wealth of the free colored population was a unique feature of Saint Domingue. The *Code Noir* placed no restrictions upon inheritance of property, and the offspring of alliances between master and slave, whether legitimate or not, freely inherited their fathers' property, land, and slaves. A royal decree dating from 1726 declared free blacks and their children and descendants incapable of receiving from whites any donation among the living or after death, under penalty of confiscation of the property, thus abrogating the *Code Noir* in this respect.[70] But this change came too late to alter the existing customs in St. Domingue, and the decree was never enforced in the colony.[71]

The courts of Saint Domingue consistently awarded contested legacies to the colored offspring of white masters. There was a case in which the party who was to inherit an estate in the event that the

[66] Moreau de St.-Méry, *Loix*, Arrêts du Conseil du Cap, May 2 and June 13, 1746.

[67] Hilliard d'Auberteuil, *Considerations sur l'état*, 2: 80, 81.

[68] *Ibid.*, p. 79 and n.

[69] Petit, *Traité sur le gouvernement*, 2: 81.

[70] Moreau de St.-Méry, *Loix*, Déclaration du roi, February 8, 1726; C. Vanufel et Champion de Villeneuve, *Code des Colons de St. Domingue* (Paris: Me Vergne, 1826), pp. 42, 43.

[71] Auguste Lebeau, *De la condition des gens de couleur libres sous l'Ancient Régime d'après des documents des archives coloniales* (Paris: Guillaumin et Cie, 1903), p. 15.

deceased left no legitimate posterity denied that a former slave wife and their legitimized children constituted legitimate posterity. The lower court had held for the mulatto children, and, although the Council of Cap reversed the lower court, the *Conseil d'État* reversed the Council of Cap in 1772, giving the inheritance to the mulatto children.[72] A judgment dating from 1775 awarded two estates and 240 slaves to the mulatto bastards of their white father, who had willed this property to them.[73] A judgment dating from 1782 awarded half of a succession to the brothers and sisters of the deceased and half to the children of Nanette Soreau, *mulatresse libre*, in accordance with the terms of the deceased's will.[74]

The free colored population increased rapidly, in spite of restrictions on emancipation and the social degradation enacted during the last half of the eighteenth century. The census taken around 1700 listed 500 *gens de couleur libres*. By 1715, their number had increased to 1,500. By 1780, the figure reached 28,000. Between 1770 and 1780, there were 7,000–8,000 individual emancipations in the colony, and marriages among *affranchis*, slaves, and French colonists were never more common.[75] It appears that the free colored elite was moving rapidly toward outnumbering, if not absorbing, the white elite during the last few years of the colony. The figures below are for free persons owning property or slaves:[76]

	1784	1788	1789
Whites	20,229	27,717	30,831
Slaves	13,257	21,848	24,848
Free Colored	297,079	405,528	434,429

The total population of Saint Domingue in 1789 was 518,000, including 40,000 whites, 28,000 free colored, and 450,000 slaves.

Writing in 1798, after the colony had exploded, P. J. Laborie, a fugitive planter, expressed the opinion that the *Code Noir* was framed too early, when experience with slavery was lacking. Emanci-

---

[72] Moreau de St.-Méry, *Loix*, Arrêt du Conseil du Cap, December 21, 1769.
[73] *Ibid.*, October 5, 1775.
[74] *Ibid.*, April 29, 1782.
[75] Moreau de St.-Méry, *Description de la partie française*, 1: 68.
[76] *Ibid.*, p. 1. The earlier figure for slaves was undercounted. Because slaves were subject to a head tax, slaveowners attempted to conceal the number of slaves they actually had. M. de Marbois, the last intendant, was more vigilant, and arrived at more accurate figures, but even these were considerably undercounted. See P. J. Laborie, *The Coffee Planter of St. Domingue* (London: T. Cadell & W. Davies, 1798), app., pp. 56–57. In one case, sixty-eight slaves were confiscated from a master who had concealed their existence from the census. See Moreau de St.-Méry, *Loix*, Ordonnance de l'intendant, June 19, 1756.

pation was unrestricted, no limits had been placed upon acquisition of property by the free colored population, and there was no discrimination against them before the law. Restrictions were imposed later, but they were not very effective.[77] It is easier to prevent the growth of a wealthy and powerful group within a society than to degrade or destroy it once it has come into existence. The wealthy, the educated *gens de couleur*, defended their interests very well, and in the process became the fuse which ignited the colony.

SOCIAL CONFLICT BETWEEN THE COLORED AND WHITE ELITES OF SAINT DOMINGUE

The Haitian Revolution was precipitated by the response of the free colored population to attempts by whites to strip them of legal protection, degrade them socially, and destroy their network of influence with persons and institutions which could offer protection in order to dispossess the free colored population of coveted land, slaves, and other property. The system of racial discrimination was gradually built up over the years and culminated with sharp discriminatory measures during the last two decades of the colony.

The basic conflict was over wealth and over power to protect wealth. Because widespread intermarriage and more informal unions resulted in the passing of some of the best lands to the mulatto offspring of white planters, the economic struggle was also manifested in sexual rivalry. Julien Raimond, eloquent representative of the colored elite of Saint Domingue in the French General Assembly, dated discrimination from shortly before the War of 1744, when the colony began to become prosperous and a large number of Europeans came over, including marriageable white women seeking to marry rich white planters. But the virtues of the white women sent over in those days by the French Government seemed "more than suspect, and their marriages with the whites did not have all the fruit that was anticipated." They were often passed over for more fertile *filles de couleur*, who also often possessed the added advantage of owning land and slaves. In spite of the presence of white women, white men continued to marry *filles de couleur*, or to choose a woman from among their slaves, "making them their wives, under the title of housekeepers." The daughters of the *gens de couleur* often married newly arrived white settlers. As the colony became more cultivated, the colored population grew rapidly and at the expense of the white population, owing to the lack of white women and to the preference for colored women.

Many white families came over after the Peace of 1749. They were jealous of the growing fortunes of the *gens de couleur*. After the Peace of 1763, there was a new wave of immigration. Educated

[77]Laborie, *Coffee Planter*, app., pp. 44–53.

gens de couleur returned from France, where they had served in the house of the king and as officers in various regiments, provoking jealousy of their accomplishments from white settlers, who pushed for the passage of humiliating and oppressive laws. Several governors, including M. Dennery and M. de Bellecombe, tried to control the hostile whites, but the result was a massacre "at Martinique, on the day of Fête-Dieu, and in the other colonies, we saw the poor whites hunting down and murdering the *gens de couleur*, accusing them of imaginary plots." Marriages between white men and *filles de couleur* were outlawed in 1768, and these women became concubines instead of wives. Many free colored landowners were deprived of their lands by "a host of tyrannical acts," but many held on to their property and slaves and maintained a strong position.[78]

The first right which came under attack was access to political positions, because political power is the ultimate arbiter of economic power, and because the denial of political rights was a precondition for denying the free colored population access to public protection. In 1706, a mulatto was appointed *procureur du roi*, despite the protest of the *doyen du conseil* that "a mulatto bastard cannot be received in any judiciary post."[79] In 1760, however, the king ordered that no *sang-melé* or white person married to a *sang-melé* could hold office in the judiciary or in the militia, or hold any other public employment in the colony.[80]

The impetus toward racial discrimination was not rooted in the French national character. "There is so little color prejudice in France," wrote Emilien Petit, "that mulattoes, quadroons, and other descendants of the black race are received in the military corps reserved for the young nobility and as magistrates."[81] Racial discrimination in Saint Domingue stemmed from the cold, calculated ambitions of the white colonists. One free colored man was sold some property by a white man who took the money for the purchase, denounced him as a slave who could not prove he was free, had him legally re-enslaved, and then refused to deliver the property purchased because a slave was incapable of making a contract.[82] Another case was that of M. Boyer, a butcher in the neighborhood of Trou who was selling meat at 1½ *escalin* per pound. Boyer had obtained from the government an exclusive monopoly for selling meat, thus closing down two free colored competitors who were selling the same quality of meat at 1 *escalin* per pound. Because this privilege ate into the pocketbooks of all purchasers of meat, the monopoly was

[78] Julien Raimond, *Observations sur l'origine et les progrès du préjugé des colons blancs contre les hommes de couleur* (Paris, 1791).
[79] Moreau de St.-Méry, *Loix*, Arrêt du Conseil du Cap, October 24, 1706.
[80] *Ibid.*, May 22, 1760.
[81] Quoted in Lebeau, *De la condition des gens de couleur libres*, p. 23.
[82] Moreau de St.-Méry, *Loix*, Ordonnance des administrateurs, February 26, 1770.

finally set aside, and the right of the free colored butchers to do business was protected.[83] The list of discriminatory laws that flowered during the last three decades of the colony is long and ludicrous.[84]

MANIPULATION OF RACIAL CONFLICT IN THE FACE OF THE INDEPENDENCE THREAT

The metropolis had no particular stake in the color of the planters of Saint Domingue. As long as the French government and French commercial interests continued to rake in countless wealth from the slave trade and from the refining and marketing of sugar, the conflict between the white and colored elites of Saint Domingue was a relatively small matter. Because the white elite had more influence at court, it succeeded in getting discriminatory measures passed. But the metropolis was not adverse to backing the colored elite in its struggle against the white elite, if the interests of France demanded it.

The American Revolution raised the specter of a successful independence movement among the white planters of Saint Domingue, and, as part of its effort to control the white planters, the metropolis attempted to abandon discrimination against the colored elite of Saint Domingue, hoping to rely upon the loyalty of the colored elite as a weapon against the independence-minded whites. A memorandum dating from the 1780s communicated the views of His Majesty that "the most thoughtful people consider the *gens de couleur* as the greatest barrier against troubles from the slaves. This class of men merits concern and care, and it leans toward tempering the established degradation and even bringing it to an end. This delicate subject demands profound thought, and should be carefully considered."[85]

Racial discrimination became intense during the last few decades of the colony, not only as a means of controlling an ever-growing slave population, but, even more important, as an instrument used by ambitious white colonists to degrade and dispossess a segment of the population which was vulnerable to attack on the

[83] *Ibid.*, Ordonnance des administrateurs touchant la boucherie au quartier du Trou, March 16, 1784.

[84] For a brief summary of some discriminatory laws, see James G. Leyburn, *The Haitian People* (New Haven, Conn.: Yale University Press, 1941), pp. 18–19. For texts of the laws, see Moreau de St.-Méry, *Loix*, Arrêt du Conseil du Cap, May 22, 1760; Ordonnance du roi, April 30, 1764; Lettre du ministre aux administrateurs, September 25, 1774; Ordonnance du roi, July 23, 1720; Ordonnance du gouverneur général, May 29, 1762; Lettre du ministre a l'intendant des Isles du Vent, December 30, 1741; Arrêt de règlement du Conseil du Cap, April 17, 1762; Arrêt du Conceil du Cap, January 23, 1769; Arrêt du Conseil du Port-au-Prince, January 13, 1770; Lettre du ministre aux administrateurs, May 27, 1771; Règlements des administrateurs, June 24 and July 16, 1773; Arrêt du Conceil du Port-au-Prince, January 9, 1778; Lettre du ministre aux administrateurs, March 13, 1778; and Règlement provisoire des administrateurs, February 9, 1779.

[85] Quoted in Gisler, *L'esclavage aux Antilles*, 98.

grounds of ancestry. Whatever one might say in favor of the current emphasis upon a psychological explanation for the origin of racial prejudice, the history of Saint Domingue confirms Antoine Gisler's conclusion that "color prejudice, with its great repercussions, had largely a political origin . . . the fruit of the methodical effort of an entire century."[86]

If it is possible to generalize from the history of Saint Domingue, we can conclude that racial antagonism is not a significant, inherent trait in mankind, but an attitude, an emotional response, which in this case was created and manipulated by the state in the interests of promoting a stable slave plantation system and of maintaining political control over a colony which was supplying the metropolis with countless wealth. The obvious implication is that the human mind is malleable, and that it is possible for the state to adopt and implement policies which bring about profound changes in racial attitudes and in social relations.

[86] *Ibid.*, pp. 98, 99.

DOUGLAS HALL

6 | Jamaica

Published accounts of free colored people[1] during slavery are fairly numerous, but they are diffuse and nearly always imprecise. Nonetheless, they leave no doubt that by the end of the eighteenth century the free colored constituted an important social class in the various British colonies of the Caribbean. Nearly every contemporary account of West Indian society then and until emancipation gave them place and described their growing wealth and numbers. When, however, we inquire more exactly how much wealth and what numbers they possessed, the data are unyielding. Brief accounts of the successes of notable individuals are to be found, but such people were not typical, and the measure of their achievements tells us little about the majority except that they were probably far less fortunate.

Population statistics are equally unreliable. In 1826, in reply to a request for figures, the governor of Jamaica explained that

> no dependence can be placed on the accuracy of any Return of the Free Population, as no Census is ever taken of their number. But with respect to the Slaves, as the registration of them takes place in the present year, I shall then be able to furnish your lordship with more accurate information with respect to their number than I could do at the present moment; for although a poll-tax is levied here on Slaves it is very frequently evaded; and no persons possessing less than four Slaves are called upon to pay that duty.[2]

Nonetheless, such estimates as are available do indicate one very important thing: from very small beginnings about the middle of the seventeenth century, the free colored on the eve of the emancipation constituted a large part of the unenslaved population of Jamaica, though they still were far outnumbered by the slaves.

U. B. Phillips referred to the American free colored people as

[1] "Free colored people" is used inclusively of "free browns" and "free blacks," to whom specific reference will be made.

[2] Quoted in "A Return of the Coloured Population in Each of the West India Colonies, as Taken in 1820, and at the Last Census; Distinguishing the Number of Slaves from Free Men and Showing Their Increase or Decrease in That Period" (House of Commons, 1 March 1827).

TABLE 6–1.   Estimates of Population in Jamaica, 1658–1861

Year	Whites	Free Colored	Slaves	Total
1658	4,500	—	1,400	—
1675	8,600	—	9,500	—
1698	7,400	—	40,000	—
1722	7,100	800	80,000	87,900
1746	10,000	—	112,400	—
1768	17,900	3,500	176,900	198,300
1775	18,700	4,500	192,800	216,000
1800	30,000	10,000	300,000	340,000
1834	—	35,000	310,000	—

Census	Whites	Colored	Blacks	
1844	15,776	68,529	293,128	377,433
1861	13,816	81,065	346,374	441,255

Sources: In compiling this table I have used (to the nearest 100) figures provided in the following accounts: R. M. Martin, *The English Colonies* (London, 1852–) vol. 4; F. W. Pitman, *The Development of the West Indies, 1700–1763* (New Haven, Conn., 1917), app. 1; and George W. Roberts, *The Population of Jamaica* (Cambridge, 1957), esp. chap. 2 and table 14 in chap. 3. It is Roberts' view that the estimates of free colored populations before 1844 are too low. There is, however, little to be gained by attempting to explain the figures given in the table, for the sources are largely in disagreement, and, where agreement seems to prevail, it usually reflects repetition rather than informed concurrence.

"an unintended but inevitable by-product of the recourse to Negro labour."[3] In other words, their first appearance was the result of natural causes, not of immigration. In this respect, they differed from the whites and from the slaves. Moreover, in Jamaica, neither whites nor slaves maintained their numbers by natural increase,[4] and for this reason alone the free colored would have appeared as a disquieting phenomenon in the view of the whites, who depended on immi-

[3] U. B. Phillips, *Life and Labor in The Old South* (Boston, 1930), p. 170.
[4] G. W. Roberts, *The Population of Jamaica* (Cambridge, 1957), chap. 2 and table 14, chap. 3. Professor Roberts estimated the average rate of increase of the colored population, 1844–61, at 1 percent per annum. On the basis of even scantier evidence, this estimate appears to be acceptable also for the earlier nineteenth century.

gration to maintain their small presence among the vastly outnumbering slaves.

This unique growth by natural increase can be explained by a number of related factors. Born in the islands, the free colored did not suffer the consequences of the middle passage or of failure to acclimatize to a new environment. As free people, they were not subject to the debilitating cruelties of slavery. And their origins were diffuse, for they were the children of white and free colored, of white and slave, free colored and slave, and free colored and free colored. They differed from the slaves because they were free; they differed from the whites because they were colored. Thus, they formed a distinct third group between the small, white elite and the mass of the enslaved.

Perhaps Jamaican society in the decades preceding emancipation could best be described as a broadly based isosceles triangle with two lines, parallel to the base, marking off a small apex, a large middle section, and a far larger base area. The small apex triangle would represent the whites; the middle section, the free colored people; and the base, the slaves. Within the apex a white could be at the very peak, among the high elite, or at the base line, among the poorest whites. Within that area he might rise or fall, but he could never fall below the base, for he was white. Similarly, though there was some social mobility within the middle area, a free colored person could not move up into the apex. The line separating the free colored from the slaves was less firmly established. Occasionally, free colored people who could not establish their status were thrust down into slavery; others escaped slavery by manumission or by self-purchase. But these movements did not affect the general separation from the others of the massive base stratum of slaves who, though having a hierarchy of their own, were the property of whites and of free colored persons.

The dividing lines between the groups were thus fundamentally different. The division between white and free colored was essentially based on color, whereas the division between free colored and slave was based on legal status. For acceptance in the white apex, a free colored had to become white. For acceptance among the free colored, a slave had to achieve freedom.

Consequently, within the class of free colored people there were grades of social standing based on complexion and on status at birth. The lightest in color were the most eligible to move up. The most recently freed were the most likely to be called upon to prove their freedom.[5] An informal but "elaborate ladder of skin colourings"

---

[5] L. Edward Brathwaite, "The Development of Creole Society in Jamaica, 1770–1820" (D.Phil. thesis, University of Sussex, 1968), p. 215. Manumitted slaves had to carry certificates of freedom and, according to Edward Long (*The History of Jamaica*, 3 vols. [London, 1774]), were supposed to wear a "blue cross" on the right shoulder to mark their freedom.

marked these gradations, though it was apparently less refined than that of the Spanish or Dutch colonies:[6]

Negro: child of Negro and Negro
Sambo: child of mulatto and Negro
Mulatto: child of white and Negro
Quadroon: child of white and mulatto
Mustee: child of white and quadroon
Mustifino: child of white and mustee
Quintroon: child of white and mustifino
Octoroon: child of white and quintroon

The law was less discriminating. Those free colored who were darker than mustifini were regarded either as Negroes or as mulattoes and were subject to all the civil disabilities imposed by successive laws in the eighteenth century. Mustifini and others of even lighter hue were, by law, deemed to be white.[7] We can, therefore, appropriately refer to the free blacks (Negroes and samboes) and the free browns (mulattoes, quadroons, and mustees) as together constituting the free colored people.

There were also, of course, various shades of color among the slaves, and this contributed to the gradations based on status at birth. There were those born into slavery who, sooner or later, by manumission or by purchase, achieved freedom.[8] There were others, born into slavery of slave women by white or free colored fathers, who were given their freedom. Some were born of free colored parents, one or both of whom had previously been slaves. Some were born of free colored parents who had never been slaves and in whose ancestry slavery was perhaps generations in the past. And some were born of free colored women by white fathers. It was these last, in particular, who most obviously threatened white supremacy: they included the lighter skinned, both their parents were free, and it was they who, partly through the generosity of their fathers, were likely to acquire sufficient wealth to participate actively in politics and to gain increasing political power as their numbers grew.

Membership in the colonial assemblies was open only to those who met certain property qualifications and were elected by constituents whose right to vote also rested on the possession of property. The

[6] Brathwaite ("Creole Society in Jamaica," pp. 213–14) quotes from the anonymous publication *Marly* (Glasgow, 1828).

[7] Bryan Edwards, *The History, Civil and Commercial, of the West Indies* (London, 1793), vol. 2, bk. 4, chap. 1, p. 17: "In Jamaica, and I believe in the rest of the Sugar Islands, the descendants of Negroes by White people, entitled by birth to all the rights and liberties of White subjects in the full extent are such as are above three steps removed in lineal digression from the Negro Venter."

[8] But the winning of freedom by either of these means was not common, except in the case of the favored children born of slaveowners by slavewomen.

laws did not at first exclude a colored man of sufficient wealth either from the electorate or from candidacy for election. Thus, the political supremacy of the whites, who owned the largest amount of colonial property in terms of land, crops, and slaves, was assured only so long as the whites remained in the colony, and so long as the non-white freemen were too poor and too few to constitute a political challenge.

The social pre-eminence of the whites rested on their control of landed property, which gave them not only political power but also the wealth with which to purchase those material and other comforts and refinements which a crude colonial agricultural society in the eighteenth century could not provide. It rested also on their ownership of black and colored slaves. When the first settlements were established in the islands, white colonists and white indentured servants labored in the fields. In the mid-seventeenth century, the introduction, however, of large-scale sugar production for export called for far more labor than colonists and indentured laborers from England could provide. In response to this demand, British slave traders marketed Africans, and whites became slaveowners, ceased to labor, and, in defense of their new and obviously preferred status, cultivated the belief that whites could not survive the rigors of physical labor in the tropics. Thus, during slavery and afterward, in wealth and in poverty, whites claimed a superiority based quite simply on their assumed right to supervisory position and their power to maintain it. Their supremacy was complete, but it was vulnerable because it rested largely on the possession of property. In an attempt to shield this vulnerability, the whites, before the mid-eighteenth century, enacted laws intended primarily to limit the opportunities of non-white freemen to acquire important position, property, or political influence.

The laws of Jamaica were, of course, peculiar to that colony, but they were representative of the general pattern of measures by which the free colored were dispossessed of certain basic rights of full citizenship in the British Caribbean colonies. In 1711 the Jamaican legislature excluded the free colored from employment in any political or public office; in 1713 it barred them from supervisory employment on the estates; in 1733 it deprived them of the right to vote; and in 1761 it forbade them either to purchase land exceeding a value of £2,000, Jamaican currency (three-fifths sterling), or to inherit property or money in excess of that amount from a white person. Other acts of the Assembly prevented the free colored from testifying in the courts of the island, from serving as "deficiency men" for slaveowners,[9] and from navigating coastal vessels, and

---

[9] The "deficiency" law required that a slaveowner employ one free (white) man for every twenty slaves in his possession. The purpose of the law was to provide a militia to defend against possible slave revolt. Free colored slaveowners were not allowed to employ the free colored as "deficiency men" and found it difficult to employ whites.

barred them from a number of other rights and privileges enjoyed by whites.[10]

Attacks on privilege spring from three identifiable sources of discontent: from those whose opposition is idealistic, based on some principle of the immorality of inequality; from others, whose antagonism is aroused because persons of privilege abuse the use of it; and from those who fight established privilege simply because they want to win it for themselves. In the long struggles of the free colored people in Jamaica to achieve equality of status with the whites there was, by definition of their aim, obviously little concern with fundamental egalitarian principle.[11] They did not attempt to unshackle the slaves; indeed, in some cases they were committed slaveowners. Nor did they try to tumble the social hierarchy.

> Had the West Indian whites been able to see it, the aims of the free coloured were strictly limited. Their methods were basically constitutional. They had no intention of overturning the society, merely of improving their own place in it. . . . They pointed out how the principles of liberalism had gone awry in their case, and asked for a restitution of their rights. This was one of their basic assumptions —that they had lost rights which were theirs originally, and which had been gradually whittled away during the eighteenth century.[12]

In short, they wished to reverse the trend of legislation by which the whites had limited the rights of the free colored. They sought equality of status and of privilege, and they recognized their exclusion as the main form of abuse exercised by whites.

Not all the free colored joined in these aspirations and complaints. Within their own ranks divisions based on color of skin, parentage, wealth, education, and other factors brought disunity between the free blacks, whose distinguishing mark was more obvious and whose parentage was generally more humble, and the free browns, who were much nearer white, were in better social standing, and generally were wealthier. Among both groups there were those who sought not so much the removal of disabilities affecting their class as their own individual recognition as the equals of whites. Thus, it is possible to distinguish two phases of the free colored response to legal discrimination against them: first, that in which individuals who had in some way advanced beyond the majority of their class sought special recognition; and, second, emerging in the early nineteenth century, that in which the free colored as a class began to

[10] They could not, for instance, join the militia cavalry or hold commissions in the militia foot. They were required to carry certificates of freedom. And there were other disabilities.

[11] The free browns, for instance, did not always find common cause with the free blacks.

[12] Sheila Duncker, "The Free Coloured and their Fight for Civil Rights in Jamaica, 1800–1830" (Master's thesis, London University, n.d.), p. 177.

press for the general removal of all disabilities inflicted on them by law.

The whites were not disposed to admit that the free colored had been dispossessed of rights. As Richard Barrett, Speaker of the Jamaican Assembly, once expressed it, the free colored had not been deprived of anything, because they had possessed no rights originally. They were "bastards" who, having no fathers, were by English law "children of the people." "Not all are English who are born in the English dominions."[13] By implication, therefore, their petitions were, properly speaking, requests for grace and favor, not demands for rights. The special-privilege acts of Jamaica certainly seem to have borne this interpretation, for their existence was not based on clearly established criteria.

The free colored petitioned the legislature in order to secure the enactment of a private bill stating that the petitioner himself, or the child or other dependent on whose behalf the petition was made, would be allowed exemption from one or more of the disabling acts affecting the free colored generally. For instance, the first two of these private bills, both of which were passed in 1707, granted to John Williams and to Manuel Bartholomew the right to be "tried according to the known laws, customs, and privileges of Englishmen"; but each bill specified that in all other respects the petitioner would "remain to all intents and purposes in the state and circumstances of a free Negro as before this Act."[14]

Nor was it enough for the petitioner simply to ask. His qualifications had to be made clear.

> That the petitioner hath caused all his natural children to be baptized, educated and instructed in the principles of the Christian religion, and intends bringing them up in a respectable manner, and to bestow on them such fortunes as to raise them above the common level of people of colour. . . .
> That by the unfortunate circumstances of their births, they are subject and liable to the same rules of government, and to the same pains and penalties, as free negroes and mulattoes are, who have no education:
> The petitioner therefore humbly prays, that the house will be pleased to give leave to bring in a bill, for the granting unto . . . the before-mentioned children, the like privileges as have been hitherto granted to persons under the same circumstances.[15]

[13] Richard Barrett, A Reply to the Speech of Dr. Lushington in the House of Commons on 12 June 1827 on the . . . Free Coloured People of Jamaica" (London, 1828).

[14] Samuel J. Hurwitz and Edith F. Hurwitz, "A Token of Freedom: Private Bill Legislation for Free Negroes in Eighteenth Century Jamaica," William and Mary Quarterly, 3rd ser. 24, no. 3 (1967).

[15] Journals of the Assembly of Jamaica, vol. VII, fol. 537, 18 December 1782, quoted in Brathwaite, "Creole Society in Jamaica," p. 218.

The stated qualifications are interesting. Baptism brought the person within the Christian church and thus both removed the stain of heathenism and gave substance to the oath sworn on the Bible. Respectable upbringing and good financial standing would lift an individual above the majority of his color.

In 1824, in his petition for special privileges, James Rowe Williamson of the parish of Saint Elizabeth pointed out that he had been well educated in England, owned considerable property in the parish, and that he had "the good fortune from correct conduct to obtain the confidence and good opinion of some of the most respectable white inhabitants of the parishes of St. Elizabeth and Manchester, and has been admitted into their society."[16]

Not all the petitioners were near-white. James Swaby, who was said to be a sambo but was probably a quadroon, owned a considerable amount of property in the parish of Manchester. He had been educated at Charter House in England, had held a commission in His Majesty's Forty-ninth Regiment of Foot, and in 1823 was living in Jamaica on half-pay. He, too, was described as "highly esteemed by the different white inhabitants of Manchester and is admitted to their society and treated in every respect as a white person."[17]

Daniel Saa was a mulatto of Spanish Town, Jamaica.[18] His father was a white mason and bricklayer, and his mother was a black slave. His father had given him his freedom and taught him the trade. He had also had him baptized. In 1810 his father died, leaving Daniel with a large family to support and debts to pay. Daniel trained the family as masons, paid off the debts, and by 1823 owned forty slaves and a house in Spanish Town valued at £2,000. In that year, with the support of many Spanish Town whites, including members of the Assembly and Council (Spanish Town was the capital and the seat of government), Daniel Saa petitioned the legislature for special privileges. This was his second such petition, an earlier one having been made in 1792.

Between 1819 and 1828 Daniel Saa worked chiefly on government contracts, and the records clearly indicate that he was a well-qualified man in his trade. As an experienced employer of a fairly large number of laborers, he occupied a supervisory position which, together with his membership in the Church of England and his apparent cultivation of white associates, identified him with whites rather than with people of his own color. In response to this identification, and in pursuit of more business, he several times, and apparently with success, petitioned the legislature for privileges. By the middle 1830s he owned imposing houses in Spanish Town, including

[16] *Votes of the Jamaica Assembly, 1824*, quoted in Duncker, "The Free Coloured," p. 39.
[17] Duncker, "The Free Coloured," p. 42.
[18] The details of Daniel Saa's achievements were taken from *ibid.*, pp. 94–100.

those rented by the rector, the inspector-general of police, and the chief justice. In addition, he was treasurer of the parish vestry and a manager of the School of Industry. He died in 1842, leaving a wife, Jane Saa, and a son, Thomas, whose mother was Anne Peeke, a free mulatto.

Between the years 1772 and 1796, petitions to the Jamaican legislature were made in behalf of 90 mustees, 245 quadroons, 176 mulattoes, and 1 Negro.[19] In 1802 the hearing of such petitions was discontinued and was not generally resumed until 1823. There are three possible explanations for the break. It may have reflected increasing anxiety in Jamaica after the revolution in Saint Domingue, as well as the subsequent immigration of French colonial refugees, who could have hardened the attitudes of Jamaican Whites against any form of allowance of increased liberty to claimants.[20] It perhaps reflected uncertainty of the loyalties of the free colored in the event of a French invasion. It probably did happen, at least in part, as a reaction to the sudden realization that the free colored were becoming numerous and increasingly wealthy. The resumption of the hearings in 1823 was very likely brought about by the growing pressure of free colored demands for the removal of all disabilities against them as a class, and the Assembly's preference for maintaining the control that the special-privilege acts gave to the legislature.[21] Between 1823 and 1830, when the disabilities of the Jamaican free colored were totally removed, petitions for special privileges were made in behalf of 200 persons.[22]

The brief account of Daniel Saa's career points to two factors that contributed to the gradual emergence of some solidarity of purpose among the free colored: their urban concentration and their growing wealth. A third factor, and one no less important, was the example and the leadership provided by individual free colored in the early nineteenth century.

In all the British colonies there was a strong tendency on the part of free colored people to concentrate in the towns.[23] They were

[19] Brathwaite, "Creole Society in Jamaica," p. 218.

[20] The extent to which revolutionary ideas and tendencies were brought to Jamaica from Haiti in the late eighteenth and early nineteenth centuries is still largely a matter of conjecture. A recent thesis by Mavis Campbell, "Edward Jordon and the Free Coloured People in Jamaica" (London, 1968), suggests a greater influence and more positive reactions than had previously been supposed.

[21] Duncker, "The Free Coloured," p. 43.

[22] Ibid., p. 48.

[23] There is much evidence of this. It appears that, of 3,408 free colored who, following the requirements of an act of 1761, applied for "certificates of freedom," 1,093 lived in Kingston. (See Roberts, The Population of Jamaica, p. 39.) The general observation is made in many other contemporary accounts —for instance, in [J. Stewart], An Account of Jamaica and Its Inhabitants (London, 1808).

not willing to labor on the sugar estates, because they had no wish to lose their identity among the mass of slaves. This unwillingness was not entirely a matter of pride. The free colored, and especially the free black, was constantly engaged in the protection of his freedom. His color identified him with the slaves rather than with the free, and it was not therefore strange that he should try to emphasize his higher status. Those who remained in rural, agricultural areas did so as skilled workers, shopkeepers, and as proprietors of land and slaves; the operation of an estate, however, brought additional difficulties. The free colored were required to employ white "deficiency" employees in proportion to the number of slaves they owned. This raised problems and complaints. The free colored found it difficult to employ whites, and, unless they could produce certificates of baptism, their qualification to give, under oath, the annual account of produce from their property was not recognized.[24]

In the towns, the free colored were largely engaged in "service" occupations and professions. They purchased slaves and earned an income by hiring them out as "jobbers"; they engaged in the retail trade as "hucksters" or "higglers" or as shopkeepers; they acquired skills and tools of trade as carpenters, masons, wheelwrights, plumbers, and other artisans; they occupied subordinate positions in the businesses of white merchants and professional men; and some who had the advantages of a more advanced education or greater financial resources were to be found working as journalists, lawyers, schoolteachers, innkeepers, and merchants on their own account.[25]

The organization of the production and marketing of sugar was such that it almost entirely by-passed the local merchants. Estates dealt directly with their merchants and agents in Britain.[26] There were certain essential supplies, however, such as lumber, staves, salted fish, and livestock, which the estates could not obtain from Britain. It was in the supply of these demands that the American–West Indian trade flourished in the eighteenth century; and because a large volume of the trade was carried on by comparatively small enterprises, visiting ships' captains and supercargoes established commercial relationships with local dealers in the individual colonies. There is evidence that in Jamaica many of these local merchants were free colored.[27]

Though American trade was for some time diminished by the War of Independence of the United States and the consequent exclu-

[24] Duncker, "The Free Coloured," pp. 30, 31.

[25] Douglas Hall, "The Social and Economic Background to Sugar in Slave Days," Caribbean Historical Review, nos. 3–4 (1955).

[26] This is amply illustrated in the works of Richard Pares and F. W. Pitman dealing with the British West Indian colonies and trade.

[27] This can be substantiated by referring to contemporary newspaper advertisements and other articles, as well as to issues of the Jamaica Almanack and Jamaica Handbook.

sion of that country from direct participation in the British imperial trade, local merchants in the Caribbean benefited from higher prices for scarce goods, from the general rise of prices during the French, Napoleonic, and Anglo-American wars, and from the extension of trade in the eighteenth century through the creation of free ports in the British Caribbean.

Because they were suppliers of essential goods to estates, these local merchants eventually became creditors of the estate owners, and, after the Napoleonic Wars, when sugar prices fell and many estates tottered on the brink of bankruptcy, they were able to use accumulated capital or credit in the acquisition of landed property in the islands. By these means, some free colored merchants became estate owners and established themselves as members, as well as providers, of the plantocracy. In so doing, they obviously strengthened their claim to social acceptance by whites; but the new relationship did not necessarily persuade the whites of anything beyond the convenience, for business reasons, of accommodating the advancement of a small number of free colored.

White support for the claims of the free colored as a class was based less upon approval than upon the fear of slave rebellions such as had occurred in the late eighteenth century in Haiti. In 1830, a letter signed "Jamaica Proprietor" was published in *The Watchman and Jamaica Free Press*,[28] a newspaper devoted to the cause of free colored advancement. The writer pointed to the growing strength of the free browns, and suggested that, in order to meet the numerical preponderance of the free blacks, "the whites should place the browns gradually on a footing with ourselves, to create a defensive alliance which may prove a security to us in our hour of need." Such an alliance, he continued, was possible because the brown people "entertain the same jealousy towards the blacks, that we do towards them."[29]

To this, Edward Jordon, the colored proprietor of the newspaper, replied that the whites had always followed a "divide and rule" policy toward the free colored people, but that it was no longer effective, for that policy had eventually served to bring the two groups into common protest against discrimination.[30] Jordon's part in creating public

[28] *The Watchman and Jamaica Free Press* was first published in 1829. The letter quoted appeared in the issue of 22 May 1830.

[29] *Ibid.*

[30] The extent to which Jordon's claim was true is still to be ascertained. There is little doubt that the free blacks and free browns were not always in agreement during slavery, and after slavery there was even more evidence of disunity. It is possible that in the last few years before emancipation the browns turned to the blacks for support in their struggles for equal rights with whites; but, again, recent research suggests that, in Jamaica, Jordon's alliance with the blacks was a matter of political expedience rather than of common belief, and that his political behavior after emancipation indicated his greater interest in maintaining white supremacy. See Campbell, "Edward Jordon."

204   DOUGLAS HALL

TABLE 6–2.   Children Attending Wolmer's Free School
in Kingston, 1814–1834

Year	White Children	Colored Children	Total
1814	87	—	87
1816	129	25	154
1818	155	38	193
1820	116	78	194
1822	93	167	260
1824	94	196	290
1826	93	176	269
1828	88	152	240
1830	88	194	282
1832	90	360	450
1834	81	420	501

Source: J. A. Thome and J. H. Kimball, *Emancipation in the West Indies*
(New York, 1838), p. 87.
Note: In 1830 the last disabilities of the free colored were removed.

opinion in support of the free colored was important. In the 1830s,
two visitors reported:

> One of the largest bookstores in the island is owned by two colored
> men (Messrs. Jordon and Osborn . . .). Connected with it is an exten-
> sive printing-office, from which a newspaper is issued twice a week.
> Another paper, under the control of colored men, is published at
> Spanishtown. These are the two principal liberal presses in Jamaica,
> and are conducted with spirit and ability. Their influence in the
> political and civil affairs of the island is very great. They are the
> organs of the colored people, bond and free, and through them any
> violation of law or humanity is exposed to the public, and redress
> demanded.[31]

Moreover, gradually in the early nineteenth century the free colored
were becoming better equipped to respond to the newspapers. In
Kingston, by 1821 the majority of the children in Wolmer's Free
School, the largest in the city, were colored.

[31] J. A. Thome and J. H. Kimball, *Emancipation in the West Indies*
(New York, 1838), p. 90.

Apart from people such as Edward Jordon and Robert Osborn, there were other free colored (of whom perhaps the most distinguished was Richard Hill of Spanish Town[32]) who, after spending his adolescence in England in school and university, had returned to Jamaica and entered the lists as a champion of the cause of the free colored. Highly praised by many who met him, Richard Hill was described in glowing terms in the 1830s:

> He is a colored gentleman, and in every respect the noblest man; white or black, whom we met in the West Indies. He is highly intelligent, and of fine moral feelings. His manners are free and unassuming, and his language in conversation fluent and well chosen. He is intimately acquainted with English and French authors, and has studied thoroughly the history and character of the people with whom the tie of color has connected him. He travelled two years in Hayti, and his letters . . . were published extensively in England.[33]

It was Richard Hill who in 1827 was permitted "within the bar" of the House of Commons in England to present the case of the free colored of Jamaica in their claim for equality with the whites.[34]

Under the influence of men such as Jordon, Osborn, and Hill, a common cause slowly began to take shape. The cause was not, however, violently expressed. The conservatism of the free colored had many bases. The restrictions imposed on them constituted a severe limitation of their civil rights; but, when they are examined in the light of their numbers and their conditions during most of the eighteenth century, it becomes clear that they would hardly have constituted a rallying cry for violent opposition to the whites. The exclusion of the colored from candidacy for membership in the assemblies or from holding public office, for instance, would have irritated only those who were qualified in both property and pretension to such position. At a time when the vote was not anywhere in the common man's possession, the poor free colored was scarcely likely to revolt in demand of it, especially in a slave society in which revolt was feared by all who were free. Exlusion from supervisory positions on the estates denied the free colored a particular occupation and thus irritated only those who would have found that way of earning a living attractive. Restrictions on land purchases beyond a certain value would have affected only those who were comparatively wealthy and planned to become landowners on a fairly large scale.

There can be little doubt that the restriction which was most generally abhorrent was the limitation on the right to testify in the

---

[32] Richard Hill was a lawyer, naturalist, historian, founder of many cultural and educational societies, and at times secretary to the Stipendiary Magistracy of the island, senior magistrate in the parish of Saint Catherine, member of the Assembly, and member of the island's Privy Council.

[33] Thome and Kimball, *Emancipation in the West Indies*, pp. 104–6.

[34] Clinton Black, *Living Names in Jamaica's History* (Kingston, n.d.).

courts, for this applied to all free colored people. Even though the law curtailed their freedom, it was to the law that they looked for the protection of those rights which remained. It is interesting to note that this restriction was one of the first to be removed, and that even in its removal an attempt was made to maintain the distinction between white and colored.[35]

The restrictions were individually and collectively oppressive, but the point to be made is that the oppression was not commonly and equally suffered; those who might have been roused to action were restrained by fear of the consequences of action. In any revolt, the free colored, and especially the free blacks, would have been the targets of whites, who would not have stopped to investigate their free status, and of slaves, who would not have been much concerned about the color of the enemy.

Much was said in Jamaica in the later eighteenth and early nineteenth centuries about the large numbers of free colored who were members of the militia and who consequently knew something of the "art of war."[36] But, even in Jamaica, where their absolute number was greatest, they could hardly have hoped to overthrow the whites and, at the same time, hold the slaves in their place. Moreover, any attempt at revolt would have brought the free colored into opposition with Britain as well as with the colonial government. This was not a risk that could be taken lightly, and, as time passed and the free colored became stronger in numbers and in wealth, they gained increasing support from British humanitarians in their protests against discrimination.

This is not to say that the free colored were always moderate in their language. In Jamaica in 1831, Edward Jordon urged the free colored to "bring down the system by the run, knock off the fetters, and let the oppressed go free." He was brought to trial and acquitted of a charge of sedition.[37] There were also less open charges of revolutionary intent. In 1823, L. C. Lecesne and J. Escoffery, signatories to a general free colored petition to the Jamaican Assembly, were deported[38] on the grounds that they sought "to place themselves on a footing with the White population" and were dangerous individuals, aliens, and members of a society "obnoxious to government."

Lecesne was the son of a white French refugee from Saint Domingue by a black woman. Escoffery's father, also a refugee from

---

[35] Until 1796 they could not testify even in cases in which they were involved, and they could not, until 1813, appear in cases involving whites.

[36] Great Britain, Hansard Parliamentary Debates (Commons), 2nd ser., "Debate . . . on Dr. Lushington's Motion respecting the Deportation of Messrs. L. C. Lecesne and J. Escoffery (Persons of Colour)," 16 June 1825.

[37] Thome and Kimball, Emancipation in the West Indies, pp. 88, 89.

[38] See note 36 above and Dr. Lushington's letter to Courtenay, 17 September 1826, bound in the same volume, for details of the Lecesne and Escoffery case.

Saint Domingue, was an Italian and his mother a sambo. Both
Lecesne and Escoffery had been born in Jamaica. Both were engaged
in trade, and Lecesne admitted to trading with Haiti, but that was
not in itself illegal. A memorial in favor of the accused had unavail-
ingly been presented by thirty-five people, including five magistrates,
the island's provost marshall, a member of the House of Assembly,
and a number of "respectable merchants." The case is especially interesting as an illustration of the attitude of the Assembly toward the
free colored, whose petition had been rejected out of hand, and because the charges against Lecesne and Escoffery, who were only two
of a number of "the most influential" free colored who had signed it,
were largely based on their French Saint Dominguan connections and
their membership in an "obnoxious" society, which they claimed was
a benevolent society. The existence of free colored "cells" is implied,
and the remaining anxiety about events in Haiti is clear.

The Haitian revolution certainly affected the British Caribbean,
but there is still much uncertainty about the extent to which individuals such as Lecesne and Escoffery, in the 1820s, and those involved in the Maroon uprising of the late eighteenth century and the
slave rebellion of 1830–31 in the western parishes of Jamaica, were
agents of revolution. In Jamaica, unlike the Windwards, there was
no military action which could be clearly ascribed either to revolutionary influences from Europe or to revolutionary intent on the part
of the free colored.

The protests of the Jamaican free colored were expressed in
petitions and memorials to the assemblies and to the crown, as well
as in growing appeals to public sentiment on the island itself. Petitions generally are not likely to succeed unless they are backed either
by large numbers or by large influence, or both; and a sustained
effort to influence public opinion requires capital as much as it demands devotion. It was not until the nineteenth century that the free
colored were sufficiently numerous, wealthy, and influential to operate successfully in these ways. The most famous of their petitions in
Jamaica was submitted in 1823, and in 1827 a great stir was made
in Parliament by Dr. Lushington in their behalf. *The Watchman and
Jamaica Free Press*, owned and edited by Edward Jordon and Robert
Osborn, was first published in 1829.

The British colonial legislatures' gradual removal of restrictive
laws began in the nineteenth century. It is clear that this yielding
was, at least in part, a consequence of the recognition of the increasing affluence and influence of the free colored. But this recognition
was not the sole cause. The first removals came in the crown colonies
in which local legislatures did not obstruct metropolitan policy and
direction. The fact that, of the islands with elected legislatures, restrictions were removed first in Jamaica, then in Barbados, and lastly
in the Leewards, suggests that the pushing of the free colored was
least resistible where they were most numerous and wealthiest. This

is not as remarkable, however, as the fact that even in Jamaica the restrictions were not totally removed until 1830; the delay suggests that a close relationship existed between the removal of free colored disabilities and the general movement toward the emancipation of the slaves. Even to the most intransigent colonial legislature it was clear that the free colored could not continue to be discriminated against when all blacks and colored would, by English law, be equal citizens with whites. No account of the success of the free colored during the early nineteenth century can ignore the influence in their behalf of the anti-slavery campaign in Britain, an influence made both stronger and more direct by the association of accomplished free colored, such as Richard Hill, with the emancipationists in Britain.

In trying to assess the contributory factors in the admission of the free colored to legal equality with whites, it is therefore necessary to recognize: the efforts made by individual free colored people who, by action or example, were champions of the cause; the simple fact that, as the free colored grew in numbers and in wealth, they began to exert pressure against the preserves of whites who were at the same time becoming fewer and poorer; the increasing number and strength of free colored challenges, by petition or debate, in the nineteenth century; the anxiety of the whites which followed the revolution in Haiti and was increased by the pre-emancipation restlessness of the slave populations; and the influence of the humanitarian movement and the turn of British policy toward emancipation. It would not be easy to determine the relative contribution of each of these, but one thing is quite clear: the whites were not morally persuaded; they surrendered. None of the pressures served to weaken in any significant measure the prejudice in favor of "pure blood."

The Colonial Acts, by which the legal disabilities of the free colored were removed, and the Acts of Abolition, by which slavery was brought to an end, removed the legal supports to those barriers which had, in slavery, separated whites, free colored, and slaves. Ex-slaves automatically became free colored people. But free colored people could not automatically become white. There was no longer any need to petition for special privilege, but it remained necessary for the free colored to seek that patronage by which they might be admitted into white society. The notion of "pure blood" still carried influence.

Very early in the history of Jamaican colonization, it had become the practice for white men to take black or colored women— slave or free—as mistresses. As I have remarked elsewhere,

> Those who came to the sugar colonies to attempt a fortune seemed to travel light, unencumbered with familial obstacles to their enterprises. When a man had made his fortune he sought a wife to give him the heir who might inherit it. Whereas the quest for sexual ad-

venture could be easily satisfied among the slave women and the poorer whites and free coloureds in a colony, the search for a wife generally led back to Britain. When whiteness of skin was one of the determinants of social excellence it was wiser, for those who wished to reach the top, whether as residents or abroad, to seek a wife whose complexion was clearly virgin, and whose pedigree was either rightfully emblazoned or easily embellished.[39]

There was no great secretiveness about these relationships between white men and colored women. Those men who could afford it were often generous to their mistresses and to the children produced by their union. Free colored women sought liaisons with white men both for the possible material advantages that might accrue and in the expectation that their children, though illegitimate, would be better off in a society in which so large a premium was placed on whiteness.

In Jamaica during the 1770s, Edward Long had voiced ineffectual disapproval of these relationships:

> [It would be far better if in Jamaica] the white men . . . would abate of their infatuated attachments to black women, and, instead of being "grac'd with a yellow offspring not their own," perform the duty incumbent on every good citizen, by raising in honourable wedlock a race of unadulterated beings.[40]

But so common was the preference of colored women for men of lighter skin that Long was led to observe that the barrenness of the few marriages he knew of between colored men and colored women seemed to indicate that mulattoes were "in this respect . . . actually of the mule-kind, and not so capable of producing from one another as from commerce with a distinct White or Black."[41]

Another, later, observer remarked on the comparatively few marriages between men and women of color:

> if the females of color are asked why they do not more generally intermarry with men of their own class, their reply is, that the greater number of the brown men are either too poor or too indolent to support a wife and family and that moreover as husbands they are prone to be jealous and tyrannical. But the truth is it is not the

---

[39] Douglas Hall, "Absentee Proprietorship in the British West Indies to about 1850," *The Jamaican Historical Review* 4 (1964): 26. The influence of absentee proprietorship on the role and function of the free colored is not treated in this paper, because even less is known about it. It is possible to suggest, however, that the free colored might have thought it more realistic to aspire to managerial position (such as was held by white estate attornies and managers, which, in the absence of the "lord of the manor," carried political and social prestige and power) than to the status of proprietors in their own right.

[40] Long, *The History of Jamaica*, 2: 327, quoted in Brathwaite, "Creole Society in Jamaica," p. 224.

[41] *Ibid.*, p. 335, quoted in Brathwaite.

custom of the country for these females to marry, and their own inclination is in unison with the prevailing interest.[42]

In clear and specific illustration of this inclination was the will of Frances Mackie, a free black woman of the parish of Westmoreland, in which she complained of the behavior of her granddaughter, Ann Delap, whom she had lately bought out of slavery, and expressed the desire that Ann should either "live as housekeeper to any creditable white person" or marry "with any decent person of colour." Should Ann fail to take either of these courses, she would forfeit her inheritance.[43]

With the exception of the few who risked, and usually sufferd, ostracism by their fellows, white men did not marry colored women. They did, however, acknowledge certain responsibilities, and, as concubinage became established as a social institution, neglect of these responsibilities brought its lesser penalties of blame. A colored mistress expected certain basic provisions for herself[44] and her children. Moreover, the general stability of these relationships was reflected in the social code by which a white man was restrained from trying to take another man's mistress.[45]

Many whites went beyond the recognized requirements and treated their colored mistresses and their children with special regard. George Girton Saunders of Saint Thomas, in eastern Jamaica, left his clothes, furniture, and carriage to "Miss Grace Lindsay who has lived with me faithfully according to the manners and customs of this country."[46] Some free colored women were left considerable property by their keepers. Those men who could afford to do so sent their colored children to England for schooling; there, some married and settled, while others, having gained professional qualification, returned to the West Indies. It was the latter in particular who drew the jealously of less qualified whites. The Reverend Thomas Cooper, who had visited Jamaica in 1817, remarked of these free colored children of white men and free brown women: "Much jealousy is entertained of them, especially when they have been educated in England, where they have been treated as men and on a footing of equality with their white brethren."[47] On the other side, much impatience prevailed among those who, having experienced such treatment in Britain, returned to their colonial birthplaces only to meet the prejudice of the slave society and its legal expression.

[42] J. Stewart, *A View of the Past and Present State of the Island of Jamaica* (Edinburgh, 1823), p. 328, quoted in Duncker, "The Free Coloured," pp. 55, 56.
[43] Duncker, "The Free Coloured," p. 57.
[44] Sheila Duncker (*ibid.*, p. 56) refers to "medical fees for his housekeeper's confinements" as "one of the recognized responsibilities of the man."
[45] *Ibid.*, p. 50 and n.
[46] *Ibid.*, pp. 59, 60.
[47] Quoted in *ibid.*, p. 125.

Edward Long, for instance, had called the mulattoes "mule-kind" and had implied the superiority of both blacks and whites over impure hybrids. As late as 1828, Richard Barrett, Speaker of the Jamaica Assembly, had declared his views and defended his prejudices in the English press:

> You hate a Jew much, a Unitarian a little more than a Jew, and a Roman Catholic you both hate and fear. We West Indians have no repugnance to sit with a Jew, but we dislike the contact and the smell of a negro. We think little of the religious doubts of the Unitarians, but we have been used from infancy to keep mulatto men at a distance. We do not puzzle ourselves much about the mummeries of popery, but, on the other hand, we love the pure blood of an English countryman better than the mixed stream that flows in the veins of the other descendants of the negro.[48]

Mr. Barrett was being at least a little hypocritical (but carefully so, for he restricted his avoidance of mulattoes to the men); at the same time, his basic attitudes were quite clearly described.

Between the "pure white," the paragon of intellectuality and high civilization, and the "pure black," the paragon of brute strength and barbarism, free colored people shifted uneasily, patronized by the whites and disliked by the slaves:

> a white and a brown child sent to Europe at the same time, and brought up together at the same school, though they may be in habits of the strictest intimacy while there, discontinue that intimacy on their growing up and returning to the West Indies; though both may be equally amiable and accomplished. The white miss disowns, with a supercilious frown, her quondam companion and school fellow, because she has been born with a deeper tinge of the brunette, and the customs and distinctions of the country forbid her cultivating such acquaintance.[49]

On the other side, "the negroes . . . are wont to say 'If me for have mistress, give me Buckera mistress, no give me Mulatto, them no use neega well.' "[50]

Social life in the colonies reflected these divisions:

> blacks had their own social life in town and on plantation; the wealthy free coloureds had theirs, mainly in the large towns; and the whites had theirs. With the exception of the theatre, coloured people, not to mention black, did not appear at public entertainment designed for the whites.[51]

[48] Barrett, "A Reply to the Speech of Dr. Lushington."
[49] [Stewart], *An Account of Jamaica*, p. 302.
[50] *Ibid.*, p. 305.
[51] Brathwaite, "Creole Society in Jamaica," p. 23.

But even in the theater the distinction was sometimes maintained:

> An Artist lately arrived from the city of Augsburg in Germany, begs
> to inform the Ladies and Gentlemen . . . that he exhibits many
> curious exercises by living Birds as performed before the Emperor of
> Germany, and His Most Christian Majesty Lewis the XVI and other
> European Courts. . . . He also performs with little dogs. Admittance
> 3s. 4d. each. Only white persons will be admitted to the above per-
> formance. Tomorrow he intends exhibiting to persons of colour.[52]

Strive as he might, the colored person, however well informed, however well apparalled, however genteel in manner, however rich, could
not enter the doors of white society without particular invitation or
allowance.

The slaves too had their own social life,[53] in which neither
whites nor free colored deigned to share. The place of the free colored
in the social hierarchy, it must be remembered, largely depended on
the extent to which they showed themselves to be different from the
slaves and nearer to the whites in color, in wealth, and in behavior
and opinion. The dislike with which they were generally reported to
be viewed by the slaves was doubtless stimulated by their insistence
on their superior status, which they said was clearly marked, not by
their skin color, but by their freedom and their claim to equality with
whites.

During the period of slavery the free colored, even more than
the masters and the slaves,

> represented the embarrassments of the slave society. The master
> possessed a woman who was a slave and who bore him a child who
> was a chattel. The father, as an individual, perhaps freed his child
> from chattel-status, but could not offend the group of white slave-
> owners by offering a coloured child a place among them. The child,
> freed from slavery, sought to achieve "white" status in order to em-
> phasize his separation from servitude. But in so doing he had both
> to undermine the common equation of "whiteness" with "suprem-
> acy," and to exemplify the capacities of the Negro from whom he
> wished to dissociate himself. And, at the same time, to mark his
> increasing age, wealth, and status he became the owner of chattel-
> slaves.[54]

The removal of free colored disabilities and the abolition of slavery
did not, could not, immediately lead to fundamental social change.
The rooted prejudices of the slave society remained to obstruct any
real progress in the "great social experiment" which the abolitionists
proclaimed as their program.

[52] Quoted in *ibid.*, p. 238.
[53] *Ibid.*, esp. chaps. 11 and 12.
[54] Douglas Hall, "Slaves and Slavery in the British West Indies," *Social
and Economic Studies* 11, no. 4 (1962): 313.

BIBLIOGRAPHICAL NOTE

The sources of information fall broadly into three categories:

Official Papers. These include the parliamentary and colonial government papers. The former are printed and are both accessible and very useful since papers relating to slave and free coloured populations were periodically collated. They contain statements of official view and policy and such factual and quantitative material as could be secured at the request of the Colonial Office.

Contemporary Accounts. Nearly every contemporary writer had something to say about the free colored. Of particular value, however, are the works of Edward Long, Bryan Edwards, and James Stewart, all intelligent observers whose works appeared in 1774, 1793, and 1808 respectively, thus giving a succession of views over a critical period of time. In addition, the colonial newspapers carried valuable and interesting reports and comments from time to time.

Recent Work. Here there is no doubt of the valuable contributions of Sheila Duncker and L. Edward Brathwaite, both of whose theses have been used, almost to the level of academic impropriety, in the present paper. Dr. Brathwaite's study, much revised in the light of more recent research (and published by Clarendon Press in 1972 under the title *The Development of Creole Society in Jamaica, 1770–1820*), includes relevant bibliographical material in greater detail and of far more consequence than these brief notes afford.

JEROME S. HANDLER AND ARNOLD A. SIO

7 | Barbados

INTRODUCTION

The first European settlement in Barbados was established in 1627. In its early years, the island's economy rested upon the production of tobacco, cotton, and indigo, which were grown on small holdings by free and indentured Europeans. Barbados became the first British possession in the Caribbean to grow sugar on a large scale, and during the 1640s its economy was transformed into one based upon plantation production and slave labor. As the plantation system expanded, thousands of Europeans left in search of land and opportunities elsewhere, and thousands of Africans were imported to take their place. By the middle of the century, the plantation slave system was firmly entrenched and the island's flourishing sugar-based economy made it (until later surpassed by Jamaica) the richest of Britain's Caribbean possessions. The fundamental social, political, and economic institutions established during the seventeenth century persisted until emancipation in 1834. Although absentee plantation owners were common, the island had many locally based (and native-born) planters and, throughout most of its history, a larger proportion of whites than did other British West Indian territories. Whites dominated and controlled the national institutions and were instrumental in perpetuating a rigid stratification system based to a considerable degree on racial origins.

Barbadian slave society conformed to the wider Caribbean model of essentially two broad social strata; although each was internally segmented, there was, on the one hand, a relatively small population of European ancestry, which controlled the island's means of production, state organization, and other national institutions, and, on the other, a slave population largely composed of persons of African descent. Gradually, over the years, a third group emerged which was comprised of persons whose racial ancestry was mixed or solely Negroid, but whose legal status was that of free persons. As free persons, white society accorded them certain privileges and rights not extended to slaves, but because of their racial ancestry they were denied other privileges and rights which white society reserved for itself. This group of freedmen, whose status was often ambiguously defined and who were frequently subjected to opposing pressures from both whites and slaves, is the subject of our study. In this paper we present an overview of a hitherto undescribed segment of Barbados slave society, and, by extension, we provide the data necessary for comparative studies of freedmen in Caribbean and New World slave societies in general.[1] We focus on the period from the end of the eighteenth century to 1834, the year of general emancipation in the British West Indies. Although we provide some discussion of the eighteenth century, there were relatively few freedmen during this time, and the major period considered falls within the first three decades of the nineteenth century.

Because there are differences in the usage of terms between, as well as among, West Indian and British scholars, on the one hand, and American scholars, on the other, and because the sources contain various terms which refer to the free non-white population, it is advisable to specify the nomenclature that we employ. *Freedman* is used to refer to any person, of either sex, whose racial ancestry was mixed or solely Negroid; such persons may have been born free or manumitted. In a few cases, where females are specifically discussed, we employ the term *freedwoman*. At times it is necessary to make phenotypic distinctions between the *free "colored,"* persons of mixed ancestry, and *free blacks*, those of Negroid ancestry alone. The sources often use *mulatto* and *Negro*, respectively. In this paper *Negro* appears in direct quotations or in a context which makes clear that we are using the term to refer to non-whites in general. We avoid using *mulatto*, and the term appears only in direct quotations. The meaning of *colored* in the sources is often ambiguous. Sometimes it refers to persons of mixed racial ancestry, sometimes to a segment of the freedman community defined in socioeconomic terms and by phenotype, and sometimes to freedmen in general. We employ *colored* for the sake of convenience, and, since the term's connotations and social implications differ in contemporary West Indian–British and American usage, we retain it within quotation marks. Finally, we use *freeman* to refer to any person, regardless of sex or racial ancestry, who is not a slave.

We regard this paper as a preliminary attempt at a systematic account of the freedmen of Barbados.[2] Despite the abundance of

[1] This paper is a greatly reduced version of one originally submitted for publication which, among other topics, included discussions of the freedman's participation in military, religious, and educational institutions. The original paper is being revised and expanded into a book-length manuscript, *The Unappropriated People: Freedmen in Barbados Slave Society*, which is to be published by The Johns Hopkins Press.

[2] For support of this research, Handler is indebted to grants from the National Institute of Mental Health, National Science Foundation, American Philosophical Society, and a Younger Scholar Fellowship from the National Endowment for the Humanities. Sio is indebted to the Fulbright Commission for two years of teaching and research in the West Indies, and to the American

216   JEROME S. HANDLER AND ARNOLD A. SIO

source materials relating to Barbados during the slave period,[3] references to freedmen are relatively infrequent and usually brief. Only a few sources by themselves provide sufficient information on any one aspect of life to permit a reasonably comprehensive account. The materials are generally sufficient for an overview of the development of the freedman's status and his participation in the island's more important institutions, but there are many areas of his cultural life and of the internal organization of his community about which we have no information, or the materials are so scant that we are reluctant to treat these areas. In several ways, then, the organization, thrust, and discussion in this paper have been markedly affected by the nature of the source materials; for want, in some instances, of even minimal evidence, we are unable to discuss (or discuss in detail) a variety of issues we consider important and relevant.

DEMOGRAPHY

The number of freedmen in Barbados increased during the nineteenth century. Of primary importance is the fact that they were a distinct minority and always formed a small percentage of the island's population. From 1809 to 1813, their number averaged 2,548, and from 1825 through 1829, 4,876. Thus, freedmen comprised from 2.8 to 4.8 percent of the total population during most of the first third of the nineteenth century, and surpassed 6 percent only in the 1830s (Table 7–1). Similarly, they formed a small segment of the non-whites (slaves and freedmen), ranging between 3.6 and 6.0 percent during the period 1809–29, and coming close to 8.0 percent by the time of emancipation. Their proportion was greater in relation to the total number of freemen (whites and freedmen), averaging 14 percent over the period 1809–13, but it was only in the mid-1820s that they achieved 25 percent of the free population.

However, freedmen formed a proportionately larger segment of the population of the parish of Saint Michael than the island-wide

Council of Learned Societies and the Colgate University Research Council for research grants. The original version of this manuscript was typed with the assistance of funds provided by the Southern Illinois University Office of Research and Projects, and the Colgate University Research Council provided funds for typing the final manuscript. We are also grateful to M. J. Chandler, S. W. Mintz, and H. A. Vaughan for their comments on the original version of this paper.

[3] See Jerome S. Handler, *A Guide to Source Materials for the Study of Barbados History, 1627–1834* (Carbondale: Southern Illinois University Press, 1971). The following abbreviations refer to the manuscript collections and/or repositories most frequently cited: BDA (Barbados Department of Archives, Barbados); CMS (Church Missionary Society Archives, London); CO (Colonial Office group, Public Record Office, London); GD (Seaforth Papers, Scottish Record Office, Edinburgh); LPL (Fulham Papers, Lambeth Palace Library, London); MMS (Methodist Missionary Society Archives, London); USPG (United Society for the Propagation of the Gospel Archives, London); WIC

numbers indicate. This parish contained, as it does today, Bridge-town, the island's capital and urban center. Most freedmen appear to have lived in Bridgetown (although we have no concrete figures on its population) and its immediate environs. Although a minority in Saint Michael (freedmen averaged about 8 percent of its popula-tion from 1809 to 1813, and 12 percent from 1825 through 1829), this group appears quite sizable if one eliminates the parish's slaves and considers only its free population: freedmen averaged 23 per-cent from 1809 to 1813, and 38 percent from 1825 through 1829 (Table 7-2).

As a group, then, freedmen tended to concentrate in Saint Michael. In 1801, about 45 percent of them lived in this parish, but, by 1809 and for the next twenty years, it contained an average of about 61 percent (Table 7-2). Although many freedmen were scat-tered throughout the ten other parishes (which were fundamentally rural) it is for Saint Michael that one finds the most evidence of an organized community and proportionately greater participation in the island's national institutions.

Some of the growth of the freedman population in Saint Michael must be attributed to natural increase and some to manumission (on the basis of limited figures, it appears that more than 50 percent of the manumitted slaves achieved their freedom in Saint Michael), but there was also a tendency for slaves manumitted in the rural areas to gravitate to Bridgetown. Rural freedmen also sought the towns, including Speightstown in Saint Peter (the island's second-largest town, but considerably smaller than Bridgetown), for the greater economic opportunities they provided.

Statistical information on the major phenotypic categories— that is, "colored" and black—is reported only for 1825–29 (Table 7-3). Over the five years 1825–29, then, the "colored" population averaged about 2,200, or 53 percent of the freedmen, while blacks averaged 1,925, or 47 percent. The figures thus indicate that by the later years of slavery a majority, but not a consequential one, of freedmen were of mixed racial ancestry.

The age distribution of freedmen is of interest because the qualitative and limited statistical information we have indicates that a considerable number of them were children. In 1802, the only year for which we have statistical data, there were 393 men and 762 women—that is, there was an adult population of 1,155; in addition, there were 499 boys and 514 girls. Thus, adults comprised about 53 percent of the freedman population and children 47 percent.[4] It is

---

(Alleyne Letters, West India Committee Library, London). Abbreviations for published materials are: PP (Parliamentary Papers, London); JBMHS (Journal of the Barbados Museum and Historical Society, Bridgetown).

[4] "Returns of Free Coloured Population . . . in Barbados, May 1802," CO 28/72. Age breakdowns are given for ten of the parishes; these contained 97 percent of the freedman population reported.

TABLE 7-1. Population of Barbados

Year	Number				Percentage				Freedmen as Percentage of	
	Freedmen	Whites	Slaves	Total	Freedmen	Whites	Slaves		Total Free	Total Non-White
1748	107	15,192	47,025	62,324	0.1	24.3	75.4		0.6	0.2
1768	448	16,139	66,379	82,966	0.5	19.4	80.0		2.7	0.6
1773	534	18,532	68,548	87,614	0.6	21.1	78.2		2.8	0.7
1786	838	16,167	62,115	79,120	1.0	20.4	78.5		4.9	1.3
1801	2,209	15,887	64,196	82,292	2.6	19.3	78.0		12.2	3.3
1809	2,663	15,566	69,369	87,598	3.0	17.7	79.1		14.6	3.6
1810	2,526	15,517	69,119	87,162	2.8	17.8	79.2		13.9	3.5
1811	2,613	15,794	69,132	87,539	2.9	18.0	78.9		14.1	3.6

Year									
1812	2,529	15,120	68,569	86,218	2.9	17.5	79.5	14.3	3.5
1813	2,412	15,561	65,995	83,968	2.8	18.5	78.5	13.4	3.5
1814	2,317	15,920	66,663	84,900	2.7	18.7	78.5	12.7	3.3
1815	3,139	16,145	69,280	88,564	3.5	18.2	78.2	16.2	4.3
1816	3,007	16,072	71,286	90,365	3.3	17.7	78.8	15.7	4.0
1825	4,524	14,630	78,096	97,250	4.6	15.0	80.3	23.6	6.0
1826	4,777	14,584	78,543	97,904	4.8	14.8	80.2	24.7	5.7
1827	4,896	14,687	79,383	98,966	4.8	14.8	80.2	25.0	5.8
1828	5,020	14,824	80,050	99,894	5.0	14.8	80.1	25.2	5.9
1829	5,146	14,959	80,086	100,191	5.1	14.9	79.9	25.5	6.0
1833–34	6,584	12,797	80,861	100,242	6.5	12.7	80.6	33.9	7.5

Sources: 1748 (CO 28/29); 1768, 1786 ("Report of the Lords," pt. 4, no. 15 and 3rd suppl. to no. 15); 1773 (CO 318/2, no. 16, cited in D. Makinson, *Barbados: A Study of North-American–West-Indian Relations, 1739–1789* [The Hague, 1964], p. 15); 1801, 1809–11 (*PP*, 1814–15, vol. 7, rept. 478); 1812–16 (compiled from statistics in: CO 28/86; *PP*, 1823, vol. 18, rept. 80; *ibid.*, 1826, vol. 26, rept. 350); 1825–29 (*ibid.*, 1830, vol. 21, rept. 674; the 1825 slave population is given as an estimate for all parishes); 1833–34 (M. Martin, *History of the Colonies of the British Empire* [London, 1843], p. 64; statistics on the white population of Saint Peter and Saint Thomas are not included).

TABLE 7-2. Population of Barbados, by Parish

Year	Saint Michael Freedmen	Saint Michael Whites	Saint Michael Slaves	Saint Michael Total	All Parishes Freedmen	All Parishes Whites	All Parishes Slaves	% Residing in Saint Michael Freedmen	% Residing in Saint Michael Whites	% Residing in Saint Michael Slaves	% Pop. of Saint Michael Freedmen	% Pop. of Saint Michael Whites	% Pop. of Saint Michael Slaves
1801	1,000	4,336	10,519	15,855	2,209	15,887	64,196	45.2	27.2	16.3	6.3	27.3	66.3
1809	1,668	5,313	12,262	19,243	2,663	15,566	69,369	62.6	34.1	17.6	8.6	27.6	63.7
1810	1,466	5,161	12,001	18,628	2,526	15,517	69,119	58.0	33.2	17.3	7.8	27.7	64.4
1811	1,551	5,406	12,293	19,250	2,613	15,794	69,132	59.4	34.2	17.7	8.0	28.0	63.8
1812	1,540	4,519	12,070	18,129	2,529	15,120	68,569	60.8	29.8	17.6	8.4	24.9	66.5
1813	1,370	4,977	11,509	17,856	2,412	15,561	65,995	56.7	31.9	17.4	7.6	27.8	64.4
1814	1,264	5,130	11,277	17,671	2,317	15,920	66,663	54.5	32.2	16.9	7.1	29.0	63.8
1815	2,071	5,374	11,558	19,003	3,139	16,145	69,280	65.9	33.2	16.6	10.8	28.2	60.8
1816	1,933	5,038	13,695	20,666	3,007	16,072	71,286	64.2	31.3	19.2	9.3	24.3	66.2
1825	2,825	4,942	17,000	24,767	4,524	14,630	78,096	62.4	33.7	21.7	11.4	19.9	68.6
1826	3,045	4,965	16,439	24,449	4,777	14,584	78,543	63.4	34.0	20.9	12.4	20.3	67.2
1827	3,065	5,001	16,722	24,788	4,896	14,687	79,383	62.6	34.0	21.0	12.3	20.1	67.4
1828	3,095	5,020	16,719	24,834	5,020	14,824	80,050	61.6	33.8	20.8	12.4	20.2	67.3
1829	3,140	5,050	16,807	24,997	5,146	14,959	80,086	61.0	33.7	20.9	12.5	20.2	67.2

Sources: Same as those for Table 7-1.

TABLE 7–3.   Freedmen of Barbados, by Phenotype

| Year | Number | | | Percentage | |
	Free "Colored"	Free Black	Total	Free "Colored"	Free Black
1825	2,066	1,760	3,829	53.9	45.9
1826	2,169	1,905	4,074	53.2	46.7
1827	2,201	1,947	4,148	53.0	46.9
1828	2,259	1,989	4,248	53.1	46.8
1829	2,313	2,027	4,340	53.2	46.7

Sources: Compiled from "Return of the White, Free Coloured, Free Black, and Slave Population of Barbados, from 1825 to 1829 Inclusive" (PP, 1830, vol. 21, rept. 674). The figures are taken from eight of the parishes (Saint Andrew, Saint Thomas, and Saint Peter are excluded), but these eight contained 85 percent of the total freedman population.

difficult to know how much of this age division persisted during the remainder of the slave period. However, birth rates (Table 7–4) and the efforts made by freed parents to manumit their still-enslaved children suggest that the number of children increased, and that they continued to form a significant proportion of the freedman population. Thus, much of our discussion implicitly focuses on the status, institutional participation, and behavior of adults, but we are, in effect, dealing with a group that was considerably smaller than is indicated by the gross population figures given in Table 7–1.

In considering the adult group, sexual composition is important, not only because participation in some national institutions was confined to males, but also because the number of freedwomen, particularly those of child-bearing age, was a variable in the rate of natural increase of the freedman population.[5] Our statistical information on sex is limited to the years 1801, 1802, 1825, 1827, and 1829.[6] During the two earlier years, females comprised 57.3 and 58.8 percent, respectively, of the freedman population. Data for the mid-1820s show that they comprised 50.0, 49.8, and 49.3 percent; that is, the population was equally divided between males and fe-

[5] Figures for 1802 are the only ones which permit a rough estimate of the number of women of child-bearing age; in this year 35 percent of the freedmen were adult females (ibid.). However, since there was a tendency to manumit older slaves, it is likely that many of these persons were beyond child-bearing age.
[6] Sources: 1801 (PP, 1814–15, vol. 7, rept. 478); 1802 (CO 28/72); 1825, 1827, and 1829 (PP, 1830, vol. 21, rept. 674).

males, thus indicating a lowering of the sex ratio over the years toward an equality of males to females. Yet, according to manumission figures for the mid-1820s, about 66 percent of the slaves manumitted were females.[7] One might thus expect the population figures for these years to indicate a greater number of females rather than an equal number of the sexes. At present, we can explain this discrepancy only by suggesting that the sources do not include manumission figures in population statistics.

With respect to population growth, as can be seen in Table 7–1, the number of freedmen had risen significantly by the end of the eighteenth century, and continued to grow steadily in the first three decades of the nineteenth. Increasing from more than 2,000 persons in 1801, to more than 5,000 in 1829, they approached 7,000 on the eve of emancipation; thus, in a little more than three decades the freedman population had tripled in size. Freedmen showed a proportionately greater rate of growth than did the island's slaves, and, while both groups increased in size, the number and proportion of whites declined. In the first decade of the nineteenth century, freedmen averaged close to 3 percent of the island's population, but by the end of the third decade this percentage had increased to 5, and it approached 7 by the early 1830s. On the other hand, slaves stayed between 79 and 80 percent (though their numbers increased) throughout the period, while whites declined from 18 percent during the first decade to 15 percent in the third.[8]

As the number of whites declined and that of freedmen increased, the latter came to form an increasingly significant minority among the island's freemen (whites and freedmen). During the first fifteen or so years of the nineteenth century, they averaged about 14 percent of the free population, an average that increased to 25 percent during the 1820s and exceeded a third by emancipation. As a percentage of the total non-white population, the increase of freedmen was from an average of 3.5 in the early years of the nineteenth century to 7.5 prior to emancipation.

It is difficult to ascertain the factors responsible for this growth —that is, to what extent it was due to natural increase (births minus deaths) and to what extent due to manumissions. What appear to be reasonably useful figures on the births and deaths of freedmen are limited to the four-year period 1826–29 (Table 7–4). During these years (we do not know how they compare to earlier ones), the annual natural increase was 127, 114, 148, and 120, respectively. Projecting these figures onto the population totals reported for each

[7] For 1824 and 1825, see PP, 1826, vol. 28, rept. 353; for 1826 and 1829, see *ibid.*, 1833, vol. 26, rept. 539.

[8] The decline of the white population appears to have been largely due to emigration; during the period 1826–29, the average annual crude rate of natural increase among whites was nil (calculated from figures given in *ibid.*, 1830, vol. 21, rept. 674).

TABLE 7-4. Freedmen of Barbados: Births and Deaths

Year	Total Population	Number of Births	Number of Deaths	Natural Increase	Crude Rates (per 1,000 population)		
					Births	Deaths	Natural Increase
1826	4,797	343	216	127	72	45	27
1827	4,896	265	151	114	54	31	23
1828	5,020	349	201	148	70	40	30
1829	5,146	373	253	120	72	49	23

Source: PP, 1830, vol. 21, rept. 674.

223

224 JEROME S. HANDLER AND ARNOLD A. SIO

successive year, the projections roughly coincide with the actual figures reported. One might thus conclude that natural increase was largely responsible for the growth of the freedman population during these years. However, other sets of figures indicate that the population during this period was also growing as a result of slave manumissions.[9] Despite the considerable difficulties involved in determining the extent to which natural increase contributed to the growth of the freedman population, it does appear that, at least during the later years of slavery, manumission played an important role.

MANUMISSION

The main forms of manumission, by will and deed, represented an exercise of the owner's property rights, and because the manumission process was subject to certain legal regulations, mainly in the form of fees, many owners freed their slaves in England, or occasionally in neighboring colonies. In Barbadian law, manumission could also occur as a reward for a slave's role in helping to prevent revolts or in defense of the island against foreign invasions.

The concern with slave revolts in Barbados in general, and with a particularly threatening plot in 1692, led to the passing of an act in that year which manumitted slaves who informed on their peers planning "to commit or abet any insurrection or rebellion."[10] This act was of little significance, however, for, despite another plot in 1702, there was no slave revolt on the island until 1816; even then, a special bill, passed early in 1817 "for manumitting certain slaves for their good conduct during and since the rebellion," resulted only in the freeing of about five or six persons. For similar reasons of security, and in recognition that "there are many Negroes and other slaves . . . who are worthy of trust and confidence . . . and therefore may be of great service" in defense of the island, the legislature in 1707 passed an act whereby any slave who killed an invading enemy would be manumitted.[11] This act also was of little significance, for the island was never invaded, despite, as in the Napoleonic Wars, occasional threats. Although unimportant as sources of manumission, the laws of 1692 and 1707 were the only ones which contained specific conditions by which freedom could be granted; both laws remained on the books until the mid-1820s, when they were repealed and their clauses were incorporated into the island's "slave consolidation act."[12] In all other cases, the conditions under which a slave was to be manumitted were the province of the slaveowner.

Manumissions by will reflected the unique desires and interests

9 *Ibid.*, 1833, vol. 26, rept. 539.
10 Richard Hall, *Acts, Passed in the Island of Barbados. From 1643 to 1762* (London, 1764), pp. 129–30.
11 *Ibid.*, p. 175.
12 Clause 50; PP, 1826–27, vol. 25 (report not numbered), no. 487.

of individual masters. In general, they were a function of a special relationship between master and slave and were granted as a reward for "fidelity," as, for example, in domestic service and/or a sexual relationship, or to a master's children by a slave woman. On the basis of our present information we cannot determine the frequency of manumissions by will, nor determine with precision the extent to which such manumissions were a source of the island's freedman population. Our impression, gained from reading a number of transcripts of early wills, is that manumission by this means was relatively infrequent, and this impression is reinforced by the limited set of figures available. From the beginning of January, 1821, to the end of December, 1825, the island's deputy secretary reported that 410 slaves were manumitted; of this number, between 3 and 6 percent were manumitted by will, the remainder by some form of deed.[13]

The decision to manumit by deed was made by the slaveowner for a variety of reasons and motives and could be effected in a number of customary ways. One type commonly reported was manumission as a favor to a slave mistress, and deed manumissions of this kind were regarded as an important source of the freedman population. In 1811, reporting on the increase of freedmen in the parish, the rector of Saint Michael pointed out that "great numbers of them obtain their freedom every year. . . . out of every four at least three are females, who obtain that privilege by becoming the favourites of white men."[14]

A practice having the same effect as manumission by deed involved white men purchasing their slave mistresses from "their owners, in many instances their own parent—and subsequently giving a certificate on the back of the deed of sale, annulling their right of property in the person of their favourite"; this gave them "a freedom not recognized in the laws, but tacitly assented to by the community."[15] This customary device was apparently also employed by freedmen who purchased their own enslaved children.

Self-purchase was another practice involved in deed manumission which was accepted in custom rather than being specified in law, and it could be initiated by the slave in negotiation with the master. "*Purchasing themselves* means the depositing in the hands of the master the sum which he values them at . . . before he can give his consent to manumission: this then may also be termed *buying consent*."[16] If consent was given, the master might allow the slave

[13] *PP*, 1826, vol. 28, rept. 353.
[14] *Ibid.*, 1814–15, vol. 7, rept. 478, p. 3; cf. J. A. Waller, *A Voyage in the West Indies* (London, 1820), p. 20.
[15] J. W. Orderson, *Cursory Remarks and Plain Facts Connected with the Question Produced by the Proposed Slave Registry Bill* (London, 1816), p. 16.
[16] [Anon.], *Letter from a Gentleman in Barbadoes to His Friend in London, on the Subject of Manumission from Slavery* (London, 1803), p. 21; italics in the original.

to "go at large"; in such cases the slave largely conducted his own life and earned his own way, but paid his master a weekly stipend, which presumably he saved from his earnings.

However, although our evidence is limited, it appears that self-purchase was relatively infrequent as a device for activating a manumission deed. Forster Clarke, a prominent planter, offered the general "opinion that very few [slaves] ever possess the means of purchasing their freedom"; he could cite only three cases within the period 1822–27 on the Codrington plantations, owned by the Society for the Propagation of the Gospel in Foreign Parts.[17] Even when the necessary funds could be acquired, owners were reluctant to permit the practice. In general, it appears that slaves who acquired the money to purchase their freedom were largely artisans or domestics—that is, those who had a greater chance of being permitted to "go at large" or to be hired out.

Self-purchase—indeed, manumission in general—was denied, however, when it fundamentally went against what the owner defined as his own self-interest, economic or otherwise. Thus, during his visit to Barbados in 1829–30, William Bell reported that the bishop of Barbados had told him "the planters objected to grant manumissions to their best and oldest servants for fear of losing their services altogether";[18] yet, when such persons became incapable of effectively performing their duties, they sometimes gained direct manumission as a "reward" for their past services, or were permitted to purchase their freedom. For similar reasons of incapacity, owners would manumit non-productive slaves whom they did not want to support; such reasons are well reflected in the laws that regulated manumission and established fees.

Although manumission occurred early in the history of slavery in Barbados, the island's legislature did not control the process until 1739, when a law was passed which established manumission fees.[19] The general reasons for this act stemmed from the long-standing practice of owners manumitting slaves who were often old and infirm. In order to provide for support of manumitted slaves, "to prevent their becoming burdensome to the parish," the manumitter was obliged to pay fifty pounds in island currency to the parish government, which in turn would provide the freed slave with an annuity of four pounds; failure to pay the fee could result in court action by the parish against the manumitter.

However, owners who wanted to manumit slaves were able to evade paying the fees. They did this "by making a conveyance of

[17] Clarke to Secretary of the Society for the Propagation of the Gospel, May 7, 1828, in Society for the Propagation of the Gospel in Foreign Parts, *Annual Report* (London, 1828), pp. 217–18.

[18] J. Boromé, ed., "William Bell and His Second Visit to Barbados, 1829–1830," *JBMHS*, 30 (1962): 22.

[19] Hall, *Acts*, pp. 323–25.

such slave or slaves ... to some insolvent person, who immediately executes a deed of manumission, by which means the parish is defrauded of the ... fifty pounds, and the person so set free deprived of the said annuity, and reduced to the necessity of seeking a dishonest means of livelihood."[20] Consequently, the 1739 act was amended in 1783 to require that the manumitter "shall actually deposit or pay into the hands of the [parish] churchwarden" the fifty pounds, and that a receipt be issued; without the latter, the manumission would be "void and of no effect," and the slave for whom the manumission was intended would remain a slave.[21]

By the end of the century the freedman population was rising, and, in 1801, Seaforth, the new governor, proposed to the Assembly a bill which "might insure to those people the means of existence when age, sickness or misfortunes render them incapable of procuring it by their own exertions."[22] The act, which raised manumission fees and the annuity for support, was passed during that year.[23] But the legislature's willingness to pass the law was based less on its desire to support freedmen than on the assumption that the "operation of the act would amount almost to a prohibition of the baneful practice of emancipation."[24] The new law raised the manumission fee to 300 pounds island currency for females and 200 pounds for males, and increased the annual subsidy to 18 and 12 pounds, respectively; all other provisions of the 1783 manumission fee law were retained.[25] The existence of fees did, indeed, inhibit manumissions under island law, but Barbadian slaves continued to be manumitted in England, where owners were permitted to avoid fee payment.

In 1816, the 1801 act was repealed, and manumission fees were reduced to the fifty pounds, annuity to the four pounds (regardless of sex), that had been specified in the1783 law.[26] The immediate stimulus to this change was

> the fidelity and good conduct of the [freedman] ... in the [slave] insurrection of 1816 [which] removed all apprehensions on that score from the minds of our legislature. . . . and as it now appeared that there was no good reason for opposing the increase of their numbers, the deposit on a manumission was reduced to a sum which was thought barely sufficient to prevent ... owners from ridding them-

[20] S. Moore, *The Public Acts in Force: Passed by the Legislature of Barbados, from May 11th 1762 to April 8th 1800* (London, 1801), p. 224.

[21] *Ibid.*, pp. 224–25.

[22] J. Poyer, *History of Barbados from 1801 to 1803 Inclusive* (Bridgetown, 1808), p. 11.

[23] CO 30/17, no. 225.

[24] Poyer, *History of Barbados*, p. 13.

[25] CO 30/17, no. 225.

[26] "An Act to Repeal an Act Entitled An Act to Increase the Sums Made Payable by Former Laws on the Manumission of Slaves for Their Better Support and Maintenance," August 19, 1816, BDA; cf. *PP*, 1823, vol. 18, rept. 80, p. 36.

selves of the burthen of maintaining their old and infirm slaves, and also for providing in some measure for the support of the enfranchised slave.[27]

By the mid-1820s, the British government had declared itself in favor of eventual emancipation and was pressuring colonial legislatures to pass ameliorative slave laws, which, by extension, also affected freedmen. A directive in 1823 urged that, among other measures, manumission fees be abolished, and one in 1826 suggested that the legislature provide that "slaves under certain conditions . . . be enabled . . . to purchase their freedom and that of their families and relations."[28] The Barbados Assembly refused to follow the 1826 directive, regarding it as an invasion of the right of private property, and not until 1831 did the legislature repeal earlier laws that had established fees.[29] By repealing manumission fees, the Assembly not only complied with the wishes of the British government but also, in effect, expanded the right of owners to freely dispose of their property. That is, owners had often regarded fees as impediments to manumission, and, even if they were not necessarily interpreted as a direct infringement on property rights, they were intended to, and did, inhibit the number of manumissions. We do not know how many slaves were refused manumission because of the existence of fees, but, to avoid paying fees, owners frequently freed their slaves in England—a device accepted by custom, but not specified in colonial law:

> English manumissions . . . are deeds of enfranchisement executed by a person in England, to whom the slaves are conveyed by their owner resident in this island. These deeds were not originally legalized by any statute of the island, but their validity has for a series of years been recognized by all our courts, and they are now considered as good and effectual for their purpose as any other form of manumission.[30]

Manumissions executed in England became a very important source of the island's freedman population. From 1808 to August 18, 1816 (when the 200- and 300-pound fees enacted in 1801 were in force), approximately 1,000 slaves were manumitted; of this number only fifteen, or about 2 percent, were manumitted in accordance with Barbadian law, the remaining manumissions being effected almost entirely in England. From August, 1816 (after the manumission fee was reduced to fifty pounds), to the end of September, 1821, approximately 700 manumissions were reported, of which 250, or about 36

---

[27] A Report of a Committee of the Council of Barbadoes, Appointed to Inquire into the Actual Condition of the Slaves in This Island (London, 1824), pp. 81–83.

[28] PP, 1831–32, vol. 47, rept. 739.

[29] CO 30/21, no. 542.

[30] Report of a Committee of the Council, pp. 82–83.

percent, were carried out under colonial law, the remainder being "with few exceptions enfranchise[ments] by persons in England."[31] Thus, from 1808 through the middle of 1816, close to 98 percent of the slaves were manumitted in England, and from 1816 to 1821 the figure was about 64 percent.

The report from which the above figures were derived permits some definitive statements about the percentage of manumissions in England, but contains statistics only on those that "are on record in the Secretary's office"; thus, the total number of Barbadian slaves manumitted was greater than the figures cited.[32] Although it is difficult to establish a precise estimate of the total number of manumissions in any given year, it is likely that by the late 1820s the number was steadily increasing. For example, in the trienniums 1824–26 and 1827–29, 322 and 670 persons, respectively, were freed,[33] and in 1830–32 a figure of 1,089 was reported.[34] Thus, by the late 1820s and early 1830s a considerable proportion of the island's freedman population was probably comprised of relatively recently manumitted slaves.

Despite their incompleteness, these manumission estimates and others available to us permit a delineation of some of the characteristics of the population manumitted. For the period from 1808 to July, 1834, we have a record (albeit for inconsecutive years) of 3,652 manumissions which contains sex identification: of this total, an average of 62 percent were females and 38 percent males, and there seem to have been no significant deviations from these percentages throughout the period.[35] Phenotypic information is restricted to 427 cases recorded during the period 1832–34, of which 270, or 63 percent, were "colored," and 157, or 37 percent, were black; of the 707 cases for which the parish of manumission was stated (also during 1832–34), 58 percent were freed in Saint Michael, while Christ Church, with the second largest number of manumissions, accounted for only 8 percent.[36] In sum, the evidence indicates that, during the period for which we have information, most of the slaves manumitted were females, of mixed racial ancestry, and living in Saint Michael.

In the vast majority of cases the manumitter was white, but freedmen manumitted slaves who were frequently their own children. We have no statistical information on this and very little on the number of freedmen manumitters; of 377 manumitters listed for the

[31] PP, 1823, vol. 18, rept. 80, p. 36.

[32] See ibid., 1826, vol. 28, rept. 353.

[33] Ibid., 1833, vol. 26, rept. 539.

[34] Ibid., rept. 700.

[35] 1808–21 (ibid., 1823, vol. 18, rept. 80); 1822 and 1824–25 (ibid., 1826, vol. 28, rept. 353); 1826 and 1829 (ibid., 1833, vol. 26, rept. 539); January, 1832–July, 1834 (Miscellaneous and Powers Record Books, RB 7/26–27, BDA).

[36] Miscellaneous and Powers Record Books, RB 7/26–27, BDA.

period January, 1832–July, 1834, only 20 are specifically indicated as free "colored" or black.[37]

Although our information is far from detailed, it suggests that freedmen frequently tried to liberate their own children; in fact, one might even speculate that it was an *expectation* that an emancipated slave would ultimately attempt to manumit his or her close kin. In so doing, the freedman was faced not only with acquiring the financial resources (a considerable chore for many emancipated slaves) but also with obtaining the consent of the owner. This consent, or agreement to sell property, was generally made under principles that governed the sale of slaves in general. That is, slaves were sold only when the owner perceived that it was in his or her own self-interest to do so.

LEGAL STATUS AND THE POLITICO-JUDICIAL SYSTEM

Until 1721 no Barbadian laws specifically concerned freedmen. Although they suffered considerable social discrimination, their legal status was, for all intents and purposes, the same as that of other freemen; all early laws that mentioned Negroes were concerned with regulating the behavior and defining the status of the island's slave population.

The earliest circumscription of the freedman's civil status was contained in a 1721 law which specified that, in order to vote, be elected to public office, and serve on juries, a person had to be a "freeholder," a male twenty-one-year-old Christian citizen of Great Britain who owned at least ten acres of land or a house having an annual taxable value of ten pounds island currency.[38] Earlier electoral codes contained similar qualifications, but this one added that a freeholder had to be a "white man" (a racial qualification which was not removed until 1831). The same law debarred anyone of "Negro" ancestry from giving testimony in courts or other legal proceedings against whites: "no person whatsoever shall be admitted as a freeholder, or an evidence in any case whatsoever, whose original extraction shall be proved to have been from a Negro, excepting only on the trial of Negroes and other slaves."[39]

Aside from denying the freedman a major protective device against mistreatment, cheating, theft, and such, this act also provided the basis for a broader principle whereby the status of free non-whites would be defined; that is, phenotypic differences were not recognized in this or any subsequent law, and, although terminological distinctions were often made between free "Negroes," or "blacks," and free "mulattoes," or "coloreds," they never had any legal implications. For legal (and, to a considerable degree, social) purposes, any-

[37] *Ibid.*
[38] Hall, *Acts*, pp. 252–69.
[39] *Ibid.*, p. 256.

one with a hint of Negroid ancestry was considered a Negro, and thus the Barbados plantocracy (as represented in its legislative bodies) devised a relatively simple method for distinguishing between free whites and free non-whites. In addition, there is no evidence that the legislature ever attempted to provide a legal definition of the point at which Caucasoid characteristics would permit a person with Negro ancestry to be defined as white.[40]

In 1739, a second law specifically relating to the freedman established manumission fees (thus indirectly attempting to control the growth of his numbers) and permitted "the evidence or testimony of any slave, where the same is supported with very good and sufficient corroborating circumstances, against any free Negro, Indian, or Mulatto."[41] Permitting slaves to testify was not a gesture designed to ameliorate their legal condition, but rather a device which made it less cumbersome for whites to recover stolen property or press charges against freedmen who engaged in illicit trade with slaves. At this early period, marketing activities with slaves were important to the freedman. The goods exchanged often involved items stolen by the slaves from their masters' properties, and quite often slaves were the only witnesses to the transactions. By establishing manumission fees and thus making legal provisions for the support of manumitted slaves, it was hoped that freedmen would be discouraged from engaging in illicit activities.

Thus, by 1739 there was a handful of provisions in the island's legal code which specifically treated the freedman, but throughout the remainder of the eighteenth century no other major laws specifically attempted to curtail his legal or civil status; for example, no laws prohibited the freedman from assuming supervisory positions on estates or from purchasing land, houses, and slaves. In addition, the majority of the laws passed during this period that did not specifically or indirectly relate to the rights of freeholders did not contain discriminatory provisions limiting the activities or legal protection of freedmen. Furthermore, where penalties were specified or sanctions imposed on legal violations, distinctions were often made between slave and free, but not among freemen themselves.[42]

It was not until the very end of the eighteenth century and the first few years of the nineteenth that the Barbados plantocracy moved again to control freedmen. Concerned with their growing numbers, in 1801 the legislature passed an act which considerably increased manumission fees and which, from its own perspective, was designed to limit their number. In addition, serious efforts were made around this time to curtail their acquisition of property, which, it was felt,

[40] Custom may have provided such a definition, but our evidence for this is tenuous and limited to only one source (see Waller, *Voyage*, p. 94); it is not corroborated elsewhere.

[41] Hall, *Acts*, pp. 323-25.

[42] See, for example, Moore, *Public Acts*, pp. 218-19, 238-47, 381-408.

could increase their influence, stimulate more of them to call for civil rights, and thus threaten the status quo. Alarmed by "the large purchases made by the coloured people ... of land and slaves," one wealthy planter (who undoubtedly reflected the views of many) wrote: "We certainly ought to open the eyes of the legislature and convince them of the immediate necessity of checking by proper measures the growing ... power of that class of people in our island, and more particularly in Bridgetown."[43] The governor was also concerned about the potential dangers he found inherent in the "strange inconsistency in our laws and customs" by which freedmen were denied "any civil right," particularly that of giving testimony, and yet were "allowed to acquire and possess land and other real property."[44] On a number of occasions he urged the legislature either to reform the laws, a move with which his own sentiments accorded, or to restrict the freedman's acquisition of property, a move which he felt would be necessary for the island's security if civil rights were not extended. It was a common feeling that, "like the Baron in feudal times," as one contemporary historian commented, "these coloured proprietors may become turbulent and dangerous."[45]

At the turn of the century, concerned about the movement to curtail their property holdings, a group of freedmen petitioned the legislature expressing this concern and at the same time requesting amelioration, particularly in the right to testify.[46] Nonetheless, in 1803, a bill passed in the Assembly which was aimed at preventing freedmen from acquiring slaves, or land and houses beyond a certain value; the bill was also designed to prevent those who already owned slaves and property from bequeathing them to relatives and children. A group of freedmen petitioned the Barbados Council to stop the bill's final passage; the petition clearly reveals the attitudes of the group toward the society of the time as well as their position in it. "We are aware," they said,

> that in a country like this it is necessary to make distinctions and lay restraints; to such restrictions as have already been laid, we have always submitted, not only without murmuring or repining, but with cheerful rejoicing that it has been our lot to live under so free and happy a constitution. ... Although we have all our lives been accustomed to the assistance of slaves, we must immediately deprive ourselves of them and perform every menial office with our own hands. ... The greatest blessing attending upon freedom is the acquirement and enjoyment of property and without that, Liberty is

[43] Alleyne to Thorne, November 20, 1801, and February 1, 1802, WIC, pp. 66, 138.
[44] Seaforth to Hobart, June 6, 1802, GD 46/7/7.
[45] Poyer, *History of Barbados*, p. 29.
[46] This petition is referred to in letters written by J. F. Alleyne in early 1802 (WIC, pp. 133, 138).

but an empty name. . . . To deprive us of our property will remove the best security of our loyalty and fidelity.[47]

There is some indication here of a growing awareness among the freedmen that the bill could be defeated by emphasizing that, as a group, they might well hold a crucial position in a confrontation between slaveowner and slave. Certainly John Beckles, an influential member of the Council who supported the petition, viewed the situation in these terms:

> It will be politic to allow them to possess property; it will keep them at a greater distance from the slaves, and will keep up that jealousy which seems naturally to exist between the free coloured people and the slaves; it will tend to our security, for should the slaves at any time attempt to revolt, the free coloured persons for their own safety and the security of their property, must join the whites and resist them: but if we are to reduce the free coloured people to a level with the slaves, they must unite with them and will take every occasion of promoting and encouraging a revolt.[48]

At any rate, disagreements over the bill's wording and provisions caused it to be buffeted between the Assembly and Council for months, and ultimately "no further action was taken in the matter,"[49] perhaps largely because of the kind of reasoning expressed by Beckles.

Thereafter, efforts to limit the freedman's property acquisitions were dropped, and there is no evidence that such efforts were seriously renewed in subsequent years. In fact, the trend from this period onward is characterized by the struggle of the freedman to gain an extension of his civil rights and by increasing pressures for amelioration from the mother country. Thus, legislative actions were directed toward the maintenance and defense of the status quo rather than toward further curtailment of the freedman's legal position.

By the turn of the century, freedmen had formally made it known that they regarded a law granting them the right to testify as vital to their interests. As noted above, Governor Seaforth also favored such a move and argued for it, "not only to the purposes of justice and humanity . . . but also . . . to the administration of justice among the whites which is often rendered difficult, sometimes impossible, through the inadmissibility of black or coloured, and the want of, white evidence."[50] The governor finally concluded, however, that reform legislation would come only through strong directives from the imperial government. But at this early stage the imperial government made little effort to interfere with what it defined as the internal affairs of a colonial government, and home pressures were not yet

[47] "Minutes of the Barbados Privy Council, November 1, 1803," BDA.
[48] *Ibid.*
[49] H. A. Vaughan, "Poyer's Last Work," *JBMHS*, 21 (1954): 172, n. 51.
[50] Seaforth to Hobart, June 6, 1802, GD 46/7/7.

sufficient to force it to take a firm position on the conditions under which non-whites lived. Thus, the intransigence of the Barbados plantocracy on the issue of amelioration continued and was not to be easily moved, although the issue was kept alive by the freedmen themselves and, as the years progressed, by a few members of the white community.

The event that tipped the scales in favor of ameliorative legislation was a slave revolt which broke out on the night of April 14, 1816. The revolt lasted for no more than a day or two, and was suppressed by British military forces and the island's militia. A few freedmen were convicted by courts-martial of being involved, but the conduct of "the most respectable of that class . . . with scarcely any exception . . . [was] highly meritorious."[51] Furthermore, the fact that the freedman companies of the island's militia carried out their assigned duties conscientiously and with dispatch helped considerably in strengthening the case for their loyalty and the removal of legal disabilities against them.[52]

A bill permitting the testimony of freedmen in legal proceedings —the first of the ameliorative laws and the one to which the freedmen themselves gave top priority—was introduced into the Assembly on October 8, 1816; three months later, after considerable amendments, it was passed. Those in the Assembly in favor of amelioration in general, and this bill in particular, stressed the freedman's loyalty

[51] *The Report from a Select Committee of the House of Assembly . . . to Inquire into the Origin, Causes, and Progress of the Late Insurrection* (Barbados, [1818]), p. 11.

[52] Throughout slavery the freedman was expected to serve in the island's militia. This had been organized on a parochial basis in the seventeenth century for protection against external attack and slave revolts. From the seventeenth century until shortly before emancipation, all laws governing the militia noted the obligation of adult freemen without making reference to racial origins; furthermore, these laws did not confine the freedman to noncombatant roles nor prohibit him from bearing arms.

Nevertheless, freedmen were placed in segregated companies during monthly drills and times of mobilization. In addition, freedmen were debarred from serving as commissioned officers in their own units. Militia officers, especially the colonels in command of each parish, were required by law to be wealthy property owners, but the relatively few freedmen who were eligible to hold commissions were prevented from doing so by the racial prejudice expressed against them. Yet, in terms of his behavior as a militiaman, the freedman was apparently obedient and compliant. There is no evidence that his military behavior was ever seriously called into question, and observers who commented on this issue invariably emphasized his conscientiousness during training and mobilization—for example, in the 1770s and in 1805, when the island feared a French invasion, and during the 1816 slave revolt.

Although we generally lack information on the number of freedmen in the militia, judging from the total population (or the number of adult males), it is clear that at all times they were a definite minority. We assume, once again on the basis of population distributions, that Saint Michael (including Bridgetown) contained the largest number of freedmen in its militia units, the remainder being scattered throughout the other ten parishes.

to white interests and his "respectability," as evidenced by his behavior during the slave revolt.[53]

Yet, the Barbados Assembly was not prepared to extend its
"favorable consideration" to all categories of freedmen, and it limited
the law's application to those who had been baptized, who had been
free for at least a year prior to being called upon to give testimony,
and who, subsequent to the passage of the act, were manumitted by
the laws of Barbados; the last two provisions were not repealed until
1830.

It is clear that this law was intended to apply to relatively few
freedmen, and primarily to those whose demeanor and life style reflected the values that whites considered appropriate and non-
threatening. We would also suggest that the bill was enacted mainly
for reasons that would insure the protection of plantocratic interests
(and, by extension, white ones in general). That is, the 1816 revolt
had profoundly shaken the white population, and had effectively
demonstrated that its traditional anxieties vis-à-vis the slaves were
well founded. The fact that a few freedmen were convicted of assuming leadership positions dramatically underscored the potential threat
of any coalition between freedmen and slaves. The fact that most
freedmen remained loyal to white interests during the revolt was
good fortune, but how long this loyalty could be assured if the freedman's basic requests for civil rights were continuously denied was
another matter. It was apparently reasoning of this kind, and not primarily liberalism or humanitarian considerations, that was instrumental in the passage of the bill.

Not long after the act was passed, a group of twelve freedmen,
on behalf of themselves and "of the free people of colour in general,"
addressed a letter to the Assembly, expressing their gratitude for "the
privilege of giving testimony on all occasions." The letter is an interesting reflection of the ideology held by at least some of the freedmen
to whom the law was primarily directed, and for this reason we quote
it at length:

> This inestimable privilege we are free to confess we were anxious
> to enjoy for without it we conceived that our lives and properties
> were not secure and that our condition was little if any thing better
> than that of slaves. We are sensible that in a country like this where
> slavery exists, there must necessarily be a distinction between the
> white and free coloured inhabitants, and that there are privileges
> which the latter do not expect to enjoy. The right of giving testi-
> mony was all we wished for, having through the justice and wis-
> dom of the legislature obtained that we are perfectly satisfied and
> contented. . . . It affords us a great satisfaction to find that our con-
> duct upon a late unfortunate occasion has met with the approbation
> of the legislature and has been thought to render us worthy of their

[53] See "Journal of the Assembly of Barbados, October 8, 1816," CO 31/47.

consideration and attention. We assure your worships that we shall be ready at all times to give proofs of our loyalty and sincere attachment to the king and constitution and to risk our lives in the defence and protection of our country, and its laws.[54]

Regardless of the sentiments expressed in this letter, the ameliorative door had been opened, and increasing pressures from Britain to reform slave codes intensified the movement to push that door open farther. In January, 1817, the Barbadian plantocracy had been all but compelled by the imperial government to pass a slave registry act, and the controversy surrounding its passage had exacerbated traditional plantocratic sensitivity concerning its own definition of colonial political rights and individual rights over private property. Especially in the early 1820s, the irritation and tension of local whites were compounded by external events that were reflected in, among other developments, the destruction of the Methodist chapel in Bridgetown by a white mob, an almost continual apprehension that another slave revolt might break out, and rumors in late 1823 "that the free coloured people were going to revolt [or] that they intended petitioning for an increase of civic rights."[55] In October, 1823, a group of twenty freedmen addressed the Assembly.

They stated their fidelity to the "land of our nativity and to the institutions and form of government under which we have hitherto had the happiest of lives," and asserted their willingness "to assist with all their power in the maintenance of subordination and good order." Although they denied a rumor that they intended to take advantage of the unsettled state of the country and "seek to obtain certain rights and privileges" of which they were deprived, there were, indeed, certain "legal disabilities" which they hoped would be removed in the near future. However, they believed that the removal of these disabilities, unless "by the general conviction of their injustice and inexpediency, . . . would only have the effect of increasing" the prejudice already in "operation amongst the white population."[56]

The petition was not greeted adversely by the Assembly, but its sentiments did not represent a consensus of the freedmen of Barbados. It had been formulated by a small, self-appointed elite, and many freedmen objected to the actions of this small group, as well as to its conservative stance on the drive for civil rights. Thus, not long afterward, at a public meeting of freedmen, a group of 373 signed a counter petition which they directed to Governor Warde; in it they set forth their objections to the earlier petition and more firmly noted that

[54] "To the Honorable John Beckles, Speaker of the House of Assembly and the Rest of the Honorable and Worshipful Members, March 4, 1817," CO 28/86.

[55] H. A. Vaughan, "Samuel Prescod: The Birth of a Hero," *New World Quarterly*, 3 (1966): 55.

[56] "Minutes of the Barbados Privy Council, October 21, 1823," BDA.

there are certain parts of our Colonial Code which exempts us from participating with our white brethren in certain privileges, and to which, as British subjects, we humbly conceive we have a claim; and that it is our intention, in a less agitated state of the Colony, to pray for a removal of such parts, which by the several enactments of the Legislature, materially affect us.[57]

The second petition succeeded only in annoying, if not infuriating, the Assembly, not only because of its general intent (which included the desire for eligibility to vote and be elected), but also because it went to the governor and was thus a direct affront to an issue upon which the Assembly was increasingly adamant—its right to determine the island's internal affairs. A resolution on the petition stated that "this House in the most positive and unequivocal manner denies that the free-coloured inhabitants . . . are entitled to any rights and privileges, except those granted to them by the Colonial legislature, the continuance of which must depend entirely on their good conduct."[58]

However, the plantocracy was increasingly put on the defensive, and circumstances continued to work in favor of ameliorating the condition of slaves and, by extension, of freedmen as well. Yet the Assembly often delayed reform legislation as long as possible and enacted it in piecemeal fashion and frequently on the minimal level it thought it could get away with and still comply with directives from the Colonial Office. This legislative policy was well reflected in the mid-1820s, during considerations over the "slave consolidation act," the most comprehensive and lengthy slave law in the island's history. The act repealed or modified dormant laws, removed inconsistencies, and introduced new measures. An early version of this law passed the Assembly and Council in March, 1825, but it did not include a number of changes desired by the Colonial Office; a new version passed the legislature, and was assented to by the governor, in October, 1826.[59] Although ultimately approved by the crown, the approval was a qualified one, and the island's government was warned that, "unless a further and more decisive progress be made in the improvement of the slave code of the Colony, His Majesty's expectations will not be satisfied."[60] Although the "slave consolidation act" was not specifically intended to apply to freedmen, a few clauses in it related to them and were thought particularly offensive and potentially debilitating to their personal security. In these clauses sanctions were applied against slaves who used "insolent language or gestures to . . . any white person," and who "shall wilfully strike or

[57] "Journal of the House of Assembly, February 3 and 18, 1824," *ibid.*

[58] Quoted in R. Schomburgk, *The History of Barbados* (London, 1848), p. 417.

[59] For the earlier version, see CO 30/20–21, no. 446; for the later one, see *PP*, 1826–27, vol. 25 (report not numbered), pp. 205–30.

[60] Huskisson to Skeete, October 18, 1827, *PP*, 1828, vol. 27 (report not numbered), pp. 37–41.

assault any white person." Thus, freedmen were denied privileges they had possessed up to that time,[61] as well as, in the words of one of their 1827 petitions, "all legal remedy against personal assaults, and other behavior tending to provoke a breach of the peace, committed by the largest class of the population of the island." The petition was drawn up in specific reaction to these clauses, and called for their repeal, but it also expressed deeper grievances and regretted that by the "slave consolidation act," the petitioners "find themselves divested of certain privileges and advantages hitherto enjoyed by them in common with their white fellow subjects; their interests slighted; the ban of political exclusion pronounced against them by former legislatures reiterated and confirmed."[62]

The climate of the times (which in general was contributed to by pressures from Great Britain) made it difficult for even the Barbados Assembly to continue the objectionable clauses that abrogated privileges formally held; and, in January, 1828, the protective clauses of the "slave consolidation act" were explicitly extended to freedmen.[63] Additional meetings were held, petitions were again forwarded to the legislature, and other ameliorative acts followed in relatively short order: in 1829, some protective clauses applying only to freeholders (which, of course, excluded many whites), clauses which had been on the books since 1672 and 1770, were repealed, and in late 1830 the right to testify in legal proceedings was extended to all freedmen, regardless of how or when they had been manumitted.[64]

Then, on June 9, 1831 (after five months of formal consideration in the Assembly and another petition by freedmen), all legal disabilities were removed.[65] Popularly known as the "brown privilege bill," the law repealed "all acts and . . . parts of acts as impose any restraints or disabilities whatsoever on His Majesty's Free Coloured and Free Black subjects . . . to which His Majesty's white subjects . . . are not liable." In addition, the law provided that "every freeman" was eligible to vote, and so forth—that is, to qualify as a freeholder, subject to age and property qualifications. But, even at this late date, although it was technically removing racial prerequisites to becoming a freeholder, the Barbadian legislature could not bring itself to qualify the small number of freedmen who would have been eligible or resist the chance to make their legal victory incomplete. What the law did was to continue undisturbed the qualifications (in effect since 1721) of existing voters (that is, whites), while requiring all

[61] For example, a 1688 law made it a crime for "any Negro or slave whatsoever" to "offer any violence to any Christian, by striking or the like," and one in 1749 made it a crime for "any Negro or other slave" to use "any insolent language or gesture to any white or free person" (Hall, *Acts*, pp. 114, 355).

[62] PP, 1828, vol. 27 (report not numbered), pp. 42–44.

[63] CO 31/21, no. 505.

[64] *Ibid.*, no. 528.

[65] *Ibid.*, no. 538.

new freeholders, if they did not possess at least ten acres of land (a luxury few freedmen had), to own a house in a town, a house whose annual taxable value was three times higher than that required by the 1721 law. Thus, white freeholders continued to be eligible to vote under previous criteria, while new freeholders were subjected to an increase in their property qualifications. It is of more than passing interest that the rise in property qualifications applied only to houses, these being the major form of property that wealthier freedmen possessed.[66]

Although many freedmen "hailed the apparent enfranchisement, and held a public rejoicing on the occasion," Samuel Prescod (who was on his way to becoming a prominent leader in the freedman community) "succeeded . . . in convincing his brethren that the new provision was a mockery of their wrongs, and that the Assembly had only added insult to past injuries."[67]

As a group, the Barbados plantocracy had resisted as long as it could the granting of civil rights to the freedman. Even the legislature's final action, in the twilight of slavery and when emancipation was already imminent, reflected its traditional intransigence and intractibility. These qualities had been primarily mollified by continued pressure from Britain as well as by the efforts the freedman had made on his own behalf. But, as will be discussed in the final section of this chapter, the integration of the freedman into the larger society of freemen and his participation in the institutional order remained limited because of the status ascribed to him on the basis of race.

OCCUPATIONAL ROLES AND THE ECONOMIC SYSTEM

The freedman engaged in a relative diversity of economic activities, but, above all, he shunned agricultural wage labor on the plantations. He could have found employment on plantations whose slave contingents were low, but his freedom, if it meant nothing else, meant that he was not compelled to engage in work that was the hallmark of slave status and subject himself to the control and arbitrary discipline of the plantation. Critics of the freedman's reluctance

[66] Yet, even by this act, relatively few of the island's freedmen were franchised. In 1833 the governor reported that 125 freedmen paid rents "from £ 10 and upwards, and . . . would enjoy the privilege of voters, if they were white; and there are only 75 voters by the present law of £ 30 qualifications" (Smith to Stanley, October 29, 1833, CO 28/111). At this time, the island's total electorate was comprised of 1,016 persons (446 in Saint Michael alone [Schomburgk, History of Barbados, p. 455]); therefore, on the eve of emancipation, freedmen constituted only 7 percent of the eligible voters, although they comprised about one-third of the total free (non-slave) population.

[67] J. A. Thome and J. H. Kimball, Emancipation in the West Indies (New York, 1838), p. 74.

to "labour in the field" would attribute this to his pride and indolence,[68] but he was apparently not adverse to agricultural work when opportunities were presented in which he had some control over his own time and labor. Thus, there were some who engaged in small-scale agriculture by working the two- or three-acre plots they were allotted as plantation militia-tenants[69] or by renting lands as "tenants annual, at will, or in fee"[70]; by the late eighteenth century there were even some individuals who, "by their industry, have been able to purchase little freeholds, and build good habitations on them."[71] Freedmen continued to engage in small-scale agriculture (sometimes supplemented by other activities) throughout the slave period, but the opportunities for them to either rent or own land were limited. Although the number of landowners apparently increased, it was probably the rare individual who could acquire more than a few acres, and we have concrete evidence of only one freedman plantation owner.[72] In general, then, agricultural activities appear to have played a relatively minor role in the economic life of the freedman population.

The freedman would occasionally hire himself out in the towns to perform unskilled tasks such as loading sugar or engaging in similar kinds of waterfront work. But such labor was traditionally and largely performed by slaves, and thus, not only were opportunities limited, but the social context of the labor was not fundamentally different from plantation work; in addition, skilled labor was in greater demand and had higher prestige value than unskilled work. Thus, if the freedman did not already possess a skill upon being emancipated, he attempted to learn one, and gravitated toward the skilled trades. By the late eighteenth century, "Many of the men

[68] See, for example, replies of Parry, Brathwaite, and the Council of Barbados to queries 5, 37, and 38 in "Report of the Lords of the Committee of Council . . . Concerning the Present State of the Trade . . . in Slaves . . .," pt. 3, PP, 1789, vol. 26, and Report of a Committee of the General Assembly [of Babados] upon the Several Heads of Enquiry, etc., Relative to the Slave Trade (London, 1790), p. 6.

[69] Plantations were obliged to send to their parochial units one militia-man for every thirty to fifty acres of plantation land; the acreage fluctuated by law, and could be reduced in contingencies, but, in return for these services, the plantation allotted two or three acres to each tenant for the cultivating of provisions and minor cash crops and the raising of small livestock. These "militia tenants," the majority of whom were poor whites, made up a considerable proportion of the island's noncommissioned men, and freedmen were sometimes allowed to perform this role when, presumably, plantations could not find a sufficient number of poor whites to meet their quotas. Not all of the freedmen in the militia were tenants, but present information prevents us from estimating how many were, or what percentage of all freedmen in the militia they comprised.

[70] Reply of Parry to query 38, "Report of the Lords."

[71] Reply of Joshua Steele to Governor Parry, PP, 1789, vol. 26, p. 33.

[72] See the deposition of Jacob Belgrave in Report from a Select Committee, pp. 38–39.

work[ed] at the various trades of smiths, carpenters, and masons,"[73] and some even made a living as musicians.

As the years progressed, more freedmen were employed in trades. Although whites had traditionally performed many skilled mechanical jobs, by the latter half of the eighteenth century, the number of slave tradesmen had increased considerably as plantation owners, for reasons of convenience, economy, and an assured labor supply, encouraged their training. In addition, such slaves were especially valuable, not only to plantation owners, but also to many landless whites in towns, for "the great profit which their labour brings in and the hire which they fetch when let out to work."[74] Gradually, competition from skilled slaves and freedmen made it increasingly difficult for "poor white artificers . . . to get bread,"[75] and many left their trades, either losing their initiative or emigrating from the island. As this trend increased, more opportunities were created for freedmen, who continued their movement into skilled occupational roles. By 1814, as an American who was then living in Bridgetown observed, "Free Negroes carried on all the lighter mechanical trades, such as tailors, shoemakers, jewellers, etc., and were expert workmen."[76] A little more than a decade later, a Barbadian critic of freedmen, alarmed at the number of poor and unemployed whites, wrote that they "have usurped and now successfully rival" whites in trades such as joinery, carpentry, masonry, painting, shoemaking, and the like.[77]

Although men were prominent in the trades, both sexes were involved in the island's internal marketing system. Many of the traders within this system, whose roots went into the seventeenth century, were slaves who sold or bartered their own food crops and small livestock, as well as goods stolen from their masters' properties. Various seventeenth- and eighteenth-century laws attempted to arrest or circumscribe their marketing activities, and quite often the traders found it more convenient and safer to deal with white hucksters, "who, in fact, are often worse than the Negroes, by receiving all stolen goods."[78] By the middle of the eighteenth century, freedmen (many of whom, it can be assumed, were continuing marketing activities they had engaged in as slaves) had assumed this role as well. As early as 1739, a law permitting slaves to testify in legal proceedings against freedmen took note of their trading with slaves in stolen

[73] Reply of Joshua Steele to Governor Parry, PP, 1789, vol. 26, p. 33.

[74] Waller, Voyage, pp. 92–93.

[75] W. Dickson, Letters on Slavery (London, 1789), pp. 26, 40–43.

[76] [B. Browne], The Yarn of a Yankee Privateer, ed. Nathaniel Hawthorne (New York, 1926), p. 103.

[77] J. W. Orderson, Leisure Hours at the Pier: Or, A Treatise on the Education of the Poor of Barbados (Liverpool, 1827), pp. 11–13 and passim; cf. E. Eliot, Christianity and Slavery (London, 1833), pp. 225–26.

[78] Alleyne to Society for the Propagation of the Gospel in Foreign Parts, December 9, 1741, USPG, vol. B8, no. 51.

goods, and complained that they were "enticing and corrupting . . . slaves to steal and rob their owners."[79] How much of the freedman's trading activities actually depended upon the disposition of stolen goods is difficult to ascertain, despite the complaints made against him. Although there is little doubt that trade in such commodities was important, it is also apparent that the freedman trader, especially in the eighteenth century, frequently acted as an agent for white shopkeepers or hucksters, who themselves encouraged the slaves "to plunder their owners of everything that is portable."[80]

In general, the trading activities of freedman hucksters shared many of the characteristics of the white and slave ones. Vegetables, meat, fish, poultry, and so on, were sold by plying the countryside, and the Negro huckster often met incoming ships and sold fresh foods to their passengers and crews. In towns, they sold from door to door, established themselves at set locations in the streets or alleys, or set up stalls in front of their houses. In Bridgetown, especially on Sundays and holidays, many hucksters sat at "the great market" with their trays or baskets, while others wandered about hawking their wares. Hucksters sometimes sold goods they themselves had produced, or they acquired vendibles from plantation slaves with whom they exchanged items (such as food delicacies) they had brought from town.

To protect the white seller and consumer, as well as to curtail the movements of slaves, a number of late eighteenth- and early nineteenth-century laws contained provisions designed to inhibit or eliminate various types of trading practices. These laws generally had limited effect, however; in most cases the practices they were designed to control continued, and the laws were later repealed or modified. Freedmen hucksters continued to create economic opportunities and to avail themselves of those that occurred. Not only was huckstering a deeply embedded aspect of their cultural life, but it was also one of the few ways in which women, in particular, could meet household and familial responsibilities, enjoy personal independence and autonomy, and make a living. Equally important to these continuing, and often uninhibited, operations was the fact that the services provided by hucksters became essential to the distribution of foods, especially to those who lived in the towns.

The proceeds saved from huckstering activities, as well as monies earned in the trades, permitted some persons to acquire the necessary capital to open shops. By the 1780s, there were a few of these, but their number increased substantially, and within a few decades in Bridgetown, as one observer noted in 1814, "many of them were shop keepers; indeed I should think that the largest number of shops were kept by them."[81] In Speightstown, by 1825 the

79 Hall, *Acts*, pp. 323–25.
80 Dickson, *Letters*, p. 42.
81 [Browne], *Yarn*, p. 103.

freedman population was substantially augmented by those coming "from other parishes, for the purpose of carrying on a small retail trade which is now almost entirely in their hands."[82]

Freedmen continued to open shops throughout the slave period, but relatively few were able to go beyond small-scale business into mercantile establishments that, in effect, competed with the larger enterprises of wealthy whites. This was especially the case during the eighteenth century. By the early nineteenth century and throughout the remaining years of slavery, however, some freedmen became relatively wealthy merchants, most of them presumably by extending their initial shopkeeping activities and some of them by using the skills they had acquired as clerks in white mercantile houses. Few details are available on such individuals, and for this reason the case of London Bourne, "a merchant of extensive business at home and abroad," is of particular interest:

> Mr. Bourne was a slave until he was twenty-three years old. He was purchased by his father, a free Negro, who gave five hundred dollars for him. His mother and four brothers were bought at the same time for the sum of two thousand five hundred dollars. He spoke very kindly of his former master. By industry, honesty, and close attention to business, Mr. B. has now become a wealthy merchant. He owns three stores in Bridgetown, lives in a very genteel style in his own house, and is worth from twenty to thirty thousand dollars. He is highly respected by the merchants of Bridgetown for his integrity and business talents.[83]

As "respected" as Bourne might have been, he and other freedmen merchants of wealth were "as far as was practicable . . . excluded [by whites] from all business connections. . . . [and] were shut out of the merchants' exchange"; in fact, one of the ironies in Bourne's case was the fact that the merchant exchange which excluded him rented the upstairs rooms in the building which he owned and in which he operated his store and lived with his family.[84]

Women who traded beyond the huckstering level were largely confined to the operation of small shops. By the late eighteenth century and during the early nineteenth, however, the few hotel-taverns in Bridgetown were the enterprises of freedwomen. It was common for a tavern proprietress to have "been the favored enamorata of some [white] man from whom she has obtained her freedom."[85] These taverns were popular rendezvous for local whites and British military personnel, and some were sufficiently profitable that their owners became relatively wealthy and acquired "considerable property, both in houses and slaves."[86] The taverns provided meals and

[82] Hinds to Husbands, November 21, 1825, *PP*, 1826, vol. 26, rept. 350.
[83] Thome and Kimball, *Emancipation*, p. 75.
[84] *Ibid.*, p. 79.
[85] G. Pinkard, *Notes on the West Indies*, 2 vols. (London, 1806), 1: 245.
[86] Waller, *Voyage*, p. 6.

lodging, and their owners sponsored "dignity balls" (or "quality balls")—formally organized supper-dances that required an admission fee—which were largely attended by "coloured" or "mulatto" females, and "to which only white men were admitted."[87]

In general, then, huckstering, shopkeeping, and work in the skilled trades were the major occupational roles by which freedmen were able to elevate their standard of living. Despite the economic success of some individuals, toward the end of the eighteenth century many freedmen were living a marginal economic existence while others lived in extreme poverty. It is difficult, however, to achieve an accurate assessment of their standard of living at this period. For example, in the late 1780s, the island's governor, among other critics, reported that "the Free Negroes . . . will not labour for their own maintenance, but become beggars, and are frequently supported by the parish they belong to."[88] An opposite evaluation was given by Joshua Steele at the same time:

> It is in general obvious to any person of observation, the Free Negroes and Mulattoes must apply themselves to some kind of industry, as they are never seen begging, either males or females; whereas the island in general is pestered with white beggars, of both sexes, and of all ages, covered with only filthy rags; while the Free Negroes and Mulattoes are well clothed and appear to be well fed.[89]

Other comparisons between the standard of living of freedmen and poor whites also varied in emphasis (some writers finding poor whites generally worse off than freedmen, others finding them slightly better off), but the sources generally give the impression that many freedmen were quite poor.

As the years passed, more freedmen came to live under "comfortable circumstances . . . some of them possessing a good deal of wealth."[90] This increasing wealth, especially in commercial ventures and property holding in Bridgetown, was reflected in the priority that freedmen gave, in their drive for ameliorative legislation, to the right to testify in the courts. As noted previously, their early petitions constantly emphasized this point. In 1830, William Bell, commenting on changes that had occurred on the island since his visit twenty years before, noted a "very perceptible change in the manners & habits of the Coloured People. Property is becoming more general amongst them. One meets them driving their carriages & riding their horses, the same as white persons."[91] Such changes were evident and observed mainly in Bridgetown. One can surmise that many freedmen, including the majority of those who lived in the rural areas, remained

---

87 [Browne], Yarn, p. 104.
88 Reply of Parry to query 37, "Report of the Lords."
89 Reply of Joshua Steele to Governor Parry, PP, 1789, vol. 26, p. 33.
90 [Browne], Yarn, p. 103.
91 Boromé, "William Bell," p. 23.

on a generally modest or low economic level, not unlike that of the island's lower-class whites.

We have little information on the extent and value of major property held by freedmen. As suggested earlier, they appear to have owned limited quantities of agricultural land, and their major forms of property seem to have been houses (and house spots) and slaves. The extent of house ownership (which would include dwellings used for shopkeeping) was most noticeable in Bridgetown. In 1816, J. W. Orderson observed that in Bridgetown "many of the best houses belong to them; and I am well persuaded that at least one-twelfth of the whole town is the actual freehold property of the coloured people."[92] This suggests the importance of houses as a form of property to the freedman, an importance that is also well reflected in the 1831 law that enfranchised him. This law, despite its formal elimination of racial barriers to voting, was still designed to inhibit the freedman's eligibility. It did this by increasing property qualifications, but only those with respect to houses. Ownership of at least ten acres of land, a qualification that had been in force for more than a hundred years, was retained, but the annual taxable value of a house was tripled. We assume that if freedmen had been landowners of any consequence the legislature would have also increased the minimal land requirements for enfranchisement; by not doing this, it indirectly asserted that houses, not land, were the most significant form of real property held by freedmen. Even so, in 1833, only seventy-five freedmen were able to satisfy the property qualifications, a fact which provides a reasonable indication of the approximate number of males who, by Barbadian standards, could be considered relatively wealthy.

Our information on slaveowning by freedmen is fragmentary. However, there is no evidence that they had any compunction against owning or employing slaves, and available information leads us to the conclusion that, when financial circumstances permitted, freedmen did not hesitate to hire or purchase them. The attitude of at least some freedmen toward slaveownership is revealed in an 1803 petition submitted to the legislature requesting it not to pass a bill that was aimed at, among other things, preventing them from acquiring slaves: "Although we have all our lives been accustomed to the assistance of slaves, we must immediately [by the proposed bill] deprive ourselves of them and perform every menial office with our hands. . . . The greatest blessing attending upon freedom is the acquirement and enjoyment of property and without that, liberty is but an empty name."[93] By 1814 it was observed that, among Bridgetown's freedmen, "many were slave owners."[94]

[92] Orderson, *Cursory Remarks*, p. 30.
[93] "Minutes of the Barbados Privy Council, November 1, 1803," BDA.
[94] [Browne], *Yarn*, p. 103.

Although it is difficult to establish the number of slaveowners among freedmen or the number of slaves each possessed, it is doubtful that the freedman group owned more than a small percentage of the island's slave population. The slaves were largely employed as house servants, shop assistants, and, occasionally, as agricultural laborers or, perhaps, hired-out tradesmen. In addition, some of the slaves owned by freedmen were their own children, whom, because they could not pay the fee, they were unable to manumit.

Again, it is difficult to assess how freedmen treated their slaves and whether this treatment was any better or worse than the treatment of slaves by whites. In the late eighteenth century, William Dickson, a critic of the Barbadian slave system and a defender of the freedman, observed that "free Negroes are generally more severe, because less enlightened, owners, than white people,"[95] but, as the years progressed, and more freedmen became slaveholders, they may have come in for a disproportionate amount of criticism; an American resident of Bridgetown in 1814 observed that freedmen

> had the reputation of being much more cruel to their slaves than the white proprietors. I had no means of knowing how much of this censure they deserved, but I suspect it must be received with many grains of allowance, for it was a character given by whites who seemed to entertain a hostile feeling against them.[96]

J. Thome and J. Kimball, who visited the island in 1837, offered a more general conclusion, for which we have found no contradictory evidence.

> We regret to add, that until lately, the colored people of Barbadoes have been far in the back ground in the cause of abolition, and even now, the majority of them are either indifferent, or actually hostile to emancipation. They have no fellow feeling with the slave. In fact, they have had prejudices against the Negroes no less bitter than those which the whites have exercised toward them. There are many honorable exceptions to this, as has already been shown; but such, we are assured, is the general fact.[97]

It should be clear that the relationship between freedman and slave was more involved than that between master and servant. In everyday life, and in a variety of institutional contexts, the two groups were often and inevitably in contact. We have already touched on their contacts in the judicial and economic systems. Although space limitations prevent our discussing other institutions, freedmen and slaves also jointly participated in churches, primarily the Anglican and Methodist, educational facilities (where whites and non-

---

95 Dickson, *Letters*, p. 55.
96 [Browne], *Yarn*, p. 103.
97 Thome and Kimball, *Emancipation*, p. 76.

whites attended separate schools), and a variety of other cultural settings.

THE FREEDMAN IN THE SOCIAL ORDER

Having discussed the development of the freedman's status and his participation in some major national institutions, we conclude with a consideration of the freedman as one of the constituent groups in Barbadian society. We will seek to locate the group in the island's social order, summarize its relationship to whites and slaves, and delineate its internal structure and cultural features. As indicated in the introduction to this paper, the source materials are least satisfactory for the major concerns of this section. Direct evidence is especially limited on the stratification and culture of freedmen, and mainly pertains to those who lived in the towns and ranked highest in their community's social hierarchy.

Non-Barbadian whites who commented on the island's social order and the place of freedmen within it stressed the importance of race as a determinant of social position, and were inclined to characterize freedmen as a caste. J. A. Waller observed that, for the white creole, "no property, however considerable, can ever raise a man or woman of colour, not even when combined with education, to the proper rank of a human being."[98] J. Sturge and T. Harvey noted how white creole ideology involved "the belief that the blacks are by nature of an inferior race, and born to servile condition; and the spirit of caste cherished between the white, mixed, and black races"; they found that "prejudice against color is stronger in Barbadoes than in any other colony."[99] Visiting the island in 1830, an English emancipationist reported "that it was a decided loss of caste, if a white person associated as a visitor with persons of colour, even if free and of unblemished character,"[100] and S. Hodgson, who was in Barbados around the same time, also observed that the effect of racial particularism on the freedman in the West Indian social order was such that wealth, refinement, reputation, travel, and education "will avail him [of] nothing; hourly will he be taunted with . . . his Negro blood, and forever will society be barred against him."[101]

As we indicated, phenotypic differences among freedmen did not result in legal distinctions defining their status, nor did these differences apparently have a significant effect upon the way in which freedmen were treated and regarded by whites. That is, regardless of phenotypic characteristics, white society defined anyone with

[98] Waller, *Voyage*, p. 95.

[99] J. Sturge and T. Harvey, *The West Indies in 1837* (London, 1838), pp. 141–42.

[100] [Anon.], *Notes on Slavery, Made During a Recent Visit to Barbadoes*, The Negro's Friend, no. 18 (London, [1830]), p. 10.

[101] S. Hodgson, *Truths from the West Indies* (London, 1838), p. 59.

even a hint of Negroid ancestry as a non-white. For example, during the apprenticeship period William Lloyd visited Samuel Prescod, a leader of the freedman community, and later pointed out that he "has no distinguishing marks of Negro complexion, and in England he would be esteemed as a gentleman, whilst in Barbadoes he is in some degree despised as a coloured man."[102]

Outside observers thus viewed Barbadian society as one stratified on the basis of racial ancestry into superordinate and subordinate groups; anyone of Negroid ancestry was defined as a member of the latter. White racist attitudes toward freedmen involved the belief that differences in racial ancestry determined social, moral, and intellectual qualities; this belief rationalized the ascription of subordinate group status to freedmen. Although the freedman group was internally differentiated by wealth, occupation, education, and general life style, these factors did not substantially alter the group's subordinate position or affect its social distance from whites. In sum, the lower caste position of the freedman was determined by the dominant white group, which defined this position by Negroid ancestry.

While supported in certain respects by our previous discussion, this conception of the freedman in the Barbadian social structure implies a clarity in the freedman's status which did not in fact exist. His status was indeterminate, in the sense that he was neither slave nor fully free. He was a person of Negroid ancestry in a society that defined slave status by racial criteria; any person of Negroid ancestry was presumed to be a slave unless he could legally establish his freedom. Slavery, not freedom, was the presumptive status of the non-white person.

The fact that he was not a slave and not fully a freeman might suggest that the freedman occupied an intermediate status between free and slave in Barbadian society. There was, however, no clearly defined intermediate legal status for him. The essentially unstable and ambiguous nature of his position in the social order resulted from the tension that arose from the difference between the definition of a freeman and the beliefs and attitudes of whites toward Negroid ancestry. Thus, a freedman was a *"free mulatto man"* or a *"free colored woman."* As a group, freedmen were exceedingly conscious of their indeterminate status. They fundamentally rejected it (though not without some ambivalence), and their efforts to maximize their free status, which involved removing disabilities attached to their Negroid ancestry, were almost continuous during the period focused upon in this paper.

The freedmen's efforts to maximize their free status tended to concentrate on their position in the law, especially the right to testify, but included attempts to extend their participation in national insti-

---

[102] W. Lloyd, *Letters from the West Indies During a Visit in the Autumn of 1836 and the Spring of 1837* (London, [1838]), p. 17.

tutions and to remove discriminatory practices in other areas of island life as well. For example, although the "brown privilege bill" of 1831 removed all legal disabilities from freedmen, the profound racism of white society continued to degrade this free status by perpetuating the social disabilities of earlier years. As late as 1833, freedmen held a public meeting to protest discrimination in general and the denial of their admission to "public situations of honour and profit" in particular; in an "address" to the governor they emphasized that "as far as legislative enactments could remove the unnatural and impolitic distinctions between us and our white fellow-subjects, those distinctions have been removed. . . . [but] the distinctions are, in reality, still kept up."[103]

Freedmen were excluded from positions of leadership and responsibility in the Anglican church, the island's dominant church organization; there were no freedman ministers throughout the slave period, and we have evidence for only one catechist. In addition, freedmen (as well as slaves) were prevented from taking communion at the same time as whites, and non-whites were confined to special seating areas within the churches. As late as the apprenticeship period, "no coloured student has yet been admitted within the walls of Codrington College,"[104] owned by the Church of England's Society for the Propagation of the Gospel. Although there were a number of other church-related schools by the 1820s, in all cases freedmen and slaves attended the same schools, and these were kept distinct from the white ones. Racial distinctions were also maintained among teachers; the few freedman teachers taught only non-whites (though white teachers taught pupils of all races) and were paid lower salaries than their white counterparts. Freedmen paid taxes levied by parish vestries, but the indigent among them were excluded from the publicly financed parochial schools and did not receive pensions provided by vestries from tax funds, as did the white poor. Freedmen were obliged to serve in the island's militia but were denied commissions in it, and the militia units themselves were segregated. Freedmen "merchants of wealth were shut out of the merchants' exchange," and "colored gentlemen were not allowed to become members of literary associations, nor subscribers to the town libraries."[105] As a young man, Samuel Prescod was ejected from the House of Assembly while simply listening to the proceedings; "this show of interest on his part was regarded as an act of presumption."[106]

For most of the slave period, freedmen were prohibited from serving on juries, testifying against whites, voting, and holding office. They were debarred from becoming magistrates and justices of the peace. "Parents, however wealthy, had no inducement to educate

[103] Quoted in Schomburgk, *History of Barbados*, p. 453.
[104] Sturge and Harvey, *West Indies*, p. 141.
[105] Thome and Kimball, *Emancipation*, p. 79.
[106] Vaughan, "Samuel Prescod," p. 56.

their sons for the learned professions, since no force of talent nor extent of acquirement could hope to break down the [barriers] . . . which prejudice had erected around the pulpit, the bar, and the bench."[107] Baptismal, burial, and marriage records designated the racial affiliation of the freedman. Illustrating how "every opportunity was maliciously seized to taunt the colored people with their complexion," Thome and Kimball reported the case of "a gentleman of the highest worth," who

> stated that several years ago he applied to the proper office for a license to be married. The license was . . . expressed in the following insulting style: "T_____ H_____, F.M., is licensed to marry H_____ L_____, F.C.W." The initials F.M. stood for *free mulatto*, and F.C.W. for *free colored woman*! The gentleman took out his knife and cut out the initials; and was then threatened with a prosecution for forging his license![108]

When addressing freedmen, whites would generally eschew titles such as Mr., Miss, or Mrs. R. R. Madden, for example, reported the indignation of a freedwoman tavern owner who had been addressed by her first name and had emphasized that she was "Miss Betsy Austin."[109] G. Pinckard observed how "the title Mrs. seems to be reserved, solely, for the ladies from Europe, and the white creoles, and to form a distinction between them and the women of colour of all classes and description—none of whom, of whatever shade or degree, are dignified by this appelation."[110]

White creoles, especially those of the middle and upper classes, had a general aversion to contacts and relations with freedmen which might imply social equality. "Social intercourse," as Thome and Kimball reported, "was utterly interdicted. To visit the houses [of high-ranking freedmen] . . . and especially to sit down at their tables, would have been a loss of caste."[111] Waller made similar observations, and also recounted how he "was once severely reprehended by a lady at Bridgetown, for having been seen walking in the street with a surgeon of a frigate who happened to be a man of colour, though brought up in England, and educated at the University of Edinburgh."[112] A missionary reported that he "once knew a young lady to say she wished not to go to heaven if people of colour are there."[113]

However, sexual relationships between white males and freedwomen were exempt from the system that socially separated mem-

[107] Thome and Kimball, *Emancipation*, p. 76.

[108] *Ibid.*, p. 79; italics in the original.

[109] R. R. Madden, *A Twelve Months' Residence in the West Indies during the Transition from Slavery to Apprenticeship*, 2 vols. (London, 1835), 1:24.

[110] Pinckard, *Notes*, 1: 249.

[111] Thome and Kimball, *Emancipation*, p. 79.

[112] Waller, *Voyage*, p. 95.

[113] Nelson to Wesleyan Missionary Society, January 12, 1822, MMS, Box 1821–22, no. 205.

bers of the two groups. Freedwomen "from the highest as well as the lowest families" participated in the system of concubinage.[114] "I was told," a visitor in 1814 reported, "that many colored parents educated their female children for this special purpose,"[115] and years later Thome and Kimball related that young freedwomen who had been educated in England "returned to the island to become the concubines of white men."[116] Such relationships were not disparaged; on the contrary, "Colored ladies have been taught to believe that it was more honorable, and quite as virtuous, to be the kept mistresses of *white gentlemen*, than the lawfully wedded wives of *colored men*."[117] Freedwomen who became involved in these relationships "were actually proud of their position in society, and considered themselves as many degrees above those who were obliged to labor."[118] For whatever reasons white creole and foreign males encouraged concubinage and white females condoned or were indifferent to it, freedwomen perceived it as a device for social mobility and material security. Concubinage remained, however, fundamentally a relationship between individuals from superordinate and subordinate groups; since it did not result in marriage, it did not challenge the hierarchical and endogamous division between the white and freedman groups, in which membership was hereditary and permanent.

In the preceding pages we noted the contacts between freedmen and slaves in various institutional settings and in the society at large. For freedmen, however, the process of maximizing their free status involved distinguishing it from the slaves' status. In 1803, John Beckles pointed to the "jealousy which seems naturally to exist between the free coloured people and the slaves,"[119] and in a late eighteenth-century address to freedmen, William Dickson observed: "Most of you may be said to hold a higher rank in society than the slaves. You justly consider yourselves, and they consider you, as their superiors."[120] The concern with distinguishing themselves from slaves is reflected in the freedmen's various efforts to alter their legal status, wherein they consistently placed highest priority on the right to testify in legal proceedings. The 1721 law which prohibited the testimony of anyone of Negroid ancestry against whites reduced the free status of the freedman, but it still allowed his testimony against slaves. A 1739 law further reduced his status, however, by explicitly permitting slave testimony against him. From the freedman's perspective, this legal disability simply reinforced his inferior position in the social order and placed him on a comparable footing with the

114 Thome and Kimball, *Emancipation*, p. 76.
115 [Browne], *Yarn*, p. 104.
116 Thome and Kimball, *Emancipation*, p. 76.
117 *Ibid.*; italics in the original.
118 [Browne], *Yarn*, p. 104.
119 "Minutes of the Barbados Privy Council, November 1, 1803," BDA.
120 Dickson, *Letters*, p. 174.

slave. Furthermore, by eliminating his testimony against whites, it thrust him more forcefully into the position of the slave, for, as in the case of the slave, he was unable to avail himself of legal redress and protection against those very abuses of power to which his subordinate social position already exposed him. The importance of the right to testify increased as freedmen expanded their participation in commercial activities and increased their acquisition of real property. This right was necessary for more than the protection of their property and economic interests, however; it was also vital to the definition of freedom, and consequently to the distinction between free and slave statuses and the removal of the disabilities associated with Negroid ancestry.

Likewise, distinguishing their status from that of the slaves is illustrated in the anxiety freedmen showed over some passages in the 1826 "slave consolidation act." For many years it had been a crime for slaves to physically attack "any Christian" (which, by implication, included baptized freedmen) or to verbally abuse "any white or free person," but with the "slave consolidation act" the freedman was excluded from legal protection against such behavior. It is doubtful that the judicial system ever actually worked in the freedman's interest along these lines. Yet, denial of any formal legal protection was of concern to freedmen because they felt not only that they were more vulnerable to aggressive behavior on the part of slaves (thus reflecting, in part, the tensions between the two groups) but also that they were now, in the words of one of their petitions, "divested of certain privileges and advantages hitherto enjoyed by them in common with their white fellow subjects"; the denial represented a diminution of their freedom and, as a consequence, brought them closer to slave status.

In general, as Thome and Kimball reported, freedmen lacked a "fellow feeling with the slave,"[121] and appear to have been either indifferent or opposed to emancipation. Because they were concerned with maximizing their status, which, as we noted, involved distinguishing it from the slave status, and because this maximization called for the attainment of rights and privileges controlled by whites, freedmen would have been risking total alienation from the plantocracy had they attacked the slave issue. Although a handful of freedmen were involved in the 1816 slave revolt, there is no evidence of a widespread desire for such fundamental changes in the social order as would have been involved in the ending of slavery. In addition, as wealth and property holdings increased among freedmen, more appear to have perceived that they had benefited from the established order and thus were less likely to challenge the slave system.

The relationship between freedmen and slaves is a topic that merits further investigation and requires more evidence than we have

---

[121] Thome and Kimball, *Emancipation*, p. 76.

at our disposal. Although obviously there were tensions between them, the cleavage may not have been as great as we suggest. Despite the frictions and apparent ambiguity in the relationship between the two groups, a shared plight and cross-cutting ties may have mitigated the more divisive factors. Many freedmen owed their freedom to manumission rather than to birth, relatively few appear to have been economically dependent upon slaveholding, and a significant number apparently had relatives, including children, in slavery. The two groups interacted on a common basis in, for example, Methodist and Anglican church services, public and Sunday schools, and the island's internal marketing system. There is also some evidence that freedmen, most probably recently emancipated slaves, participated in such various areas of slave social life as Saturday night and Sunday dances and the magico-religious system of Obeah. In addition, there undoubtedly were many sexual liaisons, as well as occasional marriages, between the two groups. They shared, to varying degrees, a degraded status defined by their common racial ancestry, and this status was controlled and perpetuated by a white group to which neither freedman nor slave could gain access.

In the early nineteenth century, Waller observed that "a great diversity prevails" among Barbadian freedmen.[122] As we indicated previously, their group was internally differentiated by phenotypic characteristics, wealth, occupation, education, church membership, and whether free status had been achieved at birth or gained through manumission. These factors were operative in stratifying the freedman community, but the sources do not permit a precise assessment of the relative importance of each factor as a determinant of rank. At present it is difficult to discuss in detail the social strata within the freedman community, the relative distinctiveness of each stratum, and the meaning that the differences between strata had for the freedmen themselves.

The plantocracy saw internal differences within the group. Its perception was reflected in the choice of freedmen to testify before a committee of the Assembly investigating the 1816 slave revolt[123] and in the first of the laws giving freedmen the right to testify, a law which made eligible those who had been baptized and born free (or who had *not* been recently manumitted). In considering his vote on this bill, one member of the Assembly made a clear distinction between "the enlightened class of the free people of colour" and "the vulgar class"; he expressed his willingness to extend the right to the former but not to the latter.[124] Arguing for the extension of legal (but not social) equality to freedmen, Orderson, a white creole,[125] distin-

---

[122] Waller, *Voyage*, p. 95.
[123] *Report from a Select Committee*, pp. 38–41.
[124] "Journal of the Assembly of Barbados, October 8, 1816," CO 31/47.
[125] The word "creole" can take on a variety of meanings. As used in this paper, it refers to anyone, regardless of racial ancestry, who was born in

guished between "free-born subjects," who, in his estimation, merited such equality with whites, and "emancipated slaves," who might ultimately merit it, but only after a period of years had elapsed since their manumission.[126] Although Orderson focused on the mode of acquiring free status in making his primary distinction, each mode implied an associated set of behavioral attributes and values. "Free-born subjects," he noted, have "advantages of early education, progressive habits of order and moral conduct, a just appreciation of the necessary restraints on the liberty of the subject, and a temperate exercise of the rights they derive from the laws."[127] The "emancipated slaves," however, are

> a heterogeneous mass ... without any of those restraints which moral habits, religious instruction, or ameliorated manners might give as security for their peaceful and orderly behavior. ... who, with all the disorderly passions incident to ignorance and sturdy insolence, place no value upon their newly-acquired power. ... their minds being inflated with strange ideas of importance, too often becoming irritable and restless, until they provoke a collision with some of the white inhabitants, or the more respectable of their own class.[128]

Orderson emphasized that this distinction "has ever prevailed among the more respectable classes of the Free people, who have invariably kept themselves aloof from those whose less moral conduct place them in a lower estimation of society."[129]

It seems clear that some class distinctions within the freedman community were recognized by freedmen as well as by whites, although each group may have placed differing emphasis upon the same variables.

By the early nineteenth century, the freedman "elite" probably was largely composed of free-born persons of wealth and education—a conservative group that felt threatened by emancipated slaves and lower-class freedmen in general.[130] Later, this "elite" was augmented in such a way that the "respectable classes" referred to above by Orderson came to be based on an expanded set of membership criteria. Although the older and more conservative group continued to exist, by at least 1823 the upper stratum of freedmen included per-

---

Barbados. Creole culture is comprised of those beliefs and behavioral patterns which developed in the New World environment. Despite the often marked resemblance of these patterns to their Old World antecedents, creole culture has its own distinctive elements and patterning.

[126] I. W. [J. W.] Orderson, *Spare Minutes at the Pier* (Barbados, 1831), *passim*.

[127] *Ibid.*, pp. 5–6.

[128] *Ibid.*, p. 9.

[129] *Ibid.*, p. 12.

[130] See Vaughan, "Samuel Prescod," p. 55.

sons who challenged the older group and provided leadership in meetings and petitions that were aimed at a more rapid amelioration of the status of freedmen.[131] This new leadership group included persons who had been born free as well as slave, were phenotypically black as well as "colored," and who represented a wider spectrum of occupational pursuits. Whatever the differences were that existed among the upper stratum of freedmen, by the time of Thome and Kimball's visit in 1837, all members of this group seem to have shared an educational level, life style, and material comfort that made the group generally distinguishable from the mass of the freedman population.

Our evidence for social groupings and cultural life within the freedman community is limited in detail, but it is clear that the community developed a set of institutional arrangements which met its own needs and in which its members participated on a relatively exclusive basis. That is, despite varying degrees of participation in the white-controlled national institutions, the social distance from whites enforced by racism and discrimination led freedmen to form a variety of groupings and organized activities which paralleled those of white society. For example, freedmen had "their Balls, Routs, and assemblies [and] they have established places of public rendezvous for Cock-fighting and other Species of Gaming."[132] As in the white community, public meetings served as forums for expressing grievances and organizing petitions to legislative bodies. Religious-fraternal associations, formed in the 1820s, met religious and social needs which could not be fulfilled within institutions dominated by whites. Freedmen also organized charity groups for the support of their own poor,[133] and in 1805 they formed a "company to act plays."[134] Although the reaction of some authorities to the latter was adverse, we do not know if the effort was completely frustrated at this time; we do know that, by 1828, freedmen had a theater of their own, the Lyceum in Bridgetown, which was of sufficient scope to require a manager.[135]

Culturally, our direct evidence pertains largely to the middle-to-upper stratum of the freedman community. In terms of behavior this stratum does not seem to have varied greatly from that of white creoles at comparable socioeconomic levels. Home visiting and recreational patterns, for example, were similar in both groups, as were church membership, acceptance of a rigid stratification system, which

[131] The presence of two leadership groups, and the cleavages between them, was reflected in the fundamentally different orientations of the two petitions in 1823; see pp. 236–37.

[132] [J. Poyer], *A Letter Addressed to . . . Francis Lord Seaforth, by a Barbadian* (Bridgetown, 1801), p. 23.

[133] See, for example, Eliot, *Christianity*, p. 226.

[134] Seaforth to Oughterson, January 7, 1805, GD 46/7/11.

[135] Vaughan, "Samuel Prescod," p. 57. A freedman newspaper, the *New Times*, was not established until the apprenticeship period.

included dependence upon domestic servants, and a general sharing of creole life styles. In the early nineteenth century, Richard A. Wyvill observed how spectators at a military parade included "the mulatto ladies and black women, with handsome umbrellas over their heads, walking in the most stately manner up and down, some even with their waiting women,"[136] and years later William Bell reported how "one meets them driving their carriages & riding their horses, the same as white persons."[137] Thome and Kimball referred to the value orientations and life style of members of the upper stratum: they sought to "acquire property," stressed "enterprise," "industry and perseverance," "respectability," and "education"; they generally led lives characterized by "a dignified air," "a genteel style," and "refinement," and practiced an elaborate and formal etiquette of "cultivated manners."[138]

It is apparent that this group of freedmen adhered to and shared a variety of values and norms with the dominant white group, and that the identification with white creole patterns was a conspicuous feature of its concern for the maximization of social and legal status. Just as, following Eugene Genovese's recent analysis of slaveholders in the Americas, the Barbadian plantocracy can be described as a colonial offshoot of the bourgeoisie of the metropolis,[139] so this group of freedmen viewed itself as an extension of the local bourgeoisie. Since this group provided the leadership for the freedman community as a whole, its sharing of the values and norms of the dominant whites must have been one important source of stability for the Barbadian social order. The identification with and orientation toward white creole patterns further suggests that psychologically, as well as socially, the freedmen did not view themselves as occupying an intermediate status in the society. Furthermore, this identification must have also been related to the emphasis freedmen placed on their differentiation as a group from the slaves. It is likely that the positive identification with white creole values and norms and the importance attached to differentiation from slaves characterized many within the freedman community and helped account for its essential social and political conservatism.

We believe this conservatism was strengthened by the increasing success of the freedman in the island's economic system, an area in which his mobility was most evident; the freedman thus came to have a vested interest in perpetuating the wider societal context within which economic behavior took place. Sharing the values of the dominant white group and lacking the power to challenge this group's

---

[136] [Major Richard A. Wyvill], "Memoirs of an Old Officer," [1814], p. 385, Manuscript Division, Library of Congress.

[137] Boromé, "William Bell," p. 23.

[138] Thome and Kimball, Emancipation, pp. 72–76 and passim.

[139] Eugene Genovese, The World the Slaveholders Made (New York, 1969), p. 26.

authority, the freedman was thus oriented toward moderating those aspects of the society which thwarted his desire for status maximization, rather than toward challenging the racial underpinning of the slave system, which had given rise to his subordinate status in the first place.

As we have indicated above, there was a hierarchy of white and freedman groups that were endogamous and in which membership was permanent. Freedmen were subordinate to whites, and they had less access to the resources of Barbadian society. At the same time, however, the two groups shared cultural values, attitudes, and linquistic and behavioral patterns. Moreover, freedmen and whites participated in the same national institutions. In addition, freedmen were not confined to a specialized occupational status. They were differentiated in terms of occupation, as well as in terms of wealth, education, phenotype, and origin of free status. Finally, the freedman community was characterized by its own status hierarchy. The position of the freedman in the social order, then, was not fully correlated with his membership in the subordinate group. While all freedmen were members of that group because of the ascriptive criterion of Negroid ancestry, they differed in terms of their rank within the freedman community itself. Thus, the position of the freedman in the Barbadian social order derived from his Negroid ancestry and from his socioeconomic status among freedmen.

Whites engaged in a wide range of discriminatory practices to reinforce and maintain the freedmen's inferior position; for most of the slave period, freedmen were excluded from many of the rights and privileges held by whites and from a variety of roles in the private and public sectors of the society. Neither extensive miscegenation nor shared cultural attributes altered their subordinate status. Thus, as members of the subordinate group, no achieved criterion of distinction—wealth, occupation, education, career, or leadership— was sufficient to place freedmen other than below whites in the hierarchy of the society at large. It was societal characteristics such as these which led contemporary observers to view the freedman as occupying a caste position in the Barbadian social order.

EUGENE D. GENOVESE

8 | The Slave States of North America

Despite protestations of loyalty and a low incidence of seditious and rebellious behavior, free Negroes inspired fear and apprehension among the whites of the Old South. In the words of Ulrich B. Phillips, "Many men of the South thought of themselves and their neighbors as living above a loaded mine, in which the negro slaves were the powder, the abolitionists the spark, and the free negroes the fuse."[1] Therefore, says Phillips, the official policy of the southern states was to reduce access to freedom and to narrow the mobility of those Negroes already free. At the same time, he adds, "The private attitude of a great number of persons toward free Negroes differed radically from the official attitude." "Men whose main concern," he continued, "was with industry and commerce and not with police were disposed to judge other men more upon their industrial ability and worth than upon their color or legal status."[2] Wherever we look, we find communities ignoring a variety of restrictions placed upon manumission and the rights of free Negroes. If it is true that in general the free Negro was, in the words of Caleb Perry Patterson, "a sort of inmate on parole,"[3] it is no less true that even after 1830—the period with which we shall be most concerned—he had just enough support from the white community to allow him to find the wherewithal to survive.

Yet, the fears and hostility of the white community as a whole constantly threatened the security and disturbed the peace of mind of the free Negroes. During the late antebellum period and early war years, pressure mounted to induce free Negroes to re-enslave themselves and to restrict further their rights. The actual change in circumstances of free Negro life that these pressures occasioned probably were not great, but the insecurity and fear that their mere public discussion induced must have been very great.[4] Legal recogni-

[1] Ulrich Bonnell Phillips, "Racial Problems, Adjustments and Disturbances," The Slave Economy of the Old South (Baton Rouge, 1968), pp. 60–61.

[2] Ibid., p. 61.

[3] Caleb Perry Patterson, The Negro in Tennessee, 1790–1865 (Austin, Tex., 1922), p. 174.

[4] See B. H. Nelson, "Some Aspects of Negro Life in North Carolina during the Civil War," North Carolina Historical Review, 25 (April, 1948): 143–66.

tion of the principle of voluntary enslavement had far-ranging implications. As in many other respects, the attitude toward the treatment of the free Negro revealed much about the ideological development of the white South and the progress of its self-consciousness. Bourgeois law necessarily prohibits the selling of one's self into slavery, just as it voids contracts made fraudulently. In both cases the equality deemed necessary as a framework for the bourgeois contract is violated; therefore, the laws pertaining to the voluntary enslavement of free Negroes reflect a major departure in ideology and social structure from the bourgeois norms of nineteenth-century American society.[5]

A number of southern states, especially in the late antebellum period, considered bills to expel all free Negroes, but these were defeated or were passed in such modified form as to negate their original purpose. The debates show two kinds of arguments against the move, the first being that most free Negroes were, contrary to reputation, industrious, loyal, and valuable members of society, and the other being that humanity forbade any such wholesale condemnation and uprooting. Whichever argument is judged the stronger, and however much the first conditioned the second, the fact remains that the ultra-Negrophobes never did get their way. They did, however, win concessions. Between 1830 and 1860 one state after another closed off manumissions altogether or insisted on the removal of freedmen from the state.[6] In the 1850s the position of the free Negro in New Orleans and some other cities rapidly deteriorated in a variety of ways: through increasingly harsh attacks in the press, police harassment, and restrictions against keeping coffee houses or entering special fields of employment.[7] The state courts, even those that acted to soften the force of the slave codes, did little or nothing to ease the plight of the free Negroes.[8] As a particularly vicious counterpart of these legal and social developments, free Negroes faced the persistent danger of being kidnapped and sold into slavery. This danger became especially great in the 1850s, when slave prices rose steeply; the position of the free Negroes was most exposed in the newly settled regions of the South.[9] Despite these difficulties, free Negro protest

[5] See the illuminating remarks of Wilbert E. Moore, "Slave Law and the Social Structure," *Journal of Negro History*, 26 (April, 1941): 194, n. 53.

[6] Missouri was an exception. There, manumission laws were liberalized. See Harrison Anthony Trexler, *Slavery in Missouri, 1804–1865* (Baltimore, 1914), pp. 210–23.

[7] Robert C. Reinders, "The Decline of the New Orleans Free Negro in the Decade before the Civil War," *Journal of Mississippi History*, 24 (April, 1962): 88–98.

[8] Donald J. Senese, "The Free Negro and the South Carolina Courts," *South Carolina Historical Magazine*, 68 (July, 1967): 140–53.

[9] Earl W. Fornell, "The Abduction of Free Negroes and Slaves in Texas," *Southwestern Historical Quarterly*, 60 (January, 1957): 369–86.

and petition for redress of grievances increased during the fifties, as did white concern for free Negro "impudence."[10]

In 1860 there were close to half a million free Negroes in the United States, roughly half of them in the slave states. In 1790 there had been fewer than 60,000, but the next decade saw an 82 percent increase; ten years later, thanks primarily to the annexation of Louisiana, the total free Negro population rose by about 72 percent. Thereafter, the rate of increase fell off sharply to 25.0 percent between 1810 and 1820; 37.0 percent during the twenties; 21.0 percent during the thirties; 12.5 percent during the forties; and finally, 12.25 percent during the fifties. In the slave states the period 1830–60 was one of increasing restrictions on manumission, expulsion of freedmen, and a general deterioration in the free Negroes' conditions of life. By the end of the antebellum period four states (Mississippi, Florida, Texas, and Arkansas) had fewer than 1,000 free Negro residents, and in the case of Mississippi that meant a drop of more than 40 percent in twenty years. Five other states (Missouri, Tennessee, Alabama, Georgia, and South Carolina) had fewer than 10,000, and Kentucky had only a few hundred more than that. For the rest, Louisiana had 18,600; North Carolina, 30,400; Virginia, 58,000; and Maryland, 83,900. To complete the story, Delaware, which had virtually ceased being a slave state, had just below 20,000. In other words, the mass of southern free Negroes were in the Southeast, from Maryland to North Carolina, with a large supplement in Louisiana.[11]

A large portion of the free Negroes lived in the cities and towns. Of the 83,900 in Maryland, almost 25,600 lived in Baltimore; of the 18,600 in Louisiana, 10,700 lived in New Orleans. Elsewhere, free Negroes tended to cluster in cities like Memphis, Natchez, Vicksburg, and Mobile. Nevertheless, a large if undetermined number did live in the countryside, especially in the Virginia-Maryland tidewater and in Arkansas and North Carolina. How many village, town, and even city free Negroes earned part of their income by occasional labor on nearby farms and plantations remains an open question, and herein lies a major clue to the ambivalence of southern whites. In the cities the labor of the free Negroes, skilled and unskilled, was needed by local white residents and by nearby farmers and planters, especially before the influx of white immigrants during the 1840s and 1850s. Similarly, the secular agricultural depression in the Virginia-Maryland tidewater created a curious shortage of labor at the very time when so many slaves were being sold south. The same economic forces that drove the planters to reduce the size of their slave force for reasons

[10] Ira Berlin, "Slaves Who Were Free: The Free Negro in the Upper South, 1776–1861" (Ph.D. diss., University of Wisconsin, 1970), *passim*, but esp. pp. 270–300.

[11] For a useful summary of the main statistics and a good introduction to the subject see E. Franklin Frazier, *The Negro in the United States*, rev. ed. (New York, 1963), esp. pp. 63–65.

of efficiency and in order to raise funds to supplement low agricultural profits also drove them to hire short-term skilled labor and to seek supplementary hands during critical periods of the crop year.[12] Under these circumstances free Negroes could find work as craftsmen and ordinary laborers in town and country. Contrary to the trend in Charleston and New Orleans, economic opportunities in eastern Virginia and Maryland seem to have improved for free Negroes during the late antebellum period, although they never became secure. In Louisiana, sugar plantations needed extra labor during peak months and found it among free Negroes as well as among whites. Free Negroes worked at both skilled and unskilled jobs, and many of the coopers were reputedly free Negroes. Thus, to some extent those demographic and economic forces which Marvin Harris credits with easing the path to freedom for the colored in Brazil and elsewhere and with inhibiting the development of a two-caste system did in fact play a role within the two-caste system of the Old South.[13]

Outside Delaware, whites presumed all Negroes—that is, black and colored—to be slaves and required those who claimed to be free to produce papers to prove it. As time went on, this presumption passed into a program of restriction, which culminated in the 1850s in a series of state laws inviting free Negroes to enslave themselves.[14] Only a few did so, but that some did suggests that often their legal and economic position was so precarious as to throw them on the mercy of some trusted white man.[15] In Georgia and Florida all free Negroes had to have white guardians, and elsewhere increasing pressures for guardianship led to one or another de facto or de jure response.[16]

In view of the racial basis of the slave regime and the attendant two-caste system, it is not surprising that free Negroes were generally excluded from the franchise. What is surprising is that they had the right to vote in North Carolina and Tennessee until 1835 and that they voted illegally in Rapides Parish, Louisiana, until the 1850s. In several counties of North Carolina and Tennessee and in Rapides

[12] Eugene D. Genovese, *The Political Economy of Slavery* (New York, 1965), chap. 6, esp. pp. 136–41; J. Carlyle Sitterson, "Hired Labor on Sugar Plantations of the Ante-Bellum South," *Journal of Southern History*, 14 (May, 1948): 192–205.

[13] See Marvin Harris, *Patterns of Race in the Americas* (New York, 1964), pp. 79–94.

[14] For a general introduction see Kenneth M. Stampp, *The Peculiar Institution* (New York, 1956), pp. 194–95, 216.

[15] Charles S. Sydnor, "The Free Negro in Mississippi before the Civil War," *American Historical Review*, 32 (July, 1927): 781; Marina Wikramanayake, "The Free Negro in Ante-Bellum South Carolina" (Ph.D. diss., University of Wisconsin, 1966); James Benson Sellers, *Slavery in Alabama* (University, Ala., 1964), p. 379.

[16] Thomas R. R. Cobb, *An Inquiry into the Law of Negro Slavery* (orig. pub. 1858; New York, 1968), pp. 314–15; Ulrich Bonnell Phillips, *Georgia and State Rights* (Washington, D.C., 1902), p. 156.

Parish they were alleged to have had the balance of power.[17] More
to the point, the free Negro had been deliberately enfranchised by the
Tennessee Constitutional Convention of 1796. Far from having been
an oversight, Negro suffrage had been the conscious will of the leading men of the state.[18] This early liberalism was all the more remarkable since Negroes had generally been denied the franchise in North
America from colonial days. Both Carolinas had forbidden Negro
voting by about 1715, but North Carolina reversed itself fifteen years
later. Virginia excluded Negroes in 1723, as did Georgia in 1761.[19]

Only Delaware and Louisiana allowed free Negroes to testify
against whites. In an act passed in 1732, Virginia had prohibited
such testimony, on the grounds that "they are people of such base
and corrupt natures."[20] During the eighteenth century Negroes seem
to have enjoyed the right in Maryland, but it did not survive into the
nineteenth century.[21] In Louisiana, the right of Negroes to testify
against whites was reaffirmed as late as 1852, when the state legislature voted down a bill to bar such testimony in criminal cases. On
the other hand, the courts accepted Negro testimony with the clear
understanding that the social status of the witness diminished his
credibility.[22]

The racist attitude of the white community appeared most
clearly in the laws against mixed marriage. Virginia forbade such
marriages in 1705, Maryland did so in 1717, but North Carolina did
not follow suit until 1838.[23] Yet, despite such laws in most southern
states and despite the stern condemnation of white public opinion,
mixed marriages did occur and were sometimes even flouted. Law or
no law, free Negroes married whites, or rather entered into common-
law arrangements with them, especially immigrants. A number of
these people felt secure enough to tell the census takers about their
domestic arrangement, and we may readily imagine how many more
kept it to themselves. Even in the countryside, interracial common-
law marriages occasionally existed in peace. In Jefferson and Orange
counties, in the extreme southeastern corner of Texas, five free Negroes, three of them men, lived openly with whites.[24]

[17] Roger Wallace Shugg, "Negro Voting in the Ante-Bellum South,"
Journal of Negro History, 21 (October, 1936): 357–64.

[18] See the analysis by Patterson, *Negro in Tennessee*, pp. 166 ff.

[19] Winthrop D. Jordan, *White Over Black* (Chapel Hill, 1968), p. 126.

[20] See John Codman Hurd, *The Law of Freedom and Bondage in the
United States*, 2 vols. (orig. pub. 1858; New York, 1968), 1: 242; but for
some qualifications see John H. Russell, *The Free Negro in Virginia, 1619–
1865* (Baltimore, 1913), p. 117.

[21] Jeffrey R. Brackett, *The Negro in Maryland* (Baltimore, 1889), pp.
190–91.

[22] Donald Edward Everett, "Free Persons of Color in New Orleans, 1803–
1865" (Ph.D. diss., Tulane University of Louisiana, 1952), p. 171.

[23] Hurd, *Law of Freedom and Bondage*, 1: 241 and 2: 88, 286.

[24] Andrew Forest Muir, "The Free Negro in Jefferson and Orange Counties, Texas," *Journal of Negro History*, 35 (April, 1950): 193.

The more frontier-like the community was, the easier the local whites' attitude toward miscegenation appears to have been, especially when white women were in short supply. Free Negroes were among the pioneer settlers of Texas. They and the manumitted offspring of unions of whites and slaves combined to produce a small but stable free Negro community in Texas as early as the days of the Republic.[25]

The extent of education among the free Negroes of the South is by no means clear, but Carter Woodson may have been correct in suggesting that, despite restrictive legislation, most could at least read and write. Certainly, in cities like Baltimore, New Orleans, and Mobile, where restrictions were fewer, they managed, through their own efforts, to get some education.[26] Negro money and talent accounted for the greater part of their modest achievement; white philanthropy helped, but does not appear to have played the overwhelming role generally assumed.[27] In Maryland, Negroes somehow managed to support their own educational programs while being taxed to help pay for white schools.[28] In Virginia and Georgia, Negro educational efforts were prohibited, but travelers and other contemporaries made it clear that many Negroes managed to learn to read and write. Southern whites might have feared free Negroes who could read, but they also needed them in many jobs that required some skill and education. In the end the laws remained only half-heartedly enforced.

If whites hindered the free Negro in his quest for an education, they raised no objection to his paying taxes. Georgia and South Carolina enacted discriminatory taxes shortly after the Revolutionary War, and other states followed suit. "Taxes and road duty," wrote John Spencer Bassett, "alone of all their functions of citizenship were at last prepared."[29] To this indignity we might add the increasing tendency to try and to punish free Negroes in a manner befitting slaves rather than free whites. The rest of the catalog is familiar. Free Negroes were pariahs who nonetheless proved too valuable to expel.

During the colonial period, economic competition between free

[25] Harold Schoen, "The Free Negro in the Republic of Texas," *Southwestern Historical Quarterly*, 39 (April, 1936): 292–308 and 40 (October, 1936): 85–113.

[26] Carter G. Woodson, *The Education of the Negro Prior to 1861* (New York, 1968), pp. 128–29; Frazier, *Negro in the United States*, p. 74. In an undeveloped slave state like Florida about 30 percent of the free Negro males and 40 percent of the females were literate, although it is difficult to know just what "literate" really meant. Russell Garvin, "The Free Negro in Florida before the Civil War," *Florida Historical Quarterly*, 46 (July, 1967): 7.

[27] Sellers, *Slavery in Alabama*, p. 363; J. Merton England, "The Free Negro in Ante-Bellum Tennessee," *Journal of Southern History*, 21 (February, 1955): 54–56.

[28] Brackett, *Negro in Maryland*, p. 197.

[29] John Spencer Bassett, *Slavery in the State of North Carolina* (Baltimore, 1899), pp. 408–9.

Negroes and whites did not reach dangerous proportions outside Charleston, Savannah, and perhaps a few other places. Winthrop D. Jordan accounts for the low level of white resentment toward Negro labor by saying that it "reflected the prevailing shortage of all kinds of labor in America."[30] Jordan notes outbursts of white resentment, especially among the skilled craftsmen of the towns, but stresses their occasional character:

> In Williamsburg, for instance, white and Negro craftsmen seem to have felt no sense of racial competition. Only in Charleston was there evidence of widespread and continuing resentment and there distaste for the Negro as a job competitor was closely linked to fear that South Carolina was running dangerously short of white men. No important movement for restricting Negroes to chores of servile drudgery developed, and of course no one tried to claim that Negroes were incapable of engaging in skilled crafts—a notion concocted after the abolition of slavery.[31]

As a matter of fact, the notion that Negroes were incapable as craftsmen grew up during the late antebellum period—in the face of overwhelming evidence to the contrary—although, as Jordan says, it did not sweep the South until after the war. It grew, along with a broader sentiment for racial exclusiveness, as two major trends unfolded in the Old South, the first being the perfection of the pro-slavery argument, which somewhat paradoxically included a stronger racist component than ever before, and the second being a marked influx of Irish and other immigrants who sought to capture the labor market of the larger towns and cities.[32]

In the light of the colonial acceptance of free Negro labor, what are we to make of the nineteenth-century legend of a free Negro population wallowing in poverty, crime, drunkenness, and depravity? First, even among contemporary slaveholders the charge always ran into stiff resistance from those who praised the free Negro's industry, sobriety, and loyalty and asked that he be left alone. Second, later generations of specialized historians, from Phillips on, generally expressed doubt that the free Negro deserved this reputation. An abundance of evidence demonstrates that the free Negro community, although poor and struggling, held an honorable and useful place in the southern economy.[33]

If a high percentage of free Negroes lived in towns, cities, and industrial villages, many nonetheless lived in the countryside. There

[30] Jordan, *White Over Black*, p. 130. For areas of friction see Ralph B. Flanders, "The Free Negro in Ante-Bellum Georgia," *North Carolina Historical Review*, 9 (July, 1932): 281.
[31] Jordan, *White Over Black*, p. 129.
[32] I am indebted to Professor Herbert Gutman for allowing me access to his raw data and unpublished analysis.
[33] Wikramanayake, "Free Negro in South Carolina," pp. 148–49. For a general assessment see Berlin, "Slaves Who Were Free," pp. 335 and *passim*.

is, as already noted, no way to know how many town and city Negroes serviced nearby farms and plantations as craftsmen and occasional farm laborers. Black labor in the countryside fell into three general categories: a small, but in some places important, class of yeomen; a somewhat larger class of tenant farmers and sub-subsistence landowners who supplemented their income by working parttime for others; and a large number with little or no land, who lived as occasional laborers and had a reputation for trading illicitly with slaves, especially in stolen goods.

In some states, notably Arkansas and North Carolina, the free Negro population was overwhelmingly rural and self-supporting.[34] In North Carolina, only about 10 percent of the free Negroes lived in towns and cities, and almost 60 percent of the farm hands were located in the big plantation counties of the eastern part of the state. Some Negroes owned their own farms, but most worked, at least partly, on the plantations and small farms of the whites. Here, as elsewhere, a substantial, if minor, portion lived with white families.[35]

Most of the large free Negro population of Maryland and Virginia lived and worked at or near tidewater. White Maryland farmers needed their labor and were quick to admit it whenever racist fanatics demanded their expulsion. Despite the large number of free Negroes, whites complained about the high wages that resulted from a shortage of labor. Some Negroes did well enough as farmers to hire others, including slaves.[36] In Virginia, free Negroes constituted a large proportion of the rural labor force in many counties. Data from Lunenberg County in 1814 suggests that more than 60 percent of the free Negroes there owned some land and that many more were in ancillary occupations.[37] Luther Porter Jackson's excellent study of the period 1830–60 demonstrates that the major component of Virginia's free Negro population, which constituted 12 percent of the total black and colored population in 1860, worked on the land and

---

[34] Orville W. Taylor, *Negro Slavery in Arkansas* (Durham, N.C., 1958), pp. 252–53; John Hope Franklin, "The Free Negro in the Economic Life of Ante-Bellum North Carolina," in *The Making of Black America*, ed. August Meier and Elliott Rudwick (New York, 1969), pp. 218–19; see also *idem, The Free Negro in North Carolina, 1790–1860* (orig. pub., 1943; New York, 1969). For an account of a free Negro artisan who owned a slave boy and used him to insure debts, who worked for leading white families but could not always find work, who married a slave and had a child by her, and who was protected by a white patron—in short, whose life exhibits the vicissitudes of existence even for a fairly secure free Negro—see *idem*, "James Boon, Free Negro Artisan," *Journal of Negro History*, 30 (April, 1945): 150–80.

[35] Franklin, "Free Negro in North Carolina," p. 217, n. 6; England, "Free Negro in Tennessee," p. 54. On tenancy in general see Richard B. Morris, "The Measure of Bondage in the Slave States," *Mississippi Valley Historical Review*, 41 (September, 1954): 219–40.

[36] Brackett, *Negro in Maryland*, pp. 180–81, 190, 224.

[37] Robert McColley, *Slavery and Jeffersonian Virginia* (Urbana, Ill., 1964), p. 74.

supplemented slave labor. Mechanics and artisans were found everywhere and in significant numbers, but the mass of the free Negro
population consisted primarily of farm hands and unskilled laborers.
Considerable tenancy and the presence of the crop lien help fill out
the rural picture. Among the small class of black yeomen there were
a few commercial farmers and a much larger number of subsistence
farmers.[38]

In Tennessee, free Negroes tended to concentrate in Memphis
and other cities and towns, but, even so, between 20 and 25 percent
were farmers or farm laborers, and another 50 percent worked in
trades that suggest possible links to the countryside.[39]

When we turn to the cities, including the big ones like New
Orleans, Charleston, Mobile, and Richmond, we find a general decline
in the economic strength of the free Negroes during the nineteenth
century. Although long entrenched as barbers, carpenters, bricklayers,
draymen, and, of course, house servants, they found themselves
pressed hard, if unevenly, by the Irish, Germans, and other immigrants during the nineteenth century. The most striking and yet
widely ignored feature of the southern cities was the growing ethnic
competition and antagonism manifested during the last few ante-
bellum decades. Gutman's figures for Mobile, for example, show that
Negroes constituted only 4 percent of the free male labor force in
1860 and that southern-born whites constituted only 18 percent. The
rest consisted of 15 percent from the North and 62 percent from
other countries. Using data from the Charleston censuses of 1848
and 1860, Gutman demonstrates a headlong decline in the absolute
as well as relative position of the free Negro workers, even in such
traditionally Negro occupations as barbers, blacksmiths, and tailors.[40]
Free Negro artisans and laborers, and slave draftsmen and hired laborers too, doggedly held on in the cities, but it is becoming clear that
by the 1850s they were losing ground, whereas their brothers in the
countryside, although perhaps more restricted, appear to have been

---

[38] Luther Porter Jackson, "The Virginia Free Negro Farmer and Property
Owner, 1830–1860," *Journal of Negro History*, 24 (October, 1939): 390–421.

[39] England, "Free Negro in Tennessee," pp. 37–58.

[40] See note 32. We know little about the life of the Negroes anywhere,
but Herbert Gutman's researches destroy at least one myth. His statistical
analyses show that, overwhelmingly, free Negroes lived in two-parent households and presumably in family units. The Negroes' economic position was
generally better in the South than in the North, but their family structure
proved to be the reverse. Although much stronger than the stereotype would
have it, the free Negro family in southern cities was weaker than its northern
counterpart. Thus, Frazier's thesis falls, for he derived his critique of the
Negro family from the presumed consequences of economic determinants. It
would seem, then, that the greater access of northern Negroes to religious and
social institutions of their own choosing had more effect than occupational
status. Unfortunately, apart from some knowledge of southern Negro efforts
to build their own churches and social clubs, we know very little about their
community life.

more secure. Indeed, one of the reasons given for the generally peaceful relations between free Negro and white laborers in Saint Louis during the 1850s was the employment of a majority of the Negroes in the surrounding countryside. Whites and blacks worked together without much antagonism on jobs in Saint Louis, but it is doubtful that the peace could have been maintained had their relative proportions been altered by a closing of the rural safety valve.[41] In any case, neither in town nor in country was there a Negro middle class of significant proportions, especially if we except New Orleans and Charleston.

One of the more interesting groups of free Negroes was that which owned slaves. They generally did so as a way of circumventing laws against manumission. In the late antebellum period one state after another passed laws that required manumitted slaves to leave the state and, at that, made manumission as difficult as possible. As a result, a free Negro who wished to purchase the freedom of a wife, husband, child, parent, or friend normally had to acquire and maintain property rights in his or her person; if this was not done, the emancipated Negro faced expulsion from the state. The great majority of Negro slaveholders—the total number of which was never large, although it has yet to be tabulated properly—owned relatives or friends as a mere formality and actually faced their slaves in a relationship such as the one Judge Manly of North Carolina described as existing between free Negroes and particular whites—that of "*patron* and *client*."[42] The frequency with which Negro slaveholders appeared as owners of their own children and grandchildren resulted from the particular difficulties attached to manumitting slaves under thirty years of age, even when manumission was still a legal possibility.[43]

The efforts, successful and unsuccessful, of slaves and free Negroes to free themselves and their loved ones often reached heroic proportions. Slaves who bought their own freedom generally had been artisans or skilled workers whose masters had permitted them to "hire their own time." Slave hiring was extensive throughout the South, especially in the cities. Despite all laws to the contrary, countless thousands of slaves were permitted to hire themselves out under circumstances that allowed them to pay rent to their master, provide for their own sustenance, and still save something, if they chose to. Similarly, the economic position of a portion of the free Negro community made small savings possible. In some cases free Negroes, themselves sometimes only recently freed, devoted their efforts to buying freedom for others and accomplished what can only be judged

[41] Russell B. Nolan, "The Labor Movement in St. Louis Prior to the Civil War," *Missouri Historical Review*, 34 (October, 1939): 18–37.

[42] Franklin, "Free Negro in North Carolina," p. 222.

[43] Joe Gray Taylor, *Negro Slavery in Louisiana* (Baton Rouge, 1963), p. 158.

as extraordinary feats of industry and selflessness.[44] To cite only one of many cases, Samuel Martin, who was called "the oldest resident of Port Gibson, Mississippi," bought his freedom in 1829 with the greatest effort and difficulty and then worked to buy six others, all of whom he freed and took to Cincinnati in 1844.[45]

Not all Negroes who owned only a few slaves were so selfless. Even among these cases some were interested solely or largely in profit-making. Thomas Bonneau of South Carolina, who founded a school for free Negroes, left two slave girls to his heir. His will stipulated that, if the girls did not behave, they were to be sold—"in that case," he added, "the money will be sure."[46] In other cases, litigation arising from disputes over the condition of the merchandise indicates that even free Negro slaveholders sometimes were merely engaged in business.[47]

Even when relatives were bought, their fate necessarily remained precarious as long as they were legally slaves. Carter Woodson found cases of husbands who bought their wives and deliberately kept them as slaves to insure their fidelity and good behavior. In one such instance, a Negro shoemaker in Charleston, South Carolina, bought his wife for $700, found her impossible to please, and so sold her some months later for $750.[48]

The sight of Negro slaveholders caused apprehension among the whites, but the most serious complaints were directed against those who were genuine slaveholders rather than against those who were merely protecting relatives. Although we cannot be certain, it would appear that the white community accepted the necessity of a few exceptions to the manumission laws and was prepared to look the other way, especially since the force of custom and local usage so often modified southern legal arrangements. The right of Negroes to own slaves had been firmly upheld by the courts in Virginia as early as 1654. Not until 1832 was this right effectively challenged,

[44] Herbert Aptheker, "Buying Freedom," *To Be Free* (New York, 1968), pp. 31–40, esp. pp. 35–36.

[45] "Some Undistinguished Negroes" (documents), *Journal of Negro History*, 3 (January, 1918): 91.

[46] Quoted in Wikramanayake, "Free Negro in South Carolina," p. 97.

[47] See "Slave Papers," no. 9, Library of Congress, Washington, D.C.

[48] Carter G. Woodson, *Free Negro Owners of Slaves in the United States in 1830* (Washington, D.C., 1924), p. vi. Woodson cites another case of interest:

The editor [he writes of himself] personally knew a man in Cumberland County, Virginia, whose mother was purchased by his father who had first bought himself. Being enamored of a man slave, she gave him her husband's manumission papers that they might escape together to free soil. Upon detecting the plot, the officers of the law received the impression that her huband had turned over the papers to the slave and arrested the freedman for the supposed offense. He had such difficulty in extricating himself from this complication that his attorney's fees amounted to $500. To pay these he disposed of his faithless wife to that amount.

and then only to the extent of limiting further purchases by Negroes to their spouses or children.[49] In North Carolina, the right of free Negroes to accumulate property was never seriously challenged except when that property consisted of slaves. Even so, the Supreme Court reaffirmed Negro slaveownership in 1833. Not until the secessionist legislature of 1860–61 was this right withdrawn, and then not retroactively.[50] Curiously, the decision of 1860–61 came when it was hardly needed. As John Hope Franklin points out, the decline in the economic condition of the free Negroes in North Carolina had reduced their efforts to buy slaves to a mere trickle in the closing decades of the antebellum period. Only Arkansas and the virtually free state of Delaware specifically prohibited Negro slaveownership, although other states increasingly created obstacles.[51]

Those Negroes who were genuinely slaveholders presented several knotty problems for white southerners. The basis of southern slavery being racial, there was necessarily something strange and disquieting about having black and brown slaveholders. This problem existed in Jamaica, Saint Domingue, Cuba, Brazil, and elsewhere, but with an important difference. Those societies recognized a three-caste system or something more fluid; consequently, the existence of a colored, as distinct from a black, class of slaveholders created fewer ideological difficulties, although we know very well that much trouble ensued anyway. Two states of the Old South stand out as having had highly visible, if small, groups of large slaveholders within the free Negro population. Louisiana was easily first in this category, with South Carolina second. It would hardly seem accidental that Louisiana was the southern state most directly influenced by French and Spanish culture and practice and that South Carolina ran a strong second so far as French influence was concerned. New Orleans and Charleston both showed a marked tendency toward the formation of a three-caste system, despite the lack of legal sanction. This cultural inheritance was reinforced by a demographic and economic pattern that left more room for an intermediate class of colored free men than was true in the South generally.[52]

---

[49] John H. Russell, "Colored Freemen and Slave Owners in Virginia" (with documents), *Journal of Negro History*, 1 (July 1916): 234–35, 241–42.

[50] Franklin, "Free Negro in North Carolina," pp. 224–25, 230.

[51] Stampp, *The Peculiar Institution*, pp. 194–95.

[52] Laura Foner, "The Free People of Color in Louisiana and St. Domingue: A Comparative Portrait of Two Three-Caste Societies," *Journal of Social History*, 3 (Summer, 1970): 406–30.

In Louisiana, ten free Negroes owned fifty or more slaves in 1830—in other words, enough to qualify not merely as planters but as big planters. By 1860 the number of such holdings had fallen to six, but they contained 493 slaves, or a mean average of 82 per holding. Every one of these big planters was a mulatto. The wealthiest of these Negro slaveholders was August Dubuclet of Iberville Parish, whose real property alone was valued at $200,000; his plantation totaled more than 1,200 acres, half of which were under cultivation, and housed 94 slaves. Antoine Decuir of Point Coupee owned more than

The existence of a small class of colored slaveholders and their reputation for cruelty, whether deserved or not, brings us to two questions: the first concerns the circumscribed three-caste system of New Orleans and Charleston, which had at least feeble echoes elsewhere; the second concerns the more general problem of free Negro relationships with slaves. A circumscribed three-caste system appeared precisely in the areas of French and Spanish influence: Louisiana, of course; Charleston and lowland South Carolina, with their early Huguenot settlers and later émigrés from Saint Domingue; and the gulf coast of Alabama, which came to the United States as part of the Florida cession.[53]

Economic circumstances strengthened the hand of the free Negroes but were far from strong enough to account for their relatively favored position. Culture and tradition more than economic advantage, it would seem, protected the free Negroes in their caste pretensions, especially the well-to-do mulattoes. What reinforced those pretensions in Louisiana (where they were strongest) was the cumulative effect of political divisions among the whites. When, for example, the Spanish took Louisiana from the French, they so feared the pro-French feeling among the whites that they deliberately set out to placate the free Negroes. By this time, in any case, the free Negroes

---

1,000 acres and 112 slaves in Iberville Parish. In general, the genuine slaveholders among the free colored of Louisiana had French names and were mulattoes who had inherited substantial wealth from white fathers. In much of Louisiana also, Negro slaveholding appears to have been a subterfuge, especially in the towns, but the existence of big planters among the Negroes, even in small numbers, drew much comment.

In South Carolina, too, one finds a core of large slaveholders among the free Negroes. At the end of the eighteenth century, for example, one free Negro owned about 200 slaves. William Ellison of the Sumter District, who was himself freed at the age of twenty-nine, rose to become a major planter, patented his own cotton gin, bought a plantation house from the governor of South Carolina, acquired about 100 slaves, was accepted into the exclusive white Episcopal church of Sumter, and upon his death was buried in the white cemetery. Both his daughters married white men of substantial means. Eventually, his children found it advisable to emigrate, but not before the highly charged 1850s. Until then they had found easy acceptance in white society.

Negro planters—that is, big slaveholders—existed elsewhere, but only in Louisiana (secondarily in South Carolina) do they seem to have been of more than symbolic importance. Even in Alabama, where special historical and legal circumstances existed around Mobile to protect free Negroes, the influence of the treaty of annexation of 1819 and prior Spanish influence are clear in this respect, as in others.

See Joseph Karl Menn, *The Large Slaveholders of Louisiana—1860* (New Orleans, 1964), p. 92, n. 2., and pp. 93–94; Everett, "Free Persons of Color," pp. 210–30; William L. Richter, "Slavery in Baton Rouge, 1820–1860," *Louisiana History*, 10 (Spring, 1969): 147–65; Wikramanayake, "Free Negro in South Carolina," pp. 100, 127–28, 240; Sellers, *Slavery in Alabama*, pp. 386–87, 392.

[53] Many of the free Negroes of Mobile had Spanish or French names; see Sellers, *Slavery in Alabama*, p. 385.

were firmly entrenched in the economy and could, with reasonable legal protection, hold their own against white immigration. Subsequently, even under the Americans, military conditions during Indian wars, slave risings, and the War of 1812 allowed the free Negroes to maintain their traditional rights by loyalty to the slaveholders' regime.[54]

The actual relationship that existed between free Negroes and slaves remains to be discovered. It would be surprising if major differences between town and country were not uncovered. In the towns, and especially in the larger cities, many slaves "hired their own time" and lived away from their masters. Although these practices were generally illegal, they were sanctioned almost everywhere, by custom and in accordance with white business interests. Consequently, free Negroes, whose freedom was always precarious, interacted every day, socially and at work, with slaves who were close to being half-free. A certain amount of intermarriage occurred, and

[54] See Foner, "Free People of Color," and Everett, "Free Persons of Color," *passim*.

The caste pretensions of these free Negroes, and especially of the mulattoes, quadroons, and octoroons, would be of purely local interest, if not a mere curiosity, had they not misled several generations of historians. Even so outstanding a scholar as E. Franklin Frazier improperly extrapolated from conditions in Charleston and New Orleans and, given his enormous prestige, taught two generations of white and black historians and sociologists to view the southern free Negro from the vantage point of the South's two small brown elites. According to Frazier: "In the cities of the South, especially in Charleston, South Carolina, and in New Orleans, the communities of free mulattoes became almost an intermediate caste between the whites and slaves. They acquired considerable wealth, including slaves; they maintained conventional standards and sex and family life; they were cultivated people who often sent their children to Europe for education and in order to escape racial prejudice." Frazier's judgment received strong support from scholars who became entranced with the Brown Fellowship Society, which arose as a highly restricted, well-to-do mulatto organization in Charleston in 1790 and lasted a hundred years. The Brown Fellowship Society emphasized white blood, free ancestry, economic success, and, in the words of its historian, E. Horace Fitchett, "a devotion to the tenets of the slave system." It is only one short step from being transfixed with this organization of fifty people or with the colored elite of New Orleans to such sweeping and false generalizations as that these groups provided postbellum leadership to the black masses; that they carried the only viable tradition of family stability among southern Negroes; or that free Negroes in general either were of this kind, at least in aspiration, or were impoverished and déclassé. In fact, these elites were exceptional, not only in the formal sense that all elites are by definition exceptional, but in the substantive sense that a prominent, large, and influential group of free Negro elites emerged in only two or three cities in the South.

See E. Franklin Frazier, *The Negro Church in America* (New York, 1962), p. 62; *idem, Negro Family,* pp. 153 ff., 198; and E. Horace Fitchett, "The Traditions of the Free Negro in Charleston, South Carolina," *Journal of Negro History,* 25 (April, 1940): 139–52. See also Constance McLaughlin Green, *The Secret City: A History of Race Relations in the Nation's Capital* (New York, 1968), p. 23, for an account of the open-handed spirit of a mulatto elite toward blacks.

little in the social setting generated antipathy. We must exclude for the moment the haughty but tiny mulatto bourgeoisie of New Orleans and Charleston and the small class of slaves who were attached as house servants to the town houses of the great white planters and took on airs from the attachment. When we look at the numerous free Negroes and urban slaves, who worked at similar skilled and unskilled jobs, we find much less evidence of caste feelings dividing the Negro population of the cities. On the contrary, as Richard B. Morris has shown, the improvement in the condition of some slaves, effected through the hiring system, was largely offset by the deterioration in the economic and social position of the free Negro working class.[55]

Yet, fragmentary evidence suggests that, with the possible exception of New Orleans, Charleston, and a few other cities, free Negroes and upwardly mobile slaves saw each other as brothers in a different legal condition rather than as competitors from rival status groups, although in those larger cities the process of stratification and caste distinction within the free Negro community appears to have gone far by 1860. This identification is less surprising when we realize that many in both groups had relations in the other, even a wife or husband. In North Carolina, for example, John Hope Franklin reports: "It was not unusual for free Negroes to live on slave plantations and to participate in the life there. Some of them had slave wives or husbands, and the benevolent master frequently permitted them to live there together, hiring the services of the free person."[56] Moreover, free Negroes and slaves faced the hostility and harsh competition of increasing numbers of European immigrants, who were quick to seize upon white racism as a way of forcing themselves into the job market.

Free Negroes in the large cities erected churches and schools, more often than not clandestine, and organized various kinds of improvement associations. The churches and, where circumstances permitted, the schools and social activities were usually open to slaves. Certainly the white community, even in cities like Charleston, believed that relations between the slaves and free Negroes were close.[57] As Ira Berlin observes:

> Some freedmen organized churches, schools, and benevolent societies. On the surface, these institutions were but a weak image of those of white society. They reflected middle class values and aped

[55] Morris, "Measure of Bondage," pp. 219–40; England, "Free Negro in Tennessee," pp. 37–58.

[56] Franklin, "Free Negro in North Carolina," p. 218. Russell (*Free Negro in Virginia*, p. 131) says that free Negro–slave marriages were common. See also Bassett, *Slavery in North Carolina*, p. 35; and Richard C. Wade, *Slavery in the Cities* (Chicago, 1964), pp. 251–52.

[57] Wade, *Slavery in the Cities*, pp. 249–52.

the structure of their white counterparts. But slowly their own special style began to emerge, so that African churches, schools, and benevolent societies not only gave their members a measure of security and a richer life, but provided a base from which to attack white racism.

From the beginning, free Negroes expressed their desire for independence by creating and controlling their own institutions.[58]

Both whites and slaves told contradictory stories about free Negroes. Some runaways remembered the free Negroes with loathing; John Little, who fled North Carolina for Canada, recalled how a free Negro had once betrayed him for $10.[59] James Redpath, the abolitionist editor, recalled a revealing conversation with a Negro, presumably a slave, in North Carolina: "He advised me not to trust the free colored population, because many of them were mean enough to go straight to the white people and tell them that a stranger had been talking to them about freedom." In other words, treachery lurked everywhere; but recognition of the presence of many informers would hardly justify our concluding that it defined the primary relationship of slaves to free Negroes. Before jumping to too many conclusions, we ought to consider the next sentence of Redpath's report: "He advised me also to be cautious with many of the slaves."[60]

White slaveholders and black abolitionists both saw the free Negro as at least potentially an ally, if not a promoter, of slave revolt. Whites from one end of the South to the other charged that free Negroes corrupted the slaves, encouraged them to steal and defect, and generally led them astray. As if to concur, David Walker, in his famous *Appeal*, attacked colonization as being designed to separate resourceful and intelligent free Negroes from the slaves whom they could teach and lead. He added that the whites realized how disturbing the mere presence of free black men was to the slave system.[61] The sight of free black caulkers in Baltimore exhibiting both class and racial militancy and celebrating John Brown's raid had to be disquieting.[62] Frederick Douglass added a special dimension to Walker's older argument. As a boy he had been taught that God made all whites masters and all blacks slaves, but he saw clearly that, in fact, all whites were not masters, and all blacks were not slaves.[63] Douglass also paid tribute to the active contribution of some free Negroes to the freedom of their brothers. He described, in particular, how some free Negroes lent free papers to runaways in order to facili-

[58] Berlin, "Slaves Who Were Free," p. 394.
[59] Benjamin Drew, *The Refugee* (New York, 1968), p. 205.
[60] James Redpath, *The Roving Editor* (New York, 1968), p. 128.
[61] David Walker *One Continual Cry: David Walker's Appeal to the Colored Citizens of the World, 1829–1830*, ed. Herbert Aptheker (New York, 1965), p. 111.
[62] Berlin, "Slaves Who Were Free," p. 595.
[63] Frederick Douglass, *Life and Times* (New York, 1967), p. 50.

tate their escape. The runaway would then mail the papers back from the free states. Douglass insists that many free Negroes gambled on their own freedom in this way. The odds were dangerous, for return of the papers depended on the runaway's making good his escape to free territory and having the presence of mind and integrity to send the papers back quickly and safely.[64]

Free Negro participation in the history of slave revolts is a cloudy story. If we were to judge by white fears and by the fierce legal retaliation after almost every insurrection scare, we would have to conclude that free Negroes were at the center of the black revolutionary impulse from Virginia to Texas. Yet, few free Negroes have ever been found in the actual revolts or in the many incipient revolts or scares. Denmark Vesey stands out as a great exception, and it is possible that one or two free Negroes joined Gabriel Prosser's movement and one or two other early risings, notably that of 1795.[65] On the other hand, free Negroes were known to have betrayed slave plots, as in the projected rising in Frederick, Maryland, in 1814.[66] During the rising in Louisiana in 1811—probably the greatest in the history of the slave South—free colored men offered their services to the governor and played an important role in the suppression of the rebellious slaves.[67] The ambivalence of the free Negro community appeared most sharply during the so-called Seminole war in Florida, which was really a Negro war more than an Indian one. Many free Negroes supported the Indian and black forces during the long struggle and in some cases fought in their ranks, whereas some others were to be found on the side of the whites.[68] During the War for Southern Independence, free colored militia units, most notably at New Orleans, offered their services to the Confederacy and then changed sides at the appropriate moment—a record which each of us may interpret for himself. Elsewhere, free Negroes worked for the Confederacy when they had to, but also identified with the cause of

[64] *Ibid.*, p. 198; Reinders, "Decline of the Free Negro," p. 218; Lyle Wesley Dorsett, "Slaveholding in Jackson County, Missouri," *Missouri Historical Society Bulletin*, 20 (October, 1963): 34. Similarly, where free Negroes secretly operated schools for slaves, they took enormous risks. See, for example, Reinders, "Decline of the Free Negro," p. 220. For a case study see Edmund Berkeley, Jr., "Prophet Without Honor: Christopher, Free Person of Color," *Virginia Magazine of History and Biography*, 77 (April, 1969): 180–90.

[65] Herbert Aptheker, *American Negro Slave Revolts* (New York, 1963), esp. p. 249; but see also McColley, *Slavery and Jeffersonian Virginia*, p. 111; Jordan, *White Over Black*, p. 401, n. 47; Gerald Mullen, "Slavery in 18th Century Virginia" (Ph.D. diss., Berkeley, 1968), pp. 356, 390; and Alice Dunbar-Nelson, "The People of Color of Louisiana," *Journal of Negro History*, 2 (January, 1917): 63.

[66] Aptheker, *Slave Revolts*, p. 92.

[67] Everett, "Free Persons of Color," p. 77.

[68] Kenneth Wiggins Porter, "Florida Slaves and Free Negroes in the Seminole War, 1835–1842," *Journal of Negro History*, 28 (October, 1943): 390–421.

freedom when Union generals sought to organize quasi–forced labor batallions.[69]

In view of the slender support given by free Negroes to slave revolts, and in view of the willingness of some—in fact, of many in Louisiana—to side with the whites against the slaves, how should we interpret the wrath poured down on them after every slave revolt? A review of the restrictive legislation on manumission and the status of free Negroes shows that the worst blows fell after slave insurrections or scares. Almost invariably, free Negroes were thought to be responsible, despite a monotonously consistent lack of evidence. The temptation is strong to put the reaction of the whites down to paranoia, especially since most of the insurrections occurred only in their own heads. As M. D. Cooper, a well-to-do planter in Tennessee, wrote his father in 1856: "We are trying our best in Davidson County to produce a negro insurrection, without the slightest aid from the negroes themselves. . . . There is in sober seriousness no shadow of foundation for any belief of domestic plot in insurrection."[70] It would be easy to ascribe these fears to southern guilt feelings, and, in fact, historians are prone to ascribe about everything of importance in the Old South to white guilt feelings, as if something could be demonstrated thereby.

Other explanations, which of course do not preclude the presence of guilt feelings among white southerners, have a good deal more to offer. Southern fears of slave insurrection were justified, and the attendant precautions, however brutal, were perfectly understandable. The whites' fear of the free Negro also was justified, even in the face of his general accommodation, and the campaign to restrict, or better still to expel, the free Negro made great sense.

Historians are fond of judging the white South as paranoid and guilt-striken because it feared slave revolts, despite infrequent occurrence. This is a wonderful point of view for those who do not have to live among oppressed and sullen people with discernible reasons for wanting to cut your throat. For such observers, statistical probabilities prove everything: the individual planter in Mississippi who looked around, saw at least some unmistakable evidence of hostility, worried about his wife and family, and resolved to take no chances must have been a guilt-striken paranoid living in mortal terror of the justifiable wrath of the Good Lord and the Quakers. In fact, he was probably a man of simple good sense who did not believe in speculating on his life and the lives of those in his charge. Of what importance are all the statistical probabilities to a man who has good reason to worry about his being the exception to the proven rule?

[69] Bell Irwin Wiley, *Southern Negroes, 1861–1865* (New Haven, Conn., 1965), pp. 111, 112, 125, 147, 160, 216.

[70] M. D. Cooper to his father, December 29, 1856, Cooper Papers, Tennessee State Library and Archives, Nashville.

The slaveholding class consisted of the sum total of such individuals and was not some historian's abstraction.

In these same terms the slaveholder had every reason to worry about the free Negroes, even when he knew very well that few of them were likely to meddle with insurrectionary or seditious plots. As a "Memorial of the Citizens of Charleston to the Senate and House of Representatives of the State of South Carolina" observed in 1822, the mere presence of free Negroes reminded the slaves of what they would like to be but could not become and rendered their own labor the more irksome. The memorial pointed out that, among other evils, the free colored population served as a transmitter of information and seditious ideas to the slaves.[71] Since almost all ideas are seditious when they are not those of the master, the claim was not so far-fetched. Elsewhere in the South the reports were the same: the presence of free Negroes disturbed the slaves; free Negroes traded illegally with slaves, usually in stolen goods; free Negroes more often than not aided and abetted runaways and in general acted like Negroes first and freemen second.[72] It rarely occurred to white southern-ers that the increasing tendency to treat slaves and free Negroes alike under the law and the successful circumscription of the incipient three-caste system of New Orleans and Charleston made the result inevitable.

We end, therefore, with a free Negro population, both black and colored, which could not afford to separate itself from its enslaved brethren and which, despite ambivalence, vacillation, and a wide range of individual behavior, proved a danger to the regime. From 1830, and in some respects much earlier, to 1861, the South moved steadily toward the view that slavery was a positive good and a permanent feature of southern life. Simultaneously, in a variety of ways it tried to render "the condition of the slave materially and spiritually more acceptable." One of the ironic corollaries of this two-fold development was the attack on the status of the free Negro. No vague and elaborate psychological thesis is necessary to explain the outcome, which flowed quite naturally from the political and social exigencies of a two-caste slave system that correctly saw itself on the defensive. For their part, the free Negroes chose to find ways of living out their lives in peace under conditions of economic deprivation, political and social discrimination, and legal outrage. If, under alto-gether unfavorable circumstances, they never rose against the regime in a suicidal gesture, neither did they ever give clear evidence of their loyalty and reliability to the master class. They kept their own coun-sel and held on to what they had as best they could. If their course

---

[71] The volumes of De Bow's Review may be consulted almost at random, but see especially Ulrich Bonnell Phillips, "The Slave Labor Problem in the Charleston District," Slave Economy, pp. 191–214.

[72] See, for example, Chase C. Mooney, Slavery in Tennessee (Bloom-ington, Ind., 1957), pp. 81, 179–80.

lacked the theatrics that nowadays pass for revolutionary heroics in middle-class circles, it nonetheless had dignity and purpose and certainly a great deal of wisdom.

BIBLIOGRAPHICAL NOTE

A full scholarly study of the free Negro in the Old South has yet to be written, but we may expect one soon from Ira Berlin. His excellent doctoral dissertation, "Slaves Who Were Free: The Free Negro in the Upper South, 1776–1861" (University of Wisconsin, 1970), is the best general study we have. I only regret not having had access to it until the first draft of this paper had been written. E. Franklin Frazier's older accounts in *The Negro in the United States*, rev. ed. (New York, 1963) and *The Negro Family in the United States*, abr. ed. (Chicago, 1966) are still valuable. The more specialized studies by John Hope Franklin on North Carolina and by Luther Porter Jackson and John H. Russell on Virginia are indispensable. The cited works by Carter Woodson on free Negro slaveownership and education were pioneering and remain valuable. Useful information may be gleaned from the many specialized articles in the scholarly journals on the free Negro in particular counties and towns and on such particular problems as legal status and occupations. Similarly, the several general studies of slavery in the states are useful, but primarily so for legal rather than social conditions. Miss Foner's comparative study on Louisiana and Saint Domingue opens new possibilities that ought to be developed.

9 | Cuba

Present-day attempts to study the role of the free non-white community in Cuban slave society immediately run into two significant problems. The first is historical and permanent; the second is political, and, hopefully, temporary. The historical problem lies in the fact that Cuba was a Spanish colony, almost, one could say, the alpha and omega of Spanish overseas imperialism. Being a Spanish colony, the island suffered from the peculiar vicissitudes of Spanish Roman Catholicism and the theoretically centralizing tendencies of the Spanish colonial bureaucracy. After a period of time, therefore, it was difficult to separate the reality from the legend.

Among other things, this situation meant that the entire social, political, and economic history of the island would reflect the traditions and characteristics of a Spanish and Catholic society. More specifically, the social influence of the evangelizing Roman Catholic church of the sixteenth century could be diluted but never lost, for, during the sixteenth century, the words and deeds of Las Casas, Sépulveda, and Palacios Rubios, as well as the papal ruling *Sublimis Deus* (1537), shaped the paternalistic principles of the church and the state. These official positions remained, even when individual churchmen and bureaucrats deviated from the principles.[1] In the same way, the paternalism which a formative overseas imperial bureaucracy espoused in an age of doubt and difficulty became legally enshrined. Even more, it became a part of the ideal of Spanish society, and as such was zealously defended with the spirit of the *reconquista*. Even the steady erosion of the moral force of the crown and the church did not substantially alter the ideal. Witness a knowledgeable, articulate, and philanthropic opponent of slavery such as Rafael María de Labra conscientiously declaring during the nine-

[1] On the religious impact on Spanish imperial expansion, see Lewis Hanke, *The Spanish Struggle for Justice in the Conquest of America* (Philadelphia, 1949); J. H. Parry, *The Spanish Theory of Empire in the Sixteenth Century* (Cambridge, 1940); and John L. Phelan, *The Millenial Kingdom of the Franciscans in the New World: A Study of the Writings of Gerónimo de Mendieta* (Berkeley and Los Angeles, 1956).

teenth century that Spanish slavery was "superior" to all others.[2] And Labra was no lone voice crying in a wilderness. All in all, therefore, the tradition of Spanish imperialism makes interpretation difficult.

On another plane, as a Spanish colony, Cuba was insulated from the rise of the plantation slave society in tropical America until nearly the end of the eighteenth century.[3] This delay forced the island to embark on an intensified agricultural revolution and involvement with the South Atlantic System in the nineteenth century, when the system as a whole was declining.[4] International interest—sometimes of a humanitarian nature—in ending the slave trade, together with significant technological changes in the production of sugar, had far-reaching effects upon Cuban slave society.[5] At the same time, the rise of pseudoscientific racism complicated and tended to undermine the perviously amicable patterns of race relations in Cuba.

If the historical problem tends to confuse the issues, the political problem of the isolation of Cuba both by U.S. policy and by official Cuban practice, seriously restricts and inhibits research concerning the island. Although a great deal of material is available in Spain dealing with this important period of Cuban history, there is a limit to its utility. Take the census returns, for example. Not only are they inadequate in supplying information—as all censuses of that age were—but also they cannot be checked against records of towns or plantations in Cuba. To cite a minor point: It is one thing to know that "x" free colored persons were proprietors, but it would be more significant to ascertain the value and the nature of the property held, especially whether it represented real estate or property in persons. Today evidence exists in Cuba which would substantially contribute to our knowledge of this and other problems. Nevertheless, there is sufficient information in Spain to enable one to proceed with an examination of the free colored community in Cuban slave society, even though all conclusions must obviously be tentative and subject to later qualification.

The New World slave society was a general phenomenon of the

[2] Rafael María de Labra y Cadrana, *La abolición de la esclavitud en las Antillas Españolas* (Madrid: J. Morete, 1869), pp. 25–63. This sentiment pervades most of Labra y Cadrana's writings and speeches.

[3] See J. H. Parry and P. M. Sherlock, *A Short History of the West Indies*, 2nd ed. (New York: St. Martin's Press, 1968), pp. 220–36.

[4] The South Atlantic System was the sociopolitical and economic complex whereby European capital and technology combined with African manpower to produce plantation crops in tropical America, primarily for the European market. As far as I can tell, the phrase belongs to Philip D. Curtin, and first occurs in his book, *Two Jamaicas: The Role of Ideas in a Tropical Colony, 1830–1865* (Cambridge, Mass.: Harvard University Press, 1955), pp. 4–6.

[5] This process is dealt with at length by Franklin W. Knight in *Slave Society in Cuba during the Nineteenth Century* (Madison: University of Wisconsin Press, 1970).

expansion of European social, cultural, political, and economic influences into the tropical world.[6] For, while slavery had always been a part of society, the slave society—that is, a social system in which slavery served more than an economic and organizational function— was a peculiarly European fabrication. It had its genesis in the sugar cane plantations of the eastern Mediterranean and reached its apogee in the islands of the Caribbean and on the tropical mainlands of North and South America.[7] Although sugar cane was not the only plantation crop, the most typical conditions for masters and slaves existed on such plantations in all areas outside the southern United States.

By the time the slave-operated sugar cane plantation had reached the tropical American lowlands, the concomitant society had assumed aspects of a mutually reinforcing society with tri-partite, caste-like divisions. At the top of the social pyramid stood those whites who either owned estates or held high managerial positions such as the overseers and attorneys—the men of the Casa Grande, to use Gilberto Freyre's felicitous phrase. Lower in social status than the owners and managers, but higher than any non-white group, were the often landless whites, a miscellaneous group of men who filled varied roles from a curious style of bookkeeping to the legal fulfillment of the Deficiency Laws, which were designed to provide psychological reinforcement for whites against a numerically superior force of non-whites. In the context of Cuban plantation society, the term "white" covered a wide spectrum of peninsular Spaniards, Cuban- and Latin American–born creoles, East Indians, Chinese, and Mexican Indians. Only after the "occupation" of Cuba by the United States at the end of the nineteenth century did the more rigid definition of color come into general usage on the island, a situation which reflected the somatic norm image of the North American continent.[8]

Lowest in social estimation, but vital for all aspects of the society, were the vast numbers of slaves. Most slaves were Africans by birth because, with the notable exception of the American South,

[6] The literature is extensive. Among the best works are: David Brion Davis, *The Problem of Slavery in Western Culture* (Ithaca, N.Y.: Cornell University Press, 1966); Eugene D. Genovese, *The World the Slaveholders Made* (New York: Random House, Pantheon Books, 1969); Winthrop Jordan, *White Over Black* (Chapel Hill: University of North Carolina Press, 1968); and H. J. Nieboer, *Slavery as an Industrial System* (The Hague: Nijoff, 1910).

[7] The best historical treatment of the migration of sugar cane is Noel Deerr, *The History of Sugar*, 2 vols. (London: Chapman & Hall, 1949–50).

[8] For example, Spanish census returns classified Mexican Indians and Chinese among the "white" population, but the first census directed by Americans, in 1907, placed them under the "colored" population. See *Censo de la République de Cuba bajo la administración provisional de los Estados Unidos, 1907* (Washington, D.C.: oficina del Censo de los Estados Unidos, 1908). In this paper, the Spanish usage of "white" prevails. On somatic norm image, see H. Hoetink, *Two Variants in Caribbean Race Relations* (Oxford: Clarendon Press, 1967).

every mature planation society exhibited a general inability to maintain its slave population. In Cuba, slaves tended to exercise most
skills associated with sugar or other plantation production and to
dominate the domestic chores, serving as maids, gardeners, and
coachmen. As economic assets, they were of paramount importance,
and they were also significant to their owners in considerations of
social index. Nevertheless, slaves almost monopolized the arduous
and non-skilled occupations, and, over a period of time, a certain
stigma was ascribed to those occupations for which they were most
suitable. In any case, the mutually reinforcing cleavages of race,
occupation, and culture were severe handicaps to the social integration and mobility of the slave masses.

The free person of color who could not be classified as "white"
and who was fortunate enough not to be enslaved occupied an ambiguous intermediate position between the fully free and the enslaved.
The free person of color, therefore, spanned a wide spectrum from
palest white to purest black. His was the ambivalent position that
resulted from miscegenation as well as varying combinations of historical circumstances. At one end the free person of color merged
into the lower echelon of white society. With a light skin color and
certain favorable circumstances—especially progeny, economic sol-
vency, or female delicacy, guile, and attractiveness—it was possible
for the free person of color to move upward into the white, privileged
elite. Indeed, rich mulattoes became quite desirable mates for impoverished white Spaniards, especially those from the army or the
lower orders of the bureaucracy who were in the colonies either to
seek a fortune or to recover one that had been lost. A fortune bol-
stered their social position, if not at home, at least overseas. These
Spaniards hardly ever married a rich black person. The order of
choice generally began with the creoles and ended with the rich mulattoes. This was especially true after the wars of independence of
the mainland colonies of Spain in the early nineteenth century drove
many unfortunate royalists, *venido a menos*, to Cuba. Notable, though
hardly exceptional in this respect, was Francisco Jacott, a magistrate
of the *audiencia* of Lima who made a boon of adversity by cleverly
marrying his daughter into the rich commercial family of Frías. His
granddaughter, Carmen, subsequently married a rich mulatto.[9]

The slave society in the Americas was essentially a coercive
and racist society. Professor Elsa Goveia has portrayed the way
racism was used to subordinate the blacks within the system of slavery to facilitate their exploitation and to provide the social stability
necessary for the physical, economic, social, and political survival of

[9] Antonio Pirala y Criado, *Anales de la guerra de Cuba*, 4 vols. (Madrid:
Felipe Rojas, 1895–98), 1: 494–95; Francisco Pérez de la Riva, *Origen y
régimen de la propiedad territorial en Cuba* (Havana: Imprenta "El Siglo XX,"
1946), pp. 129–36.

the whites in the British Leeward Islands.[10] In the same way, Professor Eugene Genovese has pinpointed the racist element in the class structure of the American South.[11] The argument could be repeated for every slave society. It is easy to disprove the dictum of Eric Williams that "slavery was not born of racism; rather racism was the consequence of slavery."[12] With the wisdom of historical hindsight, however, it is difficult to avoid the conclusion that slavery exacerbated the ethnocentricity of certain groups and eventually fostered a virulent racism. No one has expressed this more simply or more forcefully than Charles Boxer, who wrote: "One race cannot systematically enslave members of another for over three centuries without acquiring a conscious or unconscious feeling of racial superiority."[13] By the nineteenth century, racism was a prominent feature of Cuba's white society, and its most hostile manifestation was toward the free colored community.

This community had not been consistently discriminated against. Indeed, the history of this sector, in common with most aspects of Cuban history, divides naturally into a pre-plantation era and a plantation era. The pre-plantation phase, during which the colony had an essentially mixed economy based on grazing, tobacco farming, and market gardening, ended during the last quarter of the eighteenth century. The abolition of slavery in 1886 brought an end to the plantation slave society. The transition from a predominantly pastoral to an overwhelmingly plantation society had significant consequences for the intermediate social stratum of free colored persons. Contrary to the conclusion of a number of scholars, the physical, legal, social, economic, and political conditions of this group rapidly deteriorated under the structure of the plantation society. This deterioration occurred despite the legacy of Hispanic law and tradition, which is said to have protected free colored persons during the earlier colonial period.

DEMOGRAPHY

The free colored community in Cuba, as elsewhere, originated in the illegitimate offspring of the profligate sexual unions between white masters and black slaves. Miscegenation, however, transgressed

[10] Elsa Goveia, *Slave Society in the British Leeward Islands at the End of the Eighteenth Century* (New Haven, Conn.: Yale University Press, 1965), pp. 149–51. For a contemporary view of the Caribbean, see the quotation by Bryan Edwards in Genovese, *Slaveholders*, p. 162: "In countries where slavery is established, the leading principle on which the government is supported is fear: or a sense of that absolute coercive necessity which, leaving no choice of action, supersedes all questions of right."

[11] Genovese, *Slaveholders*, pp. 235–37.

[12] Eric Williams, *Capitalism and Slavery*, new ed. (New York: Russell & Russell, 1961), p. 7.

[13] Charles Boxer, *Race Relations in the Portuguese Colonial Empire, 1415–1825* (Oxford: Clarendon Press, 1963), p. 56.

the social mores of the whites. Nevertheless, some fathers—depending on individual circumstances—not only gave such children their liberty, but also left them an inheritance. "Colored," half-caste persons who got their freedom in this manner could hardly expect substantial legacies, since such were forbidden under Roman and common law. From the earliest day of the colony, however, a free colored community did exist.

Prior to the total abolition of slavery, this colored community augmented itself in three ways: by natural reproduction; by voluntary manumissions; and by the freedom granted to a limited number of illegally landed Africans who were captured and declared free by the Courts of Mixed Commission in Havana between 1820 and 1886. This last category comprised the so-called *emancipados*, who, rather than being set completely free, were left in a servile condition not far removed from total slavery. Between 1824 and 1866 (the year the slave trade apparently ended) more than twenty-six thousand Africans found on ships off the coast of Cuba became *emancipados*. These were then contracted out to persons needing labor in a never-ending rotation of deception and peculation from which few escaped alive.[14] Cristóbal Madan estimated that there were only 6,650 *emancipados* doing service by 1864.[15]

The Spanish authorities took the first census in Cuba in 1774, but the first properly scientific census came only under U.S. auspices in 1907. While the various censuses taken in the interim may not have been accurate in a strict sense, they are still useful for our purposes. "Correct" quantitative data are not as important here as are figures that illustrate the general demographic pattern of the period. Assuming that the inaccuracies are constant, the existing data will serve our purposes.

As Table 9–1 illustrates, the free colored population of Cuba increased from a little more than 36,000 persons in 1774, to considerably more than half a million persons by 1887—a ninefold increase in 113 years.

The fact that Cuba began as a settlement colony with a relatively mixed economy meant that from the very early period the free colored community was not only substantial but also obviously racially mixed. This mulatto element developed over a long period of time. Color-conscious Latin Americans, especially Brazilians, have a predilection for categorizing the various combinations on the basis of percentages of European and African racial stock. Cubans were no exception. Nevertheless, for official purposes, the free colored population usually found itself subdivided into *pardo*, or mulatto, and *moreno*, or black. "The mulattoes," wrote Jacobo de la Pezuela in 1863,

[14] For a more elaborate treatment of the *emancipados*, see Knight, *Slave Society in Cuba*, pp. 102–3.

[15] Cristóbal Madan, *El trabajo libre y el libre cambio en Cuba* (Paris, 1864), p. 2.

TABLE 9–1.   Growth of the Free Colored Population, 1774–1887

Year	Free Colored Population	Percentage of Total Island Population	Percentage of Non-White Population
1774	36,301	20.3	41.0
1792	54,154	19.0	45.6
1827	106,494	15.1	27.1
1841	154,546	15.1	25.9
1860	225,843	16.2	37.4
1877	272,478	20.0	55.7
1887	528,798	32.5	100.0

Sources: for 1774, Ramiro Guerra y Sánchez et al., Historia de la nación Cubana, 10 vols. (Havana: Instituto de Historia, 1952), 2: 78; for 1827 and 1841, Resumen del censo de la población de la isla de Cuba . . . 1841 (Havana: Imprenta del Gobierno, 1842), p. 19; for 1860, Spain: Junta general de estadística, censo de la población de España . . . 1860 (Madrid: Imprenta Nacional, 1863), pp. 798–800; for 1877, Spain: Censo de la población de España, 1877, 2 vols. (Madrid, 1883–84), 2: 679–94; and for 1887, Censo de la población de España en 1887 (Madrid: Instituto Geografía y Estadístico, 1891), pp. 770–71.

"are the children of white men and black women, or of white women and black men. However, this latter case is so rare that it is considered a phenomenon throughout the country, although it is physiologically as feasible as the former."[16]

The census categorized as mulatto nearly 34,000 of the more than 54,000 free persons of color on the island in 1791. This means that more than 3 out of every 5 free, non-white persons had some discernible white ancestry. It is quite possible that the proportion was greater at an earlier time, for both the slave population and the free colored population increased considerably in the generation before 1792. But as the plantation society expanded, the proportion of the mulattoes declined. Indeed, the free colored community in general, and the mulatto element in particular, showed a reverse trend to the slave population on the island. By 1841 the free colored population had grown nearly threefold, but the proportion of mulattoes had fallen to about 2 in 5. After 1841 the mulatto element stabilized around 50.0 percent of the free colored population until the end of the period of slavery. The increase in the proportion of mulattoes after 1841 reflects the declining activity of the slave trade and slav-

[16] Jacobo de la Pezuela, Diccionario geográfico, estadístico, histórico de la isla de Cuba, 4 vols. (Madrid: Mellado, 1863–66), 1: 153. This and all subsequent translations are the author's.

ery on the island. Beginning with the census of 1860, the Spanish authorities replaced the distinction between *pardo* and *moreno* with the undifferentiated classification of *gente de color* (colored persons). The change may have reflected the deterioration of racial and class relations on the island.

One aspect of the demography of the free colored community which cannot be ascertained from the available data is the contribution of manumission to the over-all growth rate. Reliable "hard" figures, or estimates, for the annual number of manumissions (even on an interrupted time sequence) are not available. From our general knowledge of the history of Cuban plantation society, however, we can offer some general impressions. It is possible that for a variety of reasons—religious, social, economic, or political—the practice of manumission was common during the pre-plantation era.[17] But, as the demand for labor increased toward the end of the eighteenth century and continued at a high level throughout the nineteenth century, white slaveowners became less willing and less able to grant manumission voluntarily.[18] At the same time, the legal route of *coartación*, by which a slave could eventually buy his freedom, was considerably restricted, partly as a result of greater and sharper discrimination against non-whites.[19] In any event, a traveler to Cuba in 1853 noticed that "emancipation of slaves very seldom occurs in Cuba, where they publicly shout that abolitionists are those who have no slaves."[20]

Before the application of the Moret Law of gradual abolition changed the situation in the mid 1870s, the greatest stimulus to the growth of the free non-white population came from its own healthy, natural reproductive capacity. Between 1827 and 1841, for example, the free colored population increased by more than 46,000. This increase amounted to 43.5 percent over the fourteen years, for a mean annual growth rate of 3.1 percent. This is a high rate of growth but not an unusually high one for that period; it is only slightly higher than the corresponding rate of increase of the white population. Furthermore, it is quite plausible, because 45.0 percent of all free colored males and 49.0 percent of all free colored females were in the potentially fertile age group, sixteen to forty years.[21]

[17] See Herbert S. Klein, *Slavery in the Americas: A Comparative Study of Virginia and Cuba* (Chicago: The University of Chicago Press, 1967), pp. 62–65 and 196–200.

[18] Manuel Moreno Fraginals, *El ingenio: El complejo económico social cubano del azúcar*, vol. 1, *1760–1860* (Havana: UNESCO, 1964), pp. 134–67.

[19] Knight, *Slave Society in Cuba*, pp. 130–33.

[20] Demoticus Philalethes [pseud.], *Yankee Travels Through the Island of Cuba* (New York: D. Appleton, 1856), p. 393.

[21] *Censo de la población de Cuba, 1841*. Note that the sex ratio for the one-to-fifteen age group is 1,037; for the sixteen-to-forty age group, 912; for the forty-one-to-sixty group, 1,049; and for the over sixty category, 650. The sex ratio was derived by formula: $\frac{M}{F} \times 1,000$; therefore, figures below 1,000 indicate a majority of females, and those above 1,000 a majority of males.

TABLE 9-2. Age-Sex Profile in 1841

Sex	1–15 Years	%	16–40 Years	%	41–60 Years	%	60 Years +	%
Male	27,988	37.0	34,269	45.0	10,939	15.0	2,507	3.0
Female	27,001	35.0	37,566	49.0	10,424	13.0	3,852	3.0
Total	54,989	35.6	71,835	46.5	21,363	13.8	6,359	4.1

The preponderance of free colored females over males was general for all parts of the island. There was no significant difference in the sex ratios for urban and rural zones. The areas of the greatest difference were the provinces of Puerto Príncipe, Santa Clara, Sancti-Spíritus, Trinidad, Cienfuegos, and San Juan de los Remedios, which today comprise Santa Clara. The provinces then had a ratio of 49.2 percent males to 50.8 percent females. This difference contrasts sharply with the situation of the white stratum of the population, as well as with the slave sector. White males outnumbered females in all three departments, attaining their greatest difference in the Western Department with a percentage difference of 10.8—55.4 percent males to 44.6 percent females. Differences in the sex composition of the slave population were even more pronounced. In the plantation frontier of the Central Department, 69.7 percent of the slave population was male—a ratio in excess of 2:1. The abolition of slavery produced a temporary adjustment of the sex ratio within the non-white population owing to the imbalance of the slave population.

More important than the difference in sex composition as an indication of potential population growth is the age-sex profile of the population. Following the breakdown into four major divisions as given in Table 9-2, one can make a number of observations about the population.

The most outstanding aspect of the population in 1841 was the youthfulness of the free colored sector. Approximately 82 percent of all free colored males and 84 percent of all free colored females were less than forty years of age. The potentially reproductive age group, between sixteen and forty years, included 45.0 percent of all females, with an excess female population of 3,500. The relatively high percentage of the population under 15 years of age—37.0 percent of the males and 35.0 percent of the females—clearly qualifies García de Arboleya's assertion in 1859 that "the annual population increases of the island since 1774 when the first official census was made re-

sulted more from immigration than from reproduction."[22] This statement may be valid for the white and slave sectors, but it is not so
for the free colored element. García de Arboleya failed to notice the
vital, natural growth of the free colored population.

Unfortunately, the available statistics for births, marriages, and
deaths do not differentiate between free non-white and slave. Of the
161,349 infants baptized in the five-year period, 1842–46, a total of
74,302, or less than 50 percent were non-white.[23] Of this number,
54,203, or more than two-thirds, were illegitimate. Of the 16,363 marriages that took place during the same quinquennial period, 3,973,
or almost 25 percent, involved non-white persons. Some of these were
slaves, of course, but, nevertheless, the majority were probably free,
thus reflecting an aptitude for marriage by that sector of the population. Of the 109,318 registered deaths, non-whites outnumbered
whites by 57,762 to 51,456. The real value of these figures will remain obscure, however, until more precise data, allowing for a better
breakdown to social and legal divisions, become available.

Thanks to Jacobo de la Pezuela, we have considerable data for
1860. According to the official census returns of 1860, the free colored population had grown to more than 200,000 persons, of whom
some 120,000 lived in the Western Department and the remaining
80,000 in the Eastern Department.[24] The division between *pardo* and
moreno tended to be nearly equal in the plantation zones. In the
Eastern Department, however, *pardos* outnumbered *morenos* by more
than 2:1. It is difficult to ascertain the cause of this pattern, or even
to determine what variations had occurred over time. A reasonable
assumption is that, in the pre-plantation days, *pardos* outnumbered
morenos throughout the island, as the earlier censuses indicate, but
that the rise of sugar brought an overwhelming number of blacks to
the Western Department. As the slaves gained their freedom, the
color element of the free non-white community was adjusted. The
plantation areas thus tended to be more densely black than were
areas which had not yet been absorbed into the sugar economy.

The location of the free colored population in Cuba mirrored
both the settlement pattern of the free population as a whole and the
vicissitudes created by the impact of the sugar revolution. Free colored persons tended to gravitate toward the cities and towns where
their skills were required. Because they detested legal slavery—of
which they stood in fear, and from which many had narrowly
escaped—they often avoided the areas of heaviest slave concentration. Along with the urban centers, therefore, the largest concentra-

[22] José García de Arboleya, *Manual de la isla de Cuba* (Havana: Imprenta
del Tiempo, 1859), p. 118.

[23] These figures were derived from Pezuela, *Diccionario*, 4: 240.

[24] *Censo de la población, 1860*. Pezuela (*Diccionario*, 4: 248–49) lists
inconsequential differences.

TABLE 9-3.   Population Distribution, 1861

Province	Free Non-Whites	Percent-age of Total	Slaves	White	Total
Bahia Honda	716	6.5	7,043	6,828	14,587
Baracoa	4,805	42.6	1,575	5,905	11,285
Bayamo	13,900	41.3	2,727	17,046	33,673
Bejucal	2,191	8.9	7,052	15,416	24,659
Cárdenas	3,214	5.5	24,418	28,355	57,987
Cienfuegos	7,812	14.3	16,985	29,714	54,511
Colon	3,703	5.9	33,699	26,476	62,878
Cuba	36,030	37.5	32,255	27,743	96,028
Guanabacoa	5,998	22.1	4,775	16,278	27,051
Guanajay	3,653	9.0	17,608	18,998	40,259
Guantánamo	5,627	28.7	8,561	5,331	19,619
Güines	4,473	7.2	24,817	32,630	61,920
Holguin	7,045	13.5	4,226	40,852	52,123
Jaruco	2,872	7.9	11,077	23,431	36,494
Jiguaní			NOT LISTED		
La Habana	37,765	18.4	29,013	138,445	205,223
Manzanillo	11,105	30.4	1,713	13,675	36,493
Matanzas	7,067	8.8	32,219	40,627	79,913
Nuevitas	533	8.4	1,622	4,189	6,376
Pinar del Río	10,408	15.1	14,996	43,522	68,926
Puerto Príncipe	10,786	17.2	13,185	38,556	62,527
Remedios	9,335	19.8	9,487	32,425	47,247
Sagua la Grande	2,416	4.7	19,150	30,420	51,986
San Antonio	2,022	6.5	10,737	21,127	30,886
San Cristóbal	3,289	11.3	7,771	17,917	28,977
Sancti-Spíritus	7,134	15.6	8,949	29,624	45,707
Santa Clara	11,200	21.3	6,865	34,579	52,644
Santa María del Rosario	828	10.2	2,173	5,045	8,046
Santiago de Cuba	2,041	12.9	4,507	9,302	15,850
Trinidad	9,034	24.0	10,539	17,936	37,509
Tunas	2,254	33.0	480	4,089	60,823
Totals	227,356	16.5	370,220	776,481	1,374,057

Source: Jacobo de la Pezuela, *Diccionario geográfico, estadístico, histórico de la isla de Cuba*, 4 vols. (Madrid: Mellado, 1863–66).

tion of free colored population was in the non-plantation eastern provinces, where more land was available for its use.

In 1870, when the total free colored groups of the island comprised 20.0 percent of the total population, the percentage in the ten most easterly jurisdictions, comprising the then Eastern Department, was nearly 30.0 percent. The distribution of the free colored population, therefore, roughly corresponded to a pattern diagonally opposite to those of white persons and slaves, as Ramiro Guerra y Sánchez noted in his study of the Ten Years' War.[25] In 1870, the twenty-two western provinces had 600,840 white persons, 141,677 free persons of color, and 300,989 slaves. The seven easterly provinces of Baracoa, Bayamo, Santiago de Cuba, Guantánamo, Holguín, Jiguaní and Manzanillo totaled 113,702 whites, 83,189 free colored, and 47,410 slaves.[26]

ECONOMIC ROLE AND PROPERTY HOLDING

When we turn from demographic growth and residence patterns to economic role and property holdings, we again encounter the sharp division between pre-plantation Cuba and the later plantation period. The expansion of the sugar plantation system had a far-reaching effect on the entire social and economic structure of Cuba. If sugar directly or indirectly opened more economic opportunities for the free colored (as it did for all sectors of the society), it nevertheless closed some significant avenues for mobility and advancement.

In his study of slavery in Cuba and Virginia, Herbert S. Klein has drawn a fairly representative picture of the free colored community in pre-plantation Cuban society.[27] In a sparsely settled frontier colony, urbanized for better defense and pursuing ranching and small farming to support its existence, it was not surprising that the free colored community participated in every aspect of early colonial life. Social class distinctions and status became subordinated to the harsh physical necessity of cooperating for survival against foreign interlopers and the threats and ravages of nature.

Not only did all men in this difficult colonial environment live together, but they also worked together and fought together. Common poverty and equal hardship united black men and white men on the farms and ranches, in the defense of the island, or in the pursuit of the glory of Spain in faraway places. During the seventeenth and eighteenth centuries, when Spain's territorial monopoly was being challenged in the Americas, the crown used anyone it could find to

[25] Ramiro Guerra y Sánchez, *Guerra de los Diez Años, 1868–1878* (Havana: Cultural, S.A., 1950), pp. 4–15.

[26] *Cuba desde 1850 á 1873: Colección de informes, memorias, etc. . . . que ha reunido Don Carlos de Sedano y Cruzat* (Madrid: Imprenta Nacional, 1873), pp. 152–53.

[27] Klein, *Slavery in the Americas*, pp. 194–227.

defend its possessions. Black men formed part of the Spanish military expeditions to fight the French in Florida in 1702 and at Vera Cruz in 1720. In 1762, black regiments offered substantial help in the futile defense of Havana against the English. The tradition of mobilizing the militia in time of need continued into the later nineteenth century. In 1874, the members of the colored militia fighting on the pro-Spanish side in the Ten Years' War numbered 7,216 men, forming, as one loyalist put it, "part of the columns which kept alive the glory of our flag and the integrity of the fatherland in the face of the insurgents."[28] But war produces unusual circumstances. How did the free colored community equip itself in times of normal peace?

Any assessment of the economic role or occupational position of the free colored community must take into account its legal disabilities. No person of color could become a priest, lawyer, doctor, pharmacist, businessman, or member of the royal bureaucracy. Nor could he hold any highly remunerative or socially prestigious position. Some of these legal disabilities go back to early colonial days. Others were added in the later period, and still others came during the nineteenth century.[29] The problem of status and color, however, was ambiguous for a very simple reason. The distinctions between slaves and other non-free persons such as the indentured Asians were reasonably sharp, despite the existence of such transitional categories as the *coartados* and the *emancipados*. On the other hand, no such clear distinction existed between the "white" person and the free mulatto. The mutually reinforcing cleavages which operated between free and slave did not operate to the same extent within the free society. Because color distinctions were imprecise, it is possible that infringements of the laws did take place and that some persons of color gained admission to the legally closed occupations. It is important that such persons passed as white and were never recognized in law or by their peers as persons of color, for these occupations remained exclusively white in the compilation of Jacobo de la Pezuela in 1861. In this case, therefore, the question of how many, if any, free persons of color were able to pass as whites assumes minor importance. As far as the society's view of itself was concerned, the situation had not changed; the status quo remained. Yet, if the society had changed, the laws would not have been slow to follow in outlining the distinctions between white persons and non-white persons. The sugar revolution, too, had its effect upon the law, as well as upon race relations. During the time of Captain General Gerónimo Valdés (1841–43), a law stipulated that the overseer of every rural

[28] Miguel Blanco Herrero, *La política de España en Ultramar* (Madrid: Sucesores de Rivadenegra, 1888), p. 431.

[29] See, for example, José M. Zamora y Coronado, comp., *Biblioteca de legislación ultramarina*, 7 vols. (Madrid: Alegría y Charlain, 1844–49), esp. 4: 461–68; and *Boletín oficial de la capitanía general de la isla de Cuba* (Havana, 1869–98).

farm must be a white man, "under penalty of one hundred pesos fine on any owner infringing this law, and against whom, moreover, the Government will use every coercive measure to enforce its compliance."[30]

In addition to the legal exclusion of any person of color from the professions, the Cuban system of landholding excluded non-white ownership. This system of exclusion from the ranks of the landed was a result more of the peculiar nature of the pattern of Cuban landholding than of any conspiracy or desire to deny land to the blacks. The complicated system of primarily usufructuary land tenure, called *mercedes*, did not lend itself to real estate speculation in the countryside, and urban lands had been subdivided for personal or communal use long before the population attained its nineteenth-century size.[31] At any rate, by the nineteenth century the creoles dominated property ownership and had placed themselves in the best position to exploit the agricultural potential of the island. Only those free colored persons who had fortuitously married into strategically placed creole families were able to find the capital to start an *ingenio* or *cafetal* or to extend their *vega*. They constituted an insignificant minority, however, and they were very likely mulatto.

As the sugar revolution rolled inexorably eastward from Havana and Pinar del Río, the vast majority of the free colored community, as well as the smaller white landholders and the poor landless whites, faced two options: move further east, ahead of the engulfing capitalist tide of sugar plantations and slavery, or become absorbed. Some undoubtedly escaped east, to face the consequences at a later date. But the *ingenio*, as Moreno Fraginals notes in his excellent study, blurred racial differences in the insatiable demand for laborers:

> The *ingenios* absorbed all available free labor. . . . The displacement of the tobacco growers of the lands around San Julian de los Güines [southeast of Havana] was followed by, among other eventualities, the incorporation of the peasants in the *ingenio*. The account books of the period clearly reveal how the falling and clearing of the forests, the cutting of firewood, and even a good deal of the cutting and hauling of the sugar cane was done by free laborers. Also, within the *ingenio*, in the manufacturing sector, white and black wage earners worked shoulder to shoulder with the slaves.[32]

The available statistical evidence strongly supports the contention that free colored persons had been virtually frozen out of prop-

[30] *Bando de gobernación y policía de la isla de Cuba expedido por el Excmo. Sr. D. Gerónimo Valdés, presidente, gobernador, y capitán general* (Havana: Imprenta del Gobierno, 1842), art. 77.

[31] Pérez de la Riva, *Origen y régimen*; Duvon C. Corbitt, "Mercedes and Realengos: A Survey of the Public Land System in Cuba," *Hispanic American Historical Review*, 19 (1939): 262–85.

[32] Moreno Fraginals, *El ingenio*, p. 141; see also Knight, *Slave Society in Cuba*, pp. 25–46.

erty ownership by the middle of the nineteenth century. As Table 9–4 shows, free colored property holding followed the demographic pattern. Both in terms of number and percentage, free colored property holders were concentrated in the east, with Baracoa having the densest concentration. Of the nearly 14,000 proprietors listed, the non-white community accounted for just a little more than 1,000, a ratio of roughly 1:13. But in the seven eastern provinces for which figures are available, non-white property owners amounted to 622 out of a total of 4,642, or a ratio of a little more than 1:6—roughly the ratio of both groups across the island.

Significant omissions occur in the data. No property holding figures are included in the returns for Bahia Honda, Nuevitas (a moderately large, though not densely populated, eastern province), Pinar del Río, San Cristóbal, Santa María del Rosario, and Santiago de Cuba, while Pezuela omits Jiguaní altogether. Moreover, no information on the type and volume of the property can be deduced from the evidence. Rafael María de Labra noted in 1869 that only 230 free persons of color owned slaves.[33] This is significant because ten years earlier the total number of slaveowners in Cuba was nearly 50,000.[34] Obviously, the conclusion we may draw from these figures is that very few free colored persons could afford, or even cared, to own property in persons.

Legally prohibited from the professions and the bureaucracy, and unable to establish themselves among the propertied classes, the free colored turned to the occupations in which they could succeed and for which an increasing demand existed in Cuba. The fact that the non-white sector fulfilled a substantial economic role was not, however, obvious to white Cubans in the nineteenth century.

Blinded by fear and racial prejudice, white people generally condemned the free-colored sector as "lazy," "uncivilized," and "unChristian."[35] The pro-slavery property owner Cristóbal Madan wrote in 1864:

> The people of color scarcely contribute to the effective labor of the island in proportion to their population. They do not work on the farms, but congregate in the cities and towns, where they degenerate day by day into a lazy and vicious class. Their women are habitually depraved, and it can be said of the race that it is of little or no use either to itself, or to the country in which it exists.[36]

[33] Labra y Cadrana, *La abolición*, p. 63.

[34] Archivo Histórico Nacional (Madrid), Sección de Ultramar, Subsección de Esclavitud, *leg.* 3553 (hereafter cited as AHN); see also Knight, *Slave Society in Cuba*, p. 135.

[35] See, for example, Francisco de Armas y Céspedes, *Regimen político de las Antillas Españolas* 2nd ed. (Palma: Biblioteca Popular, 1883), p. 89; Philalethes [pseud.], *Yankee Travels*, p. 33; *Thoughts upon the Incorporation of Cuba into the American Confederation . . .* , a pamphlet (Havana, 1849), p. 8.

[36] Madan, *El trabajo libre*, p. 3.

TABLE 9-4. Property Holding, 1861

Province	White	Non-White	Total
Bahia Honda		NOT LISTED	
Baracoa	386	211	597
Bayamo	274	38	312
Bejucal	195	1	196
Cárdenas	465	2	467
Cienfuegos	784	48	832
Colon	448	8	456
Cuba	650	132	782
Guanabacoa	226	—	226
Guanajay	270	9	279
Guantánamo	175	116	291
Güines	676	5	681
Holguin	450	30	480
Jaruco	30	—	30
Jiguaní		FIGURES NOT AVAILABLE	
La Habana	1,487	107	1,594
Manzanillo	132	12	144
Matanzas	323	32	355
Nuevitas		NOT LISTED	
Pinar del Río		NOT LISTED	
Puerto Príncipe	1,711	44	1,755
Remedios	196	6	202
Sagua la Grande	150	—	150
San Antonio	1,708	13	1,721
San Cristóbal		NOT LISTED	
Sancti-Spíritus	1,163	134	1,297
Santa Clara	787	59	846
Santa María del Rosario		NOT LISTED	
Santiago de Cuba		NOT LISTED	
Trinidad		NOT LISTED	
Tunas	242	39	281
Totals	12,928	1,046	13,974

Source: Same as that for Table 9-3.
Note: Includes all who were listed as *propietarios* or *hacendistas*.

José Antonio Saco desired "most ardently . . . the extinction of the black race," which jeopardized his island.[37] Writing from Paris in 1860, Francisco Frías y Jacott thought the blacks "impotent and dangerous" and a "disturbing element" in the population.[38] An anonymous pamphleteer, writing from Madrid and ironically calling himself "a conscientious Negrophile," claimed that the blacks were lazy, lacking in ambition, and "would be the worst workers to replace the slaves."[39] A visitor from the United States joined the chorus: "The great majority of negroes [sic] are addicted to vice; few evince a virtuous disposition."[40]

An examination of the facts, however, confirms the assertion of Antonio de las Barras y Prado around the middle of the nineteenth century that "the people of color serve the whites in every domestic, agricultural and industrial job."[41] According to the monumental statistical compilation of Jacobo de la Pezuela, non-whites showed an amazing versatility and industry over a wide range of occupations.[42] Owing to the different interpretations of occupational listings in the various returns of the provinces, it is not easy to arrive at an accurate statistical record of the role of the free colored community. Nevertheless, a general pattern can be discerned.

Non-white men featured prominently in the lower-skilled and non-skilled occupations, such as bakers, barbers, bricklayers, carpenters, daily wage earners in industry and agriculture, hatters, house painters, masons, muleteers, musicians, potters, saddle makers, sawyers, shoemakers, silversmiths, tailors, water carriers, and watchmen. The women dominated dressmaking, washing, and other domestic services. Very few colored persons ranked among the merchants, skilled technicians in the sugar industry and the railroads, teachers, fishermen, mayorales, or supervisors of slaves (which was illegal), or cattle dealers. Only one colored maestro de azúcar was found on the entire island.[43] And, of course, no colored person was a priest, a full-

---

[37] José Antonio Saco, Replica a la contestación . . . , a pamphlet (Madrid: La Publicidad, 1847), p. 18.

[38] Francisco Frías y Jacott [Count de Pozos Dulces], La isla de Cuba: Colección de escritos sobre agricultura, industria, ciencias y otros ramos de interés (Paris: Jorge Kugelmann, 1860), pp. 23 and 371.

[39] Cuba y Puerto Rico medios de conservar estas dos Antillas en su estado de esplendor, a "short treatise" by "a conscientious Negrophile" (Madrid: José Cruzado, 1866), pp. 92–93; this "short treatise" is 157 pages long.

[40] Philalethes [pseud.], Yankee Travels, p. 33.

[41] Antonio de las Barras y Prado, Memorias: La Habana a mediados del siglo XIX (Madrid: Ciudad Lineal, 1925), p. 107. This memoir was written sometime between 1850 and 1862, when the author left Havana for the last time.

[42] Pezuela, Diccionario.

[43] The maestro de azúcar was the chief of the boilerhouse, and had principal responsibility for the quality of the sugar produced. Relying more on experience, intuition, and guesswork than on chemical knowledge, his skill passed from father to son. In seventeenth-century Brazil, this position was

time member of the military or the police, or even a *mayordomo*, or bookkeeper, on an estate.

EDUCATION

The non-whites found themselves at the bottom of the economic ladder for free persons on the island, and their educational circumstances tended to reinforce their position over time. It is useful to note that, for some time into the nineteenth century, most persons, regardless of color, did not need any formal education to acquire the skills they practiced. Until around the middle of the century, jobs such as an estate "bookkeeper" required no qualification other than a white skin. The highly valued *maestro de azúcar* relied less on a knowledge of chemistry than on luck and intuition. Moreover, because the majority of the white population was illiterate, it was hardly likely that non-whites would find education and schooling either a possible or a desirable goal.[44] The nineteenth century was the age of mass exploitation, not mass education.

Yet, after 1838, Cuban society began to change, and the demand for at least a basic education increased accordingly. Schooling was not keeping up with the changes in the society. Moreover, the free colored community was the sector most adversely affected by the increasing need for formal training. However much a privilege it might have been considered, education offered opportunities for social, economic, and physical mobility. The figures for schooling suggest that the education of the free colored community was neither commensurate with their population increase nor appropriate to the changing economic conditions. As the sugar industry became more mechanized after the late 1830s, the demand for literate, skilled, and semiskilled persons increased. With land at a premium and capital scarce, displaced free blacks, whites, and mulattoes needed some minimum education in order to succeed in the increasingly competitive towns and *bateys* (main residential and manufacturing centers of the *ingenio*).

The figures for schooling, however, show a dramatic neglect of basic formal education. In 1817, Cuba had 192 schools, in which there were 6,651 white students and 316 non-white students, or 1 non-white student for every 21 white students.[45] By 1836, the number of non-white students had more than doubled, to 340, while the number of white students had increased to 8,442, the ratio having fallen to 1:13. The partial statistical returns for 1860, however, reflect a sharp decline in the growth of the non-white school population.

---

held by a white person. During the eighteenth century, the job was done by a slave on most British West Indian sugar islands. It reverted to the free whites in Cuba during the nineteenth century.

[44] Arthur F. Corwin, *Spain and the Abolition of Slavery in Cuba, 1817–1886* (Austin & London: University of Texas Press, 1967), p. 221.

[45] These figures are taken from Rafael Soto Paz, *La falsa cubanidad de saco, luz, y del monte* (Havana: Editorial "Alfa," 1941), p. 8.

The details provided by the census of that year allow us to look more closely at the figures. The number of schools had increased to 562. Between 1836 and 1860, the total number of students had risen from 9,082 to 21,494. The number of white students had more than doubled, to 20,347. However, the non-white students had increased from 640 to only 1,147. The ratio of non-white had dropped to nearly 1:20.

Most children went to schools which were de facto, though not de jure, segregated. Of the 562 public and private schools in Cuba in 1861, a mere 48 were racially integrated. Only two provinces—Las Tunas, with three schools; and Guantánamo, with five—had a completely racially integrated school system. In addition, racial integration was far greater in the Eastern Department than in the Western Department. Of the 105 schools listed in the Eastern Department, 37 were racially integrated, and these amounted to 77.0 percent of all the racially mixed schools on the island.

The outstanding impression which emerges from any study of the figures for the education of the free colored community, however, is not that they eschewed formal education; rather, it is that the plantation system of sugar and slavery in Cuba militated against mass education and discriminated against the education of non-white persons. Eight of the principal sugar-producing provinces—Bejucal, Cárdenas, Colon, Güines, Remedios, Sagua la Grande, Santa Clara, and Trinidad—contained a combined total of 642 of the 1,365 sugar estates on the island in 1861, but in not one of these provinces was there a single non-white scholar among the 3,607 students enrolled in 106 schools. Cienfuegos, Santiago de Cuba, Guanajay, Matanzas, and Puerto Príncipe together had 455 *ingenios* and 137 schools (of which 31 were racially integrated), with 5,814 students, yet only 458 of those pupils were non-white. The cosmopolitan city of Havana, which did not have a sugar estate within its metropolitan boundaries (but which, nevertheless, was the home of many of the sugar producers), had only 357 non-white students among a school population of 7,829.

When we look closely at the figures, we notice that mass neglect of education in 1861 coincided with the areas most involved in the production of plantation crops. Indeed, by that time the economy of the island had become extremely dependent upon the plantations. Sugar and coffee together amounted to more than 70 percent of the total agricultural produce, which was valued at 110 million pesos.[46]

[46] These figures were gleaned from the following sources: Pezuela, *Diccionario*, 1: 38–39; Carlos Rebello, *Estados relativos a la producción azucarera de la isla de Cuba* (Havana, 1860); Raul Cepero Bonilla, *Obras históricas* (Havana: Instituto de Historia, 1963), p. 31; Francisco Pérez de la Riva, *El café historia de su cultivo y explotación en Cuba* (Havana: Montero, 1944), pp. 68–75); H. E. Friedlaender, *Historia económica de Cuba* (Havana: Montero, 1944), pp. 544–48; José García de Arboleya, *Manual de la isla de Cuba* (Havana: Imprenta del Tiempo, 1859), p. 238.

TABLE 9-5.   Teachers, 1861

Province	Non-White	White	Total
Bahia Honda		NOT LISTED	
Baracoa	0	26	26
Bayamo	3	79	82
Bejucal	2	38	40
Cárdenas	4	155	159
Cienfuegos	2	151	153
Colon	0	162	162
Cuba	18	333	351
Guanabacoa	4	130	134
Guanajay	40	59	99
Guantánamo	5	17	22
Güines	4	164	168
Holguin		NOT LISTED	
Jaruco	0	13	13
Jiguaní		NOT LISTED	
La Habana	86	2,596	2,682
Manzanillo		NOT LISTED	
Matanzas	0	57	57
Nuevitas	0	5	5
Pinar del Río		NOT LISTED	
Puerto Príncipe	6	34	40
Remedios	0	10	10
Sagua la Grande	0	8	8
San Antonio	0	8	8
San Cristóbal		NOT LISTED	
Sancti-Spíritus	0	17	17
Santa Clara	0	7	7
Santa María del Rosario	0	3	3
Santiago de Cuba		NOT LISTED	
Trinidad	0	17	17
Tunas		NOT LISTED	
Totals	174 (4% of Total)	4,089	4,263

Source: Same as that for Table 9-3.

Table 9–6. Schools and Students, 1861

Province	Schools	Non-White			White			All Students
		Free	Fee-Paying	Total	Free	Fee-Paying	Total	
Bahia Honda					NOT LISTED			
Baracoa	5	17	11	28	20	26	46	74
Bayamo	12	47	9	56	148	215	363	419
Bejucal	10	0	0	0	205	168	373	373
Cárdenas	12	0	0	0	164	225	389	389
Cienfuegos	21	0	9	9	404	183	587	596
Colon	12	0	0	0	207	139	346	346
Cuba	37	238	79	317	708	619	1,327	1,644
Guanabacoa	22	0	3	3	426	238	664	667
Guanajay	18	6	7	13	287	243	530	543
Guantánamo	5	54	3	57	67	6	73	111
Güines	18	13	6	19	413	275	688	707
Holguin	7	0	0	0	192	70	262	262
Jaruco	13	0	0	0	263	50	313	313
Jiguaní					NOT LISTED			

La Habana[a]	173	62	295	357	3,263	4,209	7,472	7,829
Manzanillo	5	14	3	17	60	74	134	151
Matanzas	36	13	66	79	890	844	1,734	1,813
Nuevitas	6	3	6	9	119	53	172	181
Pinar del Río	17	0	0	0	170	291	461	461
Puerto Príncipe	25	22	18	40	650	528	1,178	1,218
Remedios	15	0	0	0	237	177	414	414
Sagua la Grande	10	0	0	0	149	158	307	307
San Antonio	13	0	0	0	292	124	416	416
San Cristóbal	6	0	0	0	81	67	148	148
Sancti-Spíritus	13	56	7	63	282	214	496	559
Santa Clara	15	0	0	0	376	139	515	515
Santa María del Rosario	7	0	10	10	85	28	113	123
Santiago de Cuba	12	0	0	0	132	110	242	242
Trinidad	14	60	3	63	290	213	503	566
Tunas	3	0	7	7	57	24	81	88
Totals	562	605	542	1,147	10,637	9,710	20,347	21,494

Source: Same as that for Table 9–3.
[a] Includes the university.

More than 25 percent of all land under cultivation was in sugar cane, and a considerable proportion of the remainder supported the *ingenio* activity. In addition, tobacco, although not really a plantation crop in Cuba, contributed 16.0 percent of the colony's agricultural production. By 1860, therefore, sugar, tobacco, and coffee were responsible for 86.0 percent of the agricultural production and for more than 93 percent of all Cuban exports. In the light of these facts it becomes impossible to argue that Cuba by the middle of the nineteenth century represented a "diversified economy," or an "integrated community."[47]

In considering the education of the free colored community, one finds a striking failure on the part of the Roman Catholic church to emulate the example of the other Christian religious sects planted in the Caribbean. While it is true that most schools were Roman Catholic (the only religious denomination tolerated in Cuba), the Catholic church reflected and reinforced the social and intellectual bias of the white sector. The absence of non-white priests was, after all, the result of a deliberate policy of legal exclusion. The vaunted equality of all persons which the church advocated meant little to the living.[48]

THE SOCIAL SITUATION OF THE FREE COLORED

The intermediate position of the free colored community in Cuban society generated friction with the other two groups. For this sector, straddling the ambiguous position between the really free and the enslaved, exhibited a disdain for slavery while remaining ethnically tied to the mass of blacks. At the same time, the deteriorating relations with the whites fomented bitterness and fear.

In the earlier period of Cuban history—the less frenetic phase of the pre-plantation society—social and legal divisions between the racial groups tended to be flexible. Distinctions were made between Spanish and non-Spanish, but the nature of Hispanic imperial expansion and the structure of the early colonial society encouraged and facilitated tolerance.[49] The Laws of the Indies stipulated the social hierarchy, and the royal bureaucracy and its imperialist ally, the Roman Catholic church, saw to it that the non-white elements of the colonial society gained accommodation within the paternalistic fold. As late as 1789, the crown in Madrid, patently out of step with the changes in the colonies, tried to revitalize the benevolent spirit of the *Siete Partidas*, thereby extending some of the privileges of the free colored community. The attempt met hostile rebuff in the colonies. Reform was illusory.

[47] Knight's *Slave Society in Cuba* deals extensively with the church.
[48] See Genovese, *Slaveholders*, pp. 49–71.
[49] Fernando Ortiz Fernandez, "Los cabildos afro-cubanos," *Revista Bimestre Cubana*, 16, no. 1 (1921): 5–39.

The development of the plantation society in Cuba during the nineteenth century eroded the earlier social tolerance and relatively amicable race relations. The free colored community, among all groups on the island, felt the greatest change. Not only did the sugar industry demand ever-increasing numbers of Africans, but also, both at home and overseas, conditions began to militate against racial harmony. On the neighboring island of Saint Domingue, the slaves revolted and threw out their French masters in 1804 and gave themselves the revolutionary human rights of liberty, equality, and a curious fraternity. In the British Antilles, the slaves won their freedom in 1833, and, when real emancipation came five years later, they justly turned their backs on the decadent sugar industry which had cruelly exploited them for centuries. Moreover, the English, in an extraordinary combination of humanitarian zeal and religious and economic self-interest, began a campaign to destroy slavery wherever it existed. By the middle decades of the century, newly emerging racist theories were suggesting to their converts in Cuba that the social handicap which the island suffered lay in the growing nonwhite element. But racism in Cuba antedated these European ideas. When the slaves organized large revolts—as they did in 1812, 1820, 1823, and 1843—and when rumors of revolt spread frequently, the white sector responded—as it did in 1844—with massive coercion and brutal regimentation of the free colored and the slave groups. Such a response, born of fear, tended to create a vicious circle of revolt, conspiracy, and more white malice toward, and suspicion of, the non-white.

One of the first casualties of the changing racial attitudes was the Afro-Cuban *cabildo*.[50] The *cabildo* was an important socioreligious organization of blacks, both slave and free. Founded in frontier Iberia, it underwent some transformation in Cuba. Based on an Africanized Catholicism, these associations served the very salutary purpose of bringing the non-white urbanized groups together. They concentrated on recreation, on mutual aid, and on relief for the sick and poor; they used their funds, which were derived from subscriptions, to purchase the liberty of slaves. These organizations regulated the free black community and provided a regular medium of communication with the white elite and with slaves.

The oldest member of the *cabildo* group was usually elected "king" or "captain" (*capataz*) and had considerable social influence within the town. He imposed fines on the members and represented the group in dealing with the town council. Beginning in 1792, however, a series of orders forced the *cabildo* to meet outside the city walls and restricted their meetings to Sundays and watch nights. At the same time, the members suddenly needed special permission to

[50] *Instrucción reglamentaria . . . de la formalidad para la llegada, circulación y salida de gentes en esta isla* (Havana: Imprenta del gobierno, 1849).

hold meetings. But the gradual suppression of the *cabildos* was only one form of the increasing legal and extra-legal discrimination against the free colored sector.

A royal order issued on March 12, 1837, prohibited the landing on the island of any person of color, slave or free.[51] Arriving non-white seamen were immediately incarcerated in Cuban ports for the duration of the visit of their ship. The *Bando de Gobernación y Policía* of Gerónimo Valdés, first issued in 1842, not only reactivated some of the old discriminatory laws but added some new ones. Certain occupations, such as farm overseers and bookkeepers, became legally designated as white men's jobs. Non-white persons had to be licensed before they could seek work or even enter farms.[52] Article 143 declared that "no colored person may carry arms permitted to white persons." Federico de Roncali (the count of Alcoy) added further restrictions on free persons of color. They could not travel after eleven o'clock at night, except in emergencies, when they could travel only with a lit lantern and after reporting to the *sereno*, or watchman. Another restriction concerned the driving of cattle by free persons: for every eight head of cattle which a free person of color led along the streets, he had to be accompanied by a white person. During this period, too, every attempt was made to separate free persons of color from the slaves. As Article 24 of the *Reglamento de esclavos* puts it: "The greatest care should be taken to eliminate excess drink or intercourse with free colored persons."

On September 30, 1844, in a confidential dispatch to the Colonial Department of the Royal Council, Captain General Leopoldo O'Donnell confessed that the racial situation was critical on the island. The white sector was becoming frightened of the numerically superior and ever-increasing combined colored element on the island. Plans to augment the white population and to segregate the colored people, even to expatriate them, proliferated. In an address to the Cuban Bureau for the Encouragement of White Immigration, Attorney General Vicente Vázquez Queipo attacked mixed marriages, probably hoping to stem the growth of the mulatto population:

> We do not think that the Real Junta has forgotten, concerning this point, the severe lesson of the neighboring island of Santo Domingo, whose loss depended to a great deal on the close intimacy in which the white inhabitants of the French part lived with their slaves, and the numerous colored population resulting from this foreboding association.[53]

José Antonio Saco joined the ranks of the racists and popularized the cry "Remember Haiti" in order to boost his scheme for ending the

[51] *Bando de gobernación*, art. 23.
[52] AHN, Ultramar, Esclavitud 3552, *leg.* 1, *ind.* 3, *no.* 3.
[53] Vicente Vázquez Queipo, *Informe fiscal sobre fomento de la población blanca en la isla de Cuba* ... (Madrid: Martin Alegría, 1845), p. 33.

slave trade, decreasing the black population, and restoring the "moral and numerical preponderance" of the white sector.[54]

The climate of suspicion and fear in Cuba reached a climax with the so-called La Escalera affair of 1844. On the basis of rumors of a massive slave revolt in Matanzas, in which it was alleged that the free people of color were fomenting rebellion, the white planters called for blood. Captain General Leopoldo O'Donnell, the corrupt friend of planters and slavocrats, responded with delight. Despite the fact that both white and free colored elements were associated with every organized slave revolt, nothing was said of white complicity on that occasion. O'Donnell exacted harsh penalties from the entire free colored community across the island. In a savage campaign in which a great number of persons lost their lives, the army arrested all the leaders of the free colored people, some of whom they brought back from abroad. Twenty-three mulattoes—including the poet Gabriel de la Concepción Valdés, otherwise known as Plácido, the doctor and linguist Andrés José Dodge, and the remarkable poet Juan Francisco Manzano—and eleven free blacks faced execution or exile, as did thousands of other non-whites.[55] The event was a sort of catharsis for the white population. Ten years later, Captain General José de la Concha, decrying the travesty of justice, declared:

> The findings of the military commission produced the execution, confiscation of property, and expulsion from the island of a great many persons of color, but it did not find arms, munitions, documents, or any other incriminating object which proved that there was such a conspiracy, much less on such a vast scale.[56]

The decade of the 1840s was the worst period for the free colored community. Legal restrictions multiplied, and the hostility of the white sector increased. Not surprisingly, therefore, the decade was a turning point in the plantation society. It opened an era in which the application of technology and even larger amounts of capital to industry foreshadowed the beginning of the decline of slavery. The physical violence and the additional legal disabilities of this period may have been calculated to maintain proper relations between the races. A few years later, Antonio de las Barras y Prado noted in this vein that

> the free negroes enjoy the same liberty as the rest of the other citizens, they may own property and even slaves, and many live from this profit; but always, the negro, whether slave or free, is obliged to

[54] Fernando Ortiz, *José Antonio Saco y sus ideas cubanas* (Havana: El Universo, 1929), pp. 73–74.

[55] For the official records of the affair, see AHN, Estado Esclavitud 8057, esp. *no.* 1. A lengthy, debatable account appears in Philip S. Foner, *A History of Cuba and Its Relations with the United States*, 2 vols. (New York: International Publishers, 1962), pp. 214–28.

[56] José de la Concha, *Memorias . . .* (Madrid, 1853), p. 15.

respect the white, for the law gives to the latter a superiority which has as its object, the preservation of moral dominance in order to subject the black race.[57]

The meaures taken during the 1840s seemed so efficacious that the marquis de la Pezuela re-established the free colored militia during the 1850s, although this measure was unpopular among the white classes.[58] By the later 1850s, mutual aid societies began to flourish within the free colored community once more.

The major trouble of the period clearly stemmed from the inconsistencies and conflicts of the plantation society. However much the whites in general opposed the free blacks and slaves, they could not agree on any measures to solve the "social problem." The richer planters wanted the free colored people tied to the plantations. Servile labor, white or black, was their main concern. Lower-class whites feared the competition of the free colored and abhorred the stigma attached to certain jobs, especially on the estates.[59] Hard physical labor was considerd the specialty of non-whites. Yet, by 1862, all forms of labor had become so racially integrated that it was fallacious to argue that only the blacks could work in agriculture. Before the Ten Years' War, attempts to use only white farmers to cultivate sugar cane met with limited success.[60] The demand for labor outstripped the supply, and would do so as long as the island did not have the eight to ten million landless people desired by Zulueta and the *Casino Español*.[61]

Despite the numerous disadvantages under which they labored, free blacks and free mulattoes formed an indispensable part of the Cuban society. As the sugar revolution increased in impact, and as the slave trade became more difficult and costly (while decreasing in efficacy), the contribution of the free colored community became increasingly more substantial. Unable to enter the professions, freedmen appeared in every occupation throughout the island. They were especially prominent in the urban services that were neglected or undersupplied by white labor, services such as cabdriving, cooking, washing, music making, and leather crafts.

[57] Barras y Prado, *Memorias*, pp. 111–12.

[58] Justo Zaragoza, *Las insurrecciones de Cuba: Apuntes para la historia política de esta isla en el presente siglo*, 2 vols. (Madrid, 1872–73), 1: 657–58.

[59] See the lengthy evaluation of the situation in AHN, Ultramar, Esclavitud 3552, *leg.* 2, *ind.* 8; Serrano al M. de la Guerra y Ultramar, 15 de abril de 1862.

[60] AHN, Ultramar, Esclavitud 3552, *leg.* 2, *ind.* 1; see also, Herminio Portell Vilá, *Historia de Cuba en las relaciones con los Estados Unidos* (Havana: Obispo, 1939), p. 195.

[61] Antonio Gallenga, *The Pearl of the Antilles* (London: Chapman & Hall, 1873), p. 106; Knight, *Slave Society in Cuba*.

As plantations gradually monopolized the land and dominated the economy, however, the free colored community tended to be placed at a further disadvantage. Ranking very low in landholding, and lacking the skills and education to master the new machines and technological advances that accompanied the new phase of sugar production in the nineteenth century, the free colored had to compete with poor whites and slaves for non-skilled jobs. Many, however, tended to migrate to the towns, displaying considerable disdain for the plantation.

The plantation culture militated against incorporation of free persons of color into the society. Rather than fostering an integrated community, the plantation engendered racial and social hostility. Even when all the races suffered the same cruel exploitation at the hands of the large Cuban and foreign capitalists, the majority of the white population exhibited considerable ignorance of, and prejudice toward, free persons of color. Many writers even saw the Ten Years' War as a "race war" rather than as an essentially nationalist campaign between Cubans and Spaniards which transcended race. While it is true that, even though some were not native Cubans, the most outstanding military leaders of the insurrection same from the free colored community—Antonio Maceo, Máximo Gómez, and Modesto Díaz—it is patently false to assert, as José de la Concha did, that "the vast majority of the rebels are negroes, mulattoes, chinese and deserters from our [that is, the Spanish] army."[62]

Perhaps the most surprising aspect of the historical experience of the free colored community during the plantation period is how little they benefitted from the royal bureaucracy and the Roman Catholic church. The dynamism and paternalism which had characterized the earlier phase of Spanish colonial expansion faded before the aggressive plantocracy of the nineteenth century. The wealthy planters, led by Miguel Aldama, Juan Poey, and Julian Zulueta in the *Casino Español*, dominated politics, the economy, and society in general. And, where the crown had failed, the church also failed. Given the fact that the church neglected free persons of color, it should not be surprising that the free colored neglected the church. H. H. Johnston, with his usual bias, described the situation in the early years of the twentieth century:

> The country negroes of Cuba are imperfectly converted to Christianity. The Spanish branch of the Church of Rome has not taken them to its bosom with any cordiality since the early nineteenth century, and they are now, with real political freedom, steadily turning

[62] José de la Concha, *Memoria sobre la guerra de la isla de Cuba . . . desde abril de 1874 hasta marzo de 1875* (Madrid: Labajas, 1875), p. 100. Many writers then and later agreed with Concha's impression, but this writer has looked in vain among the numerous bundles of papers dealing with the war in the archives in Madrid for evidence to support it.

away from that Church towards a vague and vicious heathenism—
the fetishistic religions of West Africa—or, with decided moral improvement, towards the Methodism, even the Anglicanism of the
United States and Jamaica.[63]

The free colored continually struggled in a system geared to
their methodical subordination. They were ambitious, energetic, and
often successful, but those with black skins faced monumental disadvantages. The greatest mobility accrued to those who could "pass as
white." While ample statistics exist for those whose light skin color
encouraged them to apply for royal permission to breach the color
line into the forbidden professions, tens of thousands were completely
deterred by their obvious excess of skin color. A casual reference to
twentieth-century statistics belies the impression that socioeconomic
mobility existed during the plantation period. As late as 1949, Lowry
Nelson observed that, "while there is a distribution of colored workers
among all occupations, it is clear that they are predominantly the
hewers of wood and drawers of water."[64] That remains a faithful description of the role of all Cuban non-whites, throughout the ages.
For the non-whites, social and economic recognition, along with
equality, eventually came from revolution, not from paternalistic intercession. Indeed, the status quo never dies without a struggle.

It is, of course, extremely difficult to characterize the attitudes,
aspirations, and self-conceptions of such an amorphous group as the
free colored community of nineteenth-century Cuba. The available
literature and research simply do not yield enough information. Nevertheless, it is clear that during this period the free colored people at
no time sought to redress their grievances through revolution. The
broad color and occupational span of the group and the peculiar development of the plantation society created conditions more favorable
for accommodation within the system than for the system's complete
overthrow. Each social stratum had its own internal substratification.
Within the free colored community, the mulattoes were on top, with
greater opportunities for mobility and even the prospect of eventual
absorption into the free white population. Even when black persons
did get rich, the social status to which they could aspire was sharply
limited. It seems that all free persons had the same ideals for society,
that all sought justice, political liberty, and the opportunity to earn
what they considered a respectable living. The Ten Years' War revealed that the appeal of nationalism was not restricted to the creoles.
The continuing presence of slavery and the bitter experience of the
1830s and 1840s probably gave to the free colored community such a

[63] H. H. Johnston, *The Negro in the New World* (London, 1910), p. 63;
see also [J. G. F. Wurdemann], *Notes on Cuba* (Boston, 1844).

[64] Lowry Nelson, *Rural Cuba* (Minneapolis: University of Minnesota
Press, 1950), pp. 156–57; see also, Wyatt MacGaffey and Clifford Barnett,
Cuba (New Haven, Conn.: HRAF Press, 1962), p. 49.

sophisticated sense of political and social change as to deter it from simple, violent revolution. Men resort to revolution only when they believe there is no other way to attain their goals.

The free colored community was certainly less revolutionary than the creole whites, who sought political independence from Spain, or the slaves, who sought their liberty. But it was also weaker numerically and was in a much more precarious position than either of the other groups. The division between free blacks and free mulattoes may also have vitiated group solidarity, notwithstanding such common organizations as the *cabildos* or the *sociedades de caridad y socorros mutuos de pardos y morenos*. The two groups did not face a common threat, as was the case with those *gens de couleur* of Saint Domingue after 1789. The absence of this common threat in the face of possible chaos seems to have predisposed the free colored community in Cuba to make individual decisions about politics and society rather than to resort to group action. And, with the exception of Saint Domingue, this pattern seems to have been common to all the slave societies in the Americas.

BIBLIOGRAPHICAL NOTE

No specific study exists of the free colored community in Cuba, and the best sources for any such attempt are to be found in the Biblioteca Nacional and Archive Histórico Nacional in Madrid and in the Archivo Nacional in Havana. Nevertheless, substantial material can be gained from the numerous studies which treat the subject in relation to the other groups and to the over-all development of the plantation society. Among the best of these general works are: Ramiro Guerra y Sánchez *et al.* eds., *Historia de la nación cubana*, 10 vols. (Havana: Editorial Historia de la Nación Cubana, 1952); Manuel Moreno Fraginals, *El ingenio: El complejo económico social cubano del azúcar*, vol. 1, *1760–1860* (Havana: UNESCO, 1964); Francisco Pérez de la Riva, *El café: Historia de su cultivo y explotación en Cuba* (Havana: Montero, 1944); Raul Cepero Bonilla, *Obras Históricas* (Havana: Instituto de Historia, 1963); Philip S. Foner, *A History of Cuba and Its Relations with the United States*, 2 vols. (New York: International Publishers, 1962); Herbert S. Klein, *Slavery in the Americas: A Comparative Study of Virginia and Cuba* (Chicago: The University of Chicago Press, 1967); Franklin W. Knight, *Slave Society in Cuba during the Nineteenth Century* (Madison: The University of Wisconsin Press, 1970); and Gwendolyn Midlo Hall, *Social Control in Slave Plantation Societies: A Comparison of St. Domingue and Cuba* (Baltimore: The Johns Hopkins Press, 1971). Colonial law and the operations of the bureaucracy are dealt with in the *Recopilación de leyes de Indias*, 3 vols., new ed. (Madrid: Consejo de Hispanidad, 1943); José M. Zamora y Coronado, comp., *Biblioteca de legislación ultramarina*, 7 vols. (Madrid: Alegría y Charlain, 1844–49); and Arthur F. Corwin, *Spain and the Abolition of Slavery in Cuba, 1817–1866* (Austin & London: University of Texas Press, 1967).

Keen, insightful observations of the free colored society abound in the writings of travelers and contemporary Cubans and Spaniards. The most outstanding accounts are: Fredrika Bremer, *The Homes of the New World: Impressions of America*, trans. Mary Howitt, 2 vols. (New York: Harper & Bros., 1853), recently reprinted by Negro Universities Press, 1968; Richard H. Dana, Jr., *To Cuba and Back: A Vacation Voyage* (orig. pub. 1859; Carbondale: Southern Illinois University Press, 1966); Alexander Humboldt, *The Island of Cuba*, trans. J. S. Thrasher (New York: Derby & Jackson, 1956); William H. Hurlbert, *Gan-Eden; or Pictures of Cuba* (Boston: Jewett, 1854); Rafael María de Labra y Cadrana, *La abolición de la esclavitud en el orden económico* (Madrid: Noguera, 1873); Joaquín M. Sanromá, *Mis memorias, 1828–1865*, 2 vols. (Madrid: Hernández, 1887–89); Antonio de las Barras y Prado, *Habana a mediados del siglo XIX: Memorias* ... (Madrid: Cuidad Lineal, 1925); Antonio Gallenga, *The Pearl of the Antilles* (London: Chapman & Hall, 1873).

For information on statistics of population, property holding, and labor, see: Charles Albert Page, "The Development of Organized Labor in Cuba" (Ph.D. diss., University of California, 1952); José García de Arboleya, *Manual de la isla de Cuba* (Havana: Imprenta del Tiempo, 1859); and Jacobo de la Pezuela, *Diccionario geográfico, estadístico, histórico de la isla de Cuba*, 4 vols. (Madrid: Mellado, 1863–66). Social activities are described by most travelers; they have been studied by Fernando Ortiz Fernandez, "La fiesta afro-cubana del día de reyes," *Revista Bimestre Cubana*, 15 (1920): 5–26, and "Los cabildos afro-cubanos," *ibid.*, 16 (1921): 5–39; V. Martinez Alier, "Color, clase y matrimonios en Cuba en el siglo XIX," *Revista de la Biblioteca Nacional José Martí* (Havana), no. 2, (1968), pp. 47–111; José Rivero Muñiz, "Las primeras asociaciones obreras de socorros mutuos," *Boletín del Instituto de Historia y del Archivo Nacional* (Havana), 64 (1964): 67–83.

HERBERT S. KLEIN

10 | Nineteenth-Century Brazil*

In attempting to analyze the structure of Negro slavery and the development of race relations in any New World society, it is essential to understand the condition of the free colored class. For the occupations, status, and degree of acceptance of the freedmen during slavery foreshadow the pattern of post-emancipation assimilation for the entire slave class. Even more crucially, the role of the free colored is an important indicator of the closed or open nature of a given slave regime. For the colored masses, free men of color offer alternative models to the slave role, and as a group they can also serve as intermediaries between the extremes of freedom and slavery and provide opportunities for non-master contact for the colored slaves.

To understand what role freedmen play in any particular slave society it is essential to determine their numbers, rates of growth, occupational mobility, life styles, and degree of integration into the white society. To date, only the free colored of North America have been much studied. Detailed analyses of this group in the slave South and the free North of the United States have provided significant insights into the origins of North American race relations.[1] The lack of similar studies in other major slave societies is particularly unfortunate in the case of the largest New World free colored class, that of Brazil. It is therefore necessary in dealing with this class to start with the fundamental questions of numbers, distribution, composition, social condition, and occupational structure.

But even beginning with such fundamental questions is a difficult task because of the lack of adequate materials. No national census was taken for Brazil until 1872, nor have all the scattered regional censuses of the preceding period been organized or published. Also, much of this pre-1872 manuscript and printed demo-

* Copyright © 1969 by The Regents of the University of California. Reprinted with additions and revisions from the *Journal of Social History*, 3, no. 1 (1969): 30–52, by permission of The Regents.

[1] Among the best of these studies are Luther P. Jackson, *Free Negro Labor and Property Holding in Virginia, 1830–1860* (New York, 1942), and John Hope Franklin, *The Free Negro in North Carolina, 1790–1860* (Chapel Hill, N.C., 1943). See also the bibliographical survey on this subject by Franklin in *From Slavery to Freedom*, 3rd ed. (New York, 1967), pp. 666–67.

309

graphic data is itself quite fragmentary in terms of age, color, condition, and sexual divisions, or even of completeness and comparability for a given region or time period.[2] The following study is therefore an initial attempt at ordering this disparate material to determine the general characteristics of the free colored strata under Brazilian slavery.

Prior to the first preserved manuscript censuses of the mid-eighteenth century, only minor references were made to the free colored class in Brazil, in travelers' accounts, governors' reports, and other scattered documents. Though the free colored class, like that of the mixed Indian-white grouping (known in Brazil as caboclos), was obviously slow to develop in the sixteenth century, by the early part of the seventeenth century the free colored were numerous enough to be recorded as separate fighting units in the colonial militia volunteer armies. In the wars against the Dutch in Brazil's Northeast in the first half of the century, one of the leading armies was made up of free colored and runaway slaves under the leadership of the free Negro Henrique Dias. So important was Dias and his *terço* (a unit consisting of several companies) in the ensuing reconquest of Dutch territories, that he and several of his Negro captains were rewarded with titles of nobility and admittance into Iberian military orders.[3]

By the eighteenth century, the number and size of these free colored units had increased to such an extent that they were being assigned to specialized military functions and at the same time were being strictly divided into all-Negro and all-mulatto units. They had also spread to almost all areas of the colony, so that from the first extant military census of the middle and late eighteenth century their presence is constantly recorded. Thus, in 1759, in the *capitania*, or province, of Pernambuco, for example, 2,723 (or 15 percent) of 18,026 paid and voluntary troops were free colored militiamen. There was one Terço de Henrique, the free Negro unit named after the famous Henrique Dias, with fifteen companies totaling 1,323 men

[2] For an analysis of the materials on colonial demography, see the study by Dauril Alden, "The Population of Brazil in the Late Eighteenth Century: A Preliminary Survey," *Hispanic American Historical Review* 43 (1963): 173–205; for a review of the imperial and republican periods, see Giorgio Mortara, "Demographic Studies in Brazil," in *The Study of Population: An Inventory and Appraisal* ed. Philip M. Hauser and Otis Dudley Duncan (Chicago, 1959), pp. 235–48. The best survey of the pre-1872 published materials was made by the government official who was preparing that census—see [Joaquim Norberto do Souza e Silva], *Investigações sôbre os recenseamentos da população geral do imperio*, Documentos Censitarios, ser. B, no. 1 (Rio de Janeiro: Serviço Nacional de Recenseamento, 1951). This is a reprint of a work originally published by the government in 1870.

[3] Dias was admitted to the exclusive Order of Santiago. See Antonio Gonsales de Mello, *Henrique Dias: Governador dos pretos, crioulos e mulatos* (Recife, 1954).

and one regiment of 1,400 free mulattoes.[4] According to a 1774 census, in the city of Bahia there was an artillery unit whose soldiers and officers were free mulattoes.[5] Nor were such units confined to the major cities. The town of Jaquaripe in 1792 was not atypical in having a Terço de Henrique. This unit was composed of 66 men, 7 of whom were born in Guinea, Africa, and the rest of whom were native to the village. The primary occupation of these free colored militiamen was fishing (some 56 percent of the total), the next leading occupation being farming, while about a dozen men were listed as artisans.[6]

These provincial, city, and town militia units, made up of whites and colored freedmen, played an important role in colonial society in maintaining order, countering foreign invasions, and in hunting down recalcitrant Indians and fugitive slaves. Though often onerous and time consuming, enrollment in these militia units, at least for the free colored, provided an important means of social mobility for outstanding individuals. Able colored soldiers became officers, and corresponding rights were then bestowed upon them. As officers, these men exercised considerable influence in colonial government. Aside from Henrique Dias, one of the most outstanding of these free colored officers was the mulatto Vicente Ferreira de Guedez, who was *Mestre de Campo* of a *terço* of white militia troops in Maranhão in 1783. A close associate of several governors, Guedez evoked a storm of protest because of his unique appointment to leadership of the white troops, his special connections with the reform-minded Maranhão governors of the period, and his zealous anti-establishment activities in many previous government posts. He was a leading opponent of the entrenched oligarchy of the town council of São Luis de Maranhão, with whom he fought a number of major legal battles. In the bitter and voluminous correspondence sent by his opponents to the crown, constant reference was made to the fact that he was the first mulatto ever to be appointed head of a white voluntary militia group, though innumerable mulatto *mestres de terços* had been made heads of colored militia companies, and his opponents charged him with everything from outright rebellion to being a runaway slave in dis-

[4] I[nstituto] H[istorico] e G[eografico] B[rasileiro] (Rio de Janeiro), Arquivo C[onselho] U[ltramarino], arq. 1-1-14, fol. 108, dated Recife, February 22, 1795 (hereafter cited as IHGB/CU). These troops were even sent for duty in distant provinces. Thus, a regiment of some 600 free colored troops from Pernambuco served on the island of Santa Catarina in 1777. See Fernando Henrique Cardoso and Octávio Ianni, *Côr e mobilidade social em Florianopólis* (São Paulo, 1960), p. 21.

[5] IHGB/CU, arq. 1-1-19, fols. 226–27, letter of Dom Joaquim, Archbishop of Bahia, June 20, 1774.

[6] B[iblioteca] N[acional] (R[io] de J[aneiro]), Secção de Manuscriptos, I-33, 21, 58, "Oficio de Antonio José Calmon de Sousa e Eça, Cap.-mor das Ordenancas de Vila de Jaquaripe" (hereafter cited as BNRJ).

guise.[7] As the Englishman Henry Koster, a resident of Recife in the 1810s, noted of the mulatto militia regiments of that city, "the officers are men of property, and the colonel, like the commander of any other regiment, is only amenable to the governor of the province." In fact, "the late colonel of the mulatto regiment of Recife, by name Nogueira, went to Lisbon, and returned to Pernambuco with the Order of Christ, which the Queen had conferred upon him," and this man's son was a priest. Koster noted that even in the white militia companies, light mulattoes, or, as he put it, "reputed white men," often became officers, since "very little pains are taken to prove that there is no mixture of blood," while "great numbers of the soldiers belonging to the regiments which are officered by white men, are mulattoes, and other persons of colour." In addition to serving in white militia companies, mulattoes, though not Negroes, were to be found in all ranks of the royal line regiments maintained in the city.[8]

Throughout the last years of the colonial period, the free colored class continued to grow rapidly, despite the ever-increasing tempo of slave importations, which numbered more than 20,000 per year by the last years of the eighteenth century.[9] The first manuscript censuses made available through the Rio archives date from the late 1790s and early 1800s, and they testify to the consistent and unusual importance of the free colored class. In the frontier region of Mato Grosso, for example, in a census taken in 1797, 47 percent of the colored class were listed as freedmen, and these freedmen made up 65 percent of the total free class. A year later the southern and still relatively backward *capitania* of São Paulo listed 43 percent of its colored population as free, with the freedmen making up 26 percent of the total free class. Even in the thriving slave state of Maranhão, whose rate of slave importations was among the highest in the last years of the eighteenth century, the free colored accounted for 27 percent of the colored population and 36 percent of all free inhabitants. The rough pattern which emerges from these early census materials is a high percentage of freedmen in the peripheral regions, running close to half the colored population, and a sizeable free colored minority of from 20 to 30 percent in the major slave-plantation regions—that is, in Maranhão, Bahia-Pernambuco, Minas Gerais, and Rio de Janeiro (see Table 10–1).

As the centers of vigorous plantation slavery moved south in the nineteenth century, the northeastern regions registered a constantly

[7] See, for example, several reports and letters sent to the crown from private individuals, as well as from the town council of São Luis, in 1783, in IHGB/CU, arq. 1-1-5, fols. 197–200.

[8] *Travels in Brazil* (London, 1816), p. 392. For mulattoes in a white elite regiment of Minas Gerais in the 1820s, see Auguste de Saint-Hilaire, *Voyage dans les provinces de Rio de Janeiro et de Minas Gerais*, vol. 1 (Paris, 1830), p. 380.

[9] Philip D. Curtin, *The Atlantic Slave Trade: A Census* (Madison, Wis., 1969), p. 207, table 62.

TABLE 10–1. The Colored Population in Late Colonial and
Imperial Brazil to the Census of 1872

	Date of Census	Free Colored	Slave Colored	Whites	Free Colored as Percentage of Total Colored
North					
Amazonas	1840	1,980	940	14,325[a]	67.8
	1872	8,592	979	11,211	89.7
Pará	1819	unknown	33,000	unknown	
	1872	110,556	27,458	92,634	80.1
Northeast					
Maranhão	1789	13,606	36,887	24,273	26.1
	1872	169,645	74,939	103,513	69.3
Piauí	1819	unknown	12,405	unknown	
	1872	121,527	23,795	43,447	83.6
Ceará	1819	unknown	55,439	unknown	
	1872	368,100	31,913	268,836	92.0
Rio Grande do Norte	1839	39,600	10,189	27,638	79.5
	1845	75,977	18,153	48,157	80.7
	1872	107,455	13,020	102,465	89.1
Paraíba	1798	8,897	15,852	12,328	35.9
	1804	11,926	5,926	16,012	66.8
	1811	56,161	17,633	45,208	76.6
	1872	200,412	21,526	144,721	90.3
Pernambuco	1839	126,813	68,458	88,593	64.9
	1872	449,547	89,028	291,159	83.4
Alagoas	1849	104,576	39,790	56,797	72.4
	1872	217,106	35,741	88,798	85.8
East					
Sergipe	1849–51[b]	92,716	56,564	43,542	62.1
	1872	100,755	22,623	49,778	81.6
Bahia	1819	unknown	147,263	unknown	
	1872	830,431	167,824	331,479	83.1
City of Bahia	1775	7,943	6,692	5,021	54.2
Espirito Santo	1839	6,599	9,233	6,730	41.6
	1857	16,451	11,819	14,311	57.2
	1872	27,367	22,659	26,582	54.7
Rio de Janeiro (excluding city of Rio)	1840	64,592	224,012	112,973	28.2
	1844	69,719	239,557	122,152	22.5
	1850	96,629	293,554	160,945	24.7
	1872	178,960	292,637	303,275	37.9

TABLE 10–1—*Continued*

	Date of Census	Free Colored	Slave Colored	Whites	Free Colored as Percentage of Total Colored
City of Rio de	1799	8,812	14,896	19,578	37.0
de Janeiro	1872	73,311	48,939	151,799	59.9
(= Corte after 1808)					
Minas Gerais	1814	143,080	150,489	83,671	48.7
	1872	805,967	370,459	830,987	68.5
South					
São Paulo	1800	32,086	42,209	95,349	43.1
	1803	46,913	44,131	112,965	51.5
	1811	48,004	48,150	127,888	49.9
	1815	49,225	51,272	115,203	48.9
	1822	52,850	63,697	127,888	45.3
	1836	66,265	86,933	172,879	38.3
	1872	207,845	156,612	433,432	57.0
Paraná	1811	9,760	6,840	18,340	58.7
	1836	11,037	7,153	23,895	58.3
	1854	13,300	10,189	33,633	56.6
	1872	37,377	10,560	69,698	77.9
Santa Catarina	1811	580	7,417	23,753	7.2
	1828	1,615	12,250	37,470	11.6
	1831	2,241	11,988	35,214	15.7
	1838	4,236	13,658	43,573	23.6
	1860	10,336	16,316	87,945	38.7
	1872	15,984	14,984	125,942	51.6
Rio Grande do	1807	2,758	13,469	27,107	16.9
Sul	1858	5,413	70,880	206,254	7.0
	1872	82,938	67,791	258,367	55.0
West-Central					
Goiás	1824	37,985	13,375	10,535	73.9
	1832	47,481	13,261	11,761	78.1
	1872	103,564	10,652	41,929	90.6
Mato Grosso	1797	9,669	11,910	5,257	44.8
	1815	10,564	10,898	5,812	49.2
	1828	15,532	10,122	4,278	60.5
	1872	27,989	6,667	17,237	80.7
Brazil	1872	4,245,428	1,510,810	3,787,289	73.7[e]

increasing free colored population, but even in the new coffee regions of São Paulo and Rio de Janeiro the free colored population maintained a vigorous growth, actually increasing more rapidly than the white population. Thus, between 1800 and 1872 the free colored population of São Paulo increased at almost twice the rate of the white population.

Though no single national census was carried out prior to 1872, a crude estimate of the proportion of free colored within the total colored population of Brazil would run between 40 and 60 percent by the middle decades of the century, a figure which would rise steadily to 74 percent by 1872. By any standards of New World slavery, these figures are unusually high and reveal the great role which the free

---

Sources: *Paraíba*: 1798, IHGB/CU, arq. 1-1-13, fols. 148v–149; 1804, fol. 204. *São Paulo*: 1800, A[rquivo] N[acional] (R[io] de J[aneiro]), cod. 808, IV, fol. 255; 1803, fol. 256; 1822, fol. 262; 1811, 1815, and 1826, Roger Bastide and Florestan Fernandes, *Brancos e negros em São Paulo* (São Paulo, 1959), p. 26. *Maranhão*: 1798, IHGB/CU, arq. 1-1-6, fol. 92. *Santa Catarina*, 1811: ANRJ, cod. 808, III, fol. 75; 1828, fol. 93; 1831: fol. 84; 1838: fol. 86; 1860, Cardoso and Fernando Henrique y Octávio Ianni, *Côr e mobilidade social em Florianopólis* (São Paulo, 1960), p. 86. *Rio Grande do Sul*: 1807, ANRJ, cod. 808, III, fol. 147. *Mato Grosso*: 1797, R[evista] do I[nstituto] H[istorico] e G[eografico] B[rasileiro] (Rio de Janeiro), XX (1857), 281; 1815, *ibid.*, p. 292; 1828, ANRJ, cod. 808, III, fols. 38–39. *Minas Gerais*: 1814, ANRJ, col. 808, I, fols. 130–32. *Espirito Santo*: 1839, ANRJ, cod. 808, I, fol. 35. *Goiás*: 1824, Auguste de Saint-Hilaire, *Viagem as nascentos do Rio S. Francisco e pela provincia de Goyaz*, trans. C. Ribeiro de Lessa, vol. 1 (São Paulo, 1937), pp. 296–97; 1832, ANRJ, cod. 808, I, fol. 96. *Rio de Janeiro*: 1844, ANRJ, cod. 808, II, fol. 62. *Paraná*: 1854, Octávio Ianni, *As metamorfoses do escravo: Apogeu e crise da escravatura no Brasil Meridional* (São Paulo, 1962), p. 104. *City of Bahia*: 1775, IHGB/CU, arq. 1-1-9, fol. 230. *Brazil*: 1872, Directoria Geral de Estadistica, *Recenseamento da população do Imperio do Brazil a que se procedeu no dia 1° de agosto de 1872*, 21 vols. (Rio de Janeiro, 1872–76).

All other census data: [Joaquim Norberto de Souza e Silva], *Investigações sôbre os recenseamentos da população geral do imperio*, Documentos Censitarios, ser. B, no. 1 (Rio de Janeiro: Servico Nacional de Recenseamento, 1951).

[a] In all the following statistics, the caboclo category has been omitted. In only one province, or *capitania*, did they have a preponderance in numbers, and that is in Amazonas. In the 1840 census the Indian-white mixture of caboclos and Indians together numbered 34,210 persons. In 1872 the caboclos alone numbered 36,828. In the entire nation in 1872 the caboclos numbered 386,955 persons.

[b] The 1849–51 census for Sergipe is a compilation of the free colored estimate of 1849 with the slave estimate of 1851.

[c] There is a possibility of error of from 3 to 4 percent in the figure because of the non-recording of slave children under eleven months of age as a result of the Law of Free Birth of September 28, 1871. The 3–4 percent figure is a rough estimate based on the percentage importance of the below–eleven months category in the Indian, free colored, and white populations. There are no instructions available in the U.S. Library of Congress edition of the 1872 census which I used, nor do the free colored have an inordinately high number of infants under eleven months of age, a fact which renders it virtually impossible without the birth and death rates to tell whether these slave infants (now officially considered apprentices) were included in the free colored class or not.

TABLE 10–2.   Crude Birth and Death Rates by Color and Condition
in Minas Gerais in 1814, per 1,000 Persons

	Numbers	Birth Rate	Death Rate	Natural Increase
Whites	83,671	36.6	27.4	9.2
Free Colored	143,080	41.7	34.3	7.4
Slave Colored	150,489	33.4	32.9	0.5
Total Number and Average Rates	377,240	37.3	32.3	5.0

Sources: Same as those for Table 10–1.

colored played in Brazilian society long before an abolition movement
appeared. To give some kind of comparative idea of the importance
of the free colored population of Brazil, it is estimated that the Cuban
figure for 1861 was just 35 percent,[10] while the figure for all states
in the United States, both slave and free, was only 11 percent in
1860.[11]

As for the cause of this very rapid growth of the free colored
class, only some tentative ideas can be proposed. There is little question that this was the fastest growing class in nineteenth-century
Brazilian society. Thus, of the seventeen provinces for which data are
available, eleven showed more rapid growth rates for the free colored
than for the whites. Yet, from some extremely fragmentary evidence
(see Table 10–2), it appears that the natural increase of the free colored was not as rapid as that of the whites, largely because of their
higher mortality rate.

If these Minas Gerais data are accurate and representative,[12]

[10] Herbert S. Klein, *Slavery in the Americas: A Comparative Study of
Cuba and Virginia* (Chicago, 1967), p. 236.

[11] U.S. Bureau of the Census, *Historical Statistics of the United States:
Colonial Times to 1957* (Washington, D.C., 1960), p. 9.

[12] To give some comparative idea of birth and death rates at this time
in the rest of Brazil, the city of Rio de Janeiro as a whole (totals undifferentiated by color) had a birth rate of 35.5 per thousand and a death rate of 39.4
per thousand in 1880 (Directoria Geral de Estadistica, *Recenseamento geral
da Republica dos Estados Unidos do Brazil em 31 de dezembro de 1890, Distrito
Fédéral* [Rio de Janeiro, 1895], p. xx). At the same time, comparing the crude
birth rates of the Minas Gerais whites (36.6 per thousand) to that of the
Portuguese metropolitan population in the same period, the figures are surprisingly close, with the Portuguese birth rate in the period 1815–1819 being
36.9 per thousand. The metropolitan Portuguese death rate in this period, how-

they support the thesis that natural reproduction alone could not account for the rapid growth of the free colored. It is evident that only a constant process of emancipation could have maintained the rapid expansion of the free colored strata. At the same time, the excessively high birth rate among the free colored would seem to indicate that this category was increasing through accessions from another class, most specifically from the slave group, a fact which could also account for the very low birth rate of slaves.[13] If such a thesis is correct, it can be assumed that there might have been a disproportionate male-to-female ratio in both the slave and free colored group, since such distortions would produce an unnatural birth pattern. This, in fact, is the case with the 1814 Minas Gerais data. Among the whites there were 101.6 male births for every 100 female births, whereas the free colored had a lower ratio, 98.7 males per 100 females, and the colored slaves a higher ratio, 103.3. These ratios seem to suggest that large numbers of female infant slaves were being freed at birth.

If these Minas figures reflected national trends, it could be argued that the national sexual breakdowns of the 1872 census tend to support the hypothesis of disproportionate female-to-male ratios among the free colored. Though clearly there seems to have been underenumeration of the entire female population, if this underenu-

---

ever, was considerably higher, or 31.2 per thousand, as compared to the white Minas figure of 27.4 per thousand. For the Portuguese data, see Messimo Livi Bacci, *A Century of Portuguese Fertility* (Princeton, 1971), pp. 16ff. The total crude birth rate figures are also comparable to the general rates published for Europe in the nineteenth century, which run from the mid- to the upper 30s per thousand (Michael G. Mulhall, *The Dictionary of Statistics* [London, 1892], pp. 91ff.). While this data would seem to suggest that the Minas Gerais vital ratios are compatible with other nineteenth-century estimates, recent demographic studies imply that these recorded nineteenth-century birth rates for Latin America were probably too low, given the patterns of more recent trends. Though no national vital statistics seem to have been taken for Brazil until the mid-twentieth century, one demographer has estimated that, given the similarities in the changes in their age distributions over time, the Brazilian vital rates probably most closely resembled those of Colombia, which had a crude birth rate of 43 per thousand in 1900. In the 1860s Argentina and Chile had crude birth rates of 46 per thousand, but these fell to 41 and 44 per thousand, respectively, by 1900 (O. Andrew Colver, *Birth Rates in Latin America: New Estimates of Historical Trends and Fluctuations*, Institute of International Studies, Research Series, no. 7 [Berkeley: University of California, 1965], p. 25 and table 5). Recent analysis of parish registers for the city of São Paulo in the first half of the nineteenth century (1798–1836) revealed a birth rate of 47.8 per thousand; see Maria Luiza Marcilio, *La ville de São Paulo: Peuplement et population, 1750–1850* (Rouen, 1968), p. 186.

[13] This same pattern of high birth rates among the free colored is also evident in Cuba. For a detailed analysis of the growth of the free colored of Cuba, see Herbert S. Klein, "North American Competition and the Characteristics of the African Slave Trade to Cuba, 1790 to 1794," *William and Mary Quarterly*, 3rd ser., 28, no. 1 (January, 1971).

TABLE 10–3.   Sex Ratio of the Brazilian Population by Color
and Condition in 1872

	Males per 100 Females
Whites	108.6
Free Mulattoes	101.4
Free Negroes	105.0
Slave Mulattoes	112.5
Slave Negroes	114.8
Caboclos	108.0
National Total	106.6

meration can be considered to have been random throughout all groups, then it is evident that the free mulatto strata had the highest percentage of females of any group in the entire population (see Table 10–3).

Though material is quite scarce on the family background of the free colored, one of the few breakdowns of the condition of the free colored at birth was made in the southern province of Santa Catarina in the census of 1828. This census listed some 708 free colored as *libertos*, or liberated slaves, as opposed to 907 *ingenuos*, or those born of free parents, which means that some 44 percent of the free colored entered that class after birth. In the Goiás census of 1824, the number of free colored born of slave parents was only 8 percent of the total free population. This discrepancy probably reflects the very high and low numbers of slaves, respectively, in the two provinces. Whereas Santa Catarina listed 88 percent of its colored population as slaves in 1828, only 36 percent of Goiás' colored population were slaves in 1824.

Even more decisive evidence of the origins of this class is seen when color breakdown is examined. Whereas the slaves were primarily Negroes, the free colored were overwhelmingly mulattoes, making up more than two-thirds of the total number of free colored in any given area. Given the mulattoes' domination of the free colored class, it is obvious that African-born Negroes were only moderately represented among the free colored.

From this evidence it can be inferred that a large proportion of the free colored class originated from native-born children of white fathers and slave mothers. Though older persons were being freed, and a steady stream of artisan slaves were purchasing their liberty, the primary source of new freedom was most probably free fathers

TABLE 10–4. Percentage of Mulattoes among Freedmen and
Slave Populations in Selected Provinces of Brazil

Province	Date of Census	Percentage of Mulattoes among Freedmen	Percentage of Mulattoes among Slaves
Mato Grosso	1828	79	16
Goiás	1832	79	13
Paraná	1836	92	26
São Paulo	1836	89	16
Rio de Janeiro	1840	79	6
Brazil	1872	78	32

Sources: Same as those for Table 10–1.

TABLE 10–5. African-Born Colored as a Percentage of Free and
Slave Populations in Selected Provinces of Brazil

Province	Date of Census	African-Born as a Percentage of Free Colored	African-Born as a Percentage of Slaves
Paraná	1836	8.1	31.2
Goiás	1836	1.0	14.5
São Paulo	1836	3.5	44.9
Espirito Santo	1839	0.8	30.6
Rio de Janeiro	1850	—	40.2
Brazil	1872	1.0	9.1

Sources: Same as those for Table 10–1.

who emancipated their offspring. All the published and unpublished
sources available accept this as a common occurrence. Obviously, not
all fathers freed their children, but society's mores considered such
behavior a virtuous act. So strong were church and customary attitudes on this practice that innumerable and simple ways of freeing
his children were open to the free white father. He could simply declare (usually when the child was baptized) that he was freeing his
child, or, if he himself did not wish to be compromised, he could

TABLE 10-6. Population in 1872 by Color, Condition, and Sex

	Males	Females	Total
Whites	1,971,772	1,815,517	3,787,289
Free Mulattoes	1,673,971	1,650,307	3,324,278
Free Negroes	472,008	449,142	921,150
Slave Mulattoes	252,824	224,680	477,504
Slave Negroes	552,346	480,956	1,033,302
Caboclos	200,948	186,007	386,955
Totals	5,123,869	4,806,609	9,930,478

Sources: Same as those for Table 10–1.

arrange for the child's godparents to pay for the child's freedom at baptism. Should this prove too embarrassing for a man's family relations, he could simply provide for his child to become a foundling, arranging with friends to have the child so declared and baptized as such. Since the law presumed all foundlings to be free, the white father thus freed his child but removed himself from suspicion of paternity.[14]

The need to protect the identity of the father seems to have varied considerably from family to family and region to region. From all the evidence it seems that the frontier areas, or regions where sudden wealth was being created (above all, in the gold mining zone of Minas Gerais), allowed much freer recognition of such progeny than the more established centers did, even though it was freely practiced everywhere. The open quality of the boom towns of Minas Gerais seems to have been an ideal framework for this recognition, and to such an extent that in 1723, at the height of the gold rush, the provincial governor felt threatened enough to complain bitterly to the crown on the issue. On April 20, 1723, he wrote to the Overseas Council (*Conselho Ultramarino*) "of the great ruin which is threatening these mines, because of the poor quality of the people who are swelling its population, by this I refer to the mulatto class, whose growth is caused by the lack of any but Negro women."

[14] Octávio Ianni, *As metamorfoses do escravo: Apogeu e crise da escravatura no Brasil Meridional* (São Paulo, 1962), pp. 173–74, 192–93. On the numerous ways of freeing slaves (for example, through self-purchase, voluntary manumission, purchase at baptism) and the frequency of their occurrence, see the excellent first-hand description by a long-term resident of Pernambuco, Koster (*Travels in Brazil*, pp. 404–7).

TABLE 10–7. Marital Status of the Population of the *Capitania* of São Paulo in 1800, by Percentage

	Single	Married	Widowed	Total Population
Whites				
Men	64.7	30.9	4.2	47,198
Women	64.2	30.4	5.2	48,151
Free Mulattoes				
Men	71.8	24.2	3.8	14,393
Women	70.3	23.1	6.5	14,554
Free Negroes				
Men	68.6	27.5	3.8	1,596
Women	66.4	24.4	9.0	1,543
Slave Mulattoes				
Men	82.1	16.3	1.5	5,235
Women	79.9	17.4	2.6	5,702
Slave Negroes				
Men	81.1	16.8	2.0	17,661
Women	74.1	22.1	3.6	13,511

Sources: Same as those for Table 10–1.
Note: In this and the following tables, I have not rounded off percentages; thus, totals do not add up to 100.0 percent.

He charged that white men were leaving their families in Europe or on the coast in order to work in the mines, were living in open concubinage with Negro slave women, and were bequeathing all their holdings to their mulatto children. To prevent the mulattoes from gaining complete domination over all the mines of the region, he went so far as to ask the crown to deny mulattoes—even if they were the only heirs—the right to inherit property, an act which the crown held to be completely against all the laws of the kingdom.[15]

Freed by their fathers or by masters for valiant service, old age, or having purchased their freedom, the free colored population was constantly on the increase throughout the era of heaviest slave importation, which ended in 1850. Following the effective termination of the slave trade in 1850, their numbers rose rapidly. Thus, by the time of the first national census in 1872, the free class had come decisively to outweigh the slave population, and in fact was the largest single group in the nation. Of the 5.7 million (or 58 percent) of the popula-

[15] IHGB/CU, arq. 1-1-21, fols. 208–14v, "Consultas de Rio de Janeiro," report dated August 6, 1723.

tion who were colored, some 4.2 million (or more than 70 percent) were freedmen, and this freedmen group was some 43 percent of the total population in imperial Brazilian society, while the slaves were only 15 percent. And this was fully sixteen years before complete emancipation was enacted.

As for the social condition of the free colored class, it appears that well before the end of slavery they had achieved an important life style intermediate between the white master and colored slave classes. If crude marital and legitimacy rates are any indication of such status, it appears from the fragmentary available evidence that the freedmen were midway between the two classes in terms of marriages and numbers of legitimate children. In the colonial *capitania* of São Paulo in 1800, for example, marriage rates of the free colored fall midway between the slave and free white class. Some seventy-two years later, this pattern, which had been evident in the frontier *capitania* of São Paulo, prevailed in the entire national population, as can be seen in Table 10–8. Here again, the free colored, especially the mulattoes, who formed more than two-thirds of the free colored class, were close to the white population in rates of marriage. And comparison of both the free Negroes and the free mulattoes with the mestizo caboclo group reveals that the latter had the least stable family arrangements among the free population.

If to the marriage rate we add the fragmentary data available on illegitimacy, the sociolegal status differentiation between free and slave colored becomes even more evident. Though not so high as the whites in legitimate births, the free colored were even more strongly marked off from the slaves in that more than half of the latter's births were recorded as illegitimate, just the opposite of the free colored pattern.

If legitimate birth and marriage are accepted as indicators of some social mobility, it seems evident that free colored, and especially the two-thirds who were mulattoes, did have a far better position in Brazilian society than did the slaves. One other possible indicator of such mobility is the number of interracial marriages. Though obviously such legal unions were quite rare, the fact that they occurred at all suggests some basic attitudes of acceptance on the part of white society.[16] Scattered references to such unions existed before slavery was abolished, but one of the first systematic studies of the racial composition of married couples occurred just two years after final abolition, in the city of Rio de Janeiro. A detailed survey of more than 40,000 married couples revealed the following results. While interracial marriage was clearly not a mass phenomenon, the fact

---

[16] It has recently been pointed out that the Latin American slave societies were sharply differentiated from the other New World slave regimes by their willingness to accept "intimate social relations based on social equality" between the races. For a full development of this thesis, see H. Hoetink, *The Two Variants in Caribbean Race Relations* (London, 1967).

TABLE 10–8. Marital Status by Sex, Color, and Condition
in Brazil, 1872, by Percentage

	Single	Married	Widowed	Total Number
Whites				
Men	65.4	29.9	4.5	1,822,224
Women	63.1	30.2	6.5	1,751,373
Free Mulattoes				
Men	70.6	26.0	3.2	1,673,971
Women	69.0	26.3	4.5	1,650,307
Free Negroes				
Men	75.2	19.8	4.9	442,219
Women	74.5	20.7	4.6	449,142
Caboclos				
Men	77.2	18.8	3.8	200,948
Women	74.5	20.8	4.6	186,007
Slave Mulattoes				
Men	88.6	8.5	2.8	252,824
Women	89.0	7.8	3.1	224,680
Slave Negroes				
Men	89.4	8.3	3.8	466,806
Women	89.1	8.5	4.6	427,936

Sources: Same as those for Table 10–1.

that it occurred in about 5,000 of 80,000 cases, or in 6 percent of the total marriages recorded, is some indication that tolerance was giving way to full acceptance, at least to the point of permitting a significant minority of interracial marriages, some 15 percent of which had white female partners.

Through marriage and birth records one can obtain some idea of the social position of the free colored in white society, but the material on occupational mobility is so fragmentary and unorganized that only tentative hypotheses can be proposed. While national industrial surveys are lacking, there are some materials on scattered trades and regions. Thus, for example, in 1775 the governor of Bahia reported to Portugal that, of the 1,267 free fishermen in the port, fewer

TABLE 10-9. Legitimacy of Birth by Sex, Color, and Condition
in Minas Gerais, 1844, by Percentage

	Legitimate	Illegitimate	Foundlings	Total Number
Whites				
Men	87.8	9.5	2.5	2,461
Women	84.5	13.3	2.0	2,442
Free Mulattoes				
Men	69.5	28.8	1.6	3,641
Women	66.4	32.5	1.0	3,784
Free Negroes				
Men	61.7	37.7	0.4	839
Women	60.4	39.4	0.1	763
Slave Mulattoes				
Men	41.1	58.8	—	471
Women	38.7	61.2	—	490
Slave Negroes				
Men	48.0	51.7	0.1	1,840
Women	40.8	59.1	—	1,860
Average Percentages and Total Number	66.1	32.6	1.1	18,571

Source: Quintanilla José de Silva, *Falla dirigida à assembléia legislativa provincial de Minas Gerais . . . no anno de 1846* (Ouro Preto, 1846), map no. 18.

Note: These figures represent birth statistics for 110 parishes, out of a total provincial number of 173, for the entire calendar year of 1844.

than 100 were whites, the rest being mulattoes and Negroes.[17] By 1861 the free colored seem to have gained control of the local seafaring trades of Bahia and to have been important as well in maintaining deep-sea transatlantic ships. Thus, the census of seamen of that year listed some 11 percent of the sailors engaged in long-distance shipping on Bahian ships as free colored. About 50 percent of the crews on the ships in the interprovincial trade were free colored,

[17] IHGB/CU, arq. 1-1-19, fol. 230, letter dated July 3, 1775. He also noted that of the seventy-two free persons employed in the whale fisheries outside Bahia in 1774, 85 percent were free colored; see Arquivo Historico Ultramarino (Lisbon), Bahia, catalog no. 8791.

TABLE 10–10. Racial Composition of Married Couples in the
City of Rio de Janeiro, 1890

Sex and Race		Number	Percentage
Males	Females		
White	Mulatto	1,799 ⎤	
Mulatto	White	368 ⎥	
White	Negro	334 ⎥ 2,521	5.9
Negro	White	20 ⎦	
Mulatto	Negro	313 ⎤ 586	1.3
Negro	Mulatto	273 ⎦	
Same	Race	38,644	91.3
Others[a]		558	1.3
Total		42,309	100.0

Source: Directoria Geral de Estadistica, *Recenseamento geral de Republica* . . . *de 1890, Distrito Federal* (Rio de Janeiro, 1895), pp. 258–59.
[a] This category includes caboclos and their intermarriage with the other three racial categories.

while free colored accounted for 70 percent of the free seamen in intraprovincial sea and internal river traffic.[18] In the whole province, 1856 figures on fishermen and seamen in all trades listed 2,634 free mulattoes and 1,787 free Negroes, who together made up 51 percent of the total number of seamen.[19]

From the material I have collected to date, I cannot tell how representative fishing and seafaring were of all industries, but it seems clear that the free colored represented a vital part of the artisanal element of Brazilian society. Almost all commentators, whether government officials or foreign travelers, stressed the dominance of colored laborers in all the skilled trades in Brazil. They also noted the common practice of apprenticing slave artisans, either by white master craftsmen, who owned their own slaves, or by other masters, who paid artisans to teach craft skills to their slaves. As the

[18] José Augusto Chaves, *Falla que recitou na abertura da assembléia legislativa da Bahia, o vice-predidente da provincia . . . no dia 1 de setembro de 1861* (Bahia, 1861), "Mappa demonstrativo das embarcações do longo curso . . . no corrente anno" (no page or map number).
[19] João Mauricio Wanderley, *Falla recitada na abertura da assembléia legislativa da Bahio . . . no 1 de marco de 1854* (Bahia, 1854), map no. 36.

governor of Pernambuco noted in a letter to the Overseas Council in 1772, "it is the usual custom in Brazil to send one's slaves to learn all types of skills, the result of which is that white artisans give up their trades and lead lazy and libertine lives."[20] This same pattern was noted by two German travelers in the late 1810s on their visit to Brazil. Commenting on the artisanal laborers in Rio de Janeiro, they noted that "artisans work with their own Negro slaves, [and teach them] . . . an ability and aptitude in the arts." They also noted that "the freedom which the masters of slaves have for utilizing them in any skilled trade which they determine, prevents the formation of European style artisanal associations."[21]

Given this common training of slaves in artisanal skills, the high wages and unusual freedom enjoyed by such slave laborers, and their right to purchase their freedom, it was inevitable that large numbers of them would become freedmen. And, as freedmen, Negroes and mulattoes dominated almost all the skilled trades. This dominance by colored freedmen extended even to trades that by law were specifically prohibited to them. Thus the *juiz de fora* (crown judge) of the *capitania* of Pernambuco wrote to the crown on April 25, 1732, complaining of "the excessive number of artisan goldsmiths and silversmiths who exist in Olinda, Recife and other places, the majority of them being mulattoes and Negroes, and even some being slaves, which is against the law and results in great damage to the republic."[22] These sensitive trades, which involved a large number of illicit gold operations and were zealously overseen by government officials, proved quite lucrative professions for the colored artisans. Thus, in 1803, when the governor of Bahia was canvassing for the colonelcy of the Fourth Regiment of Militia, "*dos homens pardos*" of the city of Bahia, a silversmith and a goldsmith, presented themselves as two of the several contenders. One was Captain of the Grenadiers Miguel Rodrigues de Deus Sequeira, and the other was

[20] IHGB/CU, arq. 1-1-15, fols. 20v–21, dated Recife, March 23, 1772. Translations of quoted matter throughout this essay are the author's.

[21] J. B. von Spix and C. F. P. von Martius, *Viagem pelo Brasil*, vol. 1 (Rio de Janeiro, 1938), pp. 123–24. This is a translation of the 1823 German edition. See also Fernando H. Cardoso, *Capitalismo e escravidão, no Brasil Meridional* (São Paulo, 1962), pp. 76–79. The Englishman John Luccock also commented on this training of slave artisans and wrote that, "where many [slaves] belong to one master, it is usual here [in Rio Grande do Sul], as in Rio de Janeiro, to have one of them instructed in the part of carpenter, another taught to make and mend shoes and the rest qualified for some useful occupation; and by hiring them out to those who may need their services, to make them advantageously repay the cost bestowed upon them" (*Notes on Rio de Janeiro and the Southern Parts of Brazil Taken during a Residence of Ten Years in That Country, from 1808 to 1818* [London, 1820], p. 201).

[22] Quoted in Leonidio Ribeiro, ed., *As artes plasticas no Brasil*, vol. 1 (Rio de Janeiro, 1952), p. 213. As this standard work notes, "colonial Brazilian silversmiths and goldsmiths were in the large majority, mulattoes and pretos."

Captain of the Seventh Company João Machado Peçanha, both of whom owned their own shops.[23]

Though Portuguese and European visitors bitterly complained about the lack of standards, the poor apprenticeship training, and the generally lower quality of the final goods produced by these slave and free colored artisans, in one area the artisans far excelled all others: in painting, sculpture, and the other plastic arts. As the Germans von Spix and von Martius noted, "among the native Brazilians, the mulattoes are the ones who manifest the greatest capacity and diligence for the mechanic arts, having noted among them an extraordinary talent for painting."[24]

This vital role of free and slave mulatto and Negro artists is evident in the innumerable great works of Brazilian Rococo which were created, especially in Minas Gerais, in the late eighteenth and early nineteenth centuries. It is universally agreed that the greatest of Brazil's colonial architects and sculptors was Antonio Francisco Lisbôa, also known as Aleijadinho, whose churches and statues are masterpieces of colonial Brazilian art.[25] A free mulatto, he was the son of a Negro slave mother and a white artisan father. Aleijadinho was not unique, however, for others, such as Valentim da Fonseca e Silva, another leading Minas sculptor, were of the same background, and many of their assistants were free Negroes and mulattoes.[26]

The unusually important role of the free and slave Negro and, above all, mulatto craftsmen in Minas Gerais is a reflection of the open nature of Minas society. The miners were overwhelmingly single and lived in concubinage with slave women. Then a free mulatto class rapidly arose and itself became an important economic element, not only through its own skills, but through inheritance as well. Equally important, almost all the churches and chapels of the *capitania* were built by religious brotherhoods, many of which were made up of free and slave colored men exclusively. From their own ranks came many of the artisans and architects, as well as the builders of the churches, and, at the same time, the white *irmandades* had no inhibitions about hiring colored workmen.[27] This patronage and the wealth of the region also led to the development of one of the most flourishing schools of original church music in all of colonial Latin America, which owed most of its importance to free

[23] *Ibid.*, p. 220.

[24] Spix and Martius, *Viagem*, 1:123.

[25] P. Kelemen, *Baroque and Rococo in Latin America* (New York, 1951), pp. 248–49; George Kubler and Martin Soria, *Art and Architecture in Spain and Portugal and Their American Dominions, 1500–1800* (Baltimore, Md., 1959), pp. 194–96.

[26] Nair Batista, "Valentim da Fonseca e Silva," *Revista do Serviço do Patrimonio Historico e Artistico Nacional* 4 (1940): 271–330.

[27] Francisco Curt Lange, "A música barroca," in *História geral da civilização brasileira*, ed. Sergio Buarque de Holanda, vol. 1 (São Paulo, 1960), pt. 2, pp. 124ff.

mulatto composers.[28] By the last half of the century, mulatto professors taught composition and harmony, while mulatto composers almost exclusively dominated the field of musical composition in Minas, which was richly supported by commissions from all the white and colored fraternities in honor of holidays, festivals, and other ceremonial occasions. So important were the mulattoes in this profession and so large were their numbers that the royal judge (or *desembargador*) of Minas Gerais complained to the crown in 1780 "that those few mulattoes who are not completely lazy, are employed as musicians, of which there are so many in Minas, that they certainly exceed the number of these in all of the Kingdom of Portugal."[29]

Aside from their importance in the arts and skilled trades of the major urban centers, free colored persons seem to have played an extraordinarily important role in medicine. Since no medical faculties were ever established in colonial Brazil, trained professional doctors were extremely rare. As the governor of Bahia noted in 1787, the majority of the barber-surgeons in the capital city of Bahia were either Negroes or Mulattoes who had learned their trade through apprenticeship and were the most important elements in the Bahian medical profession. The governor, in fact, claimed that, though they did not meet official Portuguese standards for the medical professions, these colored barber-surgeons were far superior to the so-called trained doctors and surgeons who came from Coimbra to the colony, and he strongly pleaded with the crown to allow these men to continue to practice in their accustomed manner.[30]

Finally, free men of color advanced rapidly in the arts, letters, and liberal professions under the empire. Padre José Mauricio (d. 1830), whose mother was of African birth, became the director of music of the royal chapel when the Portuguese court moved to Brazil in 1808. This Jesuit was Brazil's leading early imperial composer and was a court favorite.[31] Also to be mentioned was the extremely unusual career of the Rebouças family, whose father, the free black Antonio, was a self-educated lawyer and one of the first blacks to hold a seat in the provincial legislature of Bahia. Moving to Rio de Janeiro in 1846, he educated his two sons, André and Antonio, for

[28] In Ouro Preto, or Vila Rica, as it was called in the eighteenth century, there were five religious fraternities made up of free and slave colored men, each with its own church (*ibid.*, p. 129). The town of Bahia in the same period had eleven colored brotherhoods, each with its own separate cult of the Virgin (A. J. R. Russell-Wood, "Class, Creed, and Color in Colonial Brazil: A Study in Prejudice," *Race* 9 (1967): 153).

[29] Quoted in Lange, "A música barroca," p. 131. Lange cites as the most exceptional of these late eighteenth-century composers the free mulatto José Joaquim Lobo de Mesquita (*ibid.*, pp. 140–42).

[30] IHGB/CU, arq. 1-1-20, fols. 28v–30, letter from Governor Rodrigo José de Menezes, dated Bahia, May 21, 1787.

[31] M. A. Pôrto Alegre, "Apontamentos sôbre a vida e obras de Padre José Maurício Nunes Garcia," *Revista do Instituto Historico e Geografico do Brasil* 19 (1856): 354–69.

careers in engineering. The two sons eventually studied civil engineering in France in the 1860s, and both returned to lead major careers in Brazil. André proved the more important of the two as an inventor, educator, and engineer who designed many famous port and communication works. He was also a leader in technical education in Brazil and, unlike many other black intellectuals, was a leading abolitionist.[32] In fact, there were black and mulatto intellectuals (such as Luis Gama and José de Patrocinio) who were fervent abolitionists, and others (such as Tobias and Lima Barreto and José Maria Machado de Assis) who were virtually indifferent to the slave or race questions of their day. In the classic novels of Machado de Assis, unqualifiedly considered Brazil's greatest novelist, virtually no concern is expressed on these issues, though Machado de Assis was a mulatto and had important support from free colored intellectuals in his career.[33]

Unquestionably the most politically successful free man of color was Francisco de Sales Torres Homen. Born out of wedlock of a renegade priest and a black laundress, he was to become one of the most powerful political figures of the middle decades of the nineteenth century. A graduate of the medical faculty of Rio de Janeiro, he rapidly became the leader of the radical liberals and a key opponent of the Braganza monarchy. Serving in state and imperial legislatures, he was finally co-opted by the imperial family. A powerful figure even as a convinced monarchist, he rose to the office of minister of finance and served as president of the Bank of Brazil. Finally, he was rewarded with both a life peerage (*Visconde de Inhomirim*) and a permanent senate seat. Despite his color and low status background, he was exclusively a representative of classic upper-class white political opinions and stated no position on the slavery issue.[34]

This diversity of commitment on the part of leading black and mulatto intellectuals and political leaders suggests that a multiplicity of roles was open to the extremely successful few at the top of the political and intellectual hierarchy. As the simple colonial Brazilian society turned into the complex stratified society of nineteenth-century imperial Brazil, the free colored, like other elements in the society, began to fill the new professional middle classes. With the establishment of law and medical faculties, free colored persons attended Brazilian schools of higher learning. While many of these successful mulattoes and blacks were professionally oriented and were indifferent to their social setting, many engaged in a life-time

[32] See his autobiography, André Rebouças, *Diario e notas autobiograficas* (Rio de Janeiro, 1938), and the partial biography by Ignacio José Verissimo, *André Rebouças: Atraves de sua autobiografia* (Rio de Janeiro, 1939).

[33] Raymond S. Sayers, *The Negro in Brazilian Literature* (New York, 1956), pp. 201ff.

[34] R. Magalhaes Júnior, *Tres panfletarios do segundo reinado* (São Paulo, 1956).

commitment to abolitionism. It was from this professional free colored elite that much of the abolitionist movement took its force.[35]

The names of outstanding free colored professionals are known, but their total numerical importance in the liberal professions, or, for that matter, the role they played in agriculture, mining, communications, and unskilled urban occupations, is difficult to estimate on the basis of present available evidence. The large numbers of free colored in Mato Grosso and northeastern Brazil reflect the fact that the bulk of the populations in these areas were free colored by the end of the slave period and were therefore likely to be engaged in all the major economic activities of these regions. In the city of Rio de Janeiro, direct evidence exists (see Table 10–11) to show that the colored were represented in all the major industries of this primary urban center just two years after abolition.

As was expected, colored persons were overrepresented in such classically slave occupations as agriculture and domestic service. But even in these areas there was a heavy representation of whites, and in each case the Negroes were far more disproportionally represented than were the mulattoes. Given the disproportionate number of mulattoes who were free men of color, it could be argued that their comparatively more even distribution reflected the comparatively better occupational distribution of the free colored before slavery was abolished in 1888.

In terms of skilled and unskilled labor, however, the role the colored played in each industry cannot be determined on the basis of published national census data.[36] All that can be said is that the colored population of Rio de Janeiro in 1890 was found in every major urban occupation listed in the census and was neither totally excluded from, nor totally included in, any single occupation.

In other areas of Brazil, primarily the south, such occupational diversity does not seem to have prevailed. In the southern pastoral regions, where the colored populations as a whole were much smaller

---

[35] Luis Viana Filho, *O Negro na Bahia* (Rio de Janeiro, 1946), pp. 113–14; Oliveira Lima, *O movimento da independencia: O Império Brasileiro (1821–1889)*, 3rd ed. (São Paulo, n.d.), pp. 409–10; Sud Mennucci, *O precursor do abolicionismo no Brasil (Luiz Gama)* (São Paulo, 1938). For a listing of free colored professionals under the empire, see Luiz Luna, *O negro na luta contra a escravidao* (Rio de Janeiro, 1968), pp. 232–33.

[36] In no national Brazilian census are occupational categories broken down by color as they are in U.S. censuses. In the censuses of 1872 and 1890, color breakdown was given only for a branch of industry. In the 1900 and 1920 censuses, no color breakdowns whatsoever were provided. In the three censuses after 1940, color and occupational data were improved only to the extent of indicating color and its relationship to the self-employed, employees, employers, or members of a family unit by industry. The employee class, for example, is never broken down by types of occupations, skills, and so on. Until unpublished primary census materials can be studied, it will be difficult to analyze the problem of color mobility in post-emancipation society and virtually impossible to compare it with color mobility data in other New World societies.

TABLE 10–11.   Color Breakdown of Employees by Industry in the
City of Rio de Janeiro in 1890

| Industry | Percentages | | | Total Number |
	Whites	Mulattoes	Negroes	
Extractive	55.4	25.3	6.4	703
Pastoral	56.0	14.6	24.3	41
Agriculture	39.6	26.1	21.7	12,485
Manufacturing	75.9	19.7	8.9	48,661
Crafts (artisans)	53.0	22.5	5.5	5,859
Land transport	75.0	14.4	8.8	9,470
Commerce	90.7	5.7	3.0	48,048
Domestic Service	44.7	28.6	24.0	74,785
Profession Undeclared	70.5	15.4	11.6	48,100
Percentage of Total Fixed Population	62.5	21.7	12.4	

Source: Directoria Geral de Estadistica, Recenseamento geral de Republica
. . . de 1890, Distrito Federal (Rio de Janeiro, 1895), pp. 416–21.
Note: Percentages do not add up to 100, because of the caboclo category,
which has not been included.

than elsewhere in Brazil, the free colored seem to have occupied a
much more dependent role. In the southern grazing regions of Paraná, for example, the free colored were primarily important as re-
tainers in the large households of white ranchers.[37] Free men of color
also seem to have fared poorly in the coffee zones of São Paulo because of the thriving nature of plantation slavery and the early competition of immigrant labor. The city of São Paulo itself probably
witnessed a downward mobility of freedmen in the last quarter of the
nineteenth century because of its late industrial and urban growth,
which coincided with the massive arrival of competitive European
immigration after 1880.[38]

But the southern zone held only 16 percent of the national
population in 1872, and its pattern of occupational mobility for free
men of color does not seem to have been the dominant one for Brazil.

[37] Ianni, As metamorfoses do escravo, pp. 91ff.
[38] Florestan Fernandes, A integração do negro na sociedade de classes,
2 vols. (São Paulo, 1965), 1: chaps. 1 and 2; Roger Bastide and Florestan
Fernandes, Brancos e negros em São Paulo, 2nd ed. (São Paulo, 1959), chap. 1.

The major cities of Rio de Janeiro, Recife, and Bahia absorbed enormous numbers of free colored long before the arrival of competitive European immigration and at the time of their own rapid industrial and urban expansion.[39] Moreover, as Table 10–1 clearly demonstrates, large numbers of colored persons, possibly as much as half to two-thirds of the colored population, had experienced freedom for one or more generations prior to abolition. Thus, they had entered the free labor market well before the advent of massive European immigration, which did not begin until the decade of final abolition in the 1880s, and must surely have developed competitive skills which enabled them to retain their advantage in the face of this competition.

Though the question of occupational mobility is still an unresolved one, that of the social mobility of the freedmen seems to be reasonably supported. It is evident from the marriage and legitimacy materials that, in terms of white society, freedmen had a more nearly normal style of family life than did slaves. It is also evident that large numbers of freedmen were recognized by their white fathers, at least to the point of being granted their freedom. Finally, the fact that so many freedmen were being manumitted at such a constant and rapid rate in the nineteenth century, during the greatest expansion of the plantation economy, suggests that white Brazilians fundamentally accepted the possibility of a functioning interracial free labor society well before the institution of slavery itself was seriously challenged.

In stating these tentative hypotheses about the development of the free colored community in pre-abolition Brazil, certain general problems also should be noted. To begin with, although this free colored class was the largest single grouping in imperial Brazil, its existence clearly did not mean the end of racial discrimination in Brazilian society. From the colonial period on, there was constant opposition on the part of the white elite to that class's increasing self-assertiveness. Every conquest made by the black *cofradias* was bitterly contested by the white ones. When blacks or mulattoes rose socially and economically, whites demanded that they assimilate culturally and phenotypically to white norms. In this, as in many other features, Brazilian society was no different from other New World slave societies. The difference lay in where the lines were to be drawn. Talent, if it conformed to the basic norms of the system, was accepted into the society at the cost of this conformity. Access to economic resources for the talented few was not denied so long as these individuals could break through class barriers. The free colored did in fact cross these barriers, and in numbers sufficient to bring them minimal acceptance. Also, a relatively easy path to "whiteness"

[39] For the comparative urban growth of Brazil in the nineteenth century, see Pedro Pinchas Geiger, *Evolução da rede urbana brasileira* (Rio de Janeiro, 1963).

through intermarriage and "passing" was permitted which allowed for the very rapid absorption of these talented individuals into the "white" elite.[40] Such a system was open enough for mulattoes like Machado de Assis or Torres Homen to find the process of racial accommodation of little real import in their life chances and perceptions. Nevertheless, racial tensions were prominent enough for free men of color like Luis Gama and other intellectuals, especially those who were Negro, to be forced to identify with the largely black slave community for their self-realization.

It is also clear that the middle ranks of Brazilian society were relatively more open to accepting mulattoes and blacks than was the upper elite. The sheer numbers of free colored and their importance in this labor-hungry society dictated a certain minimum acceptance into this middle level. Here and among the lower classes segregation in housing or in occupations never developed. This does not mean that the artisans, skilled laborers, and small farmers were less troubled by the prevailing systems of prejudice than were the colored elites. They too were often singled out for persecution and oppression. The great cycle of slave rebellions which broke out in Bahia in the first half of the nineteenth century occasioned the deliberate attack on important elements of the free colored community in that city.[41] Nevertheless, blacks and mulattoes in this class tended to identify along class lines as often as they did along racial ones. Thus, the famous tailors plot in Bahia in 1798, the most important Brazilian response to the French Revolution, was largely made up by free black and mulatto artisans.[42] In another case, the Pernambucan independence rebellion of 1817–23 had several free colored leaders,

---

[40] It has been estimated by Brazil's leading demographer that something like 4 million persons of color (black and mulatto) "passed" into the white category between 1872 and 1940. This represents approximately 59,000 persons per annum. In contrast, the best estimates for the United States indicate that only 2,000–2,500 persons "pass" into the white category each year. The base population in the two societies was a black and mulatto population of 14.8 million in Brazil in 1940 and a Negro population of 11.8 million in the United States in 1930. The Brazilian estimate appears in [Giorgio Mortara], *Estudos sobre a composição da população do Brasil segundo a côr*, Estatistica Demografica, no. 11, (Rio de Janeiro: IBGE, 1950), p. 38. The 2,000–2,500 figure is provided in two independent studies of the U.S. population. The most demographically sophisticated of the two was a comparison made between the 1930 and 1940 censuses which used all available vital statistics, E. W. Eckard's "How Many Negroes 'Pass'?" *American Journal of Sociology* 52, no. 6 (1947): 498–500; see also John H. Burma, "The Measurement of Negro 'Passing,'" *ibid.*, no. 1, pt. (1946): 18–22.

[41] The most complete study of these great movements is Pierre Verger's *Flux et reflux de la traite des nègres entre le golfe de Benin et Bahia de todos os santos du dix-septième au dix-neuvième siècle* (Paris, 1968), chap. 9. Though much less accurate and based on secondary analysis, a useful English summary is provided by R. K. Kent, "African Revolt in Bahia: 24–25 January 1835," *Journal of Social History* 3, no. 4 (1970): 334–57.

[42] Kent, "African Revolt in Bahia," pp. 336–37.

yet it initially proclaimed support for slavery.[43] Again, some of the
key military leaders and followers of the millenarian leader of the
last days of the empire, O Conselheiro, were mulatto and black peas-
ants.[44] Though equality here, as in the 1798 revolt, was important,
it was expressed as part of a larger movement of class protest.

The one area in which a clear black and separatist consciousness can be said to have emerged is the revival and development of
African cults. Though large numbers of free blacks and mulattoes
were practicing and observant Catholics, it was largely from among
the free colored that the famous African cults emerged. Clearly developing, at least as far as the surviving data show, in the 1830s,
these sects expressed a black consciousness distinct from the white
norms of Brazilian society. The cults were even accused of fomenting
many of the slave revolts, and this remains a major possibility. But,
however these cults may have expressed the rage and sense of isolation of the free black community, even here the syncretization of the
cults with Brazilian elements and their absorption of white believers
over time tended to dissipate them as exclusive expressions of a black
consciousness and turn them more into expressions of a class consciousness.[45]

All of these experiences imply that, within the context of the
racially segmented societies created by Europeans in the Americas,
the Brazilian Empire, for all its unquestioned class harshness and
racial hostility, was still open enough to allow for an extraordinarily
wide range of reactions by free men of color. Thus, everything from
individual accommodation to African cultist rejection to mass movements of social protest in which blacks and mulattoes participated
as oppressed majorities or even oppressing minorities was possible
for the large free colored class in Brazil.

[43] Roger Bastide, *Les religions africaines au Brésil* (Paris, 1960), pp.
136–38.

[44] The chief strategist for the brilliant guerrilla tactics of the armies of
Canudos was a *preto*, João Grande. See Euclides Da Cunha, *Rebellion in the
Backlands*, trans. S. Putnam (Chicago, 1944), p. 214.

[45] The cults maintained a precarious existence in the rural and urban
centers of Brazil prior to the nineteenth century; their full development could
occur only under conditions of relative freedom. Given the time and funds
needed to run the cults, it appears that the urban free colored were their
primary supporters, and most experts date the vital growth and expansion of
the cults with the founding of the Candomblé of Engenho Velho at Bahia in
ca. 1830. See Edison Carneiro, *Ladinos e crioulos, estudos sôbre o negro no
Brasil* (Rio de Janeiro, 1964), pp. 126–27.

Population Tables

TABLE A–1.   Puerto Rico

Year	Whites	Slaves	Free Blacks	Free Mulattoes	Total Freedmen	Total Population
1775	29,263	7,487	2,823	31,687	34,510	71,260
1802	78,281	13,333	16,414	55,164	71,578	163,192
1812	85,662	17,536	15,833	63,983	79,816	183,014
1820	102,432	21,730	20,191	86,268	106,459	230,621

Source: Chapter 1 of this volume.

TABLE A–2.   Curaçao

Year	Whites	Slaves	Free Blacks	Free Mulattoes	Total Freedmen	Total Population
1700	—	2,400	—	—	—	—
1735	—	1,391	—	—	—	—
1817	2,780	6,765	2,309	2,240	4,549	14,094
1833	2,602	5,894	3,830	2,701	6,531	15,027
1863	—	*c.* 7,000	—	—	—	—

Source: Chapter 2 of this volume.

TABLE A–3. Surinam

Year	Whites	Slaves	Free Blacks	Free Mulattoes	Total Freedmen	Total Population
1738	—	—	—	—	598	—
1787	—	—	—	—	650	—
1788	—	50,000	—	—	—	55,000
1791	—	—	—	—	c. 1,950	—
1830	—	48,784	1,094	3,033	5,041	—
1863	—	31,380	—	—	c. 20,000	49,132

Source: Chapter 2 of this volume.

TABLE A–4. Brazil

Year	Whites	Slaves	Free Blacks	Free Mulattoes	Total Freedmen	Total Population
Minas Gerais						
1735	—	96,541	—	—	1,420	—
1749	—	88,286	—	—	961	—
1776	70,769	—	—	—	—	319,769
1786	65,664	174,135	42,739	80,309	123,048	362,847
1805	78,035	188,781	48,139	92,049	140,188	407,004
1808	106,684	148,772	47,927	129,656	177,583	433,039
1821	136,693	171,204	53,719	152,921	206,640	514,537
São Paulo						
1800	95,349	42,209	—	—	32,086	169,644
1815	115,203	51,272	—	—	49,225	215,700
1836	172,879	86,933	—	—	66,265	326,074

Source: Chapter 3 of this volume.
Note: For additional population figures on Brazil, see the tables in Chapter 10 of this volume.

TABLE A–5.   Martinique

Year	Whites	Slaves	Total Freedmen	Total Population
1664	2,681	—	—	—
1696	6,435	13,126	505	20,086
1700	6,597	14,225	507	21,379
1715	8,735	26,865	1,029	36,639
1726	10,959	40,403	1,304	52,666
1731	11,957	46,062	1,204	58,548
1734	12,705	53,080	810	66,595
1738	14,969	57,778	1,295	74,042
1751	12,068	65,905	1,413	79,386
1764	11,634	68,395	1,846	81,875
1776	11,619	71,268	2,892	85,779
1784	10,150	79,198	3,472	92,220
1789	10,636	83,414	5,235	96,158
1802	9,826	75,584	6,578	91,988
1816	9,298	80,800	9,364	99,462
1826	9,937	81,142	10,786	101,865
1835	9,000	78,076	29,955	116,031
1848	9,490	67,447	36,420	120,357

Source: Chapter 4 of this volume.

TABLE A–6.   Saint Domingue

Year	Whites	Slaves	Total Freedmen	Total Population
1700	—	—	c. 500	—
1715	—	—	1,500	—
1784	20,229	297,079	13,257	330,565
1788	27,717	405,528	21,848	455,093
1789	30,831	434,424	24,848	490,108

Source: Chapter 5 of this volume.

TABLE A–7.   Jamaica

Year	Whites	Slaves	Total Freedmen	Total Population
1658	4,500	1,400	—	—
1675	8,600	9,500	—	—
1698	7,400	40,000	—	—
1722	7,100	80,000	800	87,900
1746	10,000	112,400	—	—
1768	17,900	176,900	3,500	198,300
1775	18,700	192,800	4,500	216,000
1800	30,000	300,000	10,000	340,000
1834	—	310,000	35,000	—

Source: Chapter 6 of this volume.

TABLE A–8.   Barbados

Year	Whites	Slaves	Total Freedmen	Total Population
1748	15,192	47,025	107	62,324
1768	16,139	66,379	448	82,966
1773	18,532	68,548	534	87,614
1786	16,167	62,115	838	79,120
1801	15,887	64,196	2,209	82,292
1809	15,566	69,369	2,663	87,598
1815	16,072	71,286	3,007	90,365
1825	14,630	78,096	4,524	97,250
1829	14,959	80,086	5,146	100,191
1833	12,797	80,861	6,584	100,242

Source: Chapter 7 of this volume.

TABLE A-9. United States

Year	Whites	Slaves	Total Freedmen	Total Population
Upper South				
1790	1,072,424	521,169	30,158	1,629,751
1800	1,399,868	648,051	56,855	2,104,774
1810	1,791,840	651,965	94,085	2,309,772
1820	2,190,975	965,514	114,070	3,270,549
1830	2,711,743	1,159,670	151,877	4,023,290
1840	3,187,918	1,215,497	170,690	4,577,772
1850	4,085,134	1,395,283	203,702	5,684,019
1860	5,154,206	1,530,229	224,963	6,910,782
Lower South				
1790	193,064	136,358	2,199	331,621
1800	303,112	209,044	4,386	516,542
1810	416,945	353,331	14,180	784,456
1820	640,595	553,503	20,153	1,214,251
1830	949,015	845,805	30,193	1,825,013
1840	1,444,612	1,127,879	41,218	2,572,700
1850	2,137,284	1,808,768	34,485	3,980,537
1860	2,943,257	2,423,467	36,955	5,404,591

Source: U.S. Census Office, *Population of the United States in 1860* (Washington, D.C., 1864), pp. 598–604.

TABLE A-10. Cuba

Year	Whites	Slaves	Total Freedmen	Total Population
1774	96,440	38,879	36,301	171,620
1792	—	—	54,154	—
1827	311,051	286,942	106,494	704,487
1841	418,291	436,495	154,546	1,009,332
1860	793,484	370,553	225,843	1,389,214
1861	776,481	370,220	227,356	1,374,057
1877	—	—	272,478	—
1887	—	—	528,798	—

Source: Chapter 9 of this volume.

Index

African culture, survival of in colonial Brazil, 127–29

Agriculture, employment of freedmen in: in Barbados, 239–40; in colonial Brazil, 104–8; in the French Antilles, 163; in nineteenth-century Brazil, 331

Almagro, Diego de, 20–21

Almeida, Dom Pedro de (Count of Assumar), 86, 92, 95

Amsterdam Exchange, difficulties of, 60, 80

Andrés (son of Juan Antonio), 30

Antonio, Juan, 29–30

Artisans, freedmen as: in Barbados, 240–41; in colonial Brazil, 102; in colonial Spanish America, 51–52; in Cuba, 294; in nineteenth-century Brazil, 327–28

—white, in colonial Spanish America, 51–52

Arts, freedmen in: in colonial Brazil, 129; in colonial Spanish America, 50; in nineteenth-century Brazil, 327–28

Barbers, freedmen as, in colonial Brazil, 103

Barrett, Richard, 199, 211

Bartholomew, Manuel, 199

Bassett, John Spencer, 263

Beckles, John, 233

Beltron, Gonzalo Aguirre, 34, 56

Bourne, London, 243

Boxer, Charles, 282

Brotherhoods: as church builders, 327; philanthropic role of, 108

—colored, 122, 131; demand freedom for slaves, 123–25; integrative force of, 125

"Brown privilege bill," in Barbados, 238

Carlos, Baltasar, 54

Carta de alforria (certificate of freedom), in colonial Brazil, 86, 91, 95

Catholicism, relation of to slavery: in Cuba, 278, 305–6; in Curaçao, 74

Cattle ranchers, employ freedmen in colonial Brazil, 106

Cedulas de gracias al sacar (certificates of legal whiteness), 46

Church: freedmen excluded from in Barbados, 249; discriminates against freedmen in colonial Brazil, 111; slaves excluded from in the Netherlands Antilles, 77

Citizenship, denied Jamaican freedmen, 197–98

Coartición (system for purchasing freedom), in Cuba, 25, 285

Code Noir, 135, 136, 177, 184–87; regulates markets, 181; attacked by Martinique planters, 141–42

Colegio Real de San Felipe y San Marcos, 45

Commerce, employment for freedmen in, in Curaçao, 69

Concubinage, 251, 321; discouragement of in the French Antilles, 161

Conselho Ultramarino, Lisbon, 320

Corral, Juan del, 22

Craftsmen, freedmen as. See Artisans

Cunha, Manuel da, 130

Deficiency laws, in Cuba, 280

Destre, Domingo de, 28

Dias, Henrique, 310–11

Disabilities, legal, of freedmen: in Barbados, 230–39, 251; in Cuba, 290–91, 302; in the French Antilles, 153–54, 162, 167–68; in Jamaica, 198–99, 205–8; in Saint Domingue, 190; in the United States, 261–62

—social, of freedmen, in the French Antilles, 152–53, 162

Discrimination: against freedmen in

341

colonial Brazil, 109–11, 130; among freedmen in Jamaica, 196; racial, in Saint Domingue, 189–92
Douglass, Frederick, 273–74
Dutch West India Company, 65–66, 75–77

Education, in Cuba, 295–96
—for freedmen: in colonial Spanish America, 45; in the French Antilles, 158–59; in Surinam, 63; in the United States, 263
Emancipados, in Cuba, 11, 283
Emancipation. *See* Manumissions
Emigration, white, from Surinam, 80–81

Fabulé, Francisque, 179–80
Fishermen, freedmen as, in nineteenth-century Brazil, 323–24
Franchise: denied to freedmen in the United States, 261–62; extended to freedmen in Barbados, 239
Franklin, John Hope, 269, 272
Free colored: sexual composition of, 7, 31. *See also* Freedmen
Freedmen: group consciousness among, 12–13; links of with slaves, 15–16; role of in New World societies compared, 3
—in Barbados: as artisans, 240–41; composition of, 221–24; distribution of, 216–21; enfranchisement of, 239; excluded from church, 249; legal disabilities of, 230–39, 251; opportunities of in agriculture, 239–40; petitions by, 236–38; standard of living of, 244–45
—in Brazil (colonial): as artisans, 102; in the arts, 129; as city councillors, 112; on cattle ranches, 106; in commerce, 100–102; discriminated against, 109, 130; excluded from diamond district, 100; as midwives, 103; in the militia, 118–20; numbers of, 96–98; re-enslavement of, 92; tensions among, 117–19
—in Brazil (nineteenth-century): as artisans, 325–27; in the arts, 327–28; family background of, 318–19; growth in numbers of, 312–17, 321–22; in the militia, 310–12; origins of, 318–19; as plantation workers, 331; in professions, 328–30
—in colonial Spanish America: as apprentices, 51; as artisans, 51–52; in arts and crafts, 50; debarred from priesthood, 49; debarred from public office, 39, 47–48; depart from cities, 53; in education, 45–46; forbidden to own firearms, 39; group cohesiveness of, 53; hired out to Spaniards, 43; growth in numbers of, 36–38; lack of class consciousness of, 55–57; in medicine, 50; in the militia, 44, 49; as notaries, 48; obligation of to pay tribute, 38; reaction of to racial classification, 55; recognized by government, 55; regulation of dress among, 40–41; request exemption from militia duties, 43; rural life of, 34–35; as scribes, 48; as slaveholders, 52; social mobility of, 57; socioeconomic rise of, 45–47; in universities, 46
—in Cuba: as artisans, 294; growth in numbers of, 283–89; in the militia, 39, 290; residence patterns of, 288–89; as slaveholders, 292; social importance of, 304; social mobility of, 306
—in Curaçao: despised by whites, 72; in the militia, 68–69; numbers of, 71; social conditions of, 67; social intractability of, 71; special privileges granted to, 70; tensions among, 67; as threat to white security, 69
—in the French Antilles (Martinique and Guadeloupe): attitude of notables toward, 159–60; class divisions among, 166; education of, 158–59; as ferrymen, 160; growth in numbers of, 146–52; legal disabilities of, 153–54, 162; in the militia, 169; as peasant farmers, 163; in professions, 162; social disabilities of, 152–53, 162; as tavern keepers, 160
—in Jamaica: citizenship denied, 197–98; conservatism of, 205; discrimination among, 196; divisions among, 198; economic roles of, 201–3; growth in numbers of, 194–95; legal disabilities of, 196–99; petitions from, 199–201; restrictions on, 205–6; solidarity among, 201–2
—in Saint Domingue: civil rights of, 184; debarred from public office, 190; growth in numbers of, 188–89; inheritances of, 187–88; military role of, 174–76; wealth of, 187–88
—in Surinam: administrative positions of, 64; alliance of with Jews, 64–65; competition of with Jews, 64; dis-

tinctions among, 63; numbers of, 62; emigration of, 64

—in the United States: as artisans, 266; character of, 273; in cities, 264–65; education of, 263; expelled, 259; mingling of with slaves, 276; population distribution of, 260–61; re-enslavement of, 259; in rural areas, 265–66; as slaveholders, 267–69

Free Negroes. *See* Freedmen

Goveia, Elsa, 281
Guardianship: in the French Antilles, 161–62; in the United States, 261
Guedez, Vicente Ferreira de, 311
Gutman, Herbert, 264, 266

Harris, Marvin, 261
Hernández, Francisco, 53–54
Hernhutters, 64
Hill, Richard, 205, 208
Homen, Francisco de Sales Torres, 329, 333
Hucksters, role of: in Jamaica, 202; in Barbados, 242

Illegitimacy, in the French Antilles, 156
Immigration: European, to nineteenth-century Brazil, 332; of freedmen, prohibited in Cuba, 302; from India to Surinam, 60
Interracial marriages: in the French Antilles, 142–44, 154–57; in Jamaica, 210–11; in nineteenth-century Brazil, 322–23; in Saint Domingue, 186; in Surinam, 80; in the United States, 262, 271–72. *See also* Miscegenation

Jackson, Luther Porter, 265
Jacott, Francisco, 281
Jesuits, as slave teachers in colonial Brazil, 117
Jews: as allies of freedmen, 64–65; as a commercial elite, 66; as competitors of freedmen, 64; in government posts, 64; in the Netherlands Antilles, 59, 66, 69, 73
Jordan, Edward, 203–5
Jordan, Winthrop D., 264

Landero, Pedro Pérez, 48
Land tenure, pattern of, in Cuba, 291
Las Siete Partidas, 21–22, 24, 300
Laws of the Indies, 300
Lima, City Council of, 41

Lisboa, Antonio Francisco, 129, 327
Lockhart, James, 53
Long, Edward, 209, 211
Louisiana Code, 155

Madan, Cristóbal, 292
Manumissions: "delayed," 8; restrictions on, 5, 8
—in Barbados: fee for, 226–28; means of, 224–28
—in Brazil (colonial): means of, 86, 87–91, 95–96
—in Brazil (nineteenth-century): means of, 319–21
—in colonial Spanish America: acts of, 24; frequency of, 31; masters' attitudes toward, 32; by purchase, 29; as reward, 29; voluntary, 22–23
—in Cuba: means of, 283, 285
—in Curaçao: limited by government, 67–68; means of, 79–80
—in the French Antilles: legislation concerning, 139–44; means of, 137; relation of to taxation, 144
—in Saint Domingue: effects of on plantation labor, 176; encouraged by government, 173; government restrictions on, 177; tax on, 177
—in Surinam: means of, 79–80; rate of, 80
—in the United States: laws relating to, 267; means of, 267–68, 273
Manzano, Juan Francisco, 303
Margarita (slave), 21 and *n*
Maria de Labra, Rafael, 292
Marons: of Saint Domingue, 178–79; of Surinam, 61
Marriage. *See* Interracial marriages
Martinez, Cristobal, 51
Merchants, freedmen as, 203
Militia, freedmen in: in colonial Brazil, 118–20; in Cuba, 304; in Curaçao, 68; in the French Antilles, 169; in nineteenth-century Brazil, 310–12; in Saint Domingue, 176; in the United States, 274
Miscegenation: in Barbados, 251; in Cuba, 282–83; in Curaçao, 68, 72–73; in Jamaica, 209–10; in nineteenth-century Brazil, 321; in Saint Domingue, 185; in Surinam, 61, 78; in the United States, 263
Missionaries, as teachers, in colonial Brazil, 117
Mobility, occupational, of freedmen in nineteenth-century Brazil, 323–29
—social, of freedmen: in Barbados,

256–57; in colonial Brazil, 114–17; in Cuba, 306; in nineteenth-century Brazil, 322, 332–33
Moret Law, in Cuba, 285
Mörner, Magnus, 21, 42
Mulattoes. *See* Freedmen

Orderson, J. W., 253–54
Overseas Council (Portuguese), 112, 120, 121, 326, 334

Petit, Emilien, 185, 190
Petitions, by Barbadian freedmen, 236–38; by Jamaican freedmen, 199–201, 206–7
Pezuela, Jacobo de la, 287, 294
Phillips, Ulrich B., 193, 258, 264
Politics, freedmen in: in the French Antilles, 167–69; in nineteenth-century Brazil, 329; in Saint Domingue, 190
Poll tax, in the French Antilles, 153–54
Prescod, Samuel, 239, 248, 249
Property, conceptions of: in Dahomey, 181–82; in Saint Domingue, 182

Race relations, in the New World, 2, 301, 302
Racism, rationalization of: in Saint Domingue, 183–84; in slave societies, 281–82
Revolts. *See* Slave revolts
Revolution, American, effects of on Saint Domingue, 191
—French: Brazilian response to, 333; effects of on colonies, 138, 171
—Haitian: causes of, 189–90; effect of on the British Caribbean, 201, 207, 208
—Sugar. *See* Sugar Revolution

Saa, Daniel, 200–201
Santa Casa de Misericórdia, 96, 108, 124
Schools: in Cuba, 295, 296; for freedmen in the United States, 272
Slave Consolidation Act (Barbados), 237, 252
Slaveholding, by freedmen: in Barba-

dos, 245–46; in Curaçao, 66; in Cuba, 292; in the French Antilles, 165–66; in the United States, 267–69
Slave revolts: in Barbados, 234; in Cuba, 301, 303; in Curaçao, 79; in Surinam, 61; in the United States, 274, 275
Slave societies, social control in, 1, 172
Slavery: amelioration of in Barbados, 228, 233–34, 237; character of, 3, 131; in Curaçao and Surinam compared, 81–82; effect of on slave personality, 98–99; in France, 137–39; prohibited in the French Antilles, 137
Social groupings, in Barbados, 255–57
Society of Surinam, the Netherlands, 78
Soi-disant libre (nominally free), in the French Antilles, 145–46
Sugar revolution, effects of: on Barbados, 214; on Cuba, 280, 289–90; on Jamaica, 197; on Martinique, 136

"Tailors' Revolution," in colonial Brazil, 117, 125, 126
Tannenbaum, Frank, 1–3, 9
Taxation, effects of on manumission, 144
Ten Years' War, 290, 304, 306

Valdés, José Manuel, 46
Valdivia, Pedro de, 20
Valiente, Juan, 20
Vieira, Antonio, S.J., 114
Vieria, João Fernandes, 113, 114
Vilhena, Luis dos Santos, 89, 95
Voluntary enslavement, in the United States, implications of, 259

"War of Divine Liberty," 113
Williams, Eric, 282
Williams, John, 199
Woodson, Carter, 263, 268

Zambos: legal position of, 38; socioeconomic position of, 27–28

THE JOHNS HOPKINS UNIVERSITY PRESS

This book was composed in Primer text and Melior Semi-Bold display type
by Monotype Composition Company. It was printed by Universal Lithographers, Inc.
on S. D. Warren's 60-lb. Sebago paper, in a text shade, regular finish.
The book was bound by L. H. Jenkins, Inc. in Holliston Mills' Roxite vellum cloth.

Library of Congress Cataloging in Publication Data
Main entry under title:

Neither slave nor free.

(The Johns Hopkins symposia in comparative history)
"This volume grew out of a symposium . . . held at The
Johns Hopkins University on April 8 and 9, 1970. Sponsored
by the Department of History and the Institute of Southern History."
Includes bibliographical references.
1. Freedmen—Congresses. 2. Slavery in America—Congresses. I. Cohen,
David W., ed. II. Greene, Jack P., ed. III. Title. IV. Series: The Johns
Hopkins symposia in comparative history.

HT1048.N43   301.45′19′607   79-184238
ISBN 0-8018-1374-3